COOPERATIVE SYSTEMS DESIGN

Frontiers in Artificial Intelligence and Applications

Series Editors: J. Breuker, R. López de Mántaras, M. Mohammadian, S. Ohsuga and W. Swartout

Volume 107

Recently published in this series

Vol. 106. D. Bourcier (Ed.), Legal Knowledge and Information Systems – JURIX 2003: The Sixteenth Annual Conference
Vol. 105. Y. Kiyoki et al. (Eds.), Information Modelling and Knowledge Bases XV
Vol. 104. A. Abraham et al. (Eds.), Design and Application of Hybrid Intelligent Systems
Vol. 103. B. Tessem et al. (Eds.), Eighth Scandinavian Conference on Artificial Intelligence – SCAI'03
Vol. 102. C. Turchetti, Stochastic Models of Neural Networks
Vol. 101. G.L. Torres et al. (Eds.), Advances in Intelligent Systems and Robotics – LAPTEC'03
Vol. 100. I. Aguiló et al. (Eds.), Artificial Intelligence Research and Development
Vol. 99. D. Šuc, Machine Reconstruction of Human Control Strategies
Vol. 98. H. Fujita and P. Johannesson (Eds.), New Trends in Software Methodologies, Tools and Techniques – Proceedings of Lyee_W03: The Second International Workshop on Lyee Methodology
Vol. 97. H.U. Hoppe et al. (Eds.), Artificial Intelligence in Education – Shaping the Future of Learning through Intelligent Technologies
Vol. 96. S. Handschuh and S. Staab (Eds.), Annotation for the Semantic Web
Vol. 95. B. Omelayenko and M. Klein (Eds.), Knowledge Transformation for the Semantic Web
Vol. 94. H. Jaakkola et al. (Eds.), Information Modelling and Knowledge Bases XIV
Vol. 93. K. Wang, Intelligent Condition Monitoring and Diagnosis Systems – A Computational Intelligence Approach
Vol. 92. V. Kashyap and L. Shklar (Eds.), Real World Semantic Web Applications
Vol. 91. F. Azevedo, Constraint Solving over Multi-valued Logics – Application to Digital Circuits
Vol. 89. T. Bench-Capon et al. (Eds.), Legal Knowledge and Information Systems – JURIX 2002: The Fifteenth Annual Conference
Vol. 87. A. Abraham et al. (Eds.), Soft Computing Systems – Design, Management and Applications
Vol. 86. R.S.T. Lee and J.H.K. Liu, Invariant Object Recognition based on Elastic Graph Matching – Theory and Applications
Vol. 85. J.M. Abe and J.I. da Silva Filho (Eds.), Advances in Logic, Artificial Intelligence and Robotics – LAPTEC 2002
Vol. 84. H. Fujita and P. Johannesson (Eds.), New Trends in Software Methodologies, Tools and Techniques – Proceedings of Lyee_W02
Vol. 83. V. Loia (Ed.), Soft Computing Agents – A New Perspective for Dynamic Information Systems
Vol. 82. E. Damiani et al. (Eds.), Knowledge-Based Intelligent Information Engineering Systems and Allied Technologies – KES 2002
Vol. 81. J.A. Leite, Evolving Knowledge Bases – Specification and Semantics
Vol. 80. T. Welzer et al. (Eds.), Knowledge-based Software Engineering – Proceedings of the Fifth Joint Conference on Knowledge based Software Engineering
Vol. 79. H. Motoda (Ed.), Active Mining – New Directions of Data Mining
Vol. 78. T. Vidal and P. Liberatore (Eds.), STAIRS 2002 – STarting Artificial Intelligence Researchers Symposium

ISSN 0922-6389

Cooperative Systems Design

Scenario-Based Design of Collaborative Systems

Edited by

Françoise Darses

CNAM, Paris, France

Rose Dieng

INRIA, Sophia Antipolis, France

Carla Simone

Universita' di Milano Bicocca, Milano, Italy

and

Manuel Zacklad

Université de Technologie de Troyes, Troyes, France

IOS Press

Amsterdam • Berlin • Oxford • Tokyo • Washington, DC

ISBN 1 58603 422 7
Library of Congress Control Number: 2004104422

Publisher
IOS Press
Nieuwe Hemweg 6B
1013 BG Amsterdam
The Netherlands
fax: +31 20 620 3419
e-mail: order@iospress.nl

Distributor in the UK and Ireland
IOS Press/Lavis Marketing
73 Lime Walk
Headington
Oxford OX3 7AD
England
fax: +44 1865 75 0079

Distributor in the USA and Canada
IOS Press, Inc.
5795-G Burke Centre Parkway
Burke, VA 22015
USA
fax: +1 703 323 3668
e-mail: iosbooks@iospress.com

PRINTED IN THE NETHERLANDS

Preface

COOP'04 is the 6th International Conference on the Design of Cooperative Systems. The conference aims at bringing together researchers who contribute to the design of cooperative systems and their integration into organizational settings. The challenge of the conference is to advance:

- Understanding and modelling of collaborative work situations which are mediated by technical artefacts, either computational or not;
- Developing appropriate design methodologies for cooperative work analysis and cooperative systems design;
- Developing new technologies supporting cooperation;
- Evaluating and measuring the performance of cooperative systems.

The COOP conferences are predicated on the conviction that cooperative systems design requires a deep understanding of the cooperative work of groups and organizations, involving both artefacts and social practices. This is the reason why contributions from all disciplines contributing to or related to the field of cooperative systems design are considered as relevant, including computer and information sciences (computer-supported cooperative work (CSCW), group decision support systems, knowledge engineering, human-computer interaction, distributed artificial intelligence and multi-agent systems, etc.) and social sciences (organizational and management sciences, sociology, psychology, ergonomics, linguistics, etc.).

Various approaches and methodologies are considered, theoretical contributions as well as empirical studies reports or software development experiences on topics such as:

- Analysis of collaborative work situations
- Conceptual frameworks for understanding cooperative work
- Guidelines for designing cooperative systems
- Cooperation and emerging technologies
- Cooperation and new forms of organization
- Innovative technological solutions
- Innovative user interfaces.

In 2004, COOP has put a special emphasis on the area of Scenario-Based Design of Collaborative Systems, which includes the following issues (not exclusively):

- Scenarios as a means of understanding how computer systems might enhance cooperation
- Scenarios as a common language between users, developers and management
- Which scenarios for which collaborative systems?
- What is the role of a scenario-based approach in the life-cycle of cooperative systems: analysis, design, implementation, user training, evaluation
- Limits and benefits of scenario-based design for cooperative systems.

Besides papers dealing with these topics, other papers tackle different aspects of CSCW. They present new ideas in the field of awareness, models based on language acts analysis, collaborative design, ubiquity, or identify emerging trends such as the use of ontologies to make coordination and sharing of resources easier.

The Editors

Acknowledgements

Many persons and institutions have made the publication of this volume possible. We would like to thank them for their valuable effort. First we thank the members of the conference committee for their collaboration and the members of the program committee for helping the authors in improving the quality of the papers. We thank Miss Nadia Gauducheau, Post-Doc in psychology in the Tech-CICO laboratory, UTT, for her participation in the layout of the proceedings. We thank Mrs Patricia Maleyran (Acacia, INRIA), Mrs Lucie Georgeon, (Laboratory of Ergonomics, CNAM), Mrs Brigitte François (Tech-CICO, UTT) for their technical assistance, the internship students of the Tech-CICO laboratory for the design of the Web Site and the sponsors of the COOP'2004 conference for their financial support (CSTB, Conseil Régional PACA). Last but not least we thank Mr Alain Giboin and Mrs Monique Simonetti for their unfailing support to the COOP conferences.

Troyes, 26 February 2004

The Editors
Françoise Darses, Rose Dieng, Carla Simone, Manuel Zacklad

Conference Committee

Conference Chair

Rose Dieng-Kuntz
INRIA, Sophia Antipolis, France

Programme Committee Co-chairs

Françoise Darses
CNAM, Paris, France

Carla Simone
University of Milan, Italy

Local Organization Chair

Monique Simonetti
INRIA, Sophia Antipolis, France

Proceedings Chair

Manuel Zacklad
Université de Technologie de Troyes, France

Workshops Chair

Alain Giboin
INRIA, Sophia Antipolis, France

Poster Chair

Marcello Sarini
University of Milan, Italy

Doctoral Colloquium Chair

Kjeld Schmidt
IT University, Denmark

Program Committee

Programme Committee Co-Chairs

Françoise Darses
CNAM, Paris, France

Carla Simone
University of Milan, Italy

Scientific Committee

Alexandra Agostini, *Italy*
Liam Bannon, *Ireland*
Susan Bodker, *Denmark*
Jean-Francois Boujut, *France*
Béatrice Cahour, *France*
Monica Divitini, *Norway*
Gerhard Fischer, *USA*
Geraldine Fitzpatrick, *UK*
Christine Halverson, *USA*
Laurent Karsenty, *France*
Michael Koch, *Germany*
Kaari Kutti, *Finland*
Myriam Lewkowicz, *France*
Jacques Longchamp, *France*
Paul Luff, *UK*
Gloria Mark, *USA*
Keiichi Nakata, *Japan*
Wolfgang Prinz, *Germany*
Dave Randall, *UK*
Yvonne Rogers, *USA*
Pascal Salembier, *France*
Kjeld Schmidt, *Denmark*
Jean-Luc Soubie, *France*
Yngve Sunblad, *Sweden*
Régine Teulier, *France*
Bill Turner, *France*
Ina Wagner, *Austria*
Volker Wulf, *Germany*
Pascale Zaraté, *France*

Sponsors

CSTB, Conseil Régional PACA

Contents

Cooperative Systems Design
M. Zacklad et al. (Eds.)
IOS Press, 2004

Participatory Design of Community Information Systems: The Designer as Bard

John M. CARROLL
School of Information Sciences and Technology
The Pennsylvania State University
University Park, Pennsylvania 16802 USA

Introduction

One of the chief lessons in the past 30 years of design studies is the recognition of the range and amount of knowledge involved in design. This lesson was not the discrete result of a research program to determine the scope and nature of design knowledge. Indeed, one can see the so-called new design methods of the 1970s as a rather concerted effort to push toward a general (that is, domain knowledge free) kit of techniques (Jones, [3]). Nonetheless, the lesson has crept up on us over the years. No longer would customer interviews be seen as a comprehensive method for gathering design requirements. Concepts like stakeholder, tradeoffs, design rationale, emergent requirements, design patterns, tacit knowledge, and invisible work have increasingly complicated the picture. Today, users are conceptualized as embedded in communities of practice whose knowledge, including self-knowledge, is enacted rather than effable, in the traditional sense of requirements. What are we to do?

In this talk, I want to examine participatory design, in general and as applied in the domain of community information systems. Participatory design, crudely speaking, covers all design methods in which users (and perhaps other non-designer stakeholders) are independent actors in design decision making. Participatory design is an obvious way to bring more knowledge into the design process. It allows users to bring their domain knowledge to the design decision making that ultimately will impact their practices and communities.

By bringing the users themselves into the process, PD facilitates the sharing of tacit knowledge. Thus, even if a user-participant cannot explicitly state some particular work process contingency, his or her knowledge could still enter into the design deliberation through expressed preferences, envisionments and other shared design activities, and through linked discussions. Moreover, incorporating the users, as well as their knowledge, into the process does something more. It re-allocates power in technology development and adoption.

The perspective I want to develop and explore is that participatory design is best conceived as a space of related methods, rather than as some single approach. My claim is that new insights about participatory design methods and relationships can emerge from developing a taxonomic view of different approaches to participatory design. The design domain I will draw upon for illustration is community computing. One might think that the domain of community information systems might be one in which users would ipso facto control their technology. After all, these systems are part of the infrastructure for the civic, faith-based, and recreational volunteer associations that comprise one's personal life. But to a considerable extent, people are not in control of this technology. Community groups lack the resources to develop custom software components, or even to configure custom systems out of standard components. What they typically do is adapt, or adapt to, standard configurations of standard software.

1. Dimensions of participation

Broader participation by users and other stakeholders in design is not a monolithic intervention. There are a variety of ways to initiate participation, to manage and focus participatory interactions, and to learn from participation. Discussions of PD have recognized this from early on. For example, Clement and van den Besselaar [2] analyzed a collection of PD projects from the 1970s and 80s reported in conferences and workshops sponsored by IFIP Working Group 9.1 (Computers and Work). Participation took different forms across this sample of projects: In some, users became involved in the development of technology assessment criteria and guidelines. In others, users helped to create new organizational forms including support infrastructure. In half the projects studied, users were participating in the development of participatory practices!

In Table 1, I have called out six plausible dimensions of participation. I would be surprised if this is the optimal factoring of the dimensions, but it is a start.

Table 1: Six dimensions that define a space of participatory design methods

• Participatory impetus (Whose initiative led to adopting a participatory approach?) outside (university) researchers, the technology developers, the work/users, other stakeholders
• Ownership (Who controls the work activity being supported? Who authorized the design project and the participatory approach?) management in the customer organization, the technology developers, the workers/users, other parties are the owners. some mixture
• Scope of the design concern (What is the design discussion about? What is being produced?) a user interface; UI plus underlying software functionality, socio-technical work system, new PD practices or other infrastructure
• Scope of cooperation (When, how, and how long is the cooperative relationship?) a single workshop/work session, a series of workshops addressing a single development phase (e.g., requirements or design, not both), a series of workshops spanning two or more development phases (e.g., requirements and design), a series workshops spanning the entire lifecycle or a pervasive everyday work collaboration
• Expectations about learning and development (What do participants expect as outcomes beyond the specific work product?) nothing; designers expect to learn about users' task domain; users expect to learn about technology; users expect to assume responsibility for maintenance and further design

One reason it is interesting to try to construct an analysis like this is that it provides a more articulate answer to the question of what participatory design is. For example, Clement and van den Besselaar [2] enumerate five "ingredients" for participation: (1) workers must have access to relevant information, (2) workers must have the opportunity to take independent positions on issues, (3) workers must be included in the processes of decision making, (4) appropriate participatory methods must be available, and (5) sufficient organizational or technological flexibility. It is useful to move beyond this characterization to a more comprehensive and specific definition of the ways that stakeholders can become involved in participatory endeavors, the many ways these joint projects can be organized and managed, the many types of design concerns they can address, and the many kinds of outcomes they can aspire to and achieve.

Another reason it is useful to identify dimensions of participation and construct a space of possibilities is to be able to reflect more systematically on the differences among various alternative approaches to participatory design. For example, Clement and Van den Besselaar [2] reported that in most of the cases they surveyed the initiative to adopt a participatory approach originated with university researchers. This is not surprising given that they were investigating what at the time was a somewhat novel approach. However, the taxonomy helps to raise the question of what PD is like when the participatory impetus originates with the stakeholders themselves — with the developers, with the worker/users, with management — instead of with outside university researchers.

2. Community informatics

In the balance of this discussion I want to focus on a participatory design project involving community groups in Centre County Pennsylvania, a rural area of about 1,000 square miles with a population of 140,000, including the fairly cosmopolitan college town of State College (population 75,000) and the main campus of the Pennsylvania State University. Our research group is investigating and facilitating participatory design practices with the county historical society, the seniors' group, a sustainable development group, the enrichment program at the local high school, and with science teachers at one of the middle schools.

We initially formed these participatory design relationships by polling the community to find groups who were already using Internet technologies, like email and the Web, to carry out their missions, but who wanted or needed to consider learning more and doing more. For example, in our early discussions some of the groups were interested in attaining more direct control of their overall Web site design, some were interested in adding special functionalities to their Web sites (such as interactive maps), and some were interested in supporting collaborative interactions like discussion forums.

These design projects had several distinctive characteristics with respect to the taxonomy of participatory design approaches: (1) The owners are the worker/users. They control the work activity being supported. They authorize the design project and the participatory approach. (2) The scope of the design concern is fairly broad. It is not limited to a user interface or even an application program; it generally involves adaptations in the work itself (which the worker/users own). (3) The scope of the cooperation is also quite broad. These groups are not organized to take decisive action; they change slowly through trying ideas out and consensus building. Thus, participatory design relationships develop through considerable spans of time and involve mutual trust. (4) Finally, these groups are more responsible for their own technology than the workers typically studied in classic PD projects. It is a great idea to involve corporate secretaries in technology acquisition decisions that will affect their workplace, but getting their input may be enough. The secretaries will not have to maintain the new systems any more than had to maintain the old ones. For community groups, this is different. The only sustainable innovations they can make are those they can either pay for or carry out. There is no corporate infrastructure underwriting their activities. Thus, their expectations about learning and development are that they will assume responsibility for maintenance and further design.

Indeed, the community volunteer groups we are working with are quite unlike those in the classic PD projects. In those projects, PD was conceived of as a strategy for mediating the interests of workers and managers. These different interests were often themselves conceived of as adversarial. Some of most tantalizing fieldwork in CSCW describes the tension between formal lines of authority and official views of job roles and workflow, on the one hand, and the actual flow of work activity and information, on the other (Button, 2002). In the civic sector, these issues manifest differently. Unlike a business, no one is even officially in charge of a community; there is no single line of authority. Laws and officials, like a mayor or town council, have limited scope and impact. Official actions either have little consequence or tend to be planned and implemented very publicly through extensive negotiation processes.

Most of the activity in a community occurs through minimally coordinated and highly localized initiatives. When the Senior Citizens create a mentoring program, they only need the concurrence of the subgroups they wish to mentor. Communities function as confederations of largely autonomous subgroups. Groups publicize their activities to inspire themselves, to attract participation and support, and to leverage activities of peer groups. But they coordinate only to the extent of avoiding duplication of effort and minimizing conflicts over shared resources, such as the use of meeting rooms in a community center or public library. The motivation and reward structure for community network use is fundamentally different than for workplace computing, relying almost exclusively on intrinsic motivation and individual initiative-taking.

The diversity among the people constituting a community is greater than the range of job roles and relationships constituting most workplace organizations. To be sure, there are interesting distinctions and relationships among lawyers, legal assistants, and legal secretaries, but most of these can be understood in terms of a small number of role stereotypes and task dependencies. Proximate communities, in contrast, span all phases of life (children, teenagers, adults, the elderly), all personal roles (parents, siblings, friends), and all occupations (teachers, shop owners, police). Any given community member plays multiple roles; one is simultaneously an adult, a parent, a friend, a teacher, a Rotarian, a first-baseman, and so forth.

In our context, "management" corresponds to core members or officers of the groups. But these managers do not employ their constituents, and they cannot order them to do anything, rather the managers inspire and cajole the members to volunteer.

3. The role of bard

The milieu of community informatics raises a question about plausible and effective roles for technology developers in participatory design relationships.

Unlike a PD workshop involving an opportunity sample of workers, in the community informatics context the workshop includes some, or possibly all of the members of a real community – that is, a densely connected social network of individuals with a collective identity inhering in shared interests and practices. It is not plausible for the developer to expect to enter into this community on a casual or short-term basis. The community is not constituted to accommodate this. As a result, the developer will tend to stand at the periphery of the community.

This is not bad. It is not a failure. It certainly does not mean that participatory design relationships with volunteer community groups is an impossibility. But this is the way it will be unless the developer decides to become a participant – not only in the design cooperation, but in the community itself. On the other hand, fully joining and participating the community, for example becoming a full member of the local sustainable development association or of the county historical society may be no more feasible for the technology developer than is becoming a phototypesetter, or a legal secretary, or an atmospheric scientist in order to engage

This peripheral position in a group can be both good and bad. The peripheral participant has no organizational power, and this makes it difficult to take a frontal approach in discussions about courses of action for the group. However, not having power brings the luxury that no one need worry that power may be misused. The peripheral participant can often remain to one side of potentially polarizing discussions, helping the more central participants to resolve issues, and move ahead on plans for action. Peripheral participants can represent the group to itself from a particular perspective. For technology developers, this could mean presenting the group's technology needs and possibilities to the group itself.

This specific role can perhaps be uniquely useful: Community groups are not about information technology any more than they are about telecommunications. They recruit various technologies in the service of their community goals. This is pretty much analogous to all non-programmer/non-engineer users of information technology, with the strong exceptions, noted earlier, that members of community groups have little or no technology infrastructure (access to training, equipment budgets, technician support, etc.) and very weak managerial lines of authority and control. Many of these groups are barely resourced to meet standing obligations, let alone to develop and/or adopt new technology.

In this context, it is easy for them to lose sight of their own technology needs and goals. The peripheral participant can remind core members of their own needs and goals, and draw connections between current group issues and opportunities and technology plans. If this reminding is done creatively, it can become a vehicle for defining a zone of proximal development, in Vygotsky's [5] sense, with respect to technology learning and mastery. The zone of proximal development is the set of concepts, skills, and other capacities that a person or an organization can undertake with help. As an individual or an organization successfully operates within the zone of proximal development, it becomes autonomously competent with a larger set of concepts, skills, and capacities. At that point, it can articulate greater ambitions and continue to push the bounds of its own development. If the peripheral participant can remind the core members of their zone of proximal development with respect to information technology, and perhaps even provide some help so that they can operate within this zone, then the peripheral participant can become an instrument of learning and development within the community.

I have been looking for a metaphor to understand this role. My current suggestion is the role of "bard" – those fellows with lutes and plumed hats, roaming about, singing ballads in medieval courts. Bards were not knights, chancellors, or bishops; they were not even blacksmiths, tailors or farmers. They were not core members of the medieval community at any stratum. However, their songs reminded all the members of the community of their collective past exploits, of the folkways and mores that regulate and sustain them, and of their future objectives and visions. Their songs inspired other actors in the community to undertake great quests, to defend their comrades, or just to be a bit more creative and daring in their farming or whatever else they did. The bard's tools are themselves fairly unthreatening to the interests and practices of others, and at the same time participatory in the sense that a familiar or rousing ballad asks for sing-along.

Etienne Wenger (page 168-169; [6]) stresses the value of anecdote in measuring value in communities of practice: "The best way to assess the value of a community of practice is by collecting stories." He says that a good story describes how knowledge resources were produced and applied, how the community got from the germ of an idea to a documented approach, how innovation, learning, and problem-solving were achieved. It documents the outcome or result, the knowledge resource that was produced, and describes how that resource was applied in practice to create value for members of the community. I like the exotic anthropology that this suggestion conjures up; it's also a constructive suggestion about how to manage tacit knowledge that avoids Nonaka's "externalization" paradox [4].

We might elaborate Wenger's idea to add that a *really* good story also describes the antecedent triggers for the community's original mobilization to produce a knowledge resource -- the standing problems and recognized opportunities that led the community to innovate in the first place. It should also include at least a narrative rendering of identified or possible tradeoffs -- side-effects of implementing or adopting the resource. And it should include an analysis how the resource might be further improved in the future. Thus, "enhanced narratives" -- case studies, scenarios and design rationale -- might be the lingua franca for documenting and evaluating value in communities of practice.

Here I'm suggesting that we also turn this around and consider stories (or for that matter, ballads) as participatory tools for reminding, for inspiration, for focusing courses of action, and for guiding change in communities. In some participatory design contexts, and community informatics may be one, we (technology developers) may face the new challenge, not of ceding power to the worker/users, but of finding a productive role through which to contribute to projects owned and controlled by the users. And really, this seems like a far more interesting design method problem to tackle.

References

[1] Carroll, J.M., Chin, G., Rosson, M.B. & Neale, D.C. (2000). The Development of Cooperation: Five years of participatory design in the virtual school. In D. Boyarski & W. Kellogg (Eds.), *DIS'2000: Designing Interactive Systems* (Brooklyn, New York, August 17-19). New York: Association for Computing Machinery, pp. 239-251.

[2] Clement, A. & Van den Besselaar, P. (1993). A retrospective look at PD projects. *Communications of the ACM*, 36(4), 29-37.

[3] Jones, J.C., (1970). Design methods: Seeds of human futures. New York: Wiley.

[4] Nonaka, I. (1994). A Dynamic Theory of Organizational Knowledge Creation. *Organization Science, 5*(1), 14-37.

[5] Vygotsky, L.S. (1978). *Mind in society*. Cambridge, MA: Harvard University Press.

[6] Wenger, E., McDermott, R. & Snyder, W.M. (2002). *Cultivating Communities of Practice: A Guide to Managing Knowledge*. Cambridge, MA: Harvard Business School Press.

Cooperative Systems Design
M. Zacklad et al. (Eds.)
IOS Press, 2004

Getting to the Point with Participatory Video Scenarios

Salu YLIRISKU
University of Art and Design Helsinki
Hämeentie 135 C, 00550 Helsinki, Finland

Abstract. Participatory video scenarios can be used to facilitate user participation in the development of collaborative information systems. At the same time these scenarios promote the empathic understanding of the users. When scenario design is based on a contextual study of the users' work, the scenarios can be focused on the issues that are most challenging from the users' point of view. The number of scenarios can be minimized and their future relevance maximized, when the scenarios are built on key findings abstracted from the users' work.

Co-creating video scenarios in participation with users is at best both efficient and motivating. As users are experts in their field, they can relatively quickly come up with realistic and representative examples of situations for the scenarios. The richness and multimodality of video and the possiblity to augment the story afterwards with edited images and sounds support communicating the scenario performances in a vivid, detailed and emotion-evoking way. This paper describes a case study in which participatory video scenarios were used in the development of a bank's knowledge management system.

Keywords. Video scenarios, participatory design, user experience, improvised role acting, empathic design.

Introduction

Luotain - design for user experience is an ongoing research project at the University of Art and Design Helsinki (http://smart.uiah.fi/luotain). The primary objective of the project is to develop methodological tools to support user centred product concept design. Several case studies have been conducted in the Luotain project including such fields as snow sports, teleworking, patient transportation, laboratory analysis systems and knowledge management systems. This paper is about the knowledge management system case.

As people form an essential part of collaborative information systems, taking the people's point of view into account in the design of the new system is important. Achieving systems, services and products which are useful, usable and even pleasurable for people to use requires a user centered approach. User centered approaches vary in how they involve users, ranging from having the users as sources of information, as in Contextual Design [3], to having them as full participants in the development process, as in participatory design [22]. In addition to producing objective knowledge about the work system and users' roles in it, designers need to understand the more subjective side of work: what users experience, see and feel. The empathic design approach aims at seeing how users experience their material surroundings and the people in it, including themselves as key characters of their everyday lives [20]. For creating a more holistic picture about the users' point of view multiple approaches should be used to complement each other [32].

In order to create an understanding of the users they have to be involved in the process. Sanders and Dandavate emphasize that the path to the experiencer's world comes only through his or her participation [32]. In participatory design users are treated as full participants in the product design activities. Participatory design has its roots in the scandinavian design tradition, where users have been involved in design activities from the early stages on [22]. Participatory design activities are said to form a new space for design between the work domains of designers and end users [27].

Scenarios can be used to support participatory design activities [22]. Scenario use has even been considered to be the backbone of the participatory design process [8]. Scenarios as stories are not fixed to any particular media and they can be created for example with video. There are several studies in which video has been used to promote user participation in design projects [e.g. 6, 28].

In this paper a method for empathic design is presented in the context of the development of a large collaborative information system. The method uses participatory video scenarios, which are scenarios captured and edited on video co-created with potential future users.

1. Using Scenarios in Design

Scenarios have become a widely used tool for designing systems, services and products, and there is an increasing number of publications about scenario use [see e.g. 21, 9, 14, 19]. In addition, scenarios are used in futures studies to summarize the results of research about possible alternative futures [2]. Although scenarios are often assosiated with future use, scenarios can be created to describe current situations as well [6]. Due to the fact that scenarios are used for a range of purposes the definition varies considerably depending on the context. For example, there are numerous different specifying names for scenarios (e.g. type scenarios [6], brief scenarios, vignettes, elaborated scenarios and complete task scenarios [13]). This paper uses the definition by Carroll [9], which describes scenarios as stories about people and their activities including a setting, agents or actors, goals or objectives and actions or events.

The definition leaves the format and content of scenarios very open, which suits well the open nature of concept development activities. Scenarios can contain, comic strips [19], sound, moving image, toy characters [15] and they can even be presented in the form of plays acted out by real people [14]. The format of a scenario depends on the purpose and the skills of scenario creators. The format may affect where the focus is directed to, how much details there are in the scenario and how well the desired message is communicated. For example, a video scenario may direct the focus to the details of the real-time interactions between the user and the system.

Scenarios can be used throughout the design process in various phases for example for understanding users' needs and their work [31, 6], developing requirements [11], creating ideas [15, 9] and communicating product concepts [19]. Scenarios allow keeping product details in the background while setting the focus on users' activities and contexts [19]. Scenarios promote communicating the meaning of different designs by putting them in the use context including users, their motives and environment.

A scenario can explain the purpose of the system, service or product in a brief, concise and engaging way. They are good for communicating causal relationships, because unlike for example drawings or mockups, scenarios describe events happening over time. This makes scenarios ideal for communicating the utilitarian functions of a product.

In sum, scenarios have three major characteristics that make them so powerful in design of practical product concepts:

1. inclusion of the time dimension,
2. versatility of form and
3. versatility of content.

Scenarios also support cross-disciplinary communication. As new systems, services and products are usually created by teams it is not enough to concentrate merely on understanding the users' point of view and incorporating it into the design process. New product design may include such fields as marketing, engineering, industrial design and human factors. Customers, project management, network specialists, user interface designers, database specialists and usability specialists are often also involved. The need for a common language across discipline borders has been a topic for intensive research over the last decades [e.g. 1, 12, 28] and scenarios are a feasible method for facilitating cross disciplinary communication [1, 12]. The concreteness of scenarios makes them accessible to the many stakeholders in a development project [11].

Scenarios should focus on representative situations. As systems often facilitate many possible uses, not everything can be descibed with scenarios. If scenarios are directly based on empirically observed situations, the result may be a huge amount of scenarios with no internal structure making them difficult to manage [10]. Empirical scenarios are also a posteriori, they represent history. In the design of products for future use, they should also be valid in future situations. The number of scenarios should be kept at a manageable amount. User study findings must be condensed to be made into useful scenarios.

Good stories are not merely descriptions about events following each other, but build suspense as well. The suspense may, for example, result from a conflict between the protagonist's motives and her actions. Potts suggests that a set of scenarios in systems design should consider also situations or behaviour, which is not desired for the system and, thus, introduce a conflict in a scenario [31]. The inclusion of such situations in scenarios highlights the potential for design improvements and can make the design problem more engaging to work with.

2. Using Video in User Centered Design

Video can be used to support design activities in most of the design process phases. Video can be even used to study and reflect upon design activities and, thereby, develop the design practices [16]. Currently, there are numerous examples of using video in product development in phases such as user studies [e.g. 6, 33], organizing and representing user data [7, 25], ideation [26], design [28, 4], prototyping [24], scenario creation [6], communication of product and interface ideas [21] and product evaluation.

Video that is captured in a real environment is specific and rich in detail. It represents people, their acitivities, tools, environments and situations vividly. Observation videos are often considered objective records of the users' world, but on the contrary, evidence shows that video is far from objective. Going with a video camera to the users' environment is an intervention, which may change the way that users relate to their setting. What is captured on video is a selected fraction out of continuous events filtered through the limited angle of the camera lens. Thus, what is presented is a subjective account. Moreover, things that take place on video can be subject to controversial interpretations [6]. This can be seen as a weakness of the record or taken as an inspirational resource for design. Ethnographic video materials should be considered as representations rather than facts [30].

As video promotes acting by capturing what people do and say, it is a natural tool to be used in co-creating the scenarios together with the users. For example, Binder has observed that users can contribute to the design with improvised video scenarios [4]. Sperschneider and Bagger have used video in co-designing new products with users, who act in their own industrial work environment [33].

Improvised video scenarios describe users interacting with a system, service or product. They are acted out by representative people of the work domain without completely planning in advance what they say and do. Acting may follow a roughly planned plot or be fully improvised, for example, inspired by a design 'prop'.

The planning, filming and editing of the video scenarios takes a considerable amount of time, and video has had a reputation of being cumbersome to edit [e.g. 25]. Even though non-linear video editing tools have made editing more efficient, it is still time consuming. Video scenarios could be created completely without planning and editing, but they would most likely end up lacking internal structure and relevance. Moreover, they might be too rough or confusing to be useful in communicating the ideas to outsiders. Therefore, scenarios should be planned to some extent in advance and be processed after filming to make the message in the video more clear, effective and engaging.

Real product development projects are usually done under high time pressure, which increases the importance of efficient and effective communication between different parties involved in the process. Black points out that the key points of the data should be communicated in a vivid and memorable way [5]. A well created video scenario may support this goal, since it can convey a message in a rich, specific and emotion-evoking way.

2.1 Video and Required Skills

People are used to watching commercially produced movies, television programmes and advertising. This should be taken into consideration when creating video scenarios, since these experiences influence the expectations that people have. As the creators of video scenarios may not be professionals in acting, shooting, lighting, sound recording, cutting or directing, the resulting video scenarios may lack credibility or fascination. At worst, the audience sees the user as a fool, which definitely should be avoided when involving real users in the acting. Ethical issues are always important when using video in user centred activities [see e.g. 23, 30].

At best, video scenarios convey the idea in an engaging way. To succeed in this, basic skills about video storytelling are required. The producing teams should know about capturing high quality image and sound, and about how to edit and combine the material into a cohesive story which is of appropriate length.

3. Empathic Approach

The empathic design approach aims at creating a holistic understanding about how users experience products and incorporating that understanding into the creation of new products. In the Luotain project a framework has been developed about the roles of various aspects and contexts that have a role in the users' product experiences [17, 18]. The framework supports a holistic understanding of the users and their relationships with other people, acitivities, environment, artefacts and with future opportunities related to the current area of interest in order to inform and inspire product concept development. Based on the experiences of the case studies these relationships can be described in scenarios. As scenarios are about the motivations and experiences of users as well as the events [11], scenarios can be used among other tools and methods to support the empathic design approach.

Nielsen points out that the character or the user in the scenario is often poorly described [29]. This has made it difficult to engage with the user and to be able to imagine the user's actions. When a user is described as a fully developed character it helps the design team to connect with the user with empathy, she is more easily remembered and is, thereafter, more likely to be brought into the actual design process [29]. In participatory video scenarios the user is described in much detail. Furthermore, when the user improvises according to a rough pre-planned plot, she most likely reveals also some tacit aspects which characterise her and her way of interacting with people and products.

There are also difficulties in describing the user in detail. When a scenario is used for communicating a product concept idea to an audience, a detailed description of the user may draw too much attention and bias the evalution of the product concept.

4. Case Contact Center Knowledge Management

This chapter describes a case study about the concept development of a bank's knowledge management system. The aims of the 'Contact Center Knowledge Management' case study were to develop an understanding about the bank's phone service work from the workers' point of view and to provide the developers with relevant visual material about the topic. The research focused on studying whether it is possible create communicative visual material efficiently and in participation with end users to inform the strategic planning of a collaborative knowledge management system and focus on relevant issues about the topic.

The study was conducted with the Contact Center of a Scandinavian bank. The Contact Center produces services for over 200 cooperative banks serving almost 3 million people. It is the central service channel of the bank group for offering personal services via electronic media (i.e. phone service, email, internet). The case study took place in the beginning of a long development process of a new knowledge management system for the bank.

The context of a bank is challenging for research. A bank consists of multiple departments and offices, which are geographically dispersed. Information related to banking interactions is highly confidential and the privacy of the bank clients must not be compromized at any stage, which is reflected in the bank's formal organization. The knowledge domain is wide and each department has its dedicated role, tasks and tools in the whole. Therefore, for a researcher coming from the outside, it is important to set a clear focus in order to be able to help to develop the work.

4.1 Setting the Focus for the Study

The Contact Center's phone service, a central place requiring efficient knowledge management, was selected as the target for the study. The different work situations were assumed to include a wide variety of work and specific knowledge needs, which was important for creating a good basis for the scenarios. The real-time requirements of the work situations in the phone service are a challenge for knowledge management. Data must be retrieved fast. Also, it was assumed that many different kinds of situations could be observed in the phone service within the short time period of the study.

The workers saw knowledge management as an obscure monster. The bank's management wanted the workers to participate in the process to give this 'monster' a better known and friendlier form. This aim matched the project's interest on user experience. Therefore, an emphasis was set on the emotional side of the experience. Priority was given to the workers' point of view as well as to the point of view of the clients who they served.

The quality of the phone service of a bank depends both on the workers and on the system they use. Thus, in the design of a new banking knowledge management system it is essential to get the people committed to adopting the new system, otherwise the whole attempt may fail. Having the workers participate in the design of the new system was seen as a means to increase their commitment.

To be able to conduct the contextual study and analyze the material within the available time and human resources, the number of Contact Center workers participating in the study was limited to five. This was considered enough to create a sufficient understanding of the work, the environment and the people for creating scenarios about the new concept. The participants for the study were chosen from different backgrounds and roles to cover the variety of the workers and the roles in the Contact Center as well as possible.

4.2 Starting the Activities

The main activities of the case study consisted of a contextual observation and participatory workshops. The project started with an introductory session and ended with an evaluation session. The order of the activities is described in Figure 1. The contextual study was conducted with five workers. The planning was done by a team consisting of a project manager and a team leader from the bank and a researcher from the University of Art and Design Helsinki.

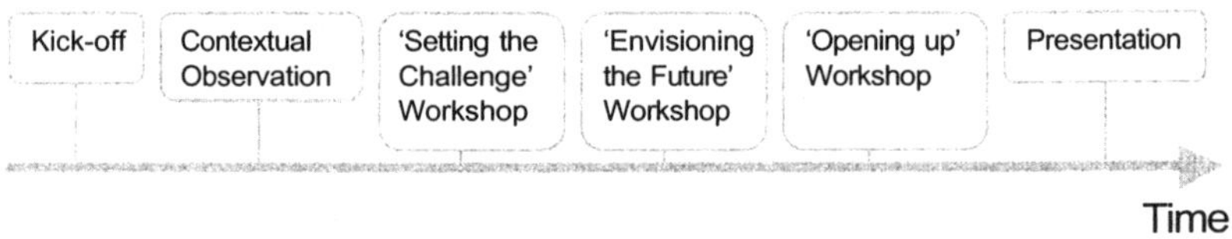

Figure 1. Time table for the case study

The case study started with an introductory kick-off session. The participants were introduced to the aims and methods of the study as well as to the researcher and a project manager from the bank. Also the workers' attitudes towards being recorded on video were discussed. This was important both ethically and for building the necessary trust between the workers and the project team. The permissions for recording video in the bank were also given in this meeting.

4.3 Contextual Observation

The phone service work was studied in the workers' real work setting. The workers were first interviewed at their workstations to get an overview of their role, artifacts, work activities, motivations and sources of good and bad feelings. After the interview the workers resumed their normal work and the observation continued for about two hours with each participant (see Figure 2).

Figure 2. The use of work related artifacts was studied during contextual observation.

The data records from the study consisted of video tapes and field notes. Some of the video tapes were first transcribed into separate text documents. There was no time to transcribe and analyze all the video material thoroughly. The rest of the user data was analyzed from the field notes.

The data from the contextual studies was analyzed in a matter of days. There were many different possible areas to focus on within the general focus of the study. For example, the focus could have been set on the problems in using current software, interactions between the workers, workers' different roles, use of the various physical and software tools related to knowledge management, the task structures, data flows and knowledge requirements of different situations. As the analysis and transcribing continued several recurring themes was identified. The findings were grouped into categories such as 'different skill requirements', 'the difference between outgoing and incoming phone calls' and 'tools and sources of information'. Unfortunately the details of these categories cannot be described here due to the confidentiality of the material.

4.4 'Setting the Challenge' Workshop

The first workshop aimed at creating a shared understanding about the current work practice and selecting a representative situation for the video scenarios. The workshop team consisted of the phone service workers and a facilitator. The workers were the same that were studied and the facilitator was the same person, who conducted the contextual study and analyzed the data.

The main findings from the contextual observation were verified with the workers. The most central findings concerned the different types of knowledge, knowledge requirements of situations, different roles in work and different work experience levels. Due to the confidentiality the findings cannot be described in more detail in this paper.

To give the participants an idea about the expectations of the workshops and what scenarios are all about, they were introduced to video scenarios in the form of a short exercise. This excercise aimed also at creating a more informal and relaxed atmosphere and at getting the participants to understand the value of scenarios in communicating an idea to people with different backgrounds.

The team acted and videotaped a story about a person who had fallen off a boat. The story was in a form of a three-act drama, which had a beginning, a middle and an end. The plot of the story was following:

```
"Beginning
Actor 1: Has fallen of the boat and is in the water shouting:
         "Help me! Help me!"
Actor 2: Is on board with a rope. She shouts to actor 1:
         "Try to hold on! I'll save you!"

Middle
Actor 2: Throws the rope to Actor 1.
         Actor 1: Ties a the rope around his back using the one-
         hand bowline.
Actor 2: Starts pulling Actor 1 from the water.

End
Both actors are onboard and smile."
```

To understand the value of scenarios in communicating a message to people accross different disciplines the participants were asked to imagine different points of view such as a shipowner's, a sailor's, a rope manufacturer's and a ship constructor's. After this it was easy for the participants to understand, that the different stakeholders could use the scenario to judge what it would mean for them if the one-hand bowline were to become the standard method for saving people in the future.

The building of the scenarios started after this warm-up excercise. The focus was set on the current practice and contrasted to the ideal situation and a possible future situation. The participants were presented the basic building blocks of the scenarios: the worker, the client, the client's situation, the problem of the client and the tools available to the worker.

To help the participants focus on a situations that are essential for knowledge management, four general criteria with some concrete examples from the contextual observation were presented. In a matter of seconds the participants came up with a real, representative and applicable situation. "In Lapland a man has lost his credit card. He is a customer of a bank in Southern Finland." Although other possible situations were discussed as well, the scenarios were built on this idea.

The facilitator's role in the creation of the scenarios was to keep the planning on the specifics of objects and events. He continuously kept asking questions like: "What is the time? What is his name and where is he calling from? He calls now. He explains his situation..... What happens next?". With the experience from the contextual study the facilitator was able to discuss details of the domain specific scenario plans with the participants.

Two scenarios were outlined to describe the current work. First one described an experienced worker's point of view and the second a novice worker's point of view. The plot was planned so that the more experienced worker could handle the situation well whereas the novice worker would fail to serve the client due to lack of knowledge about exceptional opening hours of bank offices during holidays.

The first scenario was filmed during the same day. The videotaping was done in an appropriate working context with the usual working equipment. The facilitator operated the video camera and the workers were acting. To intensify the emotional experience in the exciting points of the scenarios, the scenario was filmed from two different angles. A wider angle was taken from a side and a closer angle was taken from the front (see Figure 3). However, creating this emotional effect was difficult during editing, since the semi-improvised versions of the shots were quite different due to the improvisation.

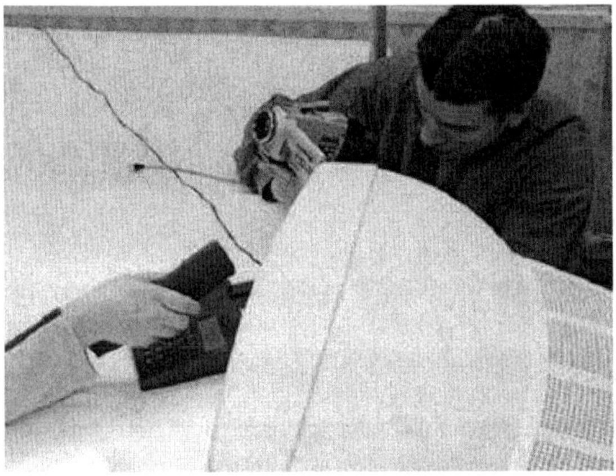

Figure 3. Shooting a front close-up for a video scenario

The customer who was hiking in Lapland could not be filmed in the appropriate context within the resources of the case study. Therefore, it was decided that the customer would be presented in a discount fashion as hand-drawn still images.

4.5 The 'Envisioning the Future' Workshop

The second workshop was held five days after the first one. The memories from the last workshop were refreshed by watching a video clip of the previous workshop. The second scenario was rehearsed once before videotaping in a similar way as the first one only the participants having different roles.

After videotaping the second scenario the story was analyzed in detail by the team. The story was studied step by step to find out the different knowledge needs and information sources in the progress of events. This analysis provided the basis for creating the ideal scenario, where all the necessary knowledge would be provided to the worker and to the client at the right moment.

It was also discussed whether the collaboration of the workers should be built into the ideal situation, since it was found during the contextual study that solving a problem in collaboration with co-workers was often considered pleasing. It also would support learning from colleagues. After all, serving the client efficiently was the most appealing solution in the ideal situation.

A realistic future scenario was based on the ideal scenario. The future scenario had a system that was able to support the worker well in the situation. Having looked at the same situation from three different points of view helped in constructing a new scenario, which combined elements from the other scenarios.

4.6 The 'Opening up' Workshop

The third workshop took place six days after the second. The goals of the workshop were to open up the designed knowledge management concept to other situations than the one presented in the scenarios and come up with the aims and development framework for the system.

The workshop started with a recap of the earlier workshops. For this purpose the facilitator had created diagrams about the different scenarios (see Figure 4). The representations showed the time that serving the client took and also the development of the client's feelings during the interaction. Video material was not used for this purpose since editing a selection of all the available material would have required too much time.

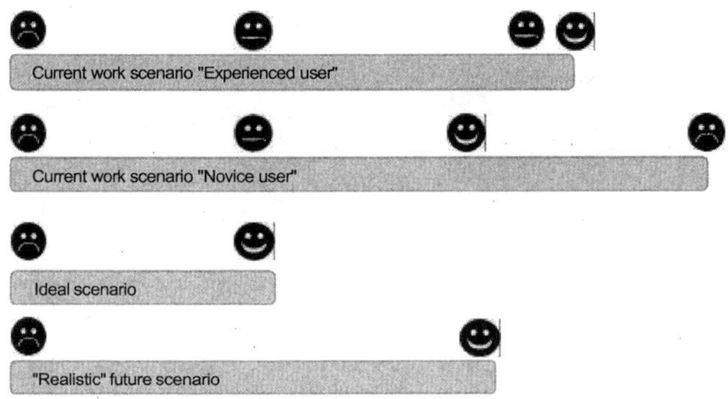

Figure 4. Diagrams showing lengths of the scenarios and the client's feelings

After the ideal and future scenarios were videotaped, the concept of design drivers was introduced to the participants. Design drivers are central values that guide design [34]. Some examples of design drivers were presented to the participants, who were then able to discuss the design drivers for the knowledge management system.

The concept of the knowledge management system presented in the future scenario was evaluated against other kinds of situations relevant to knowledge management. To support this the facilitator had selected a couple of situations from the contextual observation. The situations differed in such aspects as the frequency of occurrence and complexity.

Some screen designs were sketched out and the user's interaction with the system was designed for the different situations that had been considered so far. This provided a rough idea of the user interface for creating illustrations about the user interface for the future scenario. After considering the different situational alternatives and creating the user interface sketches, the design drivers were reviewed once again.

4.7 Editing

The editing consisted of creating images of the user interface, images of the customer, cutting, sound manipulation and sound editing. The sounds were manipulated to create the illusion of a real phone call. The participant who acted as the voice of the customer was actually sitting in the same room with the other participants during videotaping. An example of the hand-drawn images for the scenarios is presented in Figure 5.

Figure 5. The client of the bank was represented as a hand-drawn image in the video.

The facilitator was resposible for editing the video. The video editing took 14 working days including the learning of a new editing software. The final result was a video that was 20 minutes long.

4.8 Presenting and Evaluating the Scenarios

The video scenarios were presented to the workers in the project team, the managers of the knowledge management development and two professors of design. The scenarios were evaluated by 12 people in total. The evaluation was based on a questionaire, which focused on such aspects as the communicability and the emotional effects of the scenarios. The workers, managers and professors had different questionaires with some overlapping questions. The evaluation also included an informal discussion about the video scenarios and the process. The results of the evaluation of the case study and the video scenarios are summarized in the next section.

5. Results

According to the feedback from the bank's management and Contact Center workers the case study increased their understanding of the different knowledge requirements of the work situations. The specific situation on which the scenarios focused was considered central for the knowledge management domain. It was also reported that the study increased their understanding of some of the emotional effects that a knowledge management system may have on the interaction between a worker, the system and a client. Furthermore, they reported to have as a result a better understanding of the worker's as well as the client's point of view in the whole. According to the bank's project managers, the study focused on relevant issues and produced design drivers, which should guide the development of the future knowledge management system.

The participants reported that the process was motivating for them. They could influence how the observations were conducted. They participated in creating and realizing the scenarios and they planned the design drivers for the knowledge management concept. They also reported that they learned new things about their work during the study.

All the presentation session attendees reported that they liked the video scenarios. They even reported that they were willing to see the scenarios again. The audience reported emotional responses to the scenarios and the scenarios were considered engaging even by the design professors, who didn't participate in the process, but who attended the scenario presentation session. The attendees of the presentation session also commented that the scenario in which the novice worker fails to provide the client with decent service was the most exciting.

According to the feedback, all the presentation session attendees were able to understand the scenarios. The fact that some of the attendees did not have previous knowledge about the bank's knowledge management domain and some were experts in it, seems to support the claim that scenarios facilitate communication to an audience with different levels of knowledge about a topic. There was no need to develop separate material or presentation sessions for communicating the message to the management.

The situation of how the lack of information can affect the situation of a client was understood by the viewers. Especially the ones who had not participated in the process reported that they could understand, how the system affected the worker's feelings in different situations. This is in line with the observation that with video even an outsider can get the sense of how it is to interact with certain product [23].

According to the workers, the process was efficient. It took at maximum 16 hours of working time from each worker to attend the project activities. This time includes the introduction and scenario presentation sessions. The calendar time to plan and conduct the study and organize the workshops was two months and the video editing was done in a period of another two months. The case study was conducted by a researcher working on the process part time, three days a week.

In sum, in the case study it was possible to create communicative visual material in participation with the bank's workers. The result was considered relevant by the bank's project management and valid for informing the strategic planning of a collaborative knowledge management system.

6. Discussion

In this case, the scenarios were based on verified abstractions from the contextual study of the users' work. These scenarios were created together with the users and the results are

- very detailed and concrete
- realistic
- small in number
- have a good coverage of the user's different work situations (past, current and potential)
- focus on relevant things to the current area of interest
- focus on the users' point of view and support empathy for the user

In addition to communicating a pre-planned message, semi-improvised role-acting can convey some of the tacit aspects of users' work as they improvise actions similar to their own work. The participants in the case were professionals in talking, which may have affected the success of their improvised acting. There are also other studies, which show that improvised role acting can be used effectively in product development processes [14, 33].

Creating video scenarios with users requires that they are willing to act, which in some cases might not come for granted, and most likely will require facilitation. The motivation can be created in stages first observing the users in their own environment and then discussing the findings with them. They may become involved to the extent, that they are easily motivated and willing to act. This can be supported with simple warm-up excercises to relax the atmosphere. In making the users act, the facilitator has to be sensitive to the users, and they must have a way to withdraw from acting without losing their face.

Video supports user participation in the creation of the scenarios as users can be actors and scriptwriters. Moreover, using video seems to motivate the users for acting and preparing the plot. Video's effect in increasing the users' effort in striving for a good shot has been observed elsewhere also [26]. In the case study, participatory video scenarios were used to co-design with users in an efficient, effective and engaging way.

Textual and sketched scenarios lack the richness and multimodality of video. Black has pointed out that there is a need to present the data in a vivid and memorable way for the data to be utilized afterwards in the development process [5]. The richness and multimodality of video supports communicating the users' world in a specific and emotionally engaging way. Most likely, this affects the utilization of the video scenarios later in the development process.

Video scenarios can be exciting. It may result from the suspense in the story or the spectator's subjective relationship to the content of the video. People respond emotionally to a video representing themselves or a fellow worker. Salient emotions can be expected especially when a person is unaccustomed to being filmed and she sees herself acting in a projected image on the wall in front of an audience. This kind of a video can be highly personal.

The scenario in which the novice worker fails to provide the client with decent service was considered the most exciting. The conflict in the plot was the strongest. The novice worker informs the client incorrectly, which results in the client's failure to get money from a bank office. The spectators knew already from the first scenario the true nature of things and could expect the failure to happen.

The visual and aural content of the video can be manipulated to support desired emotional effects or to direct focus. This can be used to highlight for example problems in current work practice. As video can combine different media such as photos, drawn images, computer animation and music, not everything has to be recorded with a camera. This can make the scenarios more effective and the process faster and cheaper.

The editing of the video scenarios could have been done remarkably faster in this case. During the case an extensive amount of time was used to learn a new editing software, to polish the video with hand-drawn colourful images, to manipulate sounds, to find and add music and to fine tune the cutting. By doing the editing in a more 'quick&dirty' manner, the process would have been more rapid without serious loss to the message.

Basic knowledge about using video in storytelling was required for creating the video scenarios. Knowledge about issues related both to video content and technology are required for effective video use. Without appropriate experience or skill, the result will most likely to be unconvincing.

Despite that within the limits of this kind of project the amount of issues addressed is somewhat limited, the approach seems to be suitable for co-creating vivid and engaging scenarios with the users, which promote the users' point of view and at the same time focus on the central issues about the development challenge. The case study shows that this method worked in the development of a collaborative knowledge management system for a formal and complex domain of banking.

7. Future Possibilities

As processing power, data storage devices and software have all improved during the last years, high quality video editing is now possible with a mobile set of devices, which are easily brought to the users' environment. Therefore, the videos can be more easily co-edited with the users and they have better chances to affect the resulting video. As video editing tools get cheaper and more easier to use it should be possible to increase user participation in the video creation process.

Video is becoming increasingly used on digital platforms such as the internet and mobile phones, and this affects the way video will be perceived and used in the future. The appropriate length and quality of video scenarios might vary depending on the platform posing new challenges for the development of the scenarios.

Furthermore, digital platforms facilitate easier sharing of the video artifacts. As connections become faster, video scenarios can be efficiently delivered to a georaphically dispersed audience. This may well support the user centered design activities of large international companies. Thus, the development of technology will provide new possibilities to co-design and use video scenarios in the future.

Acknowledgements

Special thanks to Katja Battarbee, Turkka Keinonen, Ilpo Koskinen and Tuuli Mattelmäki for reviewing and providing helpful feedback on this paper.

References

[1] Asplund, H., Ranta, M., "Brokering based balancing of viewpoints - experiences from pre-product development of mobile services", in Proceedings of Good, Bad and Irrelevant, Helsinki, Finland, 2003, pp. 280-284.

[2] Bell, Wendell, "Foundations of Futures Studies: Human Science for a New Era", Volume 1, Transaction Publishers, USA, 1997.

[3] Beyer, H., Holtzblatt, K., "Contextual Design: Defining Customer-Centered Systems", Morgan Kaufmann Publishers, USA, 1998.

[4] Binder, T., "Setting the Stage for Improvised Video Scenarios", in extended abstracts of CHI'99 conference, Pittsburg, USA, 1999, pp. 230-231.

[5] Black, A., "Why I Work in User Experience Consulting", in Koskinen, I., Battarbee, K., Mattelmäki, T., (eds.), "Empathic Design: User Experience in Product Design", IT Press, Finland, 2003, pp. 146-152.

[6] Buur, J., Binder, T., Brandt, E., "Taking video beyond 'hard data' in User Centred Design", in proceedings of PDC2000 Participatory Design Conference, New York City, USA, 2000.

[7] Buur, J., Soendergaard, A., "Video Card Game: An augmented environment for User Centred Design discussion", in proceedings of DARE2000 conference on Designing Augmented Reality Environments, Elsinore, Denmark, 2000, pp. 63-69.

[8] Bødker, S., Iversen, O., "Staging a Professional Participatory Design Practice - Moving PD Beyond the Initial Fascination of User Involvement", in Proceedings of NordiCHI, Århus, Denmark, 2002, pp. 11-18.

[9] Carroll, J., "Making use: scenario-based design of human-computer interactions", The MIT Press, England, 2000.

[10] Carroll, J., Rosson, M., "Getting Aound the Task-Artifact Cycle: How to Make Claims and Design by Scenario", ACM Transactions on Information Systems, Vol. 10, No. 2, April, 1992, pp. 181-212.

[11] Carroll, J., Rosson, M., Chin, G., Koenemann, J., "Requirements Development in Scenario Based Design", in IEEE Transactions on Software Engineering, Vol. 24, No. 12, December, 1998, pp. 1156-1170.

[12] Erickson, T., "Notes on Design Practice: Stories and Prototypes as Catalysts for Communication", in Carroll, J., (ed.), "Scenario-based design: Envisioning Work and Technology in System Development", John Wiley & Sons, 1995, pp. 37-58.

[13] Hackos, J., Redish, J., "User and Task Analysis for Interface Design", Wiley Computer Publishing, 1998, pp. 299-337.

[14] Iacucci, G., Iacucci, C., Kuutti, K., "Imagining and experiencing in design, the role of performances", in proceedings of NordiCHI, Århus, Denmark, 2002, pp. 167- 176.

[15] Iacucci, G., Kuutti, K., Ranta, M., "On the Move with a Magic Thing: Role Playing in Concept Design of Mobile Services and Devices", in proceedings of DIS2000 conference on Desingin Interactive Systems, Brooklyn, USA, 2000, pp. 193-202.

[16] Iversen, O & Buur, J. (2002): User Centred Design through the Keyhole: Video Design Case, in proceedings of IFIP TC 13 International Conference on Human-Computer Interaction, September 1-5, Zurich, Switzerland, 2003, pp.431-438

[17] Jääskö, V., Mattelmäki, T., "Observing and Probing", in proceedings of DPPI03 conference on Designing pleasurable products and interfaces, Pittsburg, USA, 2003, pp. 126-131.

[18] Jääskö, V., Mattelmäki, T., Ylirisku, S., "The Scene of Experiences", in Proceedings of Good, Bad and Irrelevant, Helsinki, Finland, 2003, pp. 341-345.

[19] Keinonen, T., "Pieniä tarinoita pienistä puhelimista", in Keinonen (ed.) "Miten käytettävyys muotoillaan?", publication B 61, University of Art and Design, Helsinki, Finland, 2000.

[20] Koskinen, I., Battarbee, K., "Empathy in Design", in Koskinen, I., Battarbee, K., Mattelmäki M., (eds.), "Empathic Design: User Experience in Product Design", IT Press, Finland, 2003.

[21] Kolli, R., "Using Video Scenarios to Present Consumer Product Interfaces", in conference companion of INTERACT'93 and CHI'93, Amsterdam, the Netherlands, 1993, pp. 61-62.

[22] Kyng, M., "Scandinavian Design: Users in Product Development", in proceedings of CHI'94 conference on Human Factors in Conputing Systems, Boston, USA, 1994, pp. 3-9.

[23] Mackay, W., "Ethics, Lies and Videotape...", in proceedings of CHI'95 Conference on Human Factors and Computing Systems, Denver, USA, 1995, pp. 138-145.

[24] Mackay, W., "Video Prototyping: a technique for developing hypermedia systems", in CHI'88 conference companion, Washington, USA, 1988.

[25] Mackay, W., Guindon, R., Mantei, M., Suchman, L., Tatar, D., "Video: Data for Studying Human-Computer Interaction", in proceedings of CHI'88 Conference on Human Factors in Computing Systems, Washington D.C., USA, 1998, pp. 133-137.

[26] Mackay, W., Ratzer, A., Janecek, P., "Video Artifacts for Design: Bridging the Gap Between Abstraction and Detail", in proceedings of DIS2000 conference on Designing Interactive Systems, New York City, USA, 2000, pp. 72-82.

[27] Muller, M., "Participatory Design: The Third Space in Human-Computer Interaction", in "The Human-Computer Interaction Handbook", eds. Jacko, J., Sears, A., Lawrence Elbaum Associates, New Jersey, 2003, pp. 1051-1068.

[28] Muller, M., "PICTIVE - An Exploration in Participatory Design", in proceedings of CHI'91, New Orleans, USA, 1991, pp. 225-231.

[29] Nielsen, L., "From user to character - an investigation into user-descriptions in scenarios", in proceedings of DIS2000 conference on Designing Iteractive Systems, New York City, USA, 2000, pp. 99-104.

[30] Pink, S., "Doing Visual Ethnography", Sage Publications, 2001.

[31] Potts, C., "Using Schematic Scenarios to Understand User Needs", in proceedings of DIS 95 conference on Designing Interactive Systems, Ann Arbor, Michigan, USA, 1995, pp. 247-256.

[32] Sanders, E., Dandavate, U., "Design for Experiencing: New Tools", in proceedings of the First International Conference on Design and Emotion, Delft University of Technology, The Netherlands, 1999, pp. 87-92.

[33] Sperschneider, W., Bagger, K., "Ethnographic fieldwork under industrial constraints: Towards Desing-in-Context", in proceedings of NordiCHI, Stockholm, Sweden, 2000.

[34] Wikberg, H., Keinoen, T., "Design driverina off-line wearability", in Keinonen (ed.) "Miten käytettävyys muotoillaan?", publication B 61, University of Art and Design, Helsinki, Finland, 2000.

Cooperative Systems Design
M. Zacklad et al. (Eds.)
IOS Press, 2004

Stories about Asynchronous Awareness

Uta PANKOKE-BABATZ, Wolfgang PRINZ, Leonie SCHÄFER
Fraunhofer FIT
Schloss Birlinghoven
53754 Sankt Augustin, Germany
{givenname.surname]@fit.fraunhofer.de}

Abstract This paper presents a framework for asynchronous awareness. Awareness tools are potentially powerful for the support of long-term team collaboration processes. In this paper we outline the particularities of long-term awareness and introduce stories as a means to present awareness information. We show different approaches to present awareness stories and describe the results of our laboratory user testing.

Introduction

Work in distributed teams is characterised by its spatial and temporal fragmentation. Distributed teams today lack sufficient support for team work and team forming. If we compare real world and electronic collaborative environments we find considerable differences with the respect to the temporal usage pattern that can be observed. In real world collaboration being at the same location at the same point in time are essential preconditions in face-to-face collaboration. In contrast, in electronic environments we will find interaction processes which span over time. Awareness support has to acknowledge both, the spatial and the temporal distribution of interaction processes.

In a real world scenario, for example, many people are following soaps on television. Sometimes these soap-operas consist of a sequence of sequels over a long period of time. The sequels often present stories in itself, disconnected to the previous or following sequels. As a result it is often impossible for the viewer to remember all the details or even to keep the storyline of several sequels in mind. This is the reason why film producers often provide short summaries to their audience at the beginning of each sequel. Such summaries may give the story of the past by means of pictures of major actors, by spots of typical scenes and by comments of a speaker in the off. In asynchronous work situations this approach might often be useful as well. Stories could provide a means to fill the gap of information between periods of activity at the workplace. In this case stories are not used for leisure, but to provide awareness about activities at which one was not able to participate due to whatever reason, but want to join in. Stories appear appropriate to illustrate and outline the complexity and multitude of situations that can occur in asynchronous work and request particular awareness support. Thus they contribute to a requirements analysis for asynchronous awareness. Furthermore stories also appear in our daily work as a very powerful means to convey awareness information in itself.

In this paper we will tell stories about awareness support and about asynchronicity of work situations. Our stories result from a long-term collaboration process and from short-term experiments with different story presentation media. We aim at understanding what properties are necessary to make a shared electronic workspace a "place" [10] that facilitates cooperation in teams. In the first section of this paper we will introduce Barker's behavior setting theory [3] and apply it to understand the forces that become effective in electronic settings and that may support and facilitate electronic work processes. The provision of awareness appears to be essential to facilitate social forces in electronic settings, in particular when cooperative tasks are to be performed. Awareness support will contribute to facilitate the co-orientation and coordination needed in distributed work settings.

The second section will report from a long-term work process in an EU project. It will show how the awareness support available was used by the participants to facilitate work. In particular, requirements came up to present summaries of awareness information about longer periods of time. The pure temporal ordering of event streams as given in the tools available turned out not to convey the information needed. Instead, a more complex dramaturgy for such a presentation was requested. To this end, the notion of environments compiling stories to present awareness information is introduced. The third and fourth section of this paper will report from experiments we conducted with three different presentation media which are all based on the same stream of events covering one week of activity. With this approach, we could observe how the tools contributed to the test candidates' understanding of the underlying story and helped to fulfil the task given to them. Finally we will draw general conclusions for further improvements of the presentation of awareness support for long-term processes.

1. Asynchronous Awareness

The relevance of environments for teamwork is mentioned from many sources. In system requirements analysis in general, "information ecologies" have to be considered [15]. For electronic collaboration, electronic environments are requested to become "inhabited spaces" respectively electronic "places" [10]. The role of environmental and social cues for communication and cooperation are well analysed [11]. Facilitation of social presence [21] and mutual observation among the inhabitants are essential in electronic collaboration. Much work is put into the development of support for synchronous awareness [7]. To this end, video connection could be supplied [4, 13]. However, so far these approaches have not yet met the needs in distributed teams sufficiently. The relevance and needs for awareness support in long term collaboration processes need more attention.

In analogy to real world interaction we can understand team processes as located in electronic environments. We can understand the combination of media, which the team members use for interaction, as their virtual setting. This opens the opportunity to apply psychological theories about the mutual impact of environmental properties and human behaviour to virtual environments. In particular we may pay attention on how environmental properties facilitate collaboration and coordination. To this end we will use the behaviour setting theory [3] and the activity theory [12].

A behaviour setting is constituted from a milieu, its inhabitants, and standing patterns of behaviour, which are associated to properties of the milieu. A behaviour setting has a clear physical boundary. The behaviour of people within a behaviour setting differs from the behaviour of the same persons outside the boundaries. Barker called the structural similarity between the properties of the milieu and the standing patterns of behaviour "synomorphy". The milieu as well as the other inhabitants present impact on the behaviour of the people present and are forces to stimulate congruent behaviour, i.e. a milieu-behaviour-synomorphy. Physical forces of the environment stimulate congruent behaviour by means of affordance. For example, the environment determines the space for movement, and the artefacts contained open or prevent certain actions. The people's present as well as past experiences, social connotations, and culturally learned behaviour patterns also constrain the behaviour of the inhabitants. In addition, their social presence [21], the possibility of mutual observation and direct interaction contribute to motivate congruent behaviour. These latter forces originating from the respective inhabitants are called the social forces.

Although the behaviour setting theory was developed for settings where people are bodily present, this theory may well be applied to electronic settings [16, 17]. Instead of physical presence, people are mentally present in an electronic setting, they shape their action and action plans to the affordance in an electronic milieu they perceive and interact with by means of their local workstation. The source of the physical forces of an electronic setting is the functional affordance of the underlying electronic system.

When applying the behaviour setting theory to electronic collaborative situations we find a considerable lack for the support of social forces in electronic environments. Social forces are, according to Barker's synomorphy concept, an essential source to achieve congruent standing behaviour patterns in real world settings. Similarly these are requested in electronic environments for collaborative work. In electronic settings, the dynamics of social forces can become effective if participants can perceive traces or signs of presence of others [17]. Awareness support to mutually observe each other can considerably support social forces in electronic environments and thus facilitate cooperation.

1.1 Awareness facilitates social forces

In general, we can understand awareness as a particular kind of interaction between an individual and the environment. The aim of awareness is to enable users to perceive what others do. That means we have a relationship between actor and observer, which is mediated by the environment in which the action takes place and in which it is observed.

Actor → Setting → Observer

However, the asynchronicity of electronic work separates the point in time when an action takes place from the point in time when an observer perceives it. Thus awareness is double situated. The first situation occurs when a person performs action in the environment. The awareness support should record what happens in this situation. The second situation is the one of an observer when she wants to perceive what has happened. In contrast to collocated synchronous work, these two situations are temporally fragmented.

Consequently the environment should record awareness information once actions take place and present the awareness information in a way that conveys the situation that happened and that is adapted to the observer's situation. It has to acknowledge that usually an observer is not a spectator who wants to see a full performance. Instead an observer is a potential actor and her interests are based on her motives and goals [12]. Her perception of the activity in an environment is therefore focussed on what is necessary to adapt her action plans to the situation in the environment [22].

Achieving awareness in asynchronous settings requires overviews and summaries to overcome the temporal fragmentation. In interviews –see below– interviewees said, that they ask their partners or approach the place of action when more details are needed. Perceiving awareness in physical settings turns out to be a highly interactive process. It relays on the traces left in the environment and in the organization of the human memory of the partners they talked with.

In electronic settings the interaction partner that supplies awareness information should be the setting itself. Thus the awareness support in a setting has to compile awareness stories from what happened similar to what a human informant would do. From this we conclude the following general requirements to the tasks of an environment to supply awareness:

- Recording of awareness data.
- Processing, summarization, aging of awareness data and generating episodes.
- Adapting the presentation of awareness information to the medium used and to the situation of the observer.
- Reducing the level of detail based on spatial and temporal distances between the place of action and the observer.

In this study, we used an event and notification infrastructure (ENI) for the recording of awareness data, which is based on NESSIE [18]. Using this infrastructure any user action on objects in a shared workspace, e.g. create-, read-, or modify-operations on a shared document, result in events that are submitted to the ENI server. Event processing takes place in the ENI server. It stores these events in a history database and it provides a query interface to retrieve the event data of a specific period. Presentation tools may request events from ENI and process and display them [19].

1.2 Methods to study awareness

In our study we chose two approaches to study awareness needs. First we had the opportunity to study the ongoing work process in a long term EU project and, as a follow-up, also the upcoming requirements in the team. In addition, we could observe the effects of available awareness tools. In our second approach, based on these findings, we conducted a scenario-based experiment with different means to present awareness information. Both studies are reported in the following sections.

2. Awareness in a long-term team process

The requirements for awareness support in asynchronous work settings will be illustrated in the following story of a long-term work process in an EU project team. Like for many other teams, in EU-projects the spatial distances, the different local work habits all made team forming, storming and performing difficult. However, at the beginning, an electronic behaviour setting to host the team was created. It was constituted from the provision of a distribution list to be used for email communication and a shared workspace provided by the BSCW system [1]. The project team members became inhabitants of this electronic setting by being members of the distribution list as well as of the BSCW workspace.

In our study of the teamwork we paid particular attention on awareness in such a distributed setting. This related to understanding how much mutual awareness was requested, how awareness was achieved and how awareness improved cooperation in the team. The team process was studied by participating and documenting the work process, by analysing the events recorded in the electronic environment, and by discussing awareness-related questions with the team members.

In the EU project four local teams in UK and Germany were collaborating throughout 36 month. Actually the overall goal of project itself was to improve awareness support. The local teams at each site consisted of two to eight persons. In the course of time in total about 40 people became involved in the project. Staff members changed, students or guest researchers joined the teams. About 20 persons became regular team members, i.e. they have joined the project for more than one year.

2.1 Usage patterns in the electronic setting

Emerging usage patterns: From the very beginning, email and BSCW were used regularly. All relevant project material was filed in the BSCW workspace. BSCW's Daily Activity Report supplied awareness information of activities in the workspace. Glancing through it every day became a normal work habit. Email was used to distribute information to all team members, to stay in touch and to carefully learn about the other people. In the course of time we could observe that the use of email and of the BSCW workspace became tightly interwoven. This became evident when the same topics appeared in email headers and in document names in the workspace. We take the emergence of such typical usage patterns as an indication that physical and social forces of the project's electronic behavior setting were already sufficient to support some standing patterns of behavior.

Task specific patterns: Apart from this general work pattern we could observe task and work phase specific patterns. For example when reports were produced, they were filed in the workspace already in early productions stages with the intent to indicate to others that the authors were busy. But once a report was finished it was explicitly announced via email, in addition to its appearance in the BSCW's Daily Activity Report. Usually others accessed these documents only after being explicitly announced. In contrast, other documents uploaded like for example pictures from a meeting were not announced by mail, but immediately accessed once they appeared in an activity report.

Reading awareness information from email: In addition to the awareness information which was explicitly conveyed per email as in the example above, implicit awareness information was available by email. From the flow of email itself participants deduced the actual topic of interest, and the level of activity in the team, the actual presence, and involvement of people.

2.2 Temporal interaction patterns

Task specific work rhythms: In the course of the project we could observe different work processes and rhythms. For example, the start of a new design topic usually began with intensive email exchange, proposing and discussing alternative solutions. The interaction rate was quite high in such a phase. The number of new entries in the BSCW increased as proposals were filed in the BSCW workspace. Also in phases of preparing a meeting or an exposition, the interaction rates were quite high. In phases, in which documents were produced, e.g. project deliverables, several BSCW activities could be observed while the email exchange rate was rather low. In contrast, implementation phases were characterized by low email interaction rates and a low level of BSCW activities. But if an email was launched it was in many situation a request for urgently needed help. All these work phases had considerably different needs with respect to awareness. Although the Daily Activity Report was sufficient in unspecific work situations, in phases with high interaction rates, it turned out that the delivery was not frequent enough to adequately support task synchronization. In contrast, in phases with low interaction rates the report was produced in a too short time frame to reflect the progress of work.

In case of a medium term absence of a participant, we could observe that the available awareness support was not matching the participant's needs. Participants complained that the number of Daily Activity Reports accumulated after some days of absence provided too much information, that it took too much time to filter out the irrelevant and find the relevant information. We can augment this feedback from the participants with some figures from events statistics. The number of events varied between 10 and 100 per day with an average of 40. Per week the number of events varied between 60-100 in non-busy times, and went up to 200 to 500 in a very busy week. Thus it is not surprising that pure chronological presentations of such large event streams did not meet the user needs. Instead more comprehensive overviews must be provided.

Synchronicity of awareness provision: Later in the course of the project, we provided an animated 3-D world to present awareness information. This was intended to run in the background and to peripherally provide synchronous awareness information. Similar to findings from video spaces [8], synchronous supply of awareness information turned out not to meet all awareness needs of the distributed work group. Therefore these tools were extended to replay all events for user given time periods in a chronological order. This suited user needs for short term time periods, but for periods longer than a day this was not suitable either.

We conclude that different tasks and work situations need more specific awareness support. In particular, the pure chronological presentation of awareness information is not sufficient for teamwork in many situations. Therefore we experimented with other awareness presentation modes and means.

2.3 Asynchronous awareness in real world settings

At the beginning of the project we concentrated on the provision of short-term awareness for everyday work. The work study described above disclosed that particular support for awareness on medium-term and long-term activities is of high relevance. In order to learn from real world settings, we asked the participants how they achieve asynchronous awareness in their local physical work settings after a temporal absence. "Walking and talking" were named as the major means to gain awareness. While walking around they could see traces of past events in the environment and they could meet colleagues whom they asked. Interviewees said that they encouraged their colleagues to report in less than five minutes about what has happened. Thus they received summarized stories from their colleagues and they asked for more detail when needed.

Applying this to electronic settings, the human partner providing the story is usually not available. Instead, we recommend it should be the task of the environment itself to provide such stories. From our study of the work in the EU project team we conclude that users in electronic settings need meaningful overviews and summaries rather than a pure temporal stream of events. The temporal fragmentation of work as well as different work rhythms in electronic settings must be acknowledged by the awareness support. Producing stories from the event stream and presenting them adequately is one of the major requirements to awareness support for asynchronous work in electronic settings. We concluded that we have to find new ways to convey awareness information.

3. Stories as form of awareness

In a physical work environment there is a continuous flow of information in a team, between team members or colleagues. People might report to others about the progress and results of a meeting. They might give an overview on the status of the project they are currently working on or just give a summary of the latest events in their department [6].

The content of the information given away to other people can be characterized as story. Stories in a work environment usually consist of different actors, e.g. the colleagues, and follow a script, like the sequence of activities throughout a meeting.

There are many different ways to tell a story. There is a saying: "There is one truth, but thousand different ways to look at that truth." The emphasis, people set in their description of events might differ from that of other people. It depends on the current circumstances, the addressee and as well on the personality of the storyteller. Therefore the content told might result in completely different stories. The way to tell that story, to set a focus and to personalize the content, can be described as Storytelling [5]. Similarly that definition of stories and storytelling can be applied to an electronic environment. The flow of an event stream represents the actual content of information. The way the data is processed, selected and grouped by a particular presentation medium is analogous to the personal preferences and selection mechanism of the storyteller. Finally, the way the story is displayed to a user can be matched with the style a person tells a story, e.g. animated or matter-of-factly.

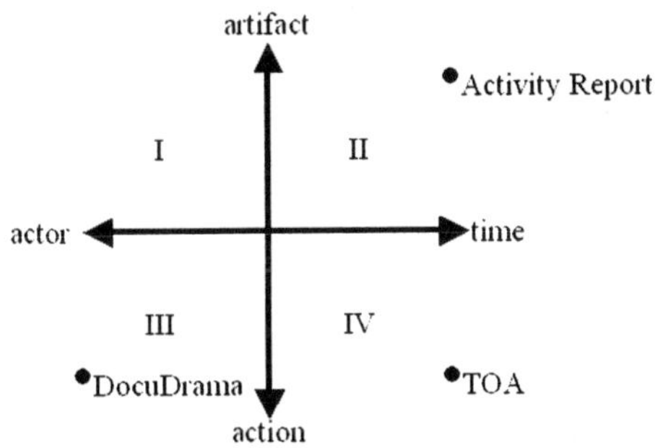

Figure 1: Dimensions of event processing and presentation

We developed three different "storytellers" to experiment with. That means, we developed three different dramaturgies and tools to present awareness information in an electronic environment. The Daily Activity Report presents activity information in a textual and chronological form. Its dramaturgy centres on artefacts, e.g. the documents, and actions. The TOA diagram, the second application, focuses on the relation between time- and object-activity. The third tool finally, DocuDrama Conversation, intends to present interaction between actors based on artefacts.

Presentation tool	Actor	Action	Artefact	Time
Activity report	Login name	Icon, keyword	Object-name	Position in list, full display
TOA-2D Diagram	Color	Icon-symbol	-	x-axis position
TOA – Tooltip for each icon	Login name	Keyword	Object-name	Full display
Docudrama	Avatar	Symbolic action	Object name in window	TextString

Table A: Representation overview

Figure 1 shows an overview on the dimensions of event processing and presentation. The sectors I – IV mark the different foci. DocuDrama Conversation is placed in sector III with focal points on actor/action relationship. The TOA diagram is in sector IV since it focuses mainly on the relation between the time and action performed. The Daily Activity Report is

located in sector II. It reports about activities on artefacts in a time-based manner. The specific foci of the tools used are laid out in table A.
Later in this paper we will introduce these presentation tools in more detail and tell stories about their usage in our user experiment.

4. Awareness experiments

In the awareness experiments described in the following we aimed to elicit more user requirements on asynchronous awareness tools. We begin with a brief introduction of the experiment and the methods used. The following stories will report from the experiments. Each story will introduce some more details of the respective tool before it reports from the experiment.

4.1 The experiment

The experiment was conducted with ten colleagues of our institution. We created the following scenario for the experiment and gave the participants the following story:

"You just returned from two weeks vacation. Together with your colleagues you want to draft a paper. Unfortunately you cannot reach your colleagues personally. The deadline for paper submission is tomorrow."

Now they were encouraged to use the awareness tools to find the relevant information to join in the text production process.

For the scenario, we had to produce the appropriate events. In order to create an realistic event stream, we chose an actual paper production process. For this process we established a BSCW workspace and four people were using it for one week to write a joint paper. They collected and uploaded material, created several subfolders and revised documents. There was one main document, which was revised several times. Other activities mostly consisted of read-actions. The work process started on Thursday, the week before the experiment. Friday and Monday had been days of high activity, while during the weekend very few events took place. Tuesday and Wednesday, the activities mostly focused on the main document and read/revise- actions.

The experiments were conducted such that each user could explore all the three presentation tools. These tools were represented in an arbitrary order such that we could see the impacts of knowing the occurring events from using the previous tools. A researcher joined each participant and told the story of the scenario, explained the task and the respective tools. After the participant finished with a tool, the researcher put questions using an interview guideline. In particular, the participants were given the task to name the most relevant document. Furthermore, they were asked whether they could detect any collaboration.

We will now describe the functionality of each tool in more detail and will report the stories conducted in the experiments.

4.2 The Daily Activity Report

The Daily Activity Report is a standard awareness feature of the BSCW system. It was already used in the EU project team process described above. It is realized as an HTML-formatted email that is sent every night to all BSCW users. The email lists all user actions that occurred in the workspaces of which the user is a member. Figure 2 shows an example of a Daily Activity Report.

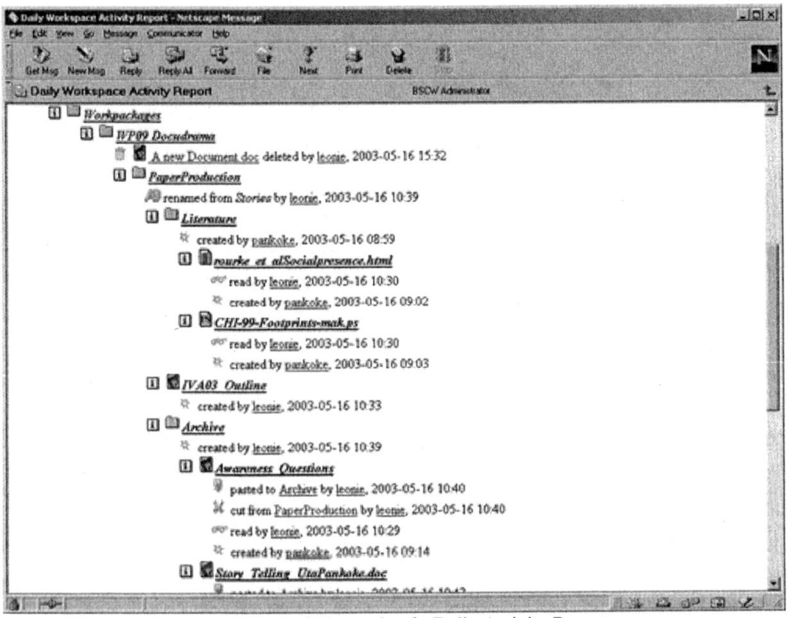

Figure 2: Example of a Daily Activity Report

The Daily Activity Report lists the events from user actions in the following sequence. First, all events are grouped by the shared folders to which the respective objects belong. The objects within a folder (documents, subfolders) are sorted alphabetically. This results in a tree-list of all objects on which user actions occurred during the last 24 hours. The actual user actions are listed in the following: an object name, an indication of the action type (read, create, modify, etc.) by a small icon as well as by a keyword, the login name of the user, and the exact date and time of the action. If more than one action were performed on the same object, the actions are sorted by time, starting with the most recent action. Thus a user gets an extract of the workspace setting reduced to the places of action.

All folder names, object names, and the user login names are represented as HTML links. Thus a user can use this link to open the respective folder, object (e.g. the document) or information about a user by a single click.

The Daily Activity Report is posted every 24 hours. In their profiles, users can configure what kinds of user actions shall be listed in the report. For example,. a user can decide to receive no information on read actions if she wants to be informed only about create or modify operations.

4.2.1 Daily Activity Report – the experiment

Almost all test users have been familiar with the Activity Report through their daily work. They stated that the report was quick and easy to scroll through and would give a good overview on the activities in a BSCW shared workspace per day. The test candidates reported that the content of the report was easy to understand and did not require cognitive workload since no symbols and signs had to be translated into meaningful content. Usually most users browsed through it and threw it away afterwards. The included HTML links are often used to go directly from the report to open the respective folder or document.

Since all users were familiar with this tool it was not surprising to observe in the experiment how eloquently they browsed through the individual activity reports. The candidates took from 2 to 5 minutes time for this task. They scrolled the individual report back and forward and appeared to have clear plans on how to read them. In the follow up interviews they could easily solve the first task and named the relevant documents. Many of them said, that the names of documents were highly important to them. The high relevance of names became also evident in particular from participants who saw BSCW as last in the sequence of tools. "Now the relation to documents becomes clear," one stated. "The name is highly relevant, there I trust my colleagues". Other criteria named to find relevant documents were the number of occurring events. It was further interesting to note that for many participants the activity report of the last day was the most relevant. They based their decisions of how to continue on the documents named in the last activity report. "I read the most recent activity report first".

However, glancing through reports from several days to get an overview about the last time period, as in our experiment, was rather unusual to them. We could observe some test candidates trying to open the activity reports all at once in order to compare them. Most candidates stated that it was difficult for them to follow a sequence of activities on a certain document across several days and reports. They would have preferred a weekly overview on the activities. With the Daily Report the continuity across the days gets lost. "I'd like to put the various activity reports aside to follow the docs across the days". "The list is nice, but I cannot recognize the processes". For example, they found it difficult to find out whether all users have read a certain document during the selected time period. The test candidates also reported that they could not clearly judge whether people collaborated on a document over a longer period of time. On a daily basis this had not been a problem, since the report lists all events on a document in a chronological order.

In general, all test candidates liked the activity report and would recommend it for future use. Several users also stated that they would gain additional benefit from a weekly activity report.

4.3 The Time-Object-Activity diagram

The time-object-activity (TOA) diagram uses a 2D representation to present user actions on objects. The x-axis denotes the time. The y-axis is used to indicate the folders in which the actions occurred. However, the structure of the folder hierarchy in the setting is not visible in this overview. An icon in the matrix represents a user action. The action time determines the position on the x-axis and the folder to which the object belongs determines the position on the y-axis. The icon itself indicates the user action, using the same symbol as the Daily Activity Report. The color of the symbol is determined by the user's login name, i.e. all actions of the same user appear in the same color. If more than one action occurred on the same object on the same day, then the icons are positioned on a single line.

A mouse-over tooltip on an icon provides firther details of the user action: user login name, object name, folder name and time of the action. By clicking on the icon, the respective object is opened. The user can configure the time span that is displayed by the TOA diagram on the x-axis and the folders that are selected for the y-axis. The TOA diagram is implemented as a JAVA application which communicates with the ENI server via the ENI program interface.

4.3.1 TOA – the experiment

Before starting with the experiment on this tool, the tool was explained briefly to the participants. However, once understood the minimized interface was easy to overlook and the participants clicked on the various icons between three to five minutes, one candidate even used 10 minutes.

The test users liked the possibility to see a longer period of time at one glance. They remarked that it was easy to detect who had been active in the selected time period. The users also pointed out that it was easy to find phases of high activity. The candidates could easily detect the days with the most activities and find out who was the most active. "One sees immediately the busy days. This was the weekend". "Easy to understand, easy to find who was active, difficult to find out relevant documents" candidates put it. The test candidates also quickly understood the symbols and could therefore easily follow a sequence of events on a document on a per-day basis. It turned out to be difficult to find information on the documents like name or type. All candidates complained that it was very difficult to find out details of the most relevant document. Not seeing the names of the documents was named as the main deficiency of this tool. "This tool is focussed on events, but my thinking is on documents" "This confused me first, I expected to see the names first". To them the names were of highest relevance for orientation in this situation. Some suggested that a more structured and longer lasting tooltip might have relieved their situation.

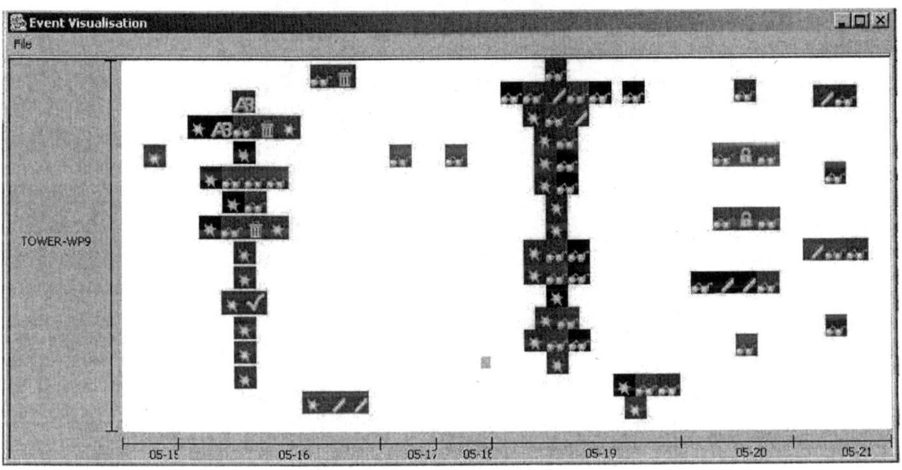

Figure 3: Example of a TOA diagram

However, all test candidates claimed that the tool would be more useful if it would be possible to follow the history of a certain document during the week[1]. Some people recommended using arrows to point from one position of a document to the document's position on the next day. But most candidates preferred to have horizontal lines for the same document such that they could find out the level of activities on the same document throughout the whole time period.

TOA, the time- and activity-based application proved to be a promising approach for the future development of overviews. Several participants expected to use the tool in the future but only if the problems mentioned above, position of documents and tooltips, would have been solved. For future use, the test users suggested the development of more variety

[1] Note: currently the visualization of all events on a single object on one line works only for a single day. I.e. if the document is used on two consecutives days, the corresponding event icons may appear on different lines. This makes it difficult to track the actions on an object. This design decision was made to reduce the vertical space needed by the drawing.

on information levels. Positive features to be considered in the design of future applications turned out to be the use of symbols and the time-based approach in form of an overview presentation.

4.4 DocuDrama Conversation

DocuDrama Conversation [20] presents awareness information in form of an animation with human-like avatars. Rules of non-verbal communication [2, 14] are employed to convey activity information.

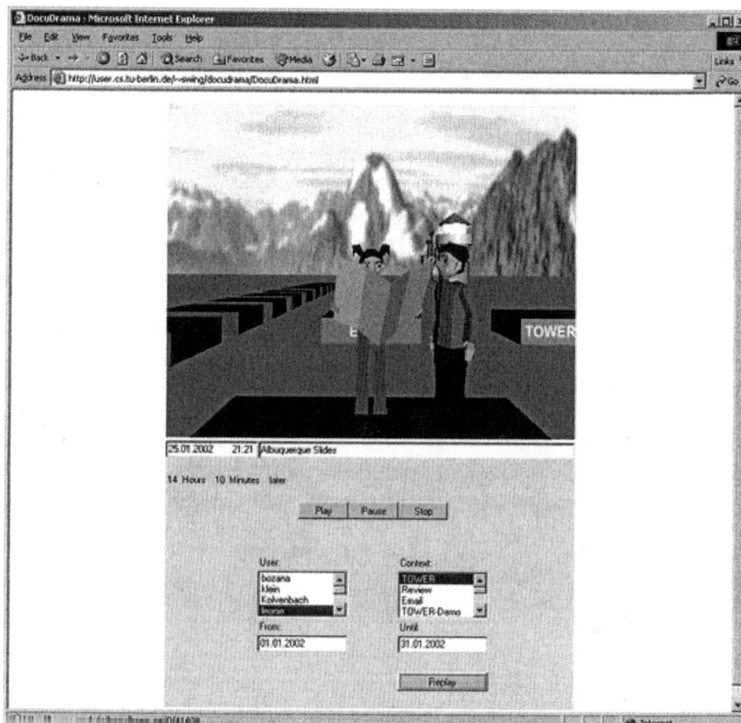

Figure 4: The DocuDrama presentation

DocuDrama Conversation aims to present the interaction between team members, which took place while collaborating on documents in a shared work workspace. This tool does not only consider collaboration in form of an immediate sequence of activities. It takes into account all events, which have occurred on a document throughout the whole time span of the collaboration process.

DocuDrama Conversation displays the sequence of activities, which have been performed on a document. The events are played out by avatars, which perform symbolic actions. The play out of actions on the same object resembles a conversation between team members. The avatars are grouped together in a circle and turn towards each other like in a conversation [9]. Figure 4 shows a scene from DocuDrama Conversation.

The DocuDrama virtual world displays the behavior setting constituted of the workspace, the actors represented by avatars. Differently coloured boxes on the ground represent folders in the team's BSCW workspace. Avatars on top of the boxes represent team members and their activities in the workspace. The position of the avatars denotes the folder of activity. The symbolic action illustrates the current activity of the owner of the avatar. Reading a newspaper, for example, symbolizes the action of opening and reading documents. Underneath the world representation DocuDrama Conversation offers text-based information on documents and events in a separate window.

The user interface offers different configuration possibilities e.g. to select a time period, to set the focus on a certain user, or to choose a context of activity. The user can also choose between the grouping of events based on the numbers of actors, on the dates, on the documents or on the types of action.

DocuDrama Conversation is implemented as JAVA application and uses the EAI package as interface with the VRML environment. The application receives its data from history log-files, which are created based on ENI events.

4.4.1 DocuDrama – the experiment

The DocuDrama tool offers a variety of different configurations and replay methods. To achieve comparable user reactions the tool was preconfigured to replay all events on a single object before the animation moves on to the next object. The replay starts with the object which shows the highest number user actions and continues with the object next in rank of user activity.

Most candidates took between three to six minutes to passively watch the DocuDrama movie very intensively, before they took the initiative to stop it. Although some candidates became impatient, they hesitated to stop it before it ended. The test candidates described the replay as entertaining. They intuitively understood the meaning of the Symbolic Actions, but demanded a greater variety in Symbolic Actions and a possibility to interact with the replay. They complained that the scenes took much too long and as a consequence they forgot what they have seen at the beginning. Some users suggested to increase the speed of the replay or to provide a user controllable fast-forward replay of the history events, combined with the possibility to take a closer look on a certain sequence of events, if a scene raised their attention.

The candidates had considerably different opinions on the manner of visualizing history events mainly with avatars. Some test candidates liked the focus on interaction between the team members, others favoured documents to be in the centre of attention. Although all users replied, that the most relevant document was the first one, many of them did not remember its name. Thus, seeing the name in separate fields underneath the movie window instead of within was irritating to them and not very helpful to become aware of the names. "Difficult to watch and to read simultaneously" a candidate commented.

The test candidates described DocuDrama Conversation as an entertaining and appealing application. They liked the virtual environment, the avatars and especially the Symbolic Actions. The users appreciated that DocuDrama showed all events on one document, even if they occurred during a longer period of time. That way it was easier to detect whether for example all team members have read a certain document or contributed to it. Non-verbal communication as a means to convey information proved to be an interesting alternative to present abstract user data, although for a longer period of time users preferred a graphical or textual overview on the sequence of events.

The main challenges for future work on DocuDrama Conversation will be to provide for more interactivity and to improve the speed of the animation. Another challenge will be to display more information on documents within the 3D replay itself.

4.5 Summary

5 minutes attention limit: We found considerable differences with respect to the time used in each presentation medium to find out the relevant information. The Daily Activity Report turned out to need the shortest time (2-5 minutes). The icon overview took a little longer (3 to 5 minutes). Most candidates also stopped watching the film after 4 to 6 minutes. In particular in the latter case not all information was conveyed before the candidates stopped. This contributes to the thesis that the time people are willing to spend for consumption of awareness information before starting their action is limited by a maximum of about five minutes. This finding nicely fits with the EU project members' stories about their habits of perceiving awareness information after a time period of absence. Usually they asked their colleagues for this information and gave them a maximum of 5 minutes.

Perceiving awareness is a matter of interaction: With the Daily Activity Report we could see how the candidates interacted by scrolling to find the relevant information. This way they switched from a more overview-like perspective to reading details. In DocuDrama they could only observe the pre-compiled movie. Some candidates said they missed to be able to move around and to focus on places, which were of relevance to them. In contrast, the time-object-activity diagram needed interaction from the very beginning since it did not convey the relevant information at first glance. This gives evidence that interaction possibilities only, do not fit the needs either.

General overview: In their comments on two of the presentation tools, the time-object-activity diagram and DocuDrama some participants said they missed the opportunity to get an overview first, before they take a closer look. Some would have preferred to move directly from an overview to locations of interest. In the time-object-activity diagram they could interact, but the overview does not convey enough information to enable them to find locations of interest. It focuses on the events, but the participants needed to locate documents easily and to map them to the workspace structure.

Actors are not so relevant: Although the DocuDrama and the time-object-activity diagram made it very easy to find out the identity of the actors and to detect places were several actors occurred, this appeared not to be of prior relevance.

Relevance of document names prior to number of events: We found, that the users focussed mainly on documents if they wanted to achieve awareness about a joint document production process. They determined the relevance of documents by its name first and secondly, by the number of occurring events. Among the names, the type of the doc - whether it is a pdf, a javascript or a word document - were considered relevant by the participants. This also becomes evident when all participants appreciated to easily perceive this information from the Daily Activity Report.

The participants preferred the Daily Activity Report to the other two tools and also recommended it to other users. "The Daily Activity Report was the most informative and the movie was the most attractive" a participant summarised.

In summary, we conclude from these experiments that in case of the task of a joint paper production, locating and knowing the relevant documents is of highest relevance to the participants. The number of occurring events as well as the identity of the respective actors is second level criteria to identify relevant information. Thus a document and workspace structure focussed presentation of awareness information is promising. We also conclude that there is not one perfect way to present awareness information. However, the overview type of presentation appeared to be useful and interaction possibilities were heavily requested to enable the user to shape the presentation to her needs.

5. Conclusions and Future Work

This work can be understood as a framework for the development of awareness support for temporally fragmented collaboration processes. Although we have not found the one most promising awareness tool, we could contribute to an improved understanding on the effects of the potential dimension for awareness support. We could study some features and their impacts in practice.

From the behaviour setting theory which we introduced in the beginning of this paper, we could conclude the relevance of awareness information to facilitate conforming behaviour in an electronic setting. Our study of a long-term team process in a EU project confirmed this assumption. In particular the emergence of standing patterns of behaviour gave evidence about the relevance of awareness support. The team study also disclosed the complexity of the needs in such temporal fragmented processes. Awareness support must provide for the double situatedness of asynchronous work i.e. it must acknowledge the situation of an actor and of a spectator. The presentation must suit the particular situation of the spectator. We found that the requirements on awareness applications differed widely depending on the situation in the setting and on the time span, which was to be covered by a review of activities. This results in different requirements on data processing and presentation.

We resume, the envisioned awareness tool of the future will not be a unified application for all users and time periods. Like in our introductory example of a soap opera, different means are requested to tell the story of the past. It should be possible to let the user configure preferences on the four dimensions – artefact, actor, action and time. For a short time period, for example, it might be advisable to focus on the dimension artefact, which might provide a summary of activities in the workspace and on the document itself. For a longer time period, the focus might change on the dimensions actor and time, e.g. in order to visualize the complete length of a collaboration process.

The presentation features like symbols or text could be used in all variations of the awareness tools, although their relevance may change. For short-term usage in which a high level of detail is requested it might be useful to rely on text. For awareness over a longer period of time, overviews are requested which convey the information at a single glance; in this case symbols turned out to be helpful. The continuous usage of one set of features might ease the handling of the tool and diminish the cognitive workload to translate the tool's awareness presentation into a meaning. However, all stories from user experiences give evidence that users need to be able to switch between different levels of detail. Thus a user may approach the place of action she is interested in. Furthermore, she must be enabled to directly interact with artefacts mentioned in the awareness stories.

In long-term work processes all the situations mentioned above may occur. Awareness support must acknowledge the specific interaction rates of the work phases as well as users' individual frequency of presence in the setting. The usability of a setting deeply depends on the flexibility of tools to provide awareness, dynamically adaptable to both the situation in the setting and the particular situation of the observer and potential actor.

In summary, electronic settings differ from real world ones with respect to the fact that the awareness information they record is not simply "footprints" and "signs of tear and wear". Instead they provide stories of happenings.

Acknowledgements

We thank all users who were involved in the documented project and in the experiments. Particular thanks goes to the designers of the tools used and to the members of the TOWER project team.

References

[1] Appelt, W., The CESAR project: Collaboration environments and service architectures for researchers, in Proceedings of the IASTED International Conferences: Internet, Multimedia Systems and Applications (IMSA '99), October 18-21, 1999, Nassau, The Bahamas, B. Furht, Editor. 1999, IASTED/ACTA Press: Anaheim. p. 325-329.

[2] Argyle, M., Bodily Communication. 2nd ed. 1990, London: Rotledge.

[3] Barker, R.G., Ecological psychology. 1968, Stanford: Stanford University Press.

[4] Bly, S., Media Spaces, in Readings in Groupware and Computer Supported Cooperative Work, R. Baecker, Editor. 1993, Morgan Kaufmann: San Manteo, CA.

[5] Branigan, E., Narrative Comprehension and Film. 1992, London: Routledge.

[6] Dixon, N.M., Common Knowledge: How Companies Thrive by Sharing What They Know. 2000: Harvard Business School Press.

[7] Erickson, T. and M.r. Laff. The Design of 'Babble' Timeline - A Social Proxy for Visualizing Group Activity over Time. In CHI 2001. 2001: ACM.

[8] Fussell, S.R., R.E. Kraut, and J. Siegel. Coordination of Communication: Effects of Shared Visual Context on Collaborative Work. In CSCW 2000. 2000. Philadelphia, PA: ACM.

[9] Garau, M., et al. The Impact of Eye Gaze on Communication using Humanoid Avatars. In CHI 2001. 2001. Seattle, Washington, USA: ACM Press New York, NY, USA.

[10] Harrison, S. and P. Dourish. Re-Place-ing Space: The Roles of Place and Space in Collaborative Systems. In CSCW '96. 1996. Cambridge, MA: ACM, New York.

[11] Heath, C. and P. Luff. Collaborative Activity and Technological Design: Task Coordination in London Underground Control Rooms. In E-CSCW '91. 1991: Kluwer.

[12] Leontjev, A.N., Activity, Consciousness, Personality. 1978: Prentice-Hall.

[13] Morikawa, O. and T. Maesako. HyperMirror: Toward Pleasant to use Video Mediated Communication System. In CSCW '98 Computer Supported Cooperative Work. 1998. Seattle: AACM Press.

[14] Morris, D., Bodytalk. Körpersprache, Gesten und Gebärden. 1997, München: Wilhelm Heyne Verlag.

[15] Nardi, B.A. and V.L. O'Day, Information Ecologies: Using Technology with heart. 1999, Cambridge, Massachusetts: The MIT Press.

[16] Pankoke-Babatz, U., Electronic Behavior Settings for CSCW. AI & Society, 2000. 14(1): p. 3-30.

[17] Pankoke-Babatz, U., Designkonzept für Systeme zur computergestützten Zusammenarbeit unter Nutzung der Behavior-Setting-Theorie. Fraunhofer Series in Information and Communication Technology. Vol. 2. 2003, Aachen: Shaker Verlag. 313.

[18] Prinz, W. NESSIE: An Awareness Environment for Cooperative Settings. In Sixth European Conference on Computer Supported Cooperative Work (ECSCW '99). 1999. Kopenhagen: Kluwer Academic Publishers.

[19] Prinz, W., et al., Presenting activity information in an inhabited information space, in Inhabited Information Spaces, E. Churchill; and D. Snowdon, Editors. 2003.

[20] Schäfer, L., E. Raybourn, and A. Oldroyd. DocuDrama Conversations. In SIGGRAPH 2002. 2002. San Antonio, Texas, USA: ACM.

[21] Short, J., E. Williams, and C. Bruce, The social psychology of telecommunications. 1976, London: John Wiley &Sons, Ltd. 195.

[22] Suchman, L., Plans and situated actions. The problem of human-machine communication. 1987, Cambridge: Cambridge University Press.

Cooperative Systems Design
M. Zacklad et al. (Eds.)
IOS Press, 2004

ThreeDmap: customizing awareness information

Fabrizio NUNNARI
Computer Science Department, University of Torino, Italy

Abstract In this paper we present ThreeDmap, an editor that allows the creation and customization of 3D graphical interfaces for the promotion of awareness information. The development of ThreeDmap is related to the recent improvements of ThreeDness, a software module promoting awareness information through a 3D graphical representation of the *context* of cooperating people. ThreeDness improvements are put in relation with presentation strategies that emerged from two research fields that, like ThreeDness, use a 3D technology: Collaborative Virtual Environments and non-WIMP user interfaces.

1 Introduction: CSCW, 3D, displays and GUIs

The concept of *awareness* has been recognized as a key concept in the field of Computer Supported Cooperative Work (CSCW). Despite of the lack consensus on its meaning and formalisation of its definition, CSCW researchers generally agree in using this term to denote "those practices through which actors tacitly and seamlessly align and integrate their distributed and yet interdependent activities" [21] and attempt to define a computational models suitable to support the exchange of *awareness information* [6] among actors.

The ThreeDness project [14] started with the aim of *promoting* awareness information produced by one of these models through a graphical representation of the *context* (the spatial, organizational, task-related and personal environment) of the cooperating actors. According to this model, the concepts of *focus* (on which task an actor is concentrated) and logical distance (how much two entities are related to each other) play a key role.

The graphical output generated by ThreeDness is based on real-time 3D graphics. The purpose is to take advantage of the greater flexibility offered by the 3D technology for the visualization of information with respect to the more traditional 2D approach. This choice is also supported by the observation that the consumer PC market gives cheap access to powerful 3D hardware technology that already gained the scientific world [3, 17]. Another goal is to provide users with an interface to perceive awareness information without being distracted from the activity they are currently focused on. For this reasons ThreeDness output is suitable to be better displayed in devices as second monitors or wide wall-screens, and not in windows of the main screen that can be easily covered by the windows of other *"focus-oriented"* applications. In this way, the user interaction with the interface can be occasional and limited in time.

The first version of the prototype [14] was based on a single reference domain made of *actors*, associated to *roles*, which have to accomplish *tasks* using *resources*. The proposed solution refers to a typical office work environment, where everyone uses a PC to advance in his *task*. The source of the promoted information (*facts*) comes directly from a simplified Workflow Management System (WFMS) organizing the relationships between the involved People, their tasks and resources. Facts are taken and processed by an *awareness engine*, based on the MoMA (Model of Modulated Awareness) model [22], that sends awareness information to ThreeDness. The latter translates them into a graphical representation that is sent back to all the users that generated the source facts. Furthermore, the representation is not the same for every user, but personalized according to each own identity.

In this paper we present ThreeDmap, a graphical editor that allows users to design and customize the way in which the awareness information is presented through the ThreeDness interface. Given an application domain, the process to decide *which* elements are useful to support awareness promotion is a hard task without neither standard methods nor rules specifying *how* such information has to be presented. This situation can be compared to how people furnish their home. Generally, architects propose solutions based on guidelines about style and comfort, however a direct intervention of the customer is always needed to adapt the proposals to particular needs and tastes. Similarly, ThreeDmap allows experts of awareness promotion to propose new visualization ideas and solutions that end-users can further customize.

The development of ThreeDmap is related to the recent improvements of ThreeDness both in terms of adaptability, through the supplied, and in terms of flexibility, through an independence from the application domain of the awareness information elaborated by the MoMA. Such improvements are based on *presentation strategies* that have been inspired by the analysis of two research fields that take advantage of real-time 3D technology to study new forms of visualization and interaction techniques: CSCW and Computer-Human Interaction. They brought to the definition of *Collaborative Virtual Environments* (CVEs) and non-WIMP User Interfaces (UIs), respectively. CVEs are the extension of single-user Virtual Reality (VR) applications to support the simultaneous interaction of multiple distributed users. Each user is immersed in a virtual world and there embodied in a digital alter-ego called avatar [4]. The term non-WIMP UIs is used to denote user interfaces based on a different paradigm with respect to the widely used *"Windows, Icons, Mouse, Pointer"* one (e.g., [13, 7]). More precisely, we consider the particular kind of non-WIMP UIs that takes advantage of real-time 3D graphics, as CVEs already do by definition, and to which we will refer as 3D-based User Interfaces (3DUIs).

The paper is organized as follows. Section 2 compares CVEs and 3DUIs. The derived presentation strategies underlying ThreeDness are then illustrated in Section 3. According to them, Section 4 presents the ThreeDmap editor and an example of its use is shown in Section 5. Finally, Section 6 sketches the ThreeDness architecture while Section 7 discusses achievements and future work.

2 The use of 3D technology in CVEs and 3DUIs

In this section we compare CVEs and 3DUIs: we identify the peculiarities of both approaches in the visualization of awareness information to highlight the principles leading to the definition of ThreeDness presentation strategies.

Because of the common use of 3D technology, these two categories are sometimes confused. In both CVEs and 3DUIs the terms *virtual world* or *virtual environment* are used to identify a freely explorable digital space, populated by virtual objects. However, the two approaches make very different use of the virtual world. CVEs are derived from VR applications, whose goal is to create a digital environment that a user, embodied in an avatar, can explore and interact with, as he would do in the real world. CVEs extend this concept by adding elements to interact and cooperate with other users, as they would normally do in real life. Hence, in CVEs the virtual world is populated by objects with the purpose to create a space that resemble a real one (e.g., [9, 5]). Unlike CVEs, 3DUIs are derived from user interfaces whose goal is to provide the user with a comfortable and easy way to interact with an application to accomplish some *task*. It is irrelevant whether the objects populating the virtual world represent real objects or not.

Sometimes these different aims are not taken into account. CVEs have been defined as "*shared three dimensional interfaces*" [23], that is, people that have to cooperatively accomplish a task can simultaneously use a CVE and interact with the objects populating it since they replace the components of traditional graphical user interfaces. Similarly, researches on 3DUIs propose models of the dialog needed for the accomplishment of a task in terms of the interaction with the objects of a navigable virtual world [13]. The problem is that often there is no need of a virtual world in order to perform a certain task, whether this is collaborative or not [15]. We believe that both 3DUIs and CVEs have to be better analysed in order to identify which are the advantages of using a 3D technology.

Following their VR root, CVEs are increasingly improving their capability to simulate the reality by supporting simultaneous collaborative object manipulation or imitating characteristics of human communication, such as gestures, body movements and facial expressions [15]. In CVEs user interaction with the virtual environment is heavily dependent on the capabilities and constraints of the embodied avatar. For example, to move an object from a place to another, a user has to position an avatar close enough to reach that object, walk through the virtual environment to the location where the object has to be placed, and finally release it. Also the navigation of the virtual world is *avatar-dependent*: users can explore the environment moving around their avatar and what they can see on their display device is just what the avatar's eyes are looking at. In summary, CVEs are *immersive* for their users and take their full attention by limiting (often eliminating) the perception of the real world. Recent researches showed that, because of the immaturity of interaction and haptic feedback devices, these approaches are still not enough satisfactory for the accomplishment of cooperative tasks (e.g., [10, 19]). However, CVEs show positive aspects for sake of awareness promotion. Firstly, the presence of a "common" virtual environment helps creating a sense of *shared-space* among the involved users, a common "shared-reality" that people naturally search for when remotely cooperating in order to accomplish shared tasks [25]. Secondly, the presence of an avatar representing every user gives a mean for the *recognition of mutual-presence* in the virtual environment [15].

The 3D approach to the creation of user interfaces can be defined as an attempt to replace WIMP components (e.g., buttons, menus, icons,...) and the related interaction mechanisms (e.g., press button, select menu item, drag icon,...) with 3D objects and a more natural interaction system thanks to the characteristics of the 3D graphics. However, this does not imply that the interface is built as a virtual environment navigable through user embodiment in an avatar. In fact, the main goal of a user interface is to provide the means for the accomplishment of tasks, thus taking the full attention of the user, i.e. his *focus*. According to [13], the advantage of using 3D graphics should be seen in the fact that an approach based on a non-WIMP paradigm naturally describes the relationship between an application and its interface in terms of *continuous relationships* between the variables characterizing the application and the interface graphic components. For example, the relationship between the mouse movement and the movement of an object in the virtual space can be described by a continuous function that maps the $\langle x, y \rangle$ mouse coordinates to a resulting $\langle x, y, z \rangle$ position. From a technical point of view, the pixel-based drawing technique, on which WIMP interfaces are based, is substituted by a vectorial-based one, as real-time 3D graphic does. In other words, the integer numbers to express pixel-based properties of the widgets (e.g., position, width, height, ...) become real numbers to express transformations of virtual objects (e.g., translation, rotation, scaling, ...) in a 3D environment. Because of their nature, vectorial engines are better suited to give to users a sense of *continuity* in the representation of information since it is possible to create the illusion of a continuous variation of the representation of information by "masking" the discretization needed to treat digital information with computers. For example, the linear movement of an object from point $\langle x_1, y_1 \rangle$ to point $\langle x_2, y_2 \rangle$ can be described by continuous function of time, while in practice it is approximated by a finite sequence of $\langle dx, dy \rangle$ variations relative to the previous position.

Any kind of application can take advantage of this approach by considering that the same continuous relationship can be applied to any kind of application variable, as for example, the priority level of a message, and not only to variables characterizing an input device.

This continuity has been evaluated to be an advantage when used for the interaction mechanisms of bi-dimensional user interfaces, such as "Zoomable UIs". In [11] users have been asked to use a zoomable interface to seek for places into a digital map. It has been noticed how the continuity (i.e. smoothness) of the zoom feature of the interface makes the users accomplish the task faster that with a discrete approach. In 3D graphics, the continuity aspect is even augmented by the presence of an additional axis that offers additional means for the positioning of objects in the space and to more effectively navigate and locate the available information [26].

As for the interaction devices proposed to the users, CVEs are better explored and "lived" through the use of gloves, shutter glasses, Head-Mounted Displays (HMDs), and any kind of device that can provide haptic force feedback [20, 2]. The research of new interaction devices is not specific of 3DUIs, where the 3D components of the interfaces can be shown in a standard PC monitor, and the interaction can be performed through traditional pointing devices. This does not mean that new interaction devices should not be considered in 3DUIs, but their primary concern is about the *task* to be accomplished, and how an interface built with the 3D technology can make it easier over a traditional WIMP one. In fact, there are situations in which a task is best performed via a traditional WIMP interface, while the 3D approach would make it harder [15]. For example, consider the task "write document" that is widely accomplished by using WIMP-based word processors. As a matter of fact, editing an electronic document is the digital counterpart of writing text over a paper. No advantage is given if the interface shows the paper flying into a virtual space rather than stuck over a digital desktop. Furthermore, concerning the interaction device, the real plastic keyboard used for typing is a widely diffused device to which people is well trained, while an exaggerated 3D approach might force the user to write on the virtual paper through the use of a virtual

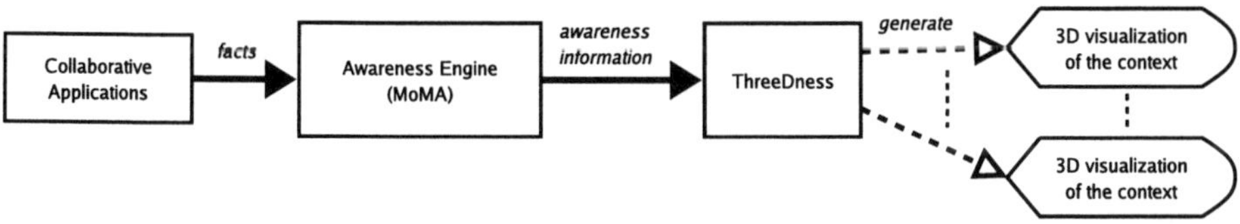

Figure 1: The architecture of the GUIs generation process.

keyboard and some kind of (un)hand(y) glove. Hence, we have to be careful in providing the users with an interface that might immerse them in a virtual world were the accomplishment of a task might become harder than in the real one.

The characteristics that emerge from the previous comparison influenced the characterization of ThreeDness presentation strategies as follows. First, recall that ThreeDness aims to provide users with an interface to "promote awareness information about the surrounding context". Since this perception should not take away the user attention from his primary activity, the interface doesn't keep his *focus*. Hence, relatively to CVEs, we neither look for an *immersive* interface, nor embody the user in an *avatar*. Instead, we appreciate the *continuity* offered by the 3DUIs approach in building interfaces, and we take inspiration from CVEs in providing the users with a *shared-space* were they can *mutually recognize their presence (and activity)*.

3 ThreeDness presentation strategies

This section goes deeper in the awareness information presentation strategies on which ThreeDness is based. To better understand them and fix a reference terminology, we describe the abstract architecture behind the generation of an interface by the ThreeDness engine. Figure 1 shows that the applications used by the cooperating people produce *facts* about their activities that are passed to an *awareness engine*. The latter interprets and elaborates these facts to generate awareness information of the *context* of cooperation, and passes the elaborated information to ThreeDness for its visualization on a distributed and possibly personalized interface. Since the elaboration of the ThreeDness engine relies on the MoMA awareness model, we briefly describe it to illustrate the kind and format of awareness information that has to be displayed.

3.1 The MoMA model

The Model of Modulated Awareness (MoMA) [22] belongs to the class of spatial models and is based on the Reaction-Diffusion metaphor. This gives the possibility to see awareness propagation as generic field propagation in the space. Since the space represents physical and logical relationships among entities, awareness information propagates along both types of relationships. MoMA space is made of *sites* linked together according to the above relationships: this defines the topology of the model. Each site can be populated by an *entity* owning a *state* and a *type* that characterizes its behavior. The latter is specified in terms of primitives specifying four basic actions. Each entity can *emit* a *field* with an initial *intensity* that decreases or increases while the field propagates according to its *propagation function* starting from the source entity site. Hence, entities at different sites can perceive the same field with different intensity values. Each entity is also characterized by a *perception function* that makes an entity *change* its *state* or *position* (moving to another site) when a certain field (with a certain intensity) is perceived. In addition, entities located at contiguous sites can *react* to change their state in a synchronous way.

3.2 Presentation: the direct and indirect interaction

The user interaction with the interface generated by ThreeDness can be *direct* or *indirect*. The former refers to the user interaction with the interface objects using an input device. The latter concerns how the interface autonomously evolves to show to the user the appropriate and customized awareness information. In applications oriented to awareness promotion, indirect interaction has a greater relevance than the direct one, because it is the mean through which the user perceives awareness information as generated by the combined action of the cooperating actors.

In most applications, awareness promotion is based on event models (e.g., [8, 16]). ThreeDness adopts a *pull-out* approach that is coherent with the *continuity* strategy described above. This approach takes inspiration from the solution proposed in [13], where the relationship between an application and the resulting 3D interface is described in terms of *links* between the application *variables* and *event handlers*. The variables hold values of the application meaningful to be displayed in the interface, while the handlers are pieces of code responsible for piloting the interface objects accordingly. In event-based mechanism the relationship between an application variable and the interface are of the type: "when variable X changes, do the following calculations" (e.g., when button A is pushed, function F is called). Instead, the proposed strategy takes an approach of this kind: "Try to maintain the following relationship to input X, whenever you have time, doing the best you can" [13].

While in the former case the interface is a passive entity that waits for changes in the application to update its display accordingly, in the latter the interface has an active role and decides when to query the application in order to *pull-out* the updated values of the variables. This approach better enables an improvement of the *quality* of the interface. In fact, an event-based mechanism discretizes the value changes of a continuous application variable in a sequence of events that inform the interface to update their representation accordingly. Since the interface has no control over the criteria governing the event generation, this process may cause scattered interface updates. In a *pull-out* approach instead, the interface itself queries the application for variables updated values by adopting the preferred updating policy (i.e., amount of time between subsequent updates), thus providing a smoother display of the awareness information.

In order to realize this approach ThreeDness has to identify a set of variables to be monitored by the interface. Moreover, to make ThreeDness a powerful awareness information representation module, these variables have to be independent of the underlying application domain. This goal is achieved thanks to the MoMA model that contains primitives elaborating awareness information in an adaptable way with respect to each specific application domain (for more details see [22]). In other words, the set of *MoMA variables* that the interface can query is defined on the basis of the MoMA model, as described in Section 4. ThreeDmap allows for the graphical editing of the mapping between such variables and the resulting graphic visualization according to additional presentation strategies described in the following sections.

3.3 Presentation: shape and appearance

It is well recognized that 3D visualization requires a particular attention on the choice of the "look" of displayed objects. In [12] the positive effect of displaying diagram symbols using 3D shaped objects instead of plain 2D ones has been documented. The recognition of 3D objects is composed by two separate mental processes: one involves the recognition of the object *shape*, the second is related to the attributes of the surface, such as the color, transparency and texture, that we call object *appearance*. The former process is about the evaluation of the shading, silhouette and structure of the solid object. It has been discovered that shape recognition is more important than appearance recognition. This consideration suggests that, in showing information using 3D objects, their shape is naturally associated to the class or type characterizing the represented entities, while the secondary attributes of the latter are represented through the change of virtual objects appearance. Moreover, other studies [23, 24] emphasize the need to support *subjective views* in CVEs, i.e., how different users of the same CVE might see it differently according to their personal needs and preferences.

Another approach to subjective views has been discussed in [27]. In Multiscale CVEs (mCVE) the scaling of avatar objects is used to reflect the level of involvement among the users populating the CVE. Again, the shape of the objects is kept unchanged, while their size, which can be seen as a *scale* attribute of their appearance, is used to customize the view of the world by each user.

In accordance with the above results, ThreeDness associates the virtual object shape to the *type* of the MoMA entity it represents, while object appearance, size and location are used to promote additional (awareness) information. For each user of the interface, the appearance of every object populating the CVE can be altered switching the object view status to *normal* (no alteration), *off* (object is hidden), *transparent* (object faces are transparent), *wireframe* (just edges are drawn), *dim* (object color is darker) or *bright* (object color is lighter). Hence, the shape and position of the objects remain the same for all users, while each user has a different view of the objects appearance.

Unlike in [23], we get rid of the limit to have only one of these attributes alterable at the same time, e.g., the object can be made either transparent, or brighter, or both together. Furthermore, as in [27], we introduce a control over the alteration level of each attribute. For example, an object can be made more or less transparent according to the *level of interest owned* by the interface users. This is in full accordance with the *continuity* offered by 3D technology discussed earlier.

3.4 Presentation: background and indicators

Another important issue that emerges from the improvement of ThreeDness regards the arrangement of the virtual objects in the interface. The objects composing ThreeDness interface are classified into *indicators* and *background*.

The *indicators* are 3D objects positioned in the interface with the purpose to represent awareness information. In relation with the MoMA, the indicators are used to represent an entity or the perception of a field by an entity. According to the strategy presented in the previous section, the shape of indicators, together with the possibility to modify their appearance, is the mean to present the awareness information. Indicators have a dynamic behavior, and may appear and disappear as well as change their appearance during the life-time of the interface. Additionally, the presence of indicators representing people gives a mean to support the *recognition of the mutual presence*, as discussed in Section 2. In fact, man-shaped objects (i.e., avatars) can be added to the scene as indicators of human presence, and changes on the attributes of the avatar objects can be used to augment the interface with information about users' activities.

The *background* is a navigable environment composed by a set of virtual objects immersed in a 3D world. Its main purpose is to give a reference and a meaning to the position of the indicators in the space instead of having them floating into the vacuum. Additionally, the background has the capability to provide the users of ThreeDness with a common referenced *shared-space*, as discussed in Section 2. Finally, the background layout can be used to recall any kind of abstract scenario (e.g. a virtual desktop, a virtual room) useful to take advantage of the spatial memory that people naturally use when looking for some information [18].

In order to enhance the visualization possibilities of ThreeDness, also the attributes of objects of the background are modifiable. For example, consider a background composed by a set of "containers", each one populated by an avatar. In order to express the level of interest between two avatars one may choose to alter the level of transparency of the avatars, hence altering their visibility. However, one may choose to alter the transparency of the containers. In this case, the visibility of the avatars is altered while their appearance still represents different kind of information concerning them. The alteration of the appearance and shape of background objects beyond the physical constraints of the real world is not new in CVEs. In [19], where people had to cooperatively move a big object in a narrow space (the *piano movers' problem*), the walls of the environment were "blinking" in order give a visual feedback when a collision between an object and a wall occurred. In [10], where people had to cooperate in order to arrange the furniture of a room, several techniques were adopted in order to give visual feedback of actors behavior: objects were drawn in wireframe when moved by someone, avatars arms were lengthening when users were analysing an object and a light cone was irradiated by the avatar's eyes to let the users easily recognize which was the field of view of the others users. These approaches served as workarounds for the lack of haptic feedback to the (real) users of the CVEs. On the contrary, since ThreeDness goal is not the simulation of the reality, we use the alteration of the appearance and shape of the virtual objects of the background as an additional mean for an effective and suggestive visualization of the awareness information.

3.5 Presentation: subjective views

A very important aim of ThreeDness is to support the users' subjective views of the same awareness information. This is achieved by making the mapping between the MoMA output and the generated interface depend on the identity of the interface user. Figure 2 illustrates an example of how the same MoMA configuration is used to generate different views from the same awareness information. In the following, we present the principles on which this strategy is based.

The end-users of the various distributed interfaces correspond to entities populating the

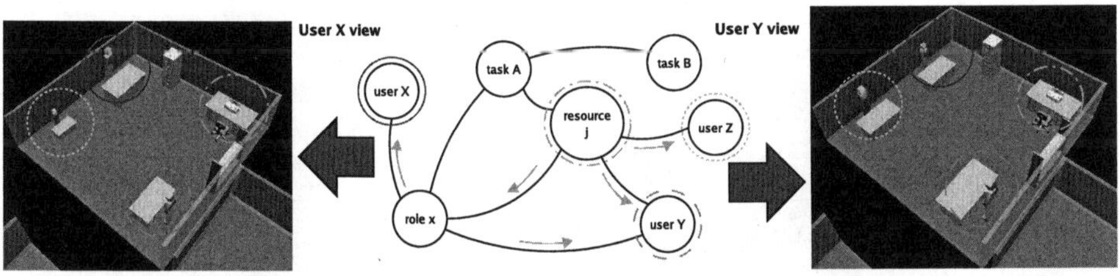

Figure 2: An example of custom views originated by the same MoMA configuration. Circles have been added to highlight the corresponding entities. Orange arrows in the MoMA graph represent the diffusion of a field.

MoMA. As for the other entities belonging to the application domain, end-users are represented in the interface by virtual objects. When drawing a user interface, the appearance of each object depends on the logical distance between the entity the object represents and the entity representing the interface user. For example, in Figure 2 the logical distance between entities corresponding to two users (i.e., the number of arcs composing the shortest path between the two entities) has been associated to the scaling attribute of the avatar objects (but it could have been associated to any other attribute, as the transparency level). In fact, the avatar representing the user Z is visualized in the interfaces of users X and Y with different dimensions. The visualization of the perception of a field is customized to different users too. When a field propagates in the logical space, it is perceived by the entities representing users with different *strength* values according to their mutual position and the field propagation function. How the field traverse the graph and how its value on each site is calculated is out of the scope of this paper and can be found in [1]. For example, when the entity representing a printer emits the field "printer is broken", such field is perceived with a higher strength by the users that are logically closer to the broken printer. As in the previous case, the different perceived values might be used to alter the attribute of the virtual objects playing as indicators for this kind of awareness information. The implementation of the strategies described above can be realized through the ThreeDmap editor that is presented in the next section.

4 The ThreeDmap editor

This section illustrates the main features of ThreeDmap editor stating from its motivations.

ThreeDmap aims to provide ThreeDness end-users with a tool to customize the presentation of awareness information. The way in which the information elaborated by the MoMA is translated into graphical components is called the *presentation logic* of ThreeDness. It contains the definition of the initial background and the description of the run-time behavior of the interface according to the strategies presented in the previous section. First, ThreeDmap is used to define a *default presentation logic*: this is provided to every end-user that starts the ThreeDness interface. Afterwards, ThreeDmap can be used by an end-user to customize the default presentation according to his preferences and needs. In both cases, the graphical interface provided by ThreeDmap gives a significant support for a quicker and easier modification of existing presentation logics or creation of new ones. This is particularly useful when ThreeDness has to be newly configured to display awareness information of an additional application domain.

Customizing Background and Shapes As illustrated in Figure 3, the user of Three-

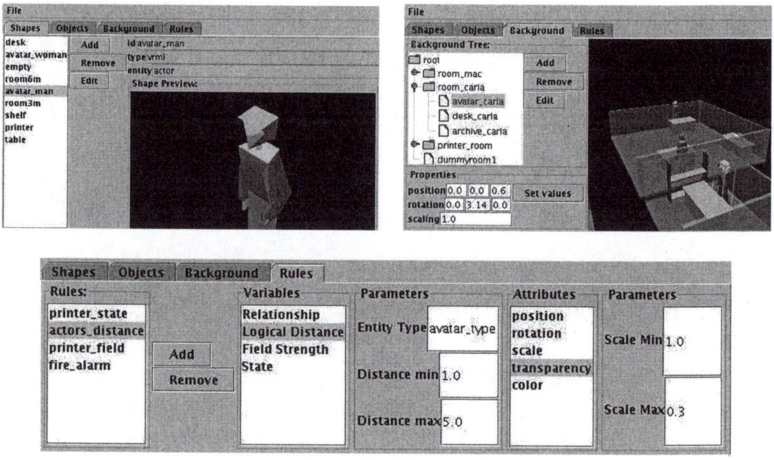

Figure 3: Screenshots of the ThreeDmap editor: Shapes, Background and Rules editing panels.

Attribute	Meaning	Range
position	x, y, z offset from the original location	$\langle -\infty, -\infty, -\infty \rangle$ to $\langle \infty, \infty, \infty \rangle$
rotation	rotation around the x, y, z reference axis	$\langle 0.0, 0.0, 0.0 \rangle$ to $\langle 2\pi, 2\pi, 2\pi \rangle$
scale	x, y, z uniform scaling	0.0 to ∞
color	Red, Green, Blue color components	$\langle 0.0, 0.0, 0.0 \rangle$ (black) to $\langle 1.0, 1.0, 1.0 \rangle$ (white)
transparency	surfaces transparency	0.0 (opaque) to 1.0 (invisible)

Table 1: Modifiable objects attributes.

Dmap is provided with an interface to define the shapes of the objects that compose the interface, and to specify if a shape represents a particular type of MoMA entity or an object of the background. Afterwards, following the strategy described in Section 3.4, the reference background can be customized. Background objects are associated with a *type* in order to facilitate their retrieval at run-time.

There are cases in which MoMA entities have to be represented by virtual objects positioned in very specific locations (e.g., the avatars representing the users have to be positioned in a room representing their office). For this reason the ThreeDmap interface is also used to populate the background with indicators representing MoMA entities. These indicators can be referenced during the run-time life of the interface in order to express the position of dynamically created indicators.

Customizing Objects Appearance As stated in Section 3.3, we aim to graphically represent information through the modification of object attributes. We identified a set of attributes that can be used to alter the appearance of each object (Table 1). Each proposed attribute can be set to a value belonging to a certain range. For example, the *transparency* level can range from 0.0 (no-transparency, or opaque objects) to 1.0 (for full-transparent, hence invisible, objects). Similarly, the *scale* can range from 0.0 (the objects are stretched at minimum and disappear), towards 1.0 (original dimensions), to a value bigger than 1.0 (objects are enlarged). The color attribute can change continuously too. Given two colors, the resulting color is obtained with a "fade" process (i.e., a linear interpolation of their RGB components). The modification of the position, rotation and scaling attributes, results in a displacement, additional-rotation and re-dimensioning of the objects from the initial location, orientation and dimension that were set when the object was created.

Although the modification of the position, orientation and scaling are not actually modifying the appearance of an object, they have been classified as "appearance attributes" since they can be effectively used to represent awareness information. For example: the objects representing a task are placed near to an avatar to indicate that the person representing that avatar has to accomplish those tasks. Then, the task objects can be displaced nearer or farther from an avatar according to their priority.

Customizing Indirect Interaction As stated in Section 3.2, we identify a set of *variables* of the MoMA to be monitored by the interface. The value of the following variables can be obtained from a MoMA configuration: *entities relationship*, *entities state*, *logical distance* and *field strength*. We used the word *query* to stress that the run-time engine is based on an approach where the interface is not passively waiting for new information to be displayed: on the contrary, the interface will *pull-out* the required awareness information as needed.

The rules panel (Figure 3) allows the editing of the presentation rules governing the dynamic behavior of the interface. They describe the mapping between the awareness information provided by the MoMA and the resulting interface adaptation. The rules are expressed in the form <*moma_query*, *interface_adaptation*>, where the *moma_query* defines which of the MoMA variables match the rule, while the *interface_adaptation* defines how the objects appearance has to change or which new indicators have to be visualized. Each rule can be interpreted as a continuous relationship between the values of the MoMA variables and the values of the object attributes.

5 An example scenario

This section presents an example scenario in order to give an overview of the possibilities offered by the rules system. We consider two applications providing the *facts* about the users context: i) a Workflow Management system defines the states and the relationships among a set of *actors* and the *tasks* to accomplished ii) a printer daemon gives information about the status of shared printers. The MoMA is configured to properly elaborate the facts in order to provide awareness information meaningful to be displayed.

The background editor has been used to create a scenario recalling the layout of the office environment where actors are located. The background has been populated with an initial set of indicators representing the actors (avatars) and the shared printers.

In the following, the rules currently supported by ThreeDmap are described. For each of them the specific instance used for the example scenario is presented. Figure 4 shows a screenshot on the generated interface.

Relationship The rules used to represent the relationships between entities take the form: <*entities_relationship*(*entity_type1*, *entity_type2*), *create_object*(*location*, *arrangement*)>. They specify that when two entities e_1 (of type *entity_type1*) and e_2 (of type *entity_type1*) form a relationship, a new object representing e_1 is created and placed in a location relative to e_2 with a certain arrangement. In our scenario, when an actor starts a task, the MoMA defines a relationship between the two involved entities. This is visualized by the rule instance <*entities_relationship*(TASK, ACTOR), *create_object*(CLOSEST "DESK", ALIGNED_ON)>, stating that an object representing the task (a book-like shaped object) has to be created and positioned next to the desk located closest to the avatar. This rule is based on the assumption that the DESK type has been associated to a proper set of virtual objects during the creation of the background. The ALIGNED_ON arrangement policy specifies that the objects are positioned over the desk and arranged next to each other. Another kind of arrangement is STACKED_ON; it arranges the objects one on the top of the other.

It has to be noticed that the application of this rule might lead to the visualization of several objects representing the same entity. In our example, when a task involves several actors for its accomplishment, it is represented by several objects, each one located next to the actor involved in its development.

Logical Distance The rules used to represent logical distance take the form: <*entity_distance* (*entity_type*, *distancemin*, *distancemax*), *set_attribute*(*attribute*, *valuemin*, *valuemax*)>. They specify how to represent the logical distance between the entity corresponding to the interface user (e_u) and an entity e_x of type *entity_type*. This is done by altering the value of the specified *attribute* for each virtual object representing the entity e_x. The attribute value is obtained through a linear interpolation of the specified boundaries according to the formula: $value = valuemin + (valuemax - valuemin) * k$, where $k = \frac{d-distancemin}{distancemax-distancemin}$ and d is the distance value. If d is below *distancemin* or above *distancemax* no interpolation is done and the respective boundaries are used. In our example, the logical distance between actors is represented by the rule: <*entity_distance*(ACTOR, 1.0, 5.0), *set_attribute*(TRANSPARENCY, 0.0, 0.7)>. It makes all the avatars become more transparent as the logical distance from the representing user grows (but limited to 0.7 when the distance is above 5.0). Since the rule implicitly uses the identity of the interface user (e_u), it produces different results in the interface of different users, thus supporting subjective views.

Field Perception The rules used to represent the perception of fields take the form: <*field_strength*(*field*, *strmin*, *strmax*), *set_attribute*(SOURCE|USER, *attribute*, *valuemin*, *valuemax*)>. They specify the *attribute* to be altered when an entity representing the *user* (e_u) perceives the specified *field*, emitted by a *source* entity. The attribute alteration can involve either the objects representing the SOURCE of the field or the USER that perceived it. The new attribute value is obtained through an interpolation like in the previous rule. In our example, a task close to a deadline starts to emit a field in order to warn actors about the critical situation. This is visualized through the rule: <*field_strength*(TASK_DEADLINE, 5.0, 10.0), *set_attribute*(SOURCE, SCALE, 1.0, 2.0)>, specifying that when a TASK_DEADLINE field is perceived, all the objects representing the source task increase their size, thus increasing their visibility.

State The rules used to represent the state of an entity take the form <*entity_state*(*entity_type*, *states*), *set_attribute*(*attribute*, *values*)>. They map the possible *states* of an entity to a set of *values* of the specified *attribute*. In our example the printer status is represented by the rule: <*entity_state*(PRINTER, {OFF, IDLE, BUSY, BROKEN}), *set_attribute*(COLOR, {GREY, GREEN, YELLOW, RED})>, specifying that each object representing an entity of type PRINTER changes its color according to the specified printer states.

Each end-user has the possibility to locally customize the default presentation logic. For example, the logical distance between users and the perception of the field TASK_DEADLINE can be represented differently by modifying the rules presented above (see Figure 4, right).

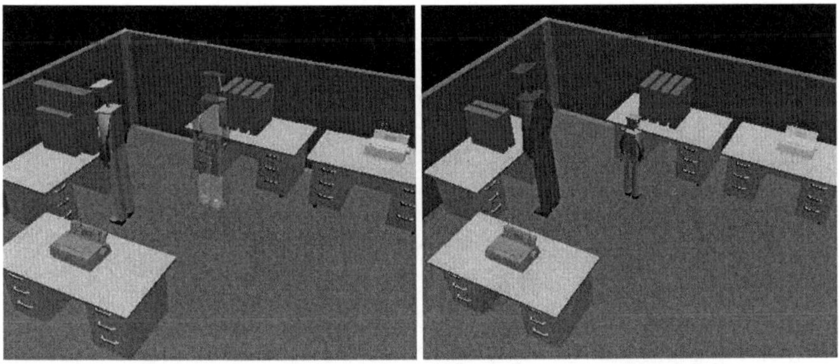

Figure 4: An example of user customized presentation. In the left figure, the awareness information is presented altering the transparency of avatars and the size of the tasks. In the right figure, the same information is presented altering the size and color of avatars.

The rule used to represent the actors logical distance becomes: <*entity_distance*(ACTOR, 1.0, 5.0), *set_attribute*(SIZE, 0.5, 1.5)>, stating that the avatar size is altered instead of its transparency. The rule used to represent the field perception becomes: <*field_strength*(TASK_DEADLINE, 5.0, 10.0), *set_attribute*(USER, COLOR, "LIGHTGRAY", "RED")>, stating that the color of the avatar is altered instead of the size of the task.

6 ThreeDness architecture

Figure 5 shows a scheme of the current ThreeDness architecture. Arrows show the logical flux of information. The architecture is based on a Client/Server structure. The upper part of the figure shows the server side, while the bottom part shows the client side. The output of the MoMA-based awareness engine, i.e. the *awareness information* is sent to the ThreeDness server and stored with an appropriate data structure. The *Client Handling Engine* keeps track of connected clients and is responsible to send them both awareness information and the presentation logic. The role of the FIFO buffer is described in Section 7.

On the server side, the *administrator* can create, through the editor, several *presentation logics* that can be used to display the same awareness information in different ways. The availability of several presentations is useful in providing end-users with different backgrounds and presentation rules suitable to their initial needs or hardware constraints. For example, users belonging to the *Marketing* and the *Research&Development* departments of the same company might want the background looking like the topology of their own department. Furthermore, if the target visualization device has limited hardware capabilities, the configuration might be simplified to render a virtual world with fewer details.

At the bottom of Figure 5 the client side of the application is represented. The balloon on the right side stresses that there are several running clients. One of them is magnified in order to analyse its content. When a client connects, a copy of one of the configurations is sent to it, together with updated awareness information that will be the input of the run-time interpreter. The run-time engine uses the local 3D engine to generate the 3D graphical interface for the user. Specifically, the identity of the person using an interface (shown in the figure by the

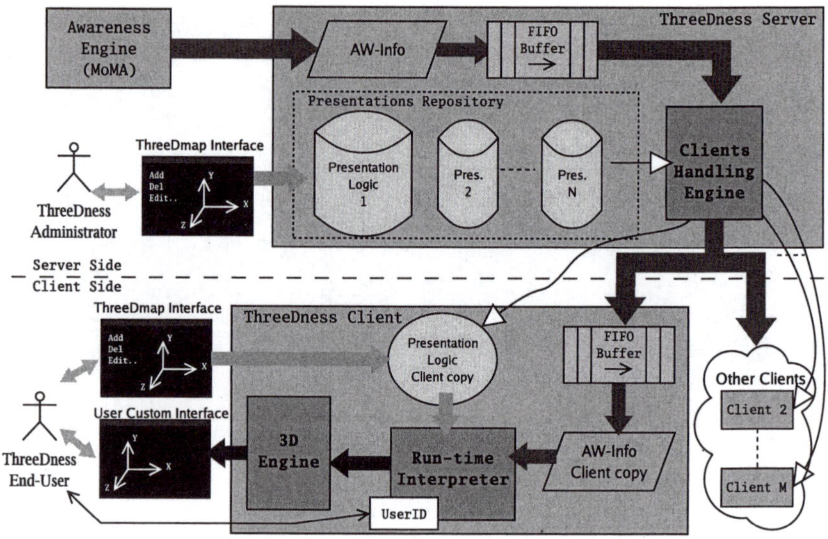

Figure 5: The ThreeDness Architecture.

UserID box) is a fundamental parameter used by the run-time engine in order to support the *subjective view* of the displayed information. Additionally, the ThreeDmap editor allows the users to customize the presentation logic according to their needs. The edited presentation can then be locally stored for future use.

The application has been written in Java language. The client/server communication has been realized taking advantage of the RMI framework and the 3D engine has been built with Java3D, an extension of Java supporting creation of real-time 3D applications. The objects populating the virtual world can be imported in VRML format.

7 Conclusions and future work

The paper presented ThreeDmap, an editor that allows the creation and customization of 3D graphical interfaces for the promotion of awareness information. The recent improvements of the ThreeDness project yielded to the definition of the components needed to describe the *presentation logics*, i.e., how the awareness information is displayed. In the current architecture, the definition of the presentation logic is solely based on the interaction with the MoMA model. Thanks to this, ThreeDness has been relieved by any domain dependency; this allows taking advantage of the flexibility offered by the MoMA in being configured to elaborate the awareness information of many application domains. ThreeDmap contributes in giving to the ThreeDness users a graphical support to easily define new presentation logics and to customize existing ones according to their personal needs and preferences.

The definition of a presentation logic is based on presentation strategies that emerged from a comparison with two research fields that, as ThreeDness, make use of 3D technology: Collaborative Virtual Environments and non-WIMP user interfaces. From this comparison emerged the necessity of an interaction mechanism between the MoMA and the interface suitable to take advantage of the continuity offered by the 3D technology; we called this a *pull-out* approach. In this approach, unlike event-based systems, the interface does not passively wait for awareness information: on the contrary, it is an active entity that "pulls" the information from the source. This results in a greater control over the interface update policies yielding to a smoother visualization of awareness information.

Currently, we are working on the combination of ThreeDness with existing applications (e.g., mail clients, Internet browsers, text editors) in order to perform a systematic evaluation. Meanwhile, some basic concerns that emerged from discussions with potential users will be considered for future improvements.

The first effort will allow users to take away their attention from the awareness interface for even long time, having the possibility to get a "summary" of what happened in the lasted period (this is similar to the DocuDrama feature of Tower [16]). This will be accomplished using a "record/play" mechanism. In normal conditions, a user sees the interface always up to date. On request, he can "scroll" the virtual space back and forward thought the past changes. Technically, this can be accomplished inserting a buffer in the client side of ThreeDness (see Section 6). Such buffer technique might be applied on the server side as well. When a new interface is started, it connects to the server and downloads a copy of the server buffer. This allows the newly connected interface to have a history of the evolution of the scenario before its connection. Moreover, this would well apply in presence of wireless networks, where connection breaks are more frequent. If a connection breaks and then resumes, all lost awareness information are sent to the client to keep it up to date.

The second effort is towards a tuning of the screen update of the ThreeDness interface. In fact, awareness information may be considered to arrive randomly over time. This might cause a random apparition and disappearance of indicators in the interface, leading to consequent confusion for the user. Hence, some techniques have to be applied in order to fine-tune the frequency used to pull-out the awareness information from the awareness model.

References

[1] Stefania Bandini and Carla Simone. Integrating forms of interaction in a distributed coordination model. *Fundamenta Informaticae*, in press.

[2] Cagatay Basdogan, Chih-Hao Ho, Mandayam A. Srinivasan, and Mel Slater. An experimental study on the role of touch in shared virtual environments. *ACM Transactions on Computer-Human Interaction (TOCHI)*, 7(4):443–460, 2000.

[3] Steve Benford, Paul Dourish, and Tom Rodden. Introduction to the special issue on human-computer interaction and collaborative virtual environments. *ACM Transactions on Computer-Human Interaction (TOCHI)*, 7(4):439–441, 2000.

[4] Steve Benford, Chris Greenhalgh, Tom Rodden, and James Pycock. Collaborative virtual environments. *Comm. of the ACM*, 44(7):79–85, 2001.

[5] Christer Carlsson and Olof Hagsand. Dive a multi-user virtual reality system. In *IEEE Virtual Reality Annual International Symposium*, pages 394–400, 1993.

[6] P. Dourish and V. Bellotti. Awareness and coordination in shared workspaces. In *Proceedings of the ACM Conference on Computer Supported Cooperative Work (CSCW'92)*, pages 107–114, Toronto, Ontario, 1992. ACM Press.

[7] Pablo Figueroa, Mark Green, and Benjamin A. Watson. A framework for 3d interaction techniques. In *CAD/Graphics 2001 (Kunming, China)*. International Academic, 2001.

[8] Geraldine Fitzpatrick. Supporting public availability and accessibility with elvin: Experiences and reflections. *CSCW Journal*, 11(3-4):447–474, 2002.

[9] C. Greenhalgh and S. Benford. Massive: a collaborative ve for tele-conferencing. *ACM TOCHI*, 2(3):239–261, 1995.

[10] Jon Hindmarsh, Mike Fraser, Christian Heath, Steve Benford, and Chris Greenhalgh. Object-focused interaction in collaborative virtual environments. *ACM TOCHI*, 7(4):477–509, 2000.

[11] Kasper Hornbæk, Benjamin B. Bederson, and Catherine Plaisant. Navigation patterns and usability of zoomable user interfaces with and without an overview. *ACM Transactions on Computer-Human Interaction (TOCHI)*, 9(4):362–389, 2002.

[12] Pourang Irani and Colin Ware. Diagramming information structures using 3d perceptual primitives. *ACM Transactions on Computer-Human Interaction (TOCHI)*, 10(1):1–19, 2003.

[13] Robert J. K. Jacob, Leonidas Deligiannidis, and Stephen Morrison. A software model and specification language for non-WIMP user interfaces. *ACM Transactions on Computer-Human Interaction*, 6(1):1–46, 1999.

[14] Fabrizio Nunnari and Carla Simone. ThreeDness: representing awareness in cooperative applications. In *COOP2002*, pages 7–22. IOS Press, 2002.

[15] Samuli Pekkola. Critical approach to 3d virtual realities for group work. In *Proceedings of the second Nordic conference on Human-computer interaction*, pages 129–138. ACM Press, 2002.

[16] W. Prinz and U. Pankoke-Babatz. Awareness of cooperative activities in mixed realities. In *Proceedings of CAST01*, pages 231–234, 2001.

[17] Theresa-Marie Rhyne. Computer games and scientific visualization. *Communications of the ACM*, 45(7):40–44, 2002.

[18] George G. Robertson, Mary Czerwinski, Kevin Larson, Daniel C. Robbins, David Thiel, and Maarten van Dantzich. Data mountain: Using spatial memory for document management. In *ACM Symposium on User Interface Software and Technology*, pages 153–162, 1998.

[19] Roy A. Ruddle, Justin C. D. Savage, and Dylan M. Jones. Symmetric and asymmetric action integration during cooperative object manipulation in virtual environments. *ACM Transactions on Computer-Human Interaction (TOCHI)*, 9(4):285–308, 2002.

[20] Eva-Lotta Sallnäs, Kirsten Rassmus-Gröhn, and Calle Sjöström. Supporting presence in collaborative environments by haptic force feedback. *ACM Transactions on Computer-Human Interaction (TOCHI)*, 7(4):461–476, 2000.

[21] Kield Schmidt. The problem with "awareness": Introductory remarks on "awareness in cscw". *Computer Supported Cooperative Work (CSCW). The Journal of Collaborative Computing*, 11(3-4):285–298, 2002.

[22] Carla Simone and Stefania Bandini. Integrating awareness in cooperative applications through the reaction-diffusion metaphor. *CSCW Journal*, 11(3-4):495–530, 2002.

[23] Gareth Smith. Cooperative virtual environments: lessons from 2d multi user interfaces. In *Proceedings of the 1996 ACM conference on Computer supported cooperative work*, pages 390–398. ACM Press, 1996.

[24] Gareth Smith and John Mariani. Using subjective views to enhance 3d applications. In *Proceedings of the ACM symposium on Virtual reality software and technology*, pages 139–146. ACM Press, 1997.

[25] Diane H. Sonnenwald, Mary C. Whitton, and Kelly L. Maglaughlin. Evaluating a scientific collaboratory: Results of a controlled experiment. *ACM Transactions on Computer-Human Interaction (TOCHI)*, 10(2):150–176, 2003.

[26] Colin Ware and Glenn Franck. Evaluating stereo and motion cues for visualizing information nets in three dimensions. *ACM Trans. Graph.*, 15(2):121–140, 1996.

[27] Xiaolong Zhang and George W. Furnas. Social interactions in multiscale cves. In *Proceedings of the 4th international conference on Collaborative virtual environments*, pages 31–38. ACM Press, 2002.

Cooperative Systems Design
M. Zacklad et al. (Eds.)
IOS Press, 2004

Distributed Trouble-Shooting

Wilfried M. Post, Sylvia A. A. van den Boogaard and Peter C. Rasker
TNO Human Factors, Dept. of Team Solutions
Kampweg 5, 3769 ZG Soesterberg, The Netherlands
e-mail: Post@tm.tno.nl

Abstract. When knowledge, required for trouble-shooting at sea, can be supplied real-time but from a distance, problems, such as with the limited availability of specialists, and the high costs of maintenance, may be tackled. Unclear is, however, how this redistribution of knowledge will work in practice. We therefore performed an experiment in which an on-shore expert and an on-board mechanic fixed technical problems together, to investigate the effect of communication means, and the amount of knowledge a mechanic needs to do his job. This paper presents the main results of this experiment. Based on a framework for remote trouble-shooting, we coded the conversation between expert and mechanic in detail. The results show that, in principle, the problems could be fixed, both by technical and non-technical personnel. Not surprisingly, distributed trouble-shooting requires more time and more communication, especially with non-technical personnel. Amazingly, working remotely with technicians requires more effort then with non-technical personnel. Unfortunately, remote maintenance is less safe

Introduction

The Royal Netherlands Navy faces a severe problem with the limited availability of highly specialised maintenance personnel. One way to solve this is to require no longer that all maintenance knowledge is available at each ship. Instead, the knowledge could be supplied by a central facility on shore, or by a specialist from another ship. For infrequently occurring tasks, such as system malfunction diagnosis, remote knowledge supply, or teleknowledge, may even result in reduced operating costs. However, not all tasks are eligible for teleknowledge, and both the crew on board and the teleknowledge specialist in the central facility will need proper communication equipment to ensure the current performance level.

Previously, we have given a view on the potential applications, requirements and limitations of teleknowledge on future navy vessels [1]. The paper addresses issues like the kind of knowledge that has to be transmitted, how this transmission must take place and what psychosocial boundaries and risks must be taken into account. In the present study we investigate the possibility of distributed trouble-shooting experimentally. Experts will guide, at a distance, mechanics through corrective maintenance cases, while measuring and observing their behaviour. Two research questions are addressed: what type of communication means is needed, and what level of expertise of the mechanic is necessary, for remote trouble-shooting becoming a success. We will make a comparison between two situations: in one situation the expert and mechanic communicate by a particular audio-visual equipment, and in the other situation they communicate by a perfect medium: they work side-by-side. The level of expertise of the mechanics is also varied: half of the subjects will be general technicians, the other half will be non-technical system operators.

Before describing the experiment, a framework for remote collaborative trouble-shooting is presented.

1. Framework

In our remote trouble-shooting framework, we approach distributed collaboration as an issue of transferring information, knowledge and instructions between agents. To set the scene, fig. 1 illustrates a typical conversation between an on-shore specialist and an on-board mechanic. The "knowledge clouds" stands for the level of expertise. The specialist has much general problem solving knowledge and also domain knowledge: the specifics of the system. The expert's knowledge cloud contains a more extensive trouble-shooting task hierarchy, a more complete trouble shouting method, and a more elaborated domain theory then the generalist's cloud. The generalist knows how to solve problems in general, but not much about the specific domain.

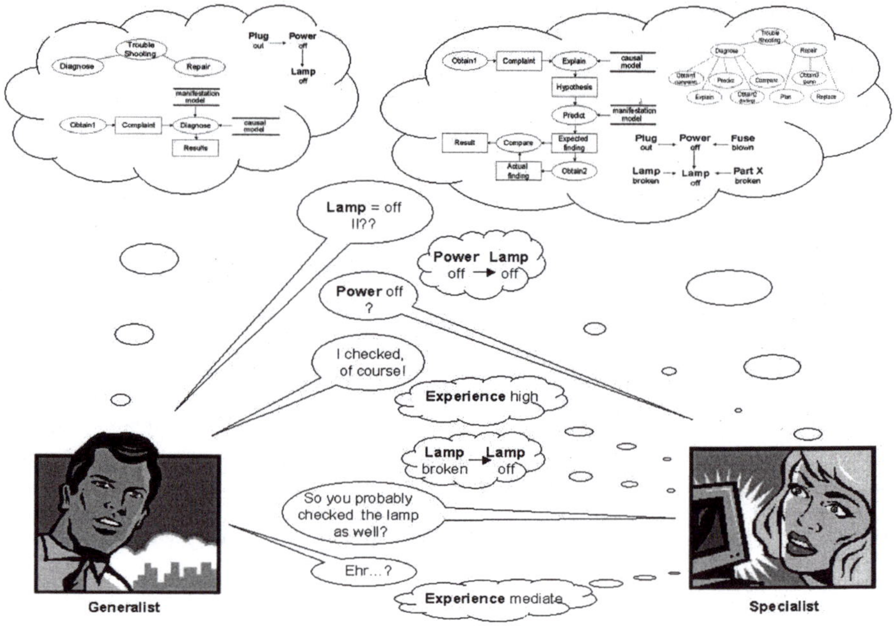

Figure 1: some aspects of communication between a general technician and a specialist.

Preceding the scene, a problem was detected, and a mechanic on board of the ship had started to fix the problem himself. He didn't succeed, so he consults a probably unknown specialist. As fig. 1 shows, the mechanic exchanges information about the problem, and the expert starts applying her knowledge, and comes up with questions. Meanwhile, she estimates the knowledge level of the mechanic, to know how to ask questions. She can ask a series of simple questions, such as "Is the plug in the socket?" followed by "Did you check the fuse?", but by doing so, possibly degrading an experienced mechanic. She may also ask the same information in one question, but with the chance that the mechanic is unfamiliar with jargon (e.g., "Do you have juice?"). It may be relevant for the specialist to notice signs of doubt, to adjust her communication, but these subtle queues are difficult to notice with the communication equipment used. Finally, when assessing the mechanic's experience as mediate, she may consider to transfer knowledge to him, enabling him to solve the problem (partially) by himself. Another way to increase his knowledge is to send him to school.

Transfer of information and knowledge during remote trouble-shooting will probably have other drawbacks as well. Some findings are hard to describe, such as tactile characteristics, smells, colours, etc. (e.g., "the pump feels pretty warm", "I smell something strange"). When the specialist cannot observe these herself, she may find a way out, by helping to specify the finding ("It should be over 40^0. Is it too hot to hold?") or by using ingenuity ("Open a can of coolant. Does it smell the same?"). Unfortunately, for some information this may be hard to do. Still another aspect is that communication is more efficient when one can refer to objects, instead of describing them (see e.g., [2;3]). Object reference is more problematic during distributed problem solving.

Summarized, distributed trouble-shooting requires information transfer and a certain distribution of knowledge. Some types of information are difficult, or even impossible, to communicate, causing that certain problems may remain unsolved. Further, it is not clear what kind of knowledge and how much an on-board mechanic requires, and whether this knowledge can be transferred during problem solving, or should be acquired at school.

1.1 Transfer between agents

For getting hold on these problems, we have first defined various aspects of the transfer of information and knowledge between specialist and mechanic, or in general, between agents (see fig. 2). Information about a problem object is about its *manifestation*, such as position, form, colour, sound, temperature, smell, etc. These can be perceived by a *sensor system* that can see, hear, feel, smell, and taste. Perception requires knowledge, otherwise the manifestations are not recognised. Information perceived is processed by a *cognitive system*, using its memory and processor. Information processing requires problem solving knowledge, such as theories, task knowledge and procedures. Information processing can result in an action, executed by a *motor system*, requiring skills. Human agents usually possess all three systems.

When two agents cooperate, they transfer *information* they have perceived, derived or remembered. They can also transfer *knowledge* in order to let the other agent derive new information, or derive what to do. They can also *instruct* the other what to do. Agents transfer in the *form* of pictures and images, sound, text, tactile information, and, indirectly, by referential information. They transfer with a *medium*, such as face-to-face, letter, telephone, e-mail, and videophone. The transfer takes place through certain *connection*, such as light, air pressure, touch, electronic, radio, etc.

As fig. 2 shows, we could improve agent cooperation in several ways. We could focus on improving the capacities of the agents, such as developing sensor systems that can smell and taste, or advanced motor systems, such as robots. We could also improve transfer, such as developing new forms, mediums or connection types. Within the scope of the present study, we will carry out our experiment with technology that becomes available in the near future. Soon, transfer between ship and shore can take place by communication and information systems with speech, data, and video services, comparable with mobile Internet. Both its virtues and restrictions will be part of the experiment. It means that we will not take all types of perceivable information into account, such as tactile information, smell and taste, although it remains possible to communicate about it indirectly. Also, we will not investigate remote perception of object manifestations, such as sensor information and electronic status of software. Although technically possible, the current machinery doesn't provide this information. In our future research, we may broaden our scope, also depending on the results of the present study.

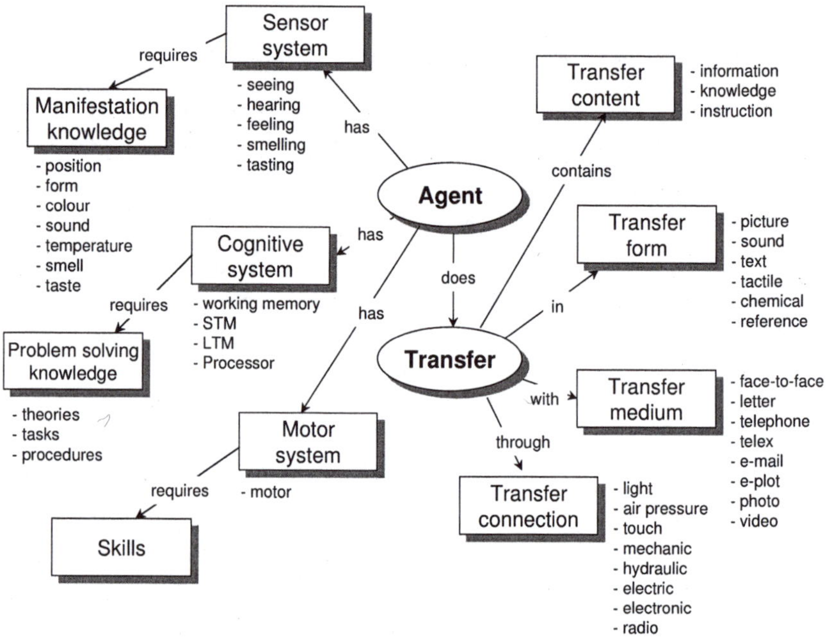

Figure 2: Agents have sensor, motor, and cognitive capabilities that require knowledge and skills. They do transfer information, knowledge and instruction, in a particular form, with a particular medium, through a particular connection.

1.2 Knowledge distribution

How can the knowledge required for problem solving best be distributed between specialist and mechanic? For trouble-shooting one needs sensor, motor, and cognitive capacities. A specialist possesses and can apply all three capacities. With his knowledge, he recognises relevant information for a problem, may knows how to come up with a solution, and what actions to perform. Further, he has the skills to execute the actions.

When a specialist has to operate from shore, the necessary information and knowledge needs to be transferred, depending on the knowledge level of the off-shore mechanic. When the mechanic is a novice, for instance an operator without technical education, then the transfer of problem information needs to be guided by the on shore specialist (see fig. 3; The symbol ● denotes the initiative taker). The novice doesn't know what information is important. He cannot even recognise the object properties (he just doesn't have the knowledge for it), and is *instructed* to provide the information. The specialist does the thinking, but the activities that need to be carried out needs to be guided in full, meaning that the specialist needs to monitor the execution and adjust the activities when necessary. [4] uses the term *situation awareness* for this monitoring process.

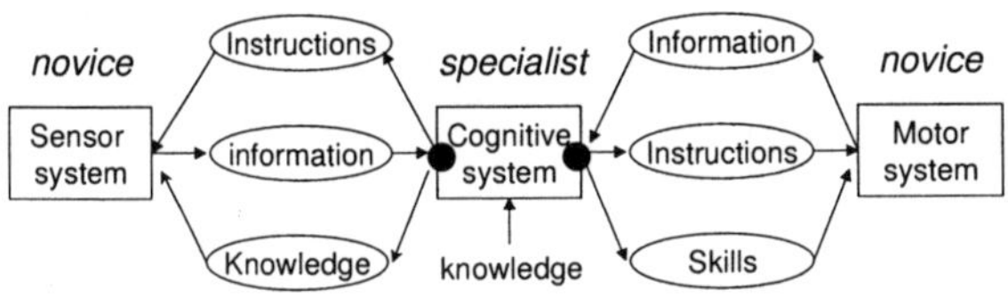

Figure 3: Distributed trouble-shooting agents need the same sensor, motor and cognitive capacities, and the proper knowledge and skills. When those are not evenly distributed knowledge and information transfer is needed, the amount of which depends on the information and knowledge the agents have available. Novices act as the eyes and the hands of the experts, but specialists need to take initiative. The symbol ● denotes the initiative taker.

When an on shore specialist collaborates with an off shore technical generalist, transfer is different (see fig. 4). The technical generalist has general knowledge of problem solving, but no specific knowledge of this particular problem. The generalist can take initiative in transferring information to the specialist. The specialist, in his turn, can transfer specific knowledge to the generalist, such as references to manuals, checklists, schema's, help on how to search the broken apparatus, etc.). This enables the generalist to provide only relevant information to the specialist. Also in repairing the problem, transfer differs from transfer between specialist and novice. The generalist can take initiative, and the specialist can monitor his actions, only intervening when an action threatens to go wrong. The specialist may also notice that the generalist lacks certain skills, and may transfer these (e.g., by "You may use some strength there", or "No, to loosen screws, always turn the driver counter-clockwise").

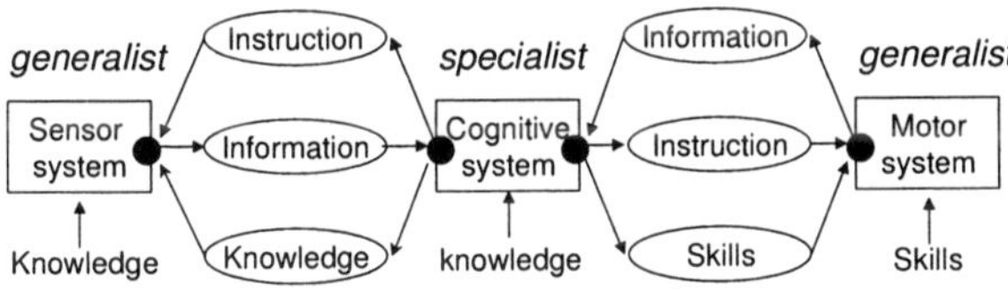

Figure 4: A knowledgeable off shore generalist can take initiative in providing information to the specialist. He is also able to assimilate new knowledge and skills. Generalists are more then the eyes and the hands of the experts.

1.3 Experiment

To find out whether distributed trouble-shooting is possible with an on shore specialist and an off shore mechanic, we performed an experiment. Two research questions were addressed: what type of *communication means* is needed, and what *level of expertise* is necessary. For the first question, we compared collaboration when mediated by full-duplex audio and video data, with perfectly mediated collaboration: working together side-by-side. The video data consist of a picture provided by the mechanic through a hand-held camera. So the video is data about the object, and not the speaker (so, *video-as-data,* and not *talking heads;* see e.g., [5]). The specialist can refer to an object by pointing to it, and sending the augmented video back to the mechanic. For the second question, we varied the level of expertise of the mechanics: half of the subjects were general technicians, the other half machine operators without technical background. The conditions are shown in table 1.

Table 1: Experimental conditions.

		Mechanic type	
		General technician	System operator
Medium type	Side-by-side		
	Audio-video		

The following hypotheses are put forward:

H1: Performance in the side-by-side condition is better than in the audio-video condition, since only a picture of the object is transferred, and not both object and overview, necessary for maintaining situation awareness.
H2: Generalists perform better then operators, regardless the type of mediation, since operators lack knowledge and skills.
H3: More communication takes place in the operator condition, since generalists take more initiative, so more instructions are transferred to the operator.
H4: More communication takes place in the audio-video condition then in the side-by-side condition, in particular the transfer of sensor information and motor instructions.

2. Method

2.1 Participants

The mechanic subjects consisted of 30 Royal Netherlands Navy functionaries, all male. Half were technicians, the other 15 were system operators. The subjects were not rewarded for their participation, but were ordered to. Two system instructors, experienced and communicative skilful, served by turns as expert. Ten subjects indicated that they have worked with the expert before, which was not surprising due to the small population of navy functionaries. Because of the hazardous type of work (e.g., part of one case consisted of measuring the functioning of a fuse with 650V current on it), one of the instructors was continuously watching the mechanic, ready to intervene in case an unsafe action was about to occur. For organisational reasons, one of two reserve safety functionaries stood in for 50% of the cases.

2.2 Design

Two variables were manipulated: medium type (side-by-side or audio-visual) and mechanic type (technical generalist or system operator). In the side-by-side condition, the expert was allowed to point at parts, but not to perform motor activities (such as pushing buttons, driving screws, etc.). A repeated measures design was used with medium type as within subject factor, and mechanic type as between-subject factor. To prevent order effects, the conditions and the cases to solve were randomised

2.3 Task / Material

The machine used for trouble-shooting was a large system for material distribution, taking up about 200 m^3 hardware and maintenance space, divided over two floors. It consists of many mechanic, electric, electronic, optic and software components. The system is located at the Royal Netherlands Navy Technical School (TOKM), where it is used for instruction. Each subject had to solve the same two cases. Before starting an experimental session, a defect was introduced. Either a fuse was replaced by a broken one, or a cable connector was plugged out. The fuse case was a typical electric problem, the cable connector case a typical mechanic problem (due to the amount of de-assembling needed).

2.4 Instruments

In the audio-visual condition, the mechanic used a hand-held camera, with a belt around his neck such that the camera could hang free when he needed both hands. The camera had an external display, necessary to know what the specialist could see. The camera was connected to a laptop, placed on a table nearby, which in its turn was wireless connected to the laptop of the specialist. The video was transferred using Windows Netmeeting 3.01. Apart from video transfer, the only function of the laptop of the mechanic was to show where the expert pointed. The head set provided duplex audio. The expert wore the same type of head set. His laptop provided the video, and with his mouse, he could refer to objects. The whole laptop desktop was transferred to the laptop of the mechanic (a feature within Netmeeting), so that both collaborators share the same picture. The picture was presented full screen (15 inch), with a resolution of 640 by 480 pixels. Fig. 5 and 6 show a mechanic and an expert collaborating at a distance.

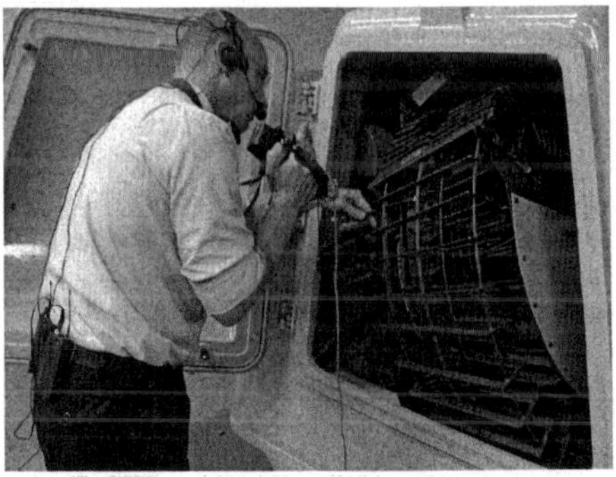

Figure 5: Mechanic at work, providing a picture to the expert with a hand-held camera.

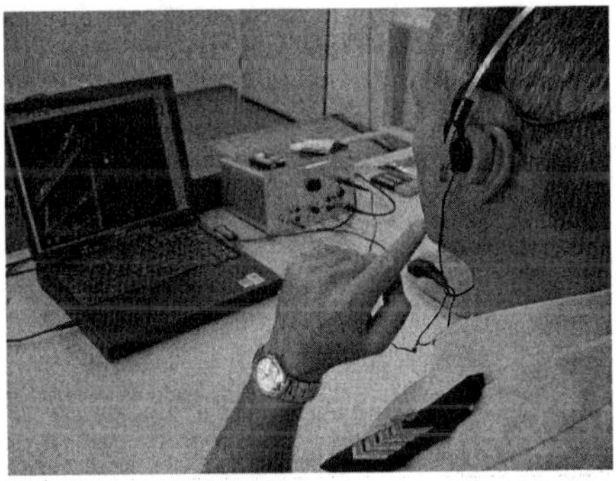

Figure 6: Expert guiding the mechanic at a distance, communicating with video and duplex audio.

2.5 Procedure

At arrival, the subjects were provided a paper introduction about the experiment. Next, they had to fill in a questionnaire about personal identifiers, technical interest, and familiarity with the goalkeeper. At the same time, the expert had to fill in a questionnaire about how well he new the subject. After that, the subjects were provided a simple training case (about fixing a problem in an amplifier), to get used to the way of collaboration, and the presence of the safety functionary. In the audio-video case they also got a short training in operating the hand-held camera. After this preparation phase, they had to solve the first problem. This process consisted of the phases orientation, hypothesis generation, hypothesis testing (inspection and de-assembling), fixing (repair and assembling), and checking. Problem solving took about 60 minutes. After problem solving, an evaluation questionnaire was provided, both to the subject as the expert. After a 60 minutes break a second case had to be solved. Again, the subjects first received a short training case, before starting the second experimental problem solving session, lasting about 60 minutes as well. Identical evaluation questionnaires were provided after the case. Finally, the subject was provided a questionnaire about how satisfied he was with the audio-visual medium. The expert had to fill in this same questionnaire at the end of all sessions. At that time they also got an exit interview.

2.6 Dependent variables

We collected dependent measures for performance and communication.

2.6.1 Performance

Duration: The duration of each session was measured in seconds.
Workload: The subjects and the experts had to indicate for both cases hum much effort they had spent. A validated 150 point scale was used for this [6].
Assistance: The observer made a note of each time the mechanic needed help from the safety functionary. The expert decided whether and when help was allowed. After each session the observer counted the number of times help was provided.
Safety assessment: During each session a safety functionary rated the behaviour of both the expert and the mechanic where safety was concerned. Rating consisted of assigning a mark between 1 and 10, with 1 meaning very bad and 10 meaning excellent.
Safety intervention: Whenever the mechanic was in immediate danger without the expert noticing it, the safety functionary took instant action. Whenever the expert noticed the mechanic being at risk, the expert himself intervened. The safety functionary wrote down these interventions on a special form. Moreover the mechanic was expected to behave in a certain way so that he would not be at risk. Examples of good behaviour are wait till you get the command to execute a task and be careful with tools. Any time the mechanic deviated from the rules without being in immediate danger the safety functionary rated the event as undesired behaviour.

2.6.2 Communication

A single experimenter coded the type of communication in real time during the experiments, using a specially designed coding interface. In total 26 complementary communication categories were used, covering 100% of the utterances. Based on our framework, described in section 1.1 and 1.2, we used the coding system presented in table 2. The interlocutor was coded too.

Table 2: Conversation categories. Remaining utterances were categorised under "others". The interlocutor was coded as well.

	Information	Knowledge	Instruction
Sensor	Perceived information about the current manifestation of objects. *"Yes, the LED is on." "The screw is missing."*	Information about the general manifestation of objects. *"Are these screws loss free?" "That's the sound of a vent"*	Instruction for obtaining sensor information. *"Turn the camera to the left" "Shall I show it to you?"*
Cognitive	Information on planning and monitoring the current work. *"First I will tell you what to do" "We found it, now we'll fix it"*	General information about plans procedures, and measures. *"Never forget the safety switch" "Always check after fixing"*	Instruction for reasoning or remembering. *"Think, what could it be?" "What would be the next step?"*
Motor	Information about current activities. *"Do you manage?" "I'm now removing the fuse"*	General information about how to perform motor activities. *"Loosening requires strength" "Fasten screws clockwise"*	Instruction to effect an objects. *"Press the stand by button" "Close the front panel"*
Social	Encouraging, thanking, complimenting, joking, etc. *"Good luck!" "Get angry, it helps!" "Well done!"*		
Internal state	Emotional expressions. *"Wow, thrilling" "Gush, it's hard work" "Pooh, dirty hands"*		
Roles	Roles and responsibilities. *"You are my eyes and hands" "Don't do it till I tell you to" "I appreciate your initiative, but discuss it with me first."*		

The literature provides many conversation coding categories. [7] for instance, use the categories "Procedural", "Task status", "Referential", "Internal state", "Acknowledgements", and "Other". "Procedural" is similar to our "Cognitive knowledge" category; "Task status" similar to "Motor Information"; "Referential" covers both "Sensor Information" and "Cognitive information"; Short "Acknowledgement" such as "OK" were not coded; longer ones, such as "OK, I will now press the button" are scored as a reaction on an utterance of the specialist (so in this case, "motor instruction, by the mechanic"); "Internal state" is identical to our "Internal State". And the category "Other" we have split up in "Social" and "Roles and responsibilities", and "Others"

Table 3 summarises the dependent variables.

Table 3: Dependent variables

Category	Variable name	Values
Performance	Duration	seconds
	Workload	a 150 point scale
	Assistance	Frequency of help
	Safety assessment	a 10 point scale
	Safety intervention	Frequency of interventions
Communication	Conversation	Frequency in 12 categories

3. Results

We discuss the main results. Details can be found in [8]. First, we examine the effects of medium and mechanic type on performance; then we compare the communication between the four conditions.

3.1 Performance

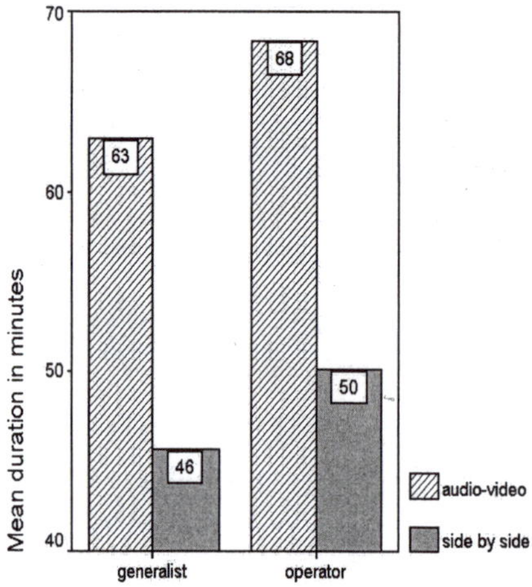

Figure 7: Duration.

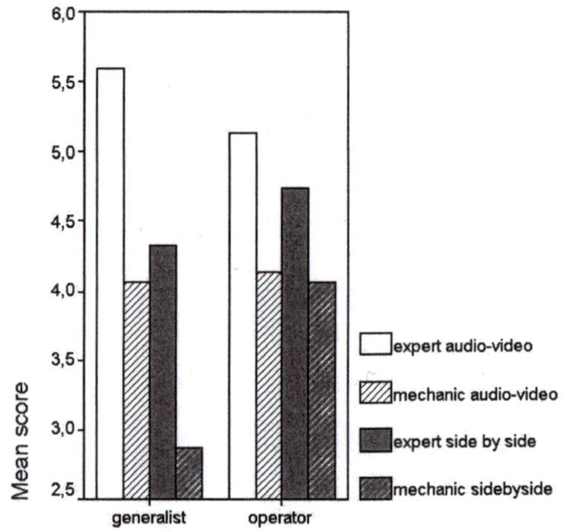

Figure 8: Workload.

Fig. 7 is a bar chart representing the joint influence of the factors mechanic type and medium on the duration. It shows that on average, the cases took slightly less then an hour to solve (57 minutes). Not shown is that the fuse case took 46 and the loose cable connection took 67 minutes to solve. The figure shows further that in the audio-visual condition, trouble-shooting took considerably longer (on average 36%) than in the side-by-side condition. Operators solved the cases slightly slower (8%) then generalist.

The effect of mechanic type and medium on workload, both for the expert and the mechanic, is shown in fig. 8. The experts experienced the most workload. In the audio-video condition they assessed workload as "quite exacting", and working side-by-side they experienced less workload. Both the experts and the generalists experienced more workload when working remotely then when working side-by-side, while the experts together with the operators assessed no workload difference between conditions.

Table 4 shows the performance in terms of safety assessments, interventions, undesirable behaviour, and required assistance. The figures show that, according to the assessments, the work was generally done safe, and that it was safer to work in the side-by-side condition then in the audio-video condition. However, the figures show also that a number of interventions were necessary to prevent hazardous situations, while each intervention is one too many. The expert had to intervene 7 times (12% of the cases), about equally often with the generalist (3 times) as with the operator (4 times). In the side-by-side condition, the expert did intervene 6 times, in the audio-video conditions only once. The safety functionary had to intervene 12 times (20 % of the cases), also about equally often with the generalist (7 times) as with the operator (5 times). In the side-by-side condition, the safety functionary had to intervene 4 times, while in the audio-video condition 8 times. This is the other way around for the expert, who intervened 6 times in the side-by-side condition, and only 1 time in with audio-video.

Table 4: Performance in terms of safety assessments, interventions, undesirable behaviour, and required help.

	Generalist		**Operator**	
	Side-by-side	Audio-video	Side-by-side	Audio-video
Safety assessment of expert	9.3	9.1	8.6	9.1
Safety assessment of mechanic	9.4	8.5	9.1	8.3
Intervention by expert	3	0	3	1
Intervention by safety functionary	1	6	3	2
Observed undesirable behaviour	2	5	3	11
Assistance by safety functionary	0	4	1	5

Further was undesirable behaviour observed 21 times (36 % of the cases), 7 times it was the generalist and 14 times the operators. In the side-by-side conditions, undesirable behaviour was observed 5 times, in the audio-video condition more often, 14 times, of which 11 times it was the operator. Finally, the safety functionary had to help the mechanic, when it took too long to do a particular task. Often this was while trying to use a tool. Assistance was almost never needed in the side-by-side condition, only in the audio-video condition, both for the generalist (4 times) and the operator (5 times). The only case in the side-by-side condition that the mechanic required help was in handling a difficult torque wrench.

3.2 Communication

Fig. 9 is a bar chart representing how much the expert and the mechanic communicated in the four conditions. On average, the expert spoke 410 times (about 7 utterances per minute), the mechanic 157 times (about 3 utterances per minute). More was said when working remotely then side by side (658 versus 476 utterances). Further, the expert said more to an operator then to a generalist (604 versus 530 utterances).

Fig. 10 represents the amount of communication in the four conditions, expressed in the 12 categories described in table 4. It shows that in all conditions, most communication is on motor instruction (about 30%), followed by sensor information (about 20%), and sensor instruction (about 10%), while there was hardly any communication on cognitive and motor knowledge, or on internal states and roles & responsibilities. It also shows that the increase of communication when working remote is due to the transfer of information and instructions, not knowledge. Further, in both conditions, working with an operator requires more information and instruction transfer then working with a generalist. Interesting to see is that the generalist requires more cognitive information in the audio-video condition then in the side-by-side condition. This difference was not found for the operator.

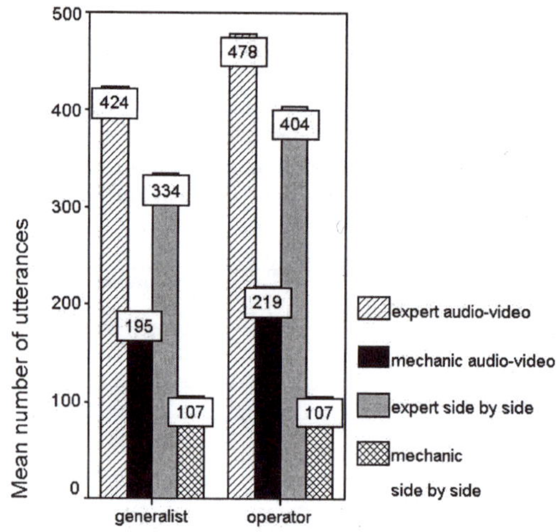

Figure 9: Communication amount by expert and mechanic.

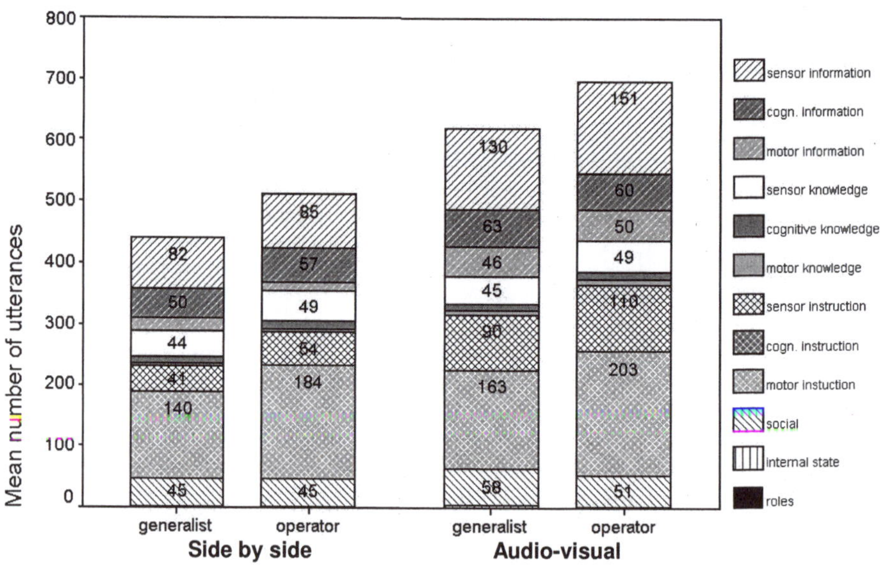

Fig. 10: Communication amount, expressed in the 12 categories (see table 4).

4. Discussion

4.1 Results

One important question is whether a mechanic can solve unfamiliar problems on board, when guided by a remote expert. The results show that in the side-by-side condition, only one mechanic couldn't solve the problem by his own and required help with handling a difficult torque wrench. We therefore may conclude that, in principle, distributed trouble-shooting can work, provided that an optimal medium and proper tools are used.

The results show also that distributed collaboration takes about 36% more time. It also requires more from the expert, who assessed workload as "quite exacting", and who had to communicate about 22% more. These results are not surprising and don't cause a practical problem. At sea, normally it doesn't matter when it takes somewhat more time, provided that it will not endanger an operation. But in times of tension, a specialist will be embarked anyway. The additional time required should be compared with time needed to fly in the expert, as now is often the case.

What is worrying is the number of safety interventions that took place, both for the general technicians and the system operators. Moreover, safety decreases when the expert monitors the mechanic from a distance. The use of safety functionaries remains important. The figures show that in the side-by-side condition, the expert intervened more often then in the audio-video condition, while this is the other way around for the interventions of the safety functionary. This may indicate that the expert didn't intervene before the safety functionary, possibly due to a lack of overview. Better communication means may contribute as well. The communication analyses revealed that much more sensor information, sensor instruction and motor information is transferred in the audio condition then in the side-by-side condition, indicating that both the situation awareness and the task awareness is not optimal, and consequently, the anticipation of unsafe behaviour is hampered. The use of both a detail and an overview video may improve this.

A final issue to discuss is the level of expertise needed. The results show that both the general technicians and the system operators finished the cases, although for the latter, it took more time and communication. That it requires more is neither surprising, but what does surprise is that the system operator can do the job as well, and equally safe. What surprised us is that distributed expert-technician co-operation required considerably more effort then side-by-side co-operation, while this effect was not found in expert-operator co-operation.

Towards the hypotheses we can conclude the following. The first hypothesis – Performance in the side-by-side condition is better than in the audio-video condition, since only a picture of the object is transferred, and not both object and overview, necessary for maintaining situation awareness – is confirmed by the results. The second one – Generalists perform better then operators, regardless the type of mediation, since operators lack knowledge and skills – is partially confirmed, and the effects is less then the effect of medium type. Technicians seem to have more problems with co-operation when they work remotely. The third hypothesis – More communication takes place in the operator condition, since generalists take more initiative, so more instructions are transferred to the operator – is confirmed as well. And also, the fourth and final hypothesis is confirmed – More communication takes place in the audio-video condition then in the side-by-side condition, in particular the transfer of sensor information and motor instructions.

4.2 Future work

This paper presented the main results of our experiment. A detailed analysis of the results is underway, but we are already planning a next experiment. Although the results of this experiment are promising, a key aspect of this study, safety, requires attention. For becoming a success, conditions for safe work needs to be addressed. We are planning to investigate whether richer audio-visual communication can improve safe work. In particular, the use of an overview picture may improve the anticipation of unsafe behaviour. We will also investigate whether dedicated safety training might improve safe work.

Due to experimental-technical reasons, we used in this experiment the same two experts repeatedly. Because of that, solving the case didn't require mental effort: the experts became familiar with the two cases. Moreover, the expert happened to be experienced instructors and very skilful communicators. We need to replicate this experiment with expert-subjects who are not familiar with the problem, especially because cognitive workload can have an impact on safety monitoring. Currently we perform an experiment with forensic experts in the lab collaborate with technical detectives at the crime scene. Cognitive workload is addressed here.

References

[1] Westermeijer, E., Post, W.M., Keijer, W. and Gillis, M.P.W. (2003). *Teleknowledge, knowledge at a distance.* Proceedings of the Thirteenth Internation Ship Control Systems Symposium (SCSS), Orlando, Florida.

[2] Clark, H. and Wilkes Gibbs, D. (1986). Referring as collaborative process. *Cognition*, 22, pp1-39.

[3] Cremers, A.H.M. (1995). *Reference to objects: an empirically based study of task-oriented dialogeus.* PhD. Thesis, Technical University of Eindhoven, The Netherlands.

[4] Endsly, M.R. (1995). Toward a theory of situation awareness in dynamic systems. *Human Factors: Special issue on situation awareness*, 1, 32-64.

[5] Whittaker, S. *Rethinking video as a technology for interpersonal communications: theory and design implications.* Int. J. Human-Computer Studies, 42, 501-529.

[6] Zijlstra, F. & meijman, T (1989). Het meten van mentale inspanning met behulp van een subjectieve methode [measuring the mental effort with a subjective method]. In Meijman, T., editor, *Mentale belasting en werkstress*, Van Gorcum. In Dutch.

[7] Kraut, R.E., Fussell, S.R. and Siegel, J. (2003). Visual information as a conversational resource in collaborative physical tasks. *Human-Computer Interaction: special issue on talking about things in mediated conversations,* 18, pp. 13-49.

[8] Post, W.M., Boogaard, S.A.A., van den, and Rasker, P.C. *Remote ship maintenance.* In preparation.

Acknowledgements

This work was funded by the Royal Netherlands Navy, and carried out in close collaboration with RNLN Technical and Operational school. We gratefully acknowledge the experts, safety functionaries, participants, and others for their co-operation during the project, especially Ad van Nimwegen, Robin de Wit, Marcel Rossen, Remy Kruijsse, Jan van den Bogert and John van den Nieuwenhuijzen.

Cooperative Systems Design
M. Zacklad et al. (Eds.)
IOS Press, 2004

A decision support for cooperation in make-to-order production

Emmanuelle Monsarrat Cyril Briand Patrick Esquirol
LAAS-CNRS, 7 avenue du colonel Roche, F-31077 Toulouse cedex 4
{monsarrat, briand, esquirol}@laas.fr

Abstract This paper proposes a method which assists the firms for cooperating in make-to-order production. The method organizes a production process which is distributed over several companies, by lowering the production stocks with the aim of decreasing production costs. In the selected approach, the global organization is achieved progressively by a set of cooperations between pairs of actors of the supply chain. We study in particular the customer-supplier relationship for which the cooperation process concerns the attributes of the orders transmitted by the customer to the supplier. We assume that the relation is governed by a cooperation contract which defines a more contractual framework to the cooperation between the decision-makers. Our objective is to design support tools that assist them during this cooperation process.

1 Introduction

Nowadays, the diversification of their production or the specialization of their trade induce the companies to collaborate with numerous partners, in the context of networks so-called *supply chains*. New communication and information technologies increase the quality and the frequency of the data exchanges and allow to ensure the coherence of information which are shared between the actors. Nevertheless, they do not solve the coherence problem between the local decisions of each partners and the global organization of the supply chain. Thus, each actor is free to change at any moment a decision, possibly inducing a global organizational instability.

To counteract this problem, the decision-maker behaviours have to be made more cooperative in the sense that any local decision which affects the organization of other external companies, has to correspond to a collaborative decision process. In the following, the set of partners involved in a collaborative decision is called a *business coalition*.

In the area of production systems, cooperation processes may have a lot of advantages which are shared by all the members of the business coalition [12]. First, they allow a better tension of the production flows, a better adaptation of the working capacities, and a better stability of the organization of the business coalition. So, they induce a global reduction of the production costs. On the other hand, the cooperation processes allow a collective management of the risk since an actor can be helped by the community to try to absorb the disturbances that affect his local organization.

First, this paper recalls the context and the problematics related to the cooperation between companies in a make-to-order production context. Then a computer-based support is described in order to facilitate the cooperation between suppliers and customers. For this kind of cooperation, a constraint-based decision-aid is proposed.

2 Context and working assumptions

2.1 Cooperation and make-to-order production

The cooperation can be defined as a collective action organized among a set of actors sharing a joint interest. With regards to a problem of organization and coordination of shared activities, several cooperative situations arise such as the definition of the collective objectives, the design of the activities, their allocation and their coordinated implementation [14]. These situations imply three complementary kinds of cooperative action [15, 7]: the *coordination* which synchronizes the individual activities required to reach a collective objective, the *collaboration* which leads several actors to work together to the design of a global activity and the *co-decision* which concerns the design of a joint decision.

Many researchers were interested in the instrumentation of the cooperation with the aim of designing adequate computer based technology to support cooperative activities [15]. The cooperation being a dynamic process, the choice of an adequate support strongly depends on the temporal, spatial and organizational frameworks which characterize each cooperative situation [5]. Moreover, as pointed out in [3], the adequacy of a support has to be evaluated with regards to the way users really use it.

The approach presented in this paper takes place in the field of make-to-order production. A make-to-order production corresponds to a small-scale production for which product routings are already known. Such a production is mainly characterized by an unpredictable demand which implies that a product manufacturing is not launched until an order has been placed by a customer. Consequently, the main production objective is to minimize the time interval between an order occurence and its completion.

In order to decrease its complexity, the production management is typically decomposed into three hierarchical functions [1]. The *planification* function builds up a medium term production plan which defines the work load of each resource on a set of elementary periods. On the base of the production plan, the *scheduling* function builds up a detailed production plan which defines in short term for each resource the starting and the finishing time of each production activity. The *real time scheduling* function implements in real time the detailed production plan, taking into account the unavoidable disturbances (resource failures, unforeseen delays, ..) related to this kind of production.

The production activities being already defined, the cooperation only concerns the organization and the synchronization of the activities among the business coalition members. Therefore two cooperative processes can be pointed out [18]. The former, described as vertical, concerns the integration of the three above-mentioned hierarchical functions. The latter corresponds to the horizontal cooperation which is involved among the actors which take part in the implementation of a particular production function.

Many research works have dealt with the instrumentation of these cooperation processes. We distinguish first a class of *centralized* approaches which assume that an entity, having a global knowledge of the characteristics of the production flows, would globally supervise the activities of the business coalition members. Related to this class of approach, a horizontal cooperation process is proposed in [6] regarding the planification function: macroscopic models are defined in order to ensure the global consistency of the load balancing among a set of companies. A vertical cooperation process is also illustrated in [10] regarding the integration of the planification and scheduling functions.

The main drawback of the centralized approach arises from the obligation for any actor to communicate the detailed characteristics of his production to the *supervisor* entity. This assumption seems unacceptable in a real application context where actors cooperate for particular activity while they are in competition for others.

To counteract this drawback, another class of research works take an interest in distributed approaches. First we distinguish the multiagent cooperative approaches for which, given a set of autonomous specialized agents, cooperative protocols are designed between agents in order to allow a self-organisation of the production processes [17, 18]. Because humans often take an active part in collaborative decisions, other approaches (such as those of [13] and [16]) prefer to propose human-centered tools and cooperation methodology in order to favour the cooperative behaviour of the actors and to aid the decision-making processes. Our approach is rather close to these works. We are also interested in using constraint-based approaches in order to provide decision-aid as it is suggested in [11, 9, 7]. In these works, the organization model corresponds to a network of *decision centers* where each decision center is characterized by a set of decision variables and a set of constraints related to theses variables. The sets of decision variables and constraints are dynamically upgraded as collective decisions are made or modified between decision centers. Therefore the cooperation can be decomposed into three functions : to *negotiate*, to *re-negotiate* and to *coordinate*. These functions involve constraint propagation mechanisms in order to maintain the consistency of the decisions all along the cooperation process.

2.2 *Working assumptions*

This paper is interested in cooperation situations which arise when several companies of a given supply chain take part in a make-to-order production process. The cooperation is here assimilated with a distributed decision process. Considering a pair of companies, two kinds of cooperation relation can be pointed out. The former corresponds to a supplier-customer relationship where the cooperation aims at organizing the production flows in order to both minimize the output stock of the supplier and the input stock of the customer. The latter corresponds to a subcontracting relationship where the cooperation aims at organizing the output production flows of the principal as well as his re-entrant production flows. This paper only takes an interest in supplier-customer relationships. We assume that the objects of the cooperation are the quantities, the deadlines and the costs related to each order. Our objective is to design computer based cooperation tools in order to support the cooperation actions and to favour the cooperative behaviours of the business coalition members.

Each of the three production management functions can be concerned with a cooperation situtation. Therefore, as the temporal and organizational frameworks related to these functions are specific, we also assume that a specific cooperation tool has to be associated with each of these functions (see figure 1). We mainly focus on the cooperation support related to the scheduling function.

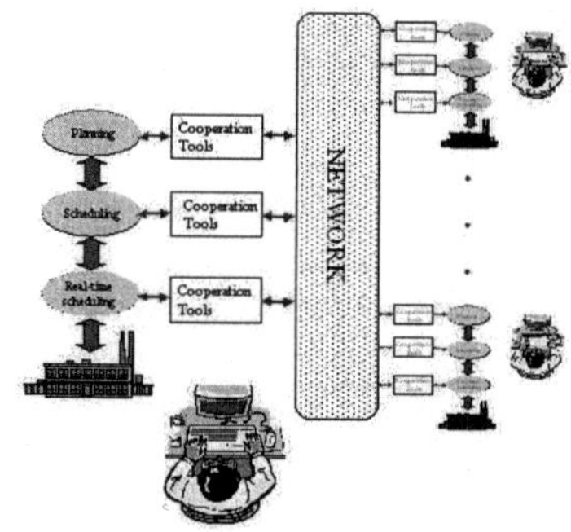

Figure 1: A cooperative architecture

As in [7], the cooperation tool is assumed to be asynchronous. Indeed, an asynchronous cooperation seems more adapted to a make-to-order production context since it does not require a simultaneous avaibility of the decision-makers. Lastly, as proposed in [9] and detailed in the next section, we organize the cooperation regarding the three decision functions : negotiation, co-ordination, renegotiation.

3 A cooperation approach for customer-supplier relationships

3.1 The notion of decision framework

Typically, the due dates of the supply that a firm communicates to its suppliers are earlier than the dates which are really necessary for its production. Indeed, a firm often prefers to maintain an input stock than to risk to delay its production. Similarly, a supplier often reserves safety margins in order to be able to react to unforeseen disturbances without delaying too many production orders. Therefore, while the production flows are locally well tightened, they are globally loose from the point of view of a supply chain (see figure 2).

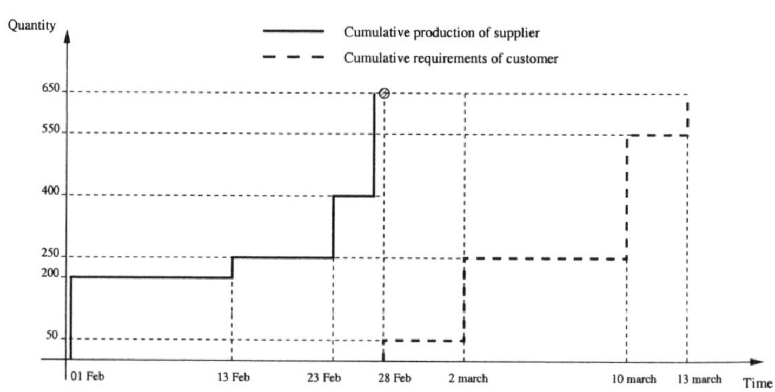

Figure 2: Production and requirements curves for a same manufacturing order

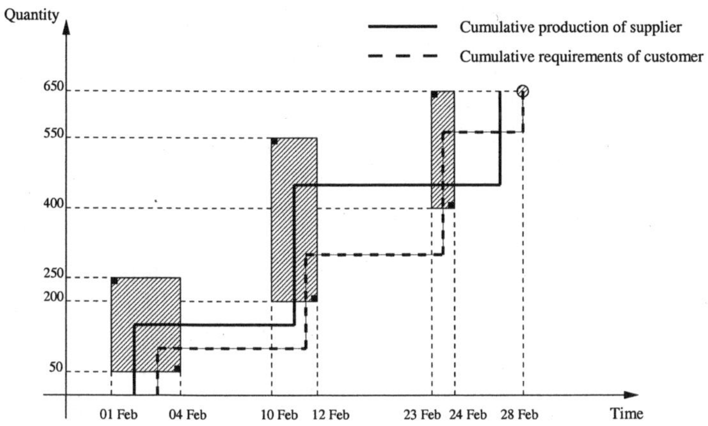

Figure 3: A decision framework

In make-to-order production, the cooperation process must lead customers and suppliers to consult each other in order to stretch the production flows that cross them. This approach could be compared to [4] and [19] in which the notion of *contract order* is used for this purpose.

In this aim, we suppose that an order between two partners is realized by a negotiation process in order to define a *decision framework*. We assume that the decision framework represents a supplier engagement to put a variable quantity of products at his customer's disposal in one or more temporal windows. Let us emphasise that the decision framework also commits the customer to remove products which are placed at his disposal. So a decision framework can be compared with a set of constraints related to the output stock levels of the supplier in some temporal intervals, or conversely, with a set of constraints related to the input stock levels of the customer. Several decision frameworks could compose an order. The figure 3 gives an example of a manufacturing order for which 650 products must be gradually supplied for February 28th. We suppose that four decision frameworks compose this order. For instance, the supplier must have produced between 200 and 550 products of the order between February 10th and February 12th. A direct representation of the decision framework by rectangle is interesting because a decision-maker can directly see his production safety margin. Moreover if the representation includes both the cumulative production of the supplier and the cumulative requirements of the customer, the decision-makers can also easily detect the decision framework incoherences which will be reduced if the partners respect these decision frameworks. For instance, in the figure 3, the decision frameworks are well respected but the third one show an incoherence.

We can notice that both the rectangle surface and the rectangle position have influence on the available flexibility of the supplier. Indeed the more important the rectangle surface is (or, if surfaces are equal, the farer from the time origin the rectangle position is), the more the supplier will easily find a production which satisfies the decision framework. Therefore, the aim of the negotiation is to size a decision framework in order to reach a trade-off which satisfies both supplier and customer objectives. Thus a decision framework must satisfy two points of view.

For example, the interface of figure 4 allows a supplier to visualize simultaneously his production (curve) and his customer supplying requirements (rectangles). Similarly, the interface of figure 5 allows a customer to observe his supplying requirements (curve) and the availability dates of products that the supplier has planned.

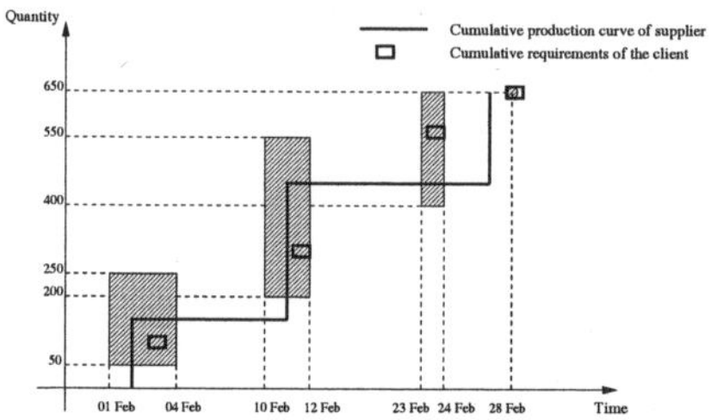

Figure 4: A coordination interface from the supplier point of view

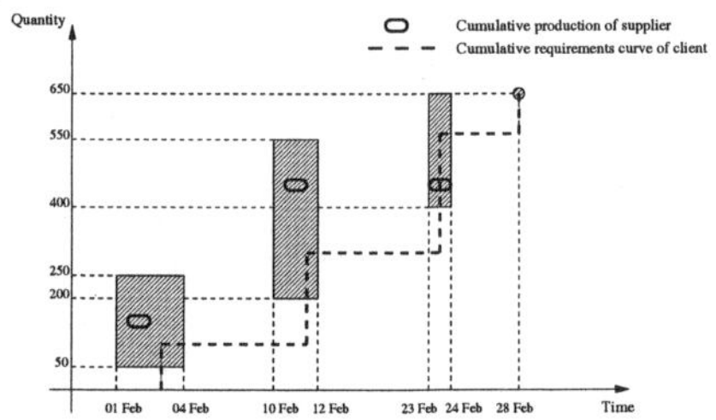

Figure 5: A coordination interface from the customer point of view

We have to notice that the decision frameworks evoluate, using renegotiation processes, while customer requirements and supplier production planning become more and more precise. We detail renegociation processes in the following section.

3.2 Description of cooperation processes

A negotiation process is initiated as one of the partners makes a new order proposal. An order proposal specifies an initial decision framework which is refined all along the negotiation process. A proposal can be issued from a customer who would like to place an order, or from a supplier who would like to propose, for instance, a commercial offer to one of his customers. Figure 6 illustrates a case where a supplier receives an order proposal from the customer *Despontin* which concerns a product *A*. This customer requires between 6 and 11 units of product *A* to be available from July 15th at 6 p.m. at the earliest, to July 16th at 6 p.m. at the latest. The partner who receives such an order proposal, can refuse or accept it, he can also generate a counterproposal. Generally, a conversation corresponds to a sequence of proposals and counterproposals, which ends either by an acceptance or by a refusal.

We distinguish two distinct types of proposals. Indeed, once accepted, a proposal can lead either to a definitive engagement of the supplier, or no engagement at all if the response only concerns the order feasibility. The first case is referred to as a *proposal for engagement*, for which the negotiation process ends either on an engagement (acceptance) or on a refusal. The second case is refered to as a *proposal for evaluation* for which the negotiation process ends either on a feasibility result (acceptance) or on an unfeasibility result (refusal). When a conversation concludes with the feasibility of a proposal, no partner is committed, since a proposal for engagement is anyway needed in order to realize a firm engagement between the two partners. Moreover a proposal for engagement will not necessarily lead to the same decision framework that the one which was determined during the feasibility analysis.

The coordination process is realized through an information message sharing. This information can concern deadlines, quantities or prices. The screen presented in figure 7 shows what could be the coordination interface of a supplier: the left-hand side is a message browser that enables to visualize the various messages already sent concerning the current set of orders; the right-hand side describes a message browser which groups the messages automati-

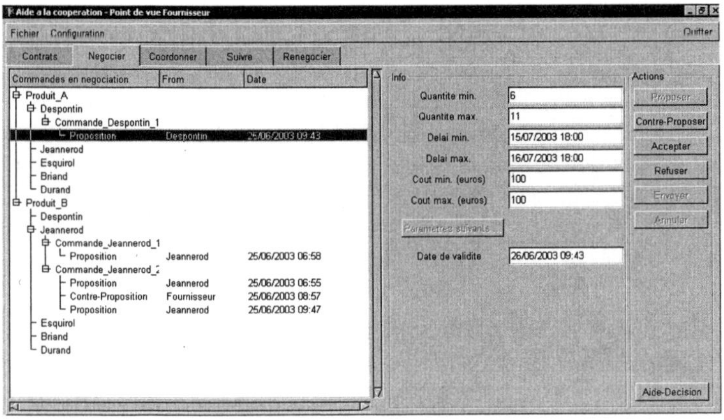

Figure 6: An interface for the negotiation

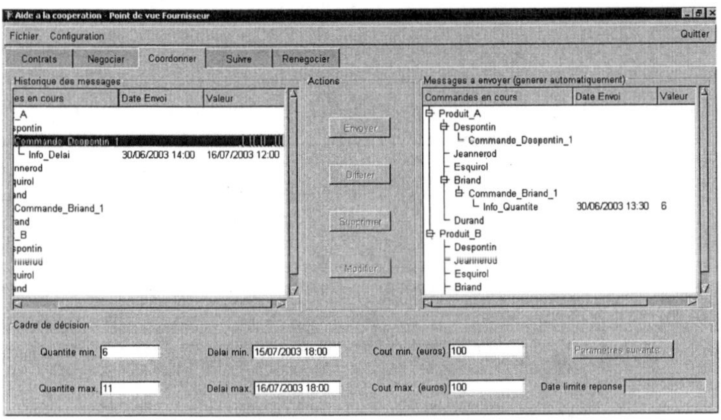

Figure 7: An interface for the coordination

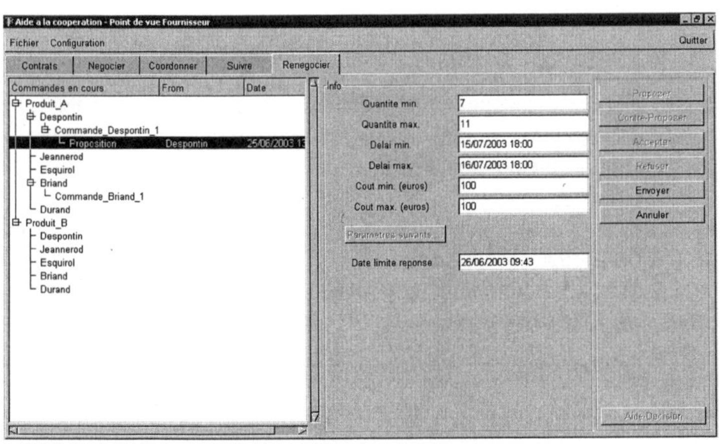

Figure 8: An interface for the renegotiation

cally proposed by the decision support tool. The decision-maker can decide either to send the generated messages, or to differ them, or to delete them, or to modify them before sending.

A renegotiation process is initiated as soon as one of the two partners wants to modify a decision framework. For instance, a supplier can ask for a modification of a decision framework when he knows that his production cannot respect it. A customer can also ask for a modification when supplies are not consistent with his requirements (see 3.1). The screen presented in figure 8 illustrates what could be the renegotiation interface of the supplier. A renegotiation request is ready to be sent from the customer *Despontin* concerning his order *Commande_1*. In order to initiate a renegotiation, the supplier sends a proposal. In this case, the customer would increase the minimal quantity of the order to be equal to 7 products instead of 6 (remember figure 6). Receiving this renegotiation request, the partner can accept, refuse, or send a counterproposal.

3.3 Contract of cooperation

In order to help supplier-customer couples to specify convenient manufacturing order, we suppose that they have agreed a cooperation contract. The clauses of this contract specify constraints that the coordination, negotiation and renegotiation processes have to satisfy. These constraints correspond to frameworks, which are different according to the considered temporal framework (see figure 9). Indeed, negotiation, coordination or renegotiation processes do not have the same constraints if they are considered at the short-term level or at the real-time level.

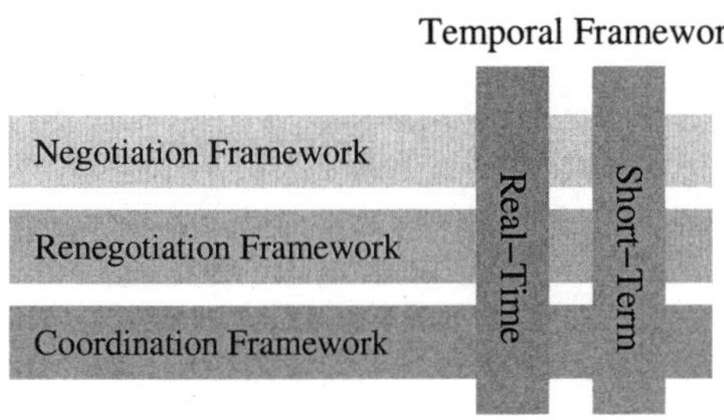

Figure 9: Frameworks of cooperation contract

We suppose that the definition of the cooperation contract is a strategic task which is realized by each pair of actors. For this reason, the contract lifetime is supposed to be longer than the decision lifetime. However a contract can be modified in order to take production context variations into account.

The negotiation framework formulates a set of constraints that any negotiation process must satisfy. For instance, it specifies minimal and maximal quantities that a process initiator can require according to the temporal framework which he depends on. It can also specifies minimal and maximal delays according to ordered quantities, and minimal and maximal product prices according to ordered quantities and deadlines. For instance, the cooperation contract illustrated in figure 10 concerns a supplier and his customer *Briand*. The negotiation framework of this contract specifies that each order must contain between 5 and 10 products

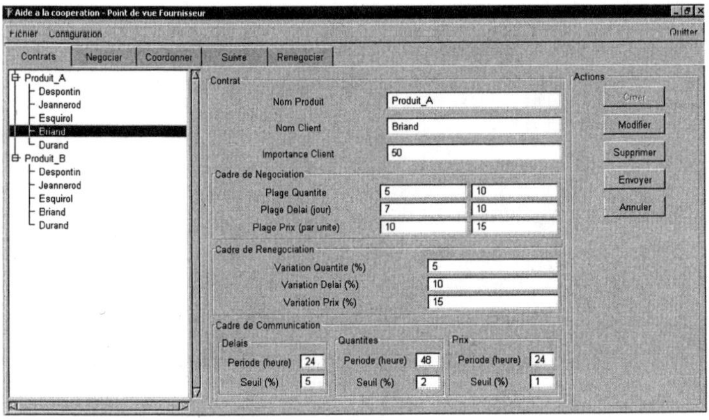

Figure 10: Illustration of cooperation contract

for a delay varying between 7 and 10 days and for a price varying between 10 and 15 euros per unit.

The coordination is also associated with a framework. This framework could specify a communication protocol which defines how partners must communicate. This protocol defines some exchange rules. For example, when an actor sends a message in order to start a communication, a rule can impose that an acknowledgement is returned in order to notify him that his request has been taken into account. The coordination framework can also define when quantities, deadlines and costs information have to be exchanged: either at periodic times (every week, every morning, etc...) or at "key" times (as soon as 90% of the quantity is produced, as soon as completion dates are 10% late, etc...). For the example on the figure 10, the coordination framework specifies that the supplier has to send an information concerning the quantity which he plans to supply to his customer every 48 hours. The supplier must also communicate this quantity as soon as it becomes more than 2% different from the last communicated quantity. The coordination concerns also delays which are communicated every 24 hours or as soon as a delay becomes more than 5% different from the last coordination delay.

When a decision framework cannot be satisfied any longer, a renegotiation process has to be initiated in order to reach a new consistent framework. This process is also constrained by a framework. This framework can concern the quantity variation, the delay variation and the price variation which are allowed between the initial decision framework and the new framework. For example in figure 10, the contract specifies that quantities, deadlines and prices cannot vary more than respectively 5%, 10%, 15% from the initial decision framework.

4 Towards a decision support system

4.1 Principle and modelling

To help the decision-makers in elaborating consistent proposals and counterproposals, the cooperation tools must offer a decision-aid in order to achieve a trade-off which satisfies both

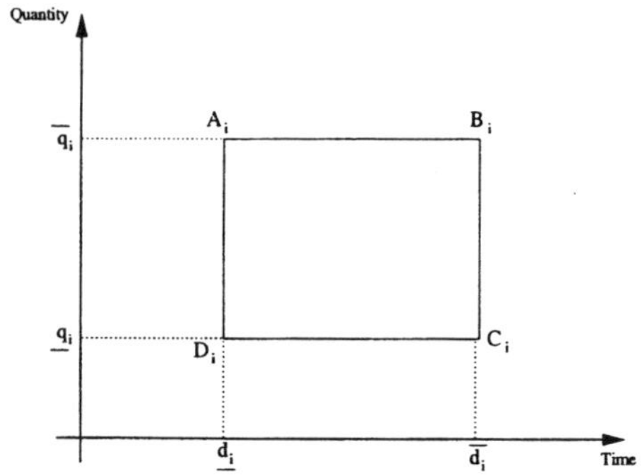

Figure 11: Decision framework of an order c

supplier objectives and customer objectives. As the result of a negotiation or a renegotiation process is a flexible decision framework, the aim of a decision-aid is to characterize its influence on the already existing orders. Indeed, orders are linked together because their implementation use shared resources. So, any decision framework modification may influence the satisfaction of the already existing frameworks. The decision-aid tools must show these impacts using a production model which defines the shared resources as well as the product routings.

By means of an example, we illustrate how a constraint approach could help either to insert or to modify a decision framework. In order to simplify, we suppose that the production model corresponds to a single ressource having a limited production rate τ for each period T.

During the period T, the quantity of completed products for the order c is denoted x_c^T, and the minimal quantity and the maximal quantity of x_c^T are denoted $\underline{x_c^T}$ et $\overline{x_c^T}$. So, we have $x_c^T \in [\underline{x_c^T}; \overline{x_c^T}], \forall T$. $X_c^n = (x_c^1, x_c^2, ..., x_c^n)$ corresponds to the production curve of c for a horizon of n periods. The corresponding problem model is given below.

$$\sum_{k=1}^{m} x_k^T \leq \tau \quad (1) \qquad X_c^n \leq P_c^n \text{ avec } P_c^n = (p_c^1, p_c^2, ..., p_c^n) \quad (2)$$

$$\sum_{k=1}^{\underline{d_i}} x_c^k \leq \overline{q_i} \quad (3) \qquad \sum_{k=1}^{\overline{d_i}} x_c^k \leq \overline{q_i} \quad (4)$$

$$\sum_{k=1}^{\overline{d_i}} x_c^k \geq \underline{q_i} \quad (5) \qquad \sum_{k=1}^{\underline{d_i}} x_c^k \geq \underline{q_i} \quad (6)$$

For m orders, the inequation 1 represents the constraint that limites the production rate of the ressource for each period T. The inequation 2 models the constraint which is involved by the production management curve P_c^n concerning an order c.

On the figure 11, the points A_i, B_i, C_i and D_i define the decision framework of the order c. The point A_i indicates the maximal quantity ($\overline{q_i}$) which could be provided for the minimal due date ($\underline{d_i}$). B_i indicates the maximal quantity which could be provided for the maximal due date ($\overline{d_i}$). C_i indicates the minimal quantity ($\underline{q_i}$) which could be provided for the maximal due date. And D_i indicates the minimal quantity which could be provided for the minimal due date. The inequations 3, 4, 5 and 6 respectively model these constraints.

4.2 Insertion of a new decision framework

First of all, in order to insert a new framework which respects the existing decision frameworks, we determinate the point A position. This point represents the supplier production when the constraints for the existing frameworks are the less restricting. The less restricting production for a framework *i* corresponds to the point C_i. So, the point A_i of the new decision framework is found when the production curves of the other orders intercept the point C of their decision framework. The point B and the point D of the new order are determined when the production management curves of the other orders are respected. Finally, the position of the point C is deduced from the positions B and D previously found.

In order to illustrate the insertion of a new decision framework, we propose an example. We suppose that the considered supplier has only one order to complete which is characterized by the decision framework *1* so that :

$$\sum_{k=1}^{10} x_1^k \leq 50 \qquad (7) \qquad\qquad \sum_{k=1}^{18} x_1^k \geq 20 \qquad (8)$$

We assume that the production rate of the shared ressource is equal to 5 units of product by period T. Additionnaly, we suppose that the production management curve of this order is:

$$P_1^{18} = (3,3,2,2,2,2,2,2,2,2,2,2,2,2,0,0,0,0)$$

The inequation 2 imposes the constraint : $X_1^{18} \leq P_1^{18}$. So, the management production anticipate to supply 30 product at the most for the period 14.

We consider a scenario in which a customer asks how many products the supplier could complete for the end of the period 14. A second decision framework must be created such as $\underline{d_2} = 14$. Therefore, the quantity $\overline{q_2} = \sum_{k=1}^{14} \overline{x_2^k}$ can be determined by propagating the constraints on the model :

$$\sum_{k=1}^{18} x_1^k = 20 \qquad (9) \qquad\qquad x_1^T + x_2^T \leq 5, \forall T \qquad (10)$$

On the figure 12, the production curve, which intercepts the point C_1, illustrates the constraint 9. Any curve on top of it respects the constraint 8. The constraints 9 and 10 allow to deduce the domain of x_2^T for each period T. We obtain $\overline{q_2} = 70$. We can determine now the quantity $\underline{q_2}$ and the due date $\overline{d_2}$ such as $\underline{q_2} = \sum_{k=1}^{14} \overline{x_2^k}$ and $\sum_{k=1}^{\overline{d_2}} \overline{x_2^k} = \overline{q_2}$.

By propagating on the model the constraints

$$X_1^{18} = (3,3,2,2,2,2,2,2,2,2,2,2,2,2,0,0,0,0) \text{ and } x_1^T + x_2^T \leq 5,$$

we obtain $\underline{q_2} = 40$ and $\overline{d_2} = 20$.

4.3 Modification of an existing decision framework

If the decision-maker modifies a decision framework *i* so that it becomes less restricting, then the modification does not impact the other framework. In the other case, by propagating the

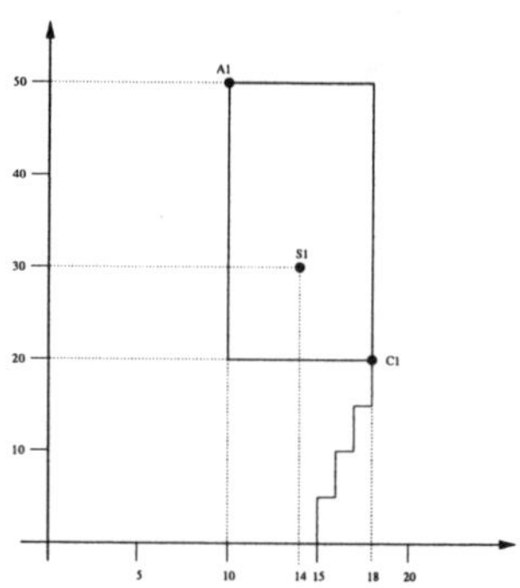

Figure 12: Decision Framework 1

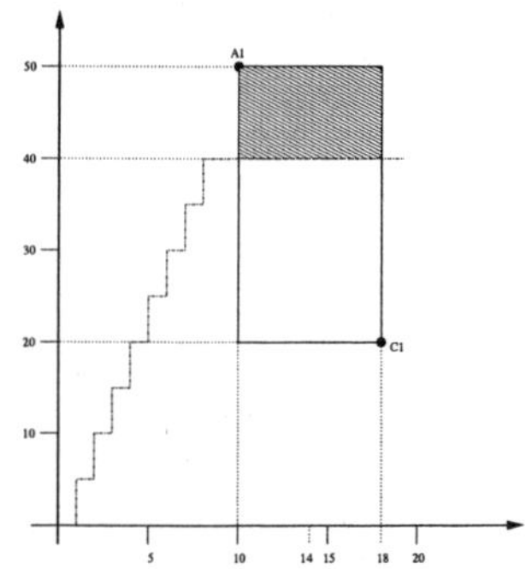

Figure 13: Modification impact of the order 2 on the order 1

new constraints, we can determine the impact of this modification on the other frameworks.

With the example of the section 4.2, we can illustrate this. We suppose a scenario in which the decision-maker would like to decrease the maximal due date of the decision framework *2* such as $\underline{d_2} = 18$. By propagating this new constraint, the decision framework *2* is now modeled by the inequations 11, 12, 13 and 14 :

$$\sum_{k=1}^{14} x_2^k \leq 70 \quad (11) \qquad \sum_{k=1}^{18} x_2^k \leq 70 \quad (12)$$

$$\sum_{k=1}^{18} x_2^k \geq 50 \quad (13) \qquad \sum_{k=1}^{14} x_2^k \geq 50 \quad (14)$$

The constraints 10 and 13 then induce $\sum_{k=1}^{18} x_1^k \leq 40$. The dimmed area of the decision framework *1* is no more accessible. Then the decision-maker may accept or refuse the modification of the decision framework *2*.

5 Conclusion

In this paper, a cooperation support is proposed in order to instrument the supplier-customer relationship in a make-to-order production context. We assume that the cooperation underlies three decision functions (to negotiate, to co-ordinate, to renegotiate). A cooperation contract specifies the collective rules that the decision-makers have to respect while perfoming these functions. The cooperative actions mainly concern the initialization and the modification of a decision framework. A decision framework corresponds to a shared object which defines the parameters (quantities, deadlines, costs) of any order which is placed by a customer with a supplier. The initialization of a decision framework leads the partners to collectively and explicitly defines the flexibility that each of them wants to reserve concerning the implementation of an order. The negotiation support presented in this paper allows to favour the supplier-customer conversations which are required during the initialization of a decision framework. A decision framework being initialized, a co-ordination support is also described which proposes to automatically send synchronization messages between suppliers and customers all along the production process, so that inconsistent situations can be easily detected. When such an inconsistent situation is detected, a re-negotiation support has been proposed in order to adapt the decision framework so that it turns back consistent with the current forecast production state.

Since the decision frameworks are locally interdependent, a decision aid should be available in order to facilitate both the initialization and the modification of a decision framework. Using constraint propagation mechanisms, such a decision aid has been sketched out considering a rather simple production model. In this approach, any decision-framework is characterized by decision variables, related to quantities and deadlines, which are linked together by a set of constraints. The constraints express the limited capacity of the resources, the current characteristics of the forecast production plan and the flexibility associated with each decision framework. Thus the initialization or the modification of a decision framework leads to define new decision variables and/or new contraints which can be propaged on the model in order to measure the impact on the other decision frameworks.

The man-machine interfaces presented in this paper have been used for specifying the interfaces of a cooperation prototype which is currently under development. This protoype will incorporate the cooperation supports and the decision aid which have been proposed in this paper. Moreover, the constraint model of the prototype will be more realistic in order to take the multi-product and multi-resource features of the production into account. Once the prototype completed, an evaluation stage should be started in order to validate that the computer-based cooperation tools are really consistent with the real cooperation requirements of the actors.

References

[1] C. Artigues, C. Briand, J.-C. Portmann, F. Roubellat, Pilotage d'atelier basé sur un ordonnancement flexible, in MÉTHODE DU PILOTAGE DES SYSTÈMES DE PRODUCTION, directed by P. Pujo and J.-P Kieffer, Hermes Sciences, (2002) 61-97.

[2] Z. Bahroun, Contribution à la planification et à la gestion dynamique des systèmes de production cyclique, Thèse de doctorat, University of Franche-Comté, France, Besançon (2000).

[3] K. Baker, S. Greenberg, C. Gutwin, Heuristic evaluation of groupware based on the mechanics of collaboration, Proceedings of the 8th IFIP Working Conference on Engineering for Human-Computer Interaction (EHCI'01), Canada, Toronto, (2001) 11-13.

[4] Y. Bassok, A. Bixby, R. Srinivasan, H.Z. Wiesel, Design of component-supply contract with commitment-revision flexibility, IBM JOURNAL OF RESEARCH AND DEVELOPMENT **41** (1999).

[5] J.-F. Boujut, J.-B. Cavaillé, A. Jeantet, Instrumentation de la coopération, in COOPÉRATION ET CONNAISSANCE DANS LES SYSTÈMES INDUSTRIELS, directed by R. Soënen and J. Perrin, Hermes Sciences, (2002) 91-109.

[6] J.-P. Bourrières, T. Lecompte, J.-C. Deschamps, R. Alami, Un cadre formel de décision pour la planification multiniveau des systèmes de production distribués, APII-JESA **35** (2001) 859-883.

[7] J.-P. Camalot, Aide à la décision et à la coopération en gestion du temps et des ressources, Thèse de doctorat, Institut National des Sciences Appliquées, France, Toulouse (2000).

[8] J.-P. Campagne, O. Sénéchal, Les nouvelles exigences de coopération, in COOPÉRATION ET CONNAISSANCE DANS LES SYSTÈMES INDUSTRIELS, directed by R. Soënen and J. Perrin, Hermes Sciences, (2002) 51-67.

[9] J. Erschler, Approche par contraintes pour l'aide à la décision et à la coopération : une nouvelle logique d'utilisation des modèles formels, in COOPÉRATION ET CONCEPTION, directed by G. De Terssac G. and E. Friedberg, Octares Editions, (1996) 137-147.

[10] A. Guinet, A multi-site production management approach, APII-JESA **34** (2000) 367-377.

[11] M.-J. Huguet, Approche par contraintes pour l'aide à la décision et à la coopération en gestion de production, Thèse de doctorat, Institut National des Sciences Appliquées, France, Toulouse (1994).

[12] H.L. Lee, V. Padmanabhan, S. Whang, Information Distortion in a supply Chain : The Bullwhip Effect, MANAGEMENT SCIENCE **43** (1997) 546-558.

[13] T. Monteiro, Conduite distribuée dúne coopération entre entreprises : le cas d'une relation donneurs d'ordres- fournisseurs, Thèse de doctorat, Institut National Polytechniques, France, Grenoble (2001).

[14] J.-C. Sardas, J. Erschler, G. De Terssac, Coopération et organisation de l'action collective, in COOPÉRATION ET CONNAISSANCE DANS LES SYSTÈMES INDUSTRIELS, directed by R. Soënen and J. Perrin, Hermes Sciences, (2002) 69-89.

[15] F. Sposito, CSCW, Groupware and social issues - Applications, analytical perspectives and possible solutions in an ever-changing and critical study field, HUMAN-COMPUTER INTERACTION LESSON, download in http://citeseer.nj.nec.com.

[16] O.Telle, Gestion des chaînes logistiques dans le domaine aéronautique : Aide à la coopération au sein d'une relation donneur d'ordres/fournisseurs, Thèse de doctorat, École Nationale Supérieure de l'Aéronautique et de l'Espace, France, Toulouse (2003).

[17] E. Tranvouez, B. Espinasse, A. Ferrarini, Résolution coopérative et distribuée de problèmes : application multi-agents au réordonnancement d'atelier, Proceedings of the 3th Congrès International de Génie Industriel, l'intégration des ressources humaines et des technologies : le défi, Montréal (1999).

[18] D. Trentesaux D., N. Moray, C. Tahon, Integration of the human operator into responsive discrete production management systems, EUROPEAN JOURNAL OF OPERATIONNAL RESEARCH **109** (1998) 342-361.

[19] A.A Tsay, W.S. Lovejoy, Quantity Flexibility Contracts and Supply Chain Performance, MANUFACTURING & SERVICE OPERATIONS MANAGEMENT **1** (1999) 89-111.

Cooperative Systems Design
M. Zacklad et al. (Eds.)
IOS Press, 2004

Characterization of Collaborative Design and Interaction Management Activities in a Distant Engineering Design Situation

Françoise DETIENNE
EIFFEL Research Group
INRIA - Domaine de Voluceau, Rocquencourt- B.P 105, 78 153 Le Chesnay Cedex, France
e-mail: Francoise.Detienne@inria.fr

Jean-François BOUJUT
Laboratoire GILCO
ENSGI – INPG, 46 ave Félix Viallet, 38031 Grenoble Cedex France
e-mail: *jean-francois.boujut@gilco.inpg.fr*

Betty HOHMANN
EIFFEL Research Group
INRIA - Domaine de Voluceau, Rocquencourt- B.P 105, 78 153 Le Chesnay Cedex France
e-mail: hohmann_betty@yahoo.com

Abstract. This paper presents an empirical research to study synchronous and asynchronous collaborative design in a technology-mediated situation. In this experiment we wanted to create a design situation where four distant designers had to communicate using commercial software and standard hardware configurations. Our methodological approach gave us the opportunity to examine two main lines of research questions concerning: (1) the specificities of technology-mediated design meetings that contrast to those of face-to-face design meetings; (2) the differences between synchronous and asynchronous collaborative work in mediated design engineering situations. Our approach stresses on some important aspects related to the management of the synchronous activity in a distant mediated situation. The originality of the approach relies on the hybrid characterization of both solution and problem management on one hand, and activity management (e.g. speech turns, meeting agenda) on the other hand.

Keywords: distributed design, engineering design, protocol analysis.

Understanding the fundamental nature of group activity in order to support it implies : «Extending our understanding of the dimensions by which the important aspects of the situation, the task, the technology and the group composition affect collaborative work » and « Constructing methodological tools to analyze and assess collaborative situations» [1].

Today, distributed design situations are becoming natural design situations for a great number of engineers. This is mainly due to the market globalisation that leads the companies to reorganise their design activities in global development teams often scattered over the world. Development cycles reduction also greatly influences the design practices and foster the development of technology-mediated design. Today information technologies enable easy distant communications and effective data transfer. Besides, synchronous communications using video conferencing facilities and application sharing are now both user friendly and robust enough for a wide professional use. However, few studies have addressed this question in the field of engineering design, and the need for specific results pointing out the specific requirements in terms of mediating tools remains important. However the study of such situations is tricky and raises many methodological issues that cannot be addressed in a single paper. Rather, our purpose is to study collaborative work in mediated design engineering situations and provide results characterising the specificities of such activities, including our methodological approach especially our analysis framework.

Collaborative work may be involved in various spatio-temporal situations. The temporal dimension may be synchronous or asynchronous. The space may be the same (co-location) or different (distant location). For each spatio-temporal situation, various tools may be involved as described in the typology of Johansen [2].

Our objective is to examine the collaborative design activities and the interaction management activities involved in a technology-mediated engineering design project. The design project studied here requires alternating between two mediated situations: synchronous distant meetings and asynchronous distant design work. Two lines of questions will be examined: (a) the specificities of technology-mediated design meetings that contrast to those of face-to-face design meetings (as reported in the literature); (b) the differences between synchronous and asynchronous collaborative work in technology-mediated engineering design situations.

1 Theoretical framework

1.1 Collaborative design activities

Previous studies on face-to-face design meetings have analyzed collaborative activities occurring during such meetings: for example, in the development of local area networks [3], of software [4] [5] [6] [7], of aerospace structures [8], of mechanical devices [9] or of a backpack-to-mountain-bike attachment [10]. In face-to-face design meetings, authors have identified various types of collaborative activities.

One type of activity, related to the object of the design task, concerns the evolution of the design problem and solution:

- design activities, i.e. elaboration , enhancements of solutions and of alternative solutions;
- evaluation activities , i.e. evaluation of solutions or alternative solutions, on the basis of criteria. These activities may be supported by argumentation;

Another type of activity, related to the object of the design task, concerns the construction of a common referential by the group of actors: cognitive synchronization (often referred to as "clarification") activities, i.e. construction of a shared representation of the current state of the solution [11].

Furthermore, group management activities, related to process issues, are also involved:

- project management activities, i.e. allocation and planning of tasks;
- meeting management activities, i.e. ordering, postponing of topics in the meeting;

Most of these studies tend to show the predominance of cognitive synchronization activities in such meetings. Stempfle and Badke-Schaub [9] found that some teams bypassed cognitive synchronisation (referred to as "analysis") and that this led them to premature evaluation of design ideas. Indeed, these collaborative activities do not occur only during formal meetings and a lot of work has illustrated the importance of informal communication in design teams [12].

1.2 Interaction management activities

The characteristics of grounding activities in communication media have been analyzed by Clark and Brennan [13]. These authors have identified several constraints, related to the spatio-temporal settings and the tools available to communicate, which affect interaction management activities and common grounding: e.g. co-presence, visibility, and simultaneity.

Collocation is assumed to facilitate these activities. Several key characteristics of collocated synchronous interactions have been identified by Olson and Olson [14]:

- rapid feedback: It allows for rapid corrections when there are misunderstanding or disagreements;
- multiple channels (visual, oral, etc.): it allows for several ways to convey complex message and provides redundancy;
- shared local context: a shared frame on the activities allows for mutual understanding about what is in other's mind;
- co-reference: gaze and gestures can easily identify the referent of deictic terms;
- impromptu interactions: opportunistic exchanges can take place;
- spatiality of reference: both people and ideas (work objects) can be referred to spatially.

A question is how far distance may affect the ease of interaction management activities.

1.3 Intermediary objects and actions on technical

This category relates to the activity of direct physical interaction with the design artefact. In that case the role played by the graphical representations of the design artefact is essential in collaborative design. Boujut and Laureillard [15] or Schmidt and Wagner [16] propose the concepts of cooperative features, coordinative artefacts or intermediary objects to characterize the particular role these representations play in the collaborative processes. These intermediate representations may support co-design, argumentation, explanation, simulation or be an external memory of design rationale. Sharing these representations between distributed groups via shared electronic and physical media may also support awareness in remote collaboration [17]. Schmidt & Wagner [16]) distinguish between different functions of the artefacts involved in a cooperative process: construction of a common ground about a design principle, a task, etc.; reminders of design principles, open problems, etc.; traces of activities; representation of design decisions. Boujut and Laureillard [15] propose to characterize specific artefacts called "cooperative features" which are involved during cooperative sessions as mediations between the designers. During cooperative sessions the designers create their own shared representation (mainly using sketched signs). Boujut and Blanco [18] observed co-located meetings and analyzed the roles of the objects involved in such situations. The issue raised by the involvement of such intermediate representations in a virtual environment remains important. This aspect has been explicitly addressed in Ruiz-Dominguez et al. [19] and the reader can refer to this publication for a detailed analysis. However, we stress here the importance of integrating this dimension within the analysis framework.

2 Research questions

Two main lines of research questions will be examined in this paper. The first line of questions relates to the specificities of technology-mediated design meetings that contrast to those of face-to-face design meetings. This question can be decomposed into two sub-questions distinguishing collaborative design activities from interaction management activities.

The first sub-question concerns the nature of the collaborative design activities involved in technology-mediated design meetings compared with face to face design meetings (as reported in the literature). Previous studies on face-to-face design meetings tend to show the predominance of cognitive synchronization activities in such meetings. We will examine whether or not the same trend can be found in technology-mediated design meetings.

The second sub-question concerns whether or not all the key characteristics of face-to-face design meetings are important to reproduce in technology-mediated design meetings. Several key characteristics of collocated synchronous interactions have been identified by Olson and Olson [14]. We will examine whether these characteristics are important in technology-mediated design meetings and, to what extent, specific interaction management activities appear in the new situation.

The second line of questions concerns the differences between synchronous and asynchronous collaborative work in technology-mediated engineering design situations. We will examine whether or not the same collaborative design activities occur in these two work modes. We will also analyze whether or not the same uses of the technical devices (specifically shared graphical representations) occur in these two temporal modes: we will distinguish between several ways intermediary objects support collaborative work: supporting on-line co-production, guiding explanation, supporting argumentation, supporting tracing, and supporting simulation.

In order to address these questions, we have extended a methodological framework based on previous research in cognitive ergonomics and social psychology [20] [21].

3 Experimental setting

The experiment was carried out in four different French universities, namely Belfort, Grenoble, Nancy and Nantes. The four universities are involved in a research program which aims at setting up distributed design experiments in the field of engineering design. The experimental protocol we present here has been jointly developed by the four universities mentioned.

In this experiment we wanted to create a design situation where four distant designers had to communicate using commercial software and standard hardware configurations.

3.1 The design task

The designers had to develop a new model of a children's trailer (see Figure 1).

Figure 1: example of a children's trailer

The input to the design process was a report of a preliminary study. The designers were asked to develop a solution that could be industrialized, defining the manufacturing requirements, describing the technical solutions and providing suitable CAD models.

The study was carried out during the early detailed design phases. This allowed us to identify the difficulties of communication between different domains. Manufacturing constraints are traditionally difficult to introduce during design, and we wanted to focus on this aspect. Negotiations were necessary in order for the participants to agree on the solution. The other point we wanted to raise was the process of building CAD models, sharing the results or collectively modifying the models during synchronous communications. We wanted to observe the evolutions of the CAD models as a medium for design communication, and the way CAD software was involved in the process: the design task therefore centred on embodiment and early detailed design.

The designers were given a design brief including:

- general requirements on the product;
- a rough project description (organization, communication protocols, specialties involved, etc.);
- preliminary schedule setting the different design meetings;
- list of the preliminary documents;
- list of the deliverables.

The preliminary design report included a functional analysis of the product detailing the functional requirements, a proposition of a technical solution and some preliminary plans detailing the solution.

As a preliminary task, the designers had to produce the various CAD models of the preliminary solution. The deliverables were specific to each domain.

3.2 The designers and their roles

The designers were four master students in engineering design. Therefore they were quite familiar with CAD systems and specific design support tools (except the project manager). A preliminary interview showed that the designers were familiar with all the software but the collaborative environment (Netmeeting®). Besides, they were rewarded and were working under a precise contract defining the conditions of their involvement. We deliberately choose this option in order to create a situation as close as possible to a professional working condition. Figure 2 displays pictures of two designers in their design environments.

Four roles were prescribed:

- a project manager;
- an industrial designer;
- an engineering designer, 1;
- an engineering designer, 2.

The project manager was in charge of the overall consistency of the solution. He also had the responsibility of the digital mock up and the agenda. The industrial designer was in charge of the usability constraints, and the ergonomic aspects of the product. The engineering designers were in charge of the technical and industrial aspects; they were responsible for two different areas of the product.

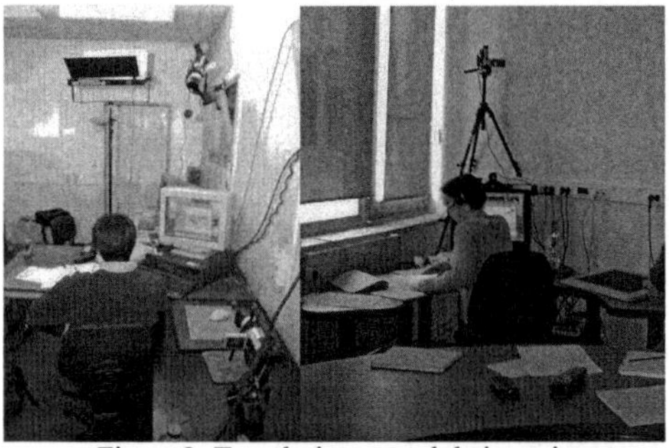

Figure 2: Two designers and their environment

3.3 Design work modes

Two work modes were distinguished during the product design process: synchronous and asynchronous modes (see Table 1).

- Synchronous mode or design meetings. Four meetings of two hours each were held in March 2002 (7, 14, 21 and 28 March), representing 8 hours of synchronous work (Table 1). The designers were in four cities : Nantes, Grenoble, Belfort and Nancy.
- Asynchronous mode or distributed design. The designers had to work at least 4 hours per week. This work was mainly individual. Communication was allowed with other designers via electronic mail.

A phase of familiarization with the communication and CAD tools was set up previous to the experiment to ensure that the participants would know the functionalities put at their disposal.

Date	**Modality**	**Time**
Meeting 1	synchronous	2 hours
1 week	asynchronous	4 hours
Meeting 2	synchronous	2 hours
1 week	asynchronous	4 hours
Meeting 3	synchronous	2 hours
1 week	asynchronous	4 hours
Meering 4	synchronous	2 hours
1 week	asynchronous	4 hours
Debriefing	Face to face meeting	4 hours

Table 1: Planning of synchronous/ asynchronous work

3.4 Technical aspects

3.4.1 Software aspects

The software available for communication were: Microsoft Netmeeting® for videoconference, Eudora® for e-mail and Ftp soft for file transfer. In addition we provided an FTP account for storing information and sharing the data. For carrying out the technical aspects the designers could use Solidworks® for 3D modeling and a local software for basic material strength analysis.

3.4.2 Hardware aspects

We used a French academic network providing speed transfer of 100 Mbytes/s. The four centers were connected to a server where Solidworks were running in order to save CPU resources on the users' workstations. Netmeeting was running on each computer and all the participants were connected to the server. Everyone was sharing the same CAD software located in the server.

3.5 Data Gathering

3.5.1 Video-recording of technology-mediated meetings

Two types of Video-recording were performed:

- Workstation view (Private space). The designers' face and local environment were video-recorded. This shows the designers movements in their private space and their use of the objets they had at hand.

- Screen view (Public and private space). A second video recorded the designers' screens. This is both private and public data because applications, programs, etc, could be open on a designer's screen, some of them in private space and the others in public space.

Finally, we obtained a 64-hour corpus: two views per four designers per four 2 hour meetings.

3.5.2 Pre and post-questionnaires

Two questionnaires were prepared to find out how the designers felt during synchronous /asynchronous work. The designers answered a questionnaire before and after each distant design meeting (pre and post design questionnaire). The questionnaires are divided into two parts: the first part deals with asynchronous work, whereas the second part deals with synchronous work. The main subjects dealt with in the pre and post questionnaire interviews are displayed in Table 2.

Pre questionnaire Interview	**Post questionnaire interview**
Asynchronous period ¬ Work planning ¬ Problems the group met ¬ Technical Functionality (use & problems)	**Asynchronous period** ¬ Work planning ¬ Designers goals
Synchronous period ¬ Work planning ¬ Problems to tackle ¬ Technical Functionality (use & problems) ¬ Suggestions to be made	**Synchronous period** ¬ Work planning ¬ Solutions adopted ¬ Technical Functionality (use & problems) ¬ Constraints and assessment of solutions

Table 2: Main Subjects dealt with in the pre and post questionnaire interviews

4 Data analysis methodology

4.1 Analysis of a technology-mediated design meeting

As a preliminary work on our 64-hour corpus, we focused on only one meeting in order to develop and apply our analysis methodology. We chose to analyze the third meeting, as it was the one in which the widest range of activities was observed and we also found that the learning process (especially regarding the tools) was quite stabilized at this stage of the design process. We then transcribed the whole corpus of this meeting.

We adopted and extended a coding scheme based on previous research in cognitive ergonomics and social psychology [20] [21] [22] [23]. The reliability of our coding scheme as been tested in D'Astous et al. [24] in which we hound that he degree of accordance between the two coders was quite good, as measured by two statistical tests: the kappa of Cohen and the index of fiability of Perrault and Leigh.

Our coding schema has two levels. At the first level, the coding is done to analyze the activities involved during the synchronous meeting. Three types of activity categories are distinguished: collaborative design activities (Table 3), interaction management activities (Table 4), and activities belonging to a relational register.

	Description
Meeting management	Organizing the actual meeting regarding the time available and the tasks to be done.
Project management	Planning the design: this involves organizing and distributing tasks according to the designers' skills.
Cognitive synchronization	Ensuring that team members share a common representation of a concept, projects goals, constraints, design strategy, solutions, etc.
Argumentation	Describing why a solution should or shouldn't be adopted.
Assessment of solution(s)	Evaluating positively or negatively a proposed solution.
Assessment of constraint(s)	Evaluating positively or negatively a constraint.
Proposing Solution(s)	Proposing, explaining a solution or an alternative solution.
Enhancing a solution	Enunciating supplementary and complementary ideas to develop a solution.

Table 3: Collaborative design activities categories

	Description
Technical resource management	Taking care that all the group shares the same technical resources, the same software in a private or shared space at a given time T. This ensures that a local context is shared.
Audio management	Ensuring that team members can hear the other members clearly.
Management of turn taking	Managing turn taking distribution.
Information resource Management	Ensuring that team members are aware of the information under discussion, and have the same document version (in their private or public spaces). This supports co-reference.
Regulator	Verbal utterances from the members who are listening, to indicate their continued presence and attention. For example: « Mmh », « Yes ».
Screen management	Ensuring that team members have a good visibility of the documents on the screen (like sketches). This supports both co-reference and ensures that a local context is shared.
Technical problem management	Help offered from one member to one or several members to give access to data that they can't open for some reason. These problems could be due to software, telecommunication failure, etc.

Table 4: Interaction management activities categories

Referring to Vacherand-Revel [21], we distinguish activities belonging to the relational register. We consider the relational register as an affective dimension. We only consider it for exchanges which are not directly about work. These kinds of exchanges allow the co-designers to share emotional affects (e.g. at the beginning of design meeting; "It's ok, we are all tired, there is no problem!").

At the second level, the coding focus is on the designers' *actions on technical devices*. Five categories were distinguished (Table 5).

	Description
Online co-producing	One or several team members use the technical device to produce together, develop a solution, a document.
Supporting argumentation	A member develops argumentation concerning a solution with an open file shared by the group (over the network).
Guiding explanation	A member uses the screen to focus on a field of the solution in order to support her/his explanation by moving the mouse to show a specific field of the solution on the screen.
Simulating	A member describes a procedure by simulating its execution. This may be for various reasons: technical failure, difficulties in finding a document, a resource, etc.
Tracing	A member keeps or seeks a trace of documents to remind the group of a decision, solution etc;

Table 5: Actions on technical devices

An excerpt of the coded corpus is shown in Annex 1.

4.2 *Synchronous versus asynchronous work*

The questionnaires revealed which activities were done and which tools were used during synchronous versus asynchronous work. Our analysis involved two phases. Firstly we systematically counted the tools reported to be used by each designer. Secondly a content analysis revealed which activities and which functionalities were associated to the tools used.

Then, the results obtained were interpreted for those tools which were used by at least three designers in order to gain a representative view of their use.

5 Results

5.1 *Global distribution of activities*

Figure 3 displays the global distribution of activities between our categories of the first level of analysis. It appears that collaborative design activities represent the most frequent exchanges (71%) occurring during the design meeting.

Interaction management activities represent 24% of the exchanges. This proportion is relatively important if we consider that no technical problems appeared during the design meeting.

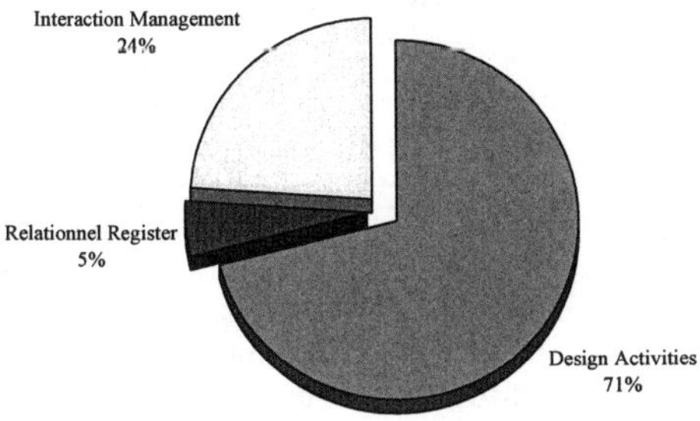

Figure 3: Global distribution of activities

Activities belonging to the relational register do not occur frequently (5%). These activities appeared mostly at the beginning, before and after break time and at the end of the meeting in order to initiate and close designers exchange.

5.2 *Face-to face design meetings versus technology-mediated design meetings*

Figure 4 displays the distribution of collaborative design activities in the technology-mediated design meeting. Cognitive synchronization (41%) was the most frequently occurring activity with respect to other collaborative design activities: assessment (23%); argumentation (18%); proposition/enhancement (12%); management (6%). So the mediated characteristic of the meeting does not seem to affect the nature of collaborative design activities involved in the meeting. So, with respect to the literature, we found the same predominance of cognitive synchronization in our technology-mediated design meeting as in face-to-face design meetings.

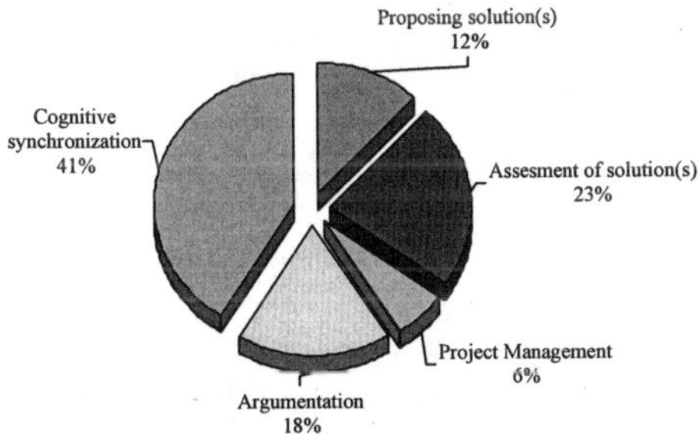

Figure 4: Collaborative design activities

We found that interaction management activities were relatively important in our technology-mediated meeting representing 24% of all activities. Figure 5 displays the distribution of interaction management activities in our meeting. The occurrence of these activities shows that co-reference is difficult. This is reflected by the importance of particular interaction management activities: information resource management (38% of interaction management activities) and screen management (17% of interaction management activities).

Management of turn taking (7% of interaction management activities) was principally made by the project leader in our technology-mediated meeting. In face-to-face design this is not usually the case, as turn taking is done on the basis of non verbal cues and does not require explicit management activities. Impromptu interactions or side discussions, which may reveal opportunistic data gathering, for further phases of the task, were not observed unlike in face-to-face meetings. These two results are similar to those found in computer-mediated communication [25].

Furthermore, the absence of visual modality was regretted by the co-designers (as reported in the questionnaires). However, other studies [26] [27] show that in a complex task, face visibility is disturbing whereas functional visibility is helpful. We can assume that, in our technology-mediated design situation, functional visibility would have allowed a local context to be shared and co-reference to be easier.

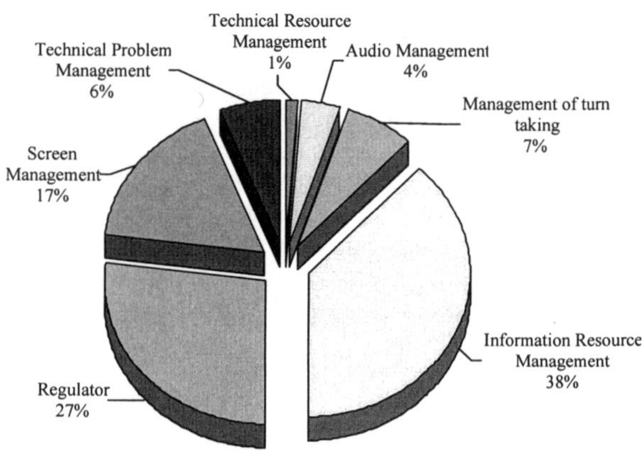

Figure 5: Interaction management activities

5.3 *Synchronous versus asynchronous collaborative work in design*

Based on the analysis of the questionnaires and of one design meeting, we found that both design activities and the use of tools varied according to the temporal mode, synchronous *versus* asynchronous, of the design work.

In the asynchronous mode, reported design activities (on the basis of the questionnaires) were mostly the implementation of solutions, i.e. 3D graphical realization of the design artefact. The CAD application and the common data repository were used respectively for graphical design and for storing and consulting design files. Electronic mail was mostly used to communicate about project management.

In the synchronous mode, reported design activities (on the basis of the questionnaires) and observed design activities (in the design meeting which we analyzed) were mostly proposition/enhancement of solutions and assessment of solutions. Co-elaboration of solutions was observed. Whiteboard and shared CAD applications were used to co-produce solutions, and to support argumentation and explanation (Figure 6). The role of graphical representations of the design artefact as entities of cooperation or intermediary objects [15] was central in the collaborative design activity.

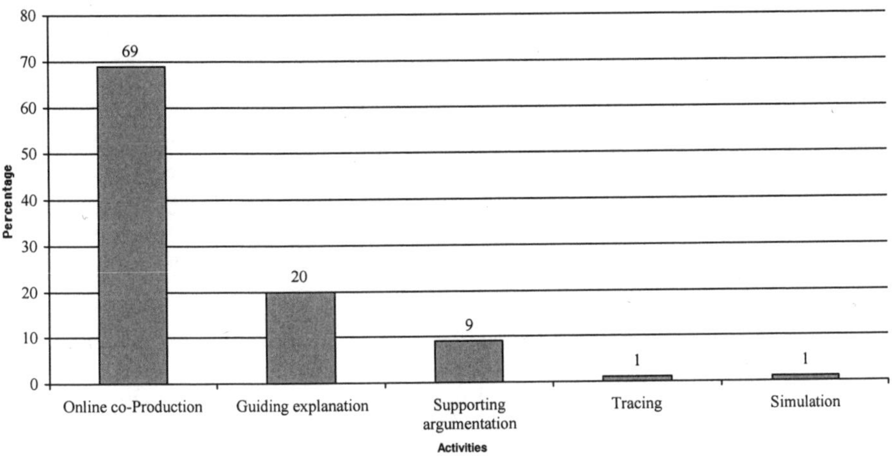

Figure 6 : Technical Devices Use (percent)

Supporting online co-production activity was the most frequently occurring use of technical devices (Figure 6). This activity was supported by computer graphics and sketches on the Netmeeting whiteboard (Table 6). Guiding explanations and supporting argumentation also had to be provided using graphics. These results show that the most widely used technical devices for mediated engineering design activities relate to graphical representations.

	Online co-producti	Guiding explicati	Supporting argumentati	Tracing	Simulatin	**Total**
Whiteboard	**177**	**62**	19	5	0	**263**
Graphics	**228**	**69**	**39**	2	0	**338**
Excel Softwar	20	8	2	0	1	**31**
Explorer	0	0	0	0	3	**3**

Table 6: Supporting tools regarding technical devices (in occurrences).

6 Discussion and further work

Our methodological framework has allowed us to analyze synchronous and asynchronous collaborative work in technology-mediated distant design situations. We found the same predominance of cognitive synchronization in our technology-mediated design meeting as in face-to-face design meetings (as reported in the literature). We found that interaction management activities were relatively important in our technology-mediated meeting. The distribution of interaction management activities shows that co-reference was difficult.

Based on the analysis of the questionnaires and of one design meeting, we found that both design activities and the use of tools varied according to the temporal mode, synchronous *versus* asynchronous, of the design work

Several limitations of our work should be highlighted. Firstly, several characteristics of our experiment limit the generality of our results: (1) the particularity of the meeting analyzed for characterizing synchronous work; (2) the designers profile; (3) the familiarity with the communication tools.

As concerns the particularity of our analyzed distant meeting, it is clear that further studies should be conducted to verify the generality of our preliminary results on synchronous distant design work.

The designers profile is also very important. In our experiment we hired students in engineering design. They were paid for their work and were working under a precise contract defining the conditions of their involvement. This question remains as to for us whether more experienced professionals would have performed differently. We plan to carry out experiments involving skilled designers and junior designers as a matter of comparison to evaluate the impact of design experience on the performance.

The skills and level of familiarity with the various communication tools is also important. We should be more careful in training the designers and/or carry out experiments with a trained team and a novice team in order to characterize a "familiarity" impact of the communication tools.

Secondly, the data recording and gathering could be improved. On the technical side videos should be more carefully synchronized in the various centres and the format should be standardized. Audio-recording is also a problem. Finally we had a 64-hour corpus that remains difficult to analyze without the help of video indexing systems. The amount of data is an issue in this kind of experiment.

Asynchronous work was analyzed on the basis of questionnaires. This analysis could be improved by a finer methodology based on gathering, other data e.g., email exchanges or computer interaction collected using specific "spy" software.

Thirdly, further development of our analysis methodology could be done. Our coding schema could be improved, in particular the categories concerning the "actions on technical devices". We felt that these categories could be refined to account for more subtle interactions through the technological tools.

Finally, the design task is a key point in the success of the experiment. A lot of experiments have been carried out in creative design phases or in early design phases [10] [28]. Exploring design solutions in a team involves 2D sketching, but when we consider embodiment design phases, the use of specific 3D modelling tools becomes necessary. Few experiments have been carried out at this stage. For us this remains an important challenge.

Acknowledgments

The design experiment mentioned in this paper has been carried out by the GRACC group, a French research group composed of four universities (Belfort, Grenoble, Nantes, Nancy). More information can be found at http://www.3s.hmg.inpg.fr/ci/gracc.

References

[1] Olson, J.S., Card, S.K., Landauer, T.K., Olson, G.M., Malone, T. & Legget, J. (1993) Computer-supported co-operative work : research issues for the 90s. *Behavior and Information Technology,* 12(2), 115-129.

[2] Johansen (1988*) Groupware: Computer support for business teams.* The Free Press, NY.

[3] Falzon, P., Darses, F., & Béguin, P. (1996) Collective design processes. *COOP'96. Second International Conference on the Design Cooperative Systems*, Juan-les-Pins, (June 2-14 1996).

[4] Herbsleb, J. D., Klein, H., Olson, G. M., Brunner, H., Olson, J. S., & Harding, J. (1995) Object-oriented analysis and design in software project teams. In F. Détienne, & R. Rist (eds): Special issue on empirical studies of object-oriented design. *Human-Computer Interaction,* 10, 2 & 3, pp 249-292.

[5] Walz, D. B., Elam, J. J., Krasner, H., & Curtis, B. (1987) A methodology for studying software design teams: an investigation of conflict behaviors in the requirements definition phase. In G. M. Olson, S. Sheppard, & E. Soloway (Eds): *Empirical Studies of Programmers: Second workshop.* Norwood, NJ: Ablex Publishing Corporation. 83-99.

[6] Olson, G.M., Olson, J.S., Carter, M. R. & Storrosten, M. (1992) Small Group Design Meetings: An Analysis of Collaboration. *Human-Computer Interaction*, 7, 347-374.

[7] D'Astous, P., Détienne, F., Robillard, P. N., & Visser, W. (2001) Quantitative measurements of the influence of participants roles during peer review meetings. *Empirical Sotware Engineering*, 6, 143-159.

[8] Visser, W. (1993) Collective design: A cognitive analysis of cooperation in practice. In N. F. M. Roozenburg (Ed.). *Proceedings of ICED 93. 9th International Conference on Engineering Design* (Volume 1) (pp. 385-392), The Hague, (August 17-19, 1993). Zürich: HEURISTA.

[9] Stempfle, J. & Badke-Schaub, P. (2002) Thinking in design teams - an analysis of team communication *Design Studies, 23*, 473-496

[10] Cross, N., Christiaans, H., & Dorst, K. (Eds.) (1996) *Analysing design activity* (Ch. 13, pp. 271-289). Chichester: Wiley.

[11] Falzon, P. (1994) Dialogues fonctionnels et activité collective. *Le Travail Humain,*, 57(4/94), 299-312.

[12] Bellotti, V., & Bly, S. (1996) Walking away from the destop computer: distributed collaboration and mobility in a product design team. *CSCW'96*, Cambridge, MA, USA.

[13] Clark, H.H. & Brennan, S. E. (1991) Grounding in communication. In L. Resnick, J-M Levine and S. D. Teasley (Eds) : *Perspectives on socially shared cognition.* (APA, Washington DC) 127-149.

[14] Olson,G.M., & Olson, J.S. (2000) Distance matters. *Human-Computer Interaction*, 15, 139-178.

[15] Boujut, J-F., & Laureillard, P. (2002) "A co-operation framework for product-process integration in engineering design. *Design studies*, 23, 497-513.

[16] Schmidt, K., & Wagner, I. (2002) Coordinative artifacts in architectural practice. In M. Blay-Fornarino, A. M. Pinna-Dery, K. Schmidt, & P. Zaraté. (Eds) : Cooperative Systems Design. IOS Press.

[17] Everitt, K. M., Klemmer, S. R., Lee, R., & Landay, J. A. (2003) Two worlds apart : bridging the gap between physical and virtuel media for distributed design collaboration. *CHI 2003*, April 5-10, Ft. Landerdale, Florida, USA.

[18] Boujut J.F., Blanco E. (2003) Intermediary Objects as a Means to Foster Co-operation in Engineering Design, *Journal of computer supported collaborative work*, vol 12 (2003), issue 2, pp. 205-219.

[19] Ruiz-Dominguez G., Diallo T., Boujut J.F., (2004) On the sequential effect induced by the use of communication tools in distant collaboration, *Proceedings of the TMCE 2004*, Edited by Horváth and Xirouchakis, Millpress, Rotterdam.

[20] Darses, F., Détienne, F., Falzon, P. & Visser, W. (2001) *COMET : A method for Analysing Collective Design Processes.* Rapport de Recherche INRIA N° 4258. Rocquencourt : INRIA.

[21] Vacherand-Revel, J. (2002). Les registres d'activités du travail coopératif médiatisé et distant de co-conception de documents scientifiques. In. E. Engrand, S. Lambolez, A. Trognon. Communication en situation de travail à distance. Collection : Langage, cognition, interaction. Presses Universitaires de Nancy.

[22] Martin, G., Détienne, F. & Lavigne, E. (2001) Analysing viewpoints in design through the argumentation process. In M. Hirose (Ed): *Proceedings of INTERACT'01*, Tokyo, Japan, July 9-13 2001, 521-529.

[23] Robillard, P. N., D'Astous, P., Détienne, F., & Visser, W. (1998). Measuring cognitive activities in software engineering. *The 20th International Conference on Software Engineering (ICES98).* Kyoto, Japan. April 19-25.

[24] D'Astous, P., Détienne, F., Visser, W. & Robillard, P. N. (in press) Changing our view on design evaluation meetings methodology: a study of software technical review meetings. *Design Studies.*

[25] Smith, M., Cadiz, J. J., & Burkhalter, B. (2000) Conversation trees and theaded chats. *CSCW'00*, December 2-6, 2000, Philadelphia, PA, USA.

[26] Tang, J.C. & Isaacs, E. (1993) Why do users like video ? Studies of multi-media supported collaboration. *Computer-supported Cooperative Work*, 1, 163-196.

[27] Wittaker, S. (1995) Rethinking video as a rechange for interpersonnel communications : theory and design implications. *International Journal of Human-Computer Studies*, 42, 501-529.

[28] Dorst K., Cross N. (2001), *Creativity in the design process: co-evolution of problem-solution,* Design Studies, 22, 425-437.

ANNEX 1

CORPUS **Designer identification**	**CORPUS** **Time**	**CORPUS** **Behavior on tools**	**CORPUS** **Verbal**	**CODING** **Activities (design or interaction management)**	**CODING** **Actions on technical device**
NC	00 :54 :19	Whiteboard (lid on screen) (drawing)	You gotta… lower it, yeah OK like that,	Cognitive synchronization	Online co-producing
NC	…	Whiteboard (lid on screen) (drawing)	and some small rubber bands to fasten it at the bottom	Proposing Solution(s)	Online co-producing
NT	…	Whiteboard (lid on screen)	No, you take it away	Proposing Solution(s)	
G	…	Whiteboard (lid on screen) (delete drawing)	You definitely take it away	Cognitive synchronization	Online co-producing
B	…	Whiteboard (lid on screen) (pointing)	We can place some small rubber bands	Proposing Solution(s)	Guiding explanation
B	…	Whiteboard (lid on screen) (pointing)	And ahhh, peace of, here you are,	Technical resource management	Guiding explanation
B	…	Whiteboard (lid on screen) (pointing)	Some small rubbers here for rolling them up if one one fully opens the window… to fasten the plastic stuff	Proposing Solution(s)	Guiding explanation
NT	00 :54 :35	Whiteboard (lid on screen)	OK	Assessment of solution	
G	00 :54 :44	Whiteboard (lid on screen) (drawing)	And instead of using a zipper couldn't we use fasteners, like this ?	Proposing Solution(s)	Online co-producing

Annex 1: excerpt of synchronous meeting coding

G, NC, NT, B: Represents the four designer

Cooperative Systems Design
M. Zacklad et al. (Eds.)
IOS Press, 2004

Backdoor Creativity – Collaborative Creativity in Technology Supported Teams

*Hillevi SUNDHOLM, #Henrik ARTMAN and *Robert RAMBERG
**Dept. of Computer and Systems Sciences*
S-164 40 Stockholm University/Royal Institute of Technology, Sweden
#Dept. of Numerical Analysis and Computer Science
S-10044 Royal Institute of Technology, Sweden

Abstract. This case study describes collaborative creativity in technology-supported teams with the task of making an interactive artefact. The teams work in the iLounge, which is designed and built with the purpose of supporting co-located collaborative work. iLounge is equipped with several vertical and horizontal large screens, called smart boards, where the team members can make their contributions available to all others. Creativity is discussed as a collaborative effort manifested in relation to technology support rather than some individual trait. Collaborative creativity is then examined and discussed as transactions between team members and their use of the workspaces. The main conclusion is that collaborative creativity is supported by using several Smart boards, and that the teams make use of the Smart boards when proposing and collectively refining ideas. Physical space also matters in terms of getting ones ideas into the discussions, but peripheral participation does not mean that one cannot be of great influence. This kind of backdoor creativity is interesting as it shows how even peripheral, in a physical sense, team members are contributing to the teams overall creative work.

Keywords: Creativity, Technological support, Situated cognition, Co-located collaboration, Interactive spaces

1. Introduction

The main entrance for creativity, as it is portrayed in media and general folklore, is the solitaire individual gushed with several innovative ideas, which takes others by astonishment. Earlier theorists within cognitive science have treated concepts such as intelligence, talent, creativity, giftedness, ability and cognition as something internal, and more particularly as traits or possessions of individual minds [5, 11]. This view on cognition and a focus on an individual mind has been criticized and rivalled by for instance situated [3, 4] – and distributed [6] perspectives on cognition. Central to these perspectives is that cognition is not placed in the heads or minds of individuals but rather in the individual-environment transaction where action (and interaction) takes place [2]. If, cognitive, social, cultural and historical external processes are to be treated as integral parts of competent action, then traditional conceptions of cognition and intelligence should be re-examined [15], as several researchers have argued, for instance Pea [11]. As stated by Barab and Plucker

> *In part, constructs such as ability and talent (or creativity) have the mixed blessing of people having widely held implicit theories of these constructs. Their unofficial definitions, therefore are often taken for granted, making definitions even more difficult* [2, pp. 174].

The authors focus on the concepts of ability and talent (or creativity, authors' remark) and theoretically ground these in situated action, activity theory, distributed cognition and legitimate peripheral participation. Barab and Plucker make a convincing argument and suggest that instead of looking upon these as properties of an individual, these should be looked upon as *"...a set of functional relations distributed across person and context, and through which the person-in-situation appears knowledgeably skilful"* [ibid pp. 174]. I.e. in the dynamic transaction among the individual, the physical environment and the socio-cultural context, ability and talent arise. In this view ability and talent are part of the individual-environment transaction and as such an opportunity that is available to all, but it may be actualized more often by some. Part of the individual-environment transaction is of course artefacts of various kinds (papers, pencils, computers etc.) that are there to support an ongoing activity. Following the line of reasoning above, an important goal for educators, designers, etc., should be to provide with environments and contexts through which talented and creative interactions can emerge.

Our research concerns co-located collaboration, where teams work in technology supported environments (called interactive spaces). The case study reported on in this paper focuses on the concept of creativity in the context of collaborative activities. We have studied two groups of students working on a design task in an interactive space for two weeks with the purpose of describing how this interactive space (as an example of an environment meant to support collaborative work) can support collaborative processes through which creative interactions can emerge.

1.1 *Creativity as Collaborative Activity*

Collaboration shares a great deal with cooperation as has been defined by Marx [cited in 16, pp. 13] as *"multiple individuals working together in a conscious way in the same production process or in different but connected production processes."* Inasmuch as this definition might be true in a general sense we would like for our purposes to refine it by adding a few features, particularly with creative teamwork in mind. The concept "conscious" may imply some intentional plan for how the cooperation is organized, but collaborative creativity cannot be fully planned. This is because it relies on close and manifest interdependence, rather than loosely coupled production processes. Even though each member might have his own area of expertise and responsibility it is only through the joint coordinated effort of their knowledge and skills that they can accomplish the task. Thus collaboration in creative teams requires the articulation of each individual's activity so that each team member can contribute with ideas, criticise or compromise the mutually shared goal. This goal, in turn, can be highly abstract and must be negotiated at all times as petite elements may change or constrain the general goal.

The constituent parts of situated collaboration can be analyzed into communication and coordination. Collaborative activity is therefore implicitly defined by the use of these two concepts. Communication is often scientifically, as well as by common sense, regarded as the passive transmission and reception of information, rather than the active process of interpretation [14, 23]. In the same commonsense manner coordination is simply considered as *"the act of working together harmoniously"* [9, pp. 358]. We expect collaborative creativity to rely more on communication breakdowns as a vehicle for innovation. Furthermore, we expect collaborative creativity, as a consequence of its manifest situatedness, to be closely connected to the layout and use of artefacts.

From these critical aspects of perspectives on creativity and collaboration, creativity can be viewed upon as one vital aspect of ongoing activities in computer supported collaborative teams. More precisely, creativity can be viewed as, and investigated as, one aspect of an ongoing dialogue in computer supported collaborative teams.

We will especially focus on how the team members interact in relation to the layout of the room, how they utilise the artefacts and how the ideas are constructed and negotiated. Viewing creativity as dialogue might help to discuss creativity as a social and communicative transaction between individuals who in some sense share a mutual goal. In this sense a communicative contribution can be viewed as objectively creative and innovative, but will only pass as creative and innovative if it at the same time finds a response in other team members [5]. An objectively creative act might thus not be viewed as creative given that others do not respond to it. At the same time a relatively mundane act (or fact) might give rise to responses that are propagated to something creative. A very strong idea can on the other hand encapsulate the creativity, for example several members reject new forms of ideas as a consequence of that these do not fit the picture. Just as communicative acts are indexed to certain contexts, creativity will be severely constrained by the interactive space and what it affords. The layout of the technology in the room might help to spread ideas but at the same time function as inhibiting people to disturb the general picture.

1.2 Supported Creativity

Creativity is bounded by external constraints either they are physical, structural, economical or social. Computers can support the creative process, and the highest chance to obtain creativity is when users are able *"to move comfortably and smoothly among the information"* [20, pp. 31].

Meeting the challenge of designing effective tools to support creativity Shneiderman [17] has constructed a framework, called a four phase's genex (generator of excellence). The four phases of the genex consists of: collect, relate, create, and donate. The phases are furthermore complemented with eight activities: searching and browsing digital data; consulting with peers and mentors; visualizing data and processes; thinking by free associations; exploring solutions; composing artefacts and performances; reviewing and replaying session histories; disseminating results. The focus of Shneiderman's work is how to support the single user in his or her creative work process through the design of the user interface (regardless of searching for information, exploring solutions or consulting with peers, etc). Our focus on the contrary is on how an environment that provides with a set of artefacts and allows for co-located collaborative work can support the emergence of creative interactions.

The eight activities described above should be supported, but the main challenge here is to design environments that support both individuals and groups. The computer supported environment should support the different individuals in the group, simplify the visualization and sharing of information for the other group members, and have a general setup for supporting the emergence of creative interactions.

1.3 Interactive Spaces

The traditional approach within human-computer interaction is to focus on the one user – one artefact situation. The workspace changes dramatically when there are many users in a space with many artefacts, and it changes even more when information can be displayed in public as well as in private. The ideas with ubiquitous computing, pervasive computing, ambient computing, and calm technology are more or less the same. More precisely, from only using desktops (or laptops) there will be technologies, that become more and more invisible, and that will be embedded in the environments. The technology disappears in the environment, but gets visible when it is needed. This is also to some extent already the case; more and more of the computers we interact with are embedded in devices. Weiser [21] defined ubiquitous computing as a "*new way of thinking about computers in the world, one that takes into account the natural human environment*" [pp. 94]. Central to his vision was interaction between humans and computers in a natural way, without the human subject thinking about it in any detail. Computers would become part of the background and indistinguishable from the fabric of everyday life. Computers are spread out in the environment and the user should get the feeling that she is interacting with the whole environment and not with separate computing devices.

By interactive spaces we mean environments that support collaborative work, co-located and distributed, where one has both public and private displays, and where there are many ways of working and sharing information with other people. One of the main strengths when working collaboratively in an interactive space is that one can easily share information with the other group members. A common problem when looking at shared digital information is that only one or a few of the group members have an appropriate representation of the information displayed [10]. However, in a space where one has public displays this problem disappears, but the problem here is to make it easy to hand information over from personal to public displays. The metaphor we have worked on when designing the interaction in interactive spaces is giving/handing a document from one person to another.

Another strength is that this workspace offers several different ways of searching and presenting data, and there is also different ways of sharing it with the other group members. When for instance having touch-sensitive displays one can interact with the computer with ordinary mouse and keyboard, but also using the fingers or pen to write, draw or navigate on the screen directly.

1.3.1 iLounge

At the Royal Institute of Technology in Kista there is an interactive space called the iLounge designed and built with the purpose of supporting co-located collaborative work. It is used both as a learning facility, and as an experimental research facility. The room has two large touch-sensitive displays known as Smart boards [18] built into a wall. In front of this wall there is a table with a horizontally embedded plasma screen, also touch-sensitive. This interactive table is large enough for 6 to 8 people to sit around. In one of the corners of the room a smaller table and three chairs are placed in front of a wall-mounted plasma display, enabling a part of the group to work separately. Figure 1 shows a plan of the room. The room has a wireless network and contains a laptop computer with a wireless LAN card. Keyboards and mice in the room are also wireless, using Bluetooth technique. Finally, the iLounge contains high quality audio and video equipment that for instance can be used when having videoconferences, or during user studies.

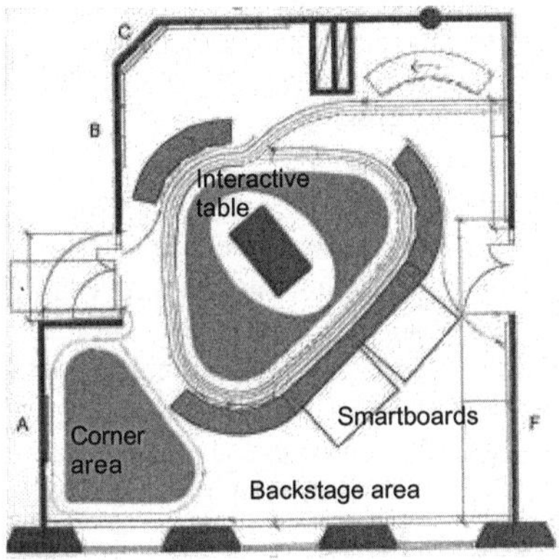

Figure 1. Plan of the room. The working areas are marked in blue.

There are many computers in the room and it is also possible to bring personal artefacts into the room, and therefore it is in no way obvious how information is shared between the different work surfaces. To facilitate and support work in the iLounge our research has been focused on the development of services that help and support the user to move data between the devices present in the room. Tipple [1] is a service with which one can open any file on any other computer that runs the Tipple service. The interface of Tipple shows icons representing all other computers running the service. If you want to start a file on another computer you drag the file icon to the icon representing the other computer (an early prototype is described in [22]). The service Multibrowse allows the user to move web content between displays in the room. When right-clicking a page or a link, the user is given the opportunity to "multibrowse" it either to or from its present location (see [7], for a more thorough description). PointRight makes it possible to use the same pointing device or keyboard on more than one computer in the room. When the pointer reaches the border of the screen it continues on the screen next to it having the service. PointRight together with iClipboard makes it possible for the user to cut or copy text between computers in the space. The text is placed on a clipboard that is shared by the computers running the service.[2]

In the study reported on in this paper we also introduced some of SMART Technologies services to the participants, specifically the virtual keyboard and Smart Notebook. Smart Notebook is an electronic whiteboard application, where one can create documents containing typed text, hand-written text, and pictures. The document is visualized as a book with pages.

1.4 Related Research

Research on creative teams at five companies [19] show that the creative teams seldom use advanced technologies. The teams rather rely on traditional equipment such as flip charts, whiteboards and overhead projectors. These teams were not reluctant to new forms of technology, but rather open to technology and new experiences. The teams would like to have access to databases for preparing meetings and sharing ideas, systems for participatory

---

[1] Tipple is developed by the FUSE group, Stockholm University/ Royal Institute of Technology, and can be downloaded at http://www.dsv.su.se/fuse/downloads.htm

[2] Multibrowse, Pointright and iClipboard are part of the iWork package and are developed by the Interactive Workspaces at Stanford University. The iWork services can be downloaded at http://iwork.stanford.edu/download.shtml.

presentations, visualizations for inspiration, and different modalities for communication. Still computers must stand in the background. The teams further want systems that are reconfigurable but at the same time invisible. Such design must include a strong aspect of learning as the reconfiguring will hardly make the computer invisible until reconfigurable practices are automatized.

In a former study of interactive spaces, with a quite similar set-up to ours, Artman & Persson [1] studied how officers in a simulated command and control unit collaborated. In that study it was found that the expected interaction between different officers representing different areas of competence was more structured around a social protocol than the possibilities to interact. The team was gathered and each officer informed the others about the states of affairs of his/hers specific units. The word was given in sequential order, by the commander, which did not admit for creative discussions. Another aspect, which seemed to inhibit general and/or in-depths discussions, was that the interactive table contained almost all aspects of the area the command and control unit, was to control. The pattern was broken when one officer produced a very simple representation of the area, which did not include all aspects. When presenting this representation to the team people started to discuss the general situation and what they could do about it. In a sense this embodied the slogan of "less is more". The present study is less tradition-bound and might give rise to different interaction patterns. The task in itself is very different as the command and control is to control an area out-there, while the groups' task in the study reported on here is to come up with an interactive system that attracts a group of unknown persons. Thus the present group is less bounded and we expect to find discussions, idea swapping and close collaborative activities – collaborative creativity.

2. Method

Five female and four male students in the ages of 21 to 45, divided in two groups, participated in the study. One group consisted of three men and one woman, and the other group of one man and four women. A couple of them in the groups knew each other from before. The students attended a course in design of interactive systems at our department. The students' task was to design a digital, multimedia guide for an exhibition "4, 5 Billion Years - The History of Earth and Life" at the Swedish Museum of Natural History. The two groups were responsible for designing the multimedia guide describing "from Big bang to first life", and "pre-historical mammals" (the mammals living before the primates). The target group was children about twelve years old. We followed the students during the conceptual design phase of their assignment. The conceptual design phase lasted two weeks and consisted of brainstorming, sketching of scenarios and the multimedia product, and information search. During this time the groups had four and five sessions, respectively, in the iLounge. Prior to this, they received an introduction to the environment and the specific services introduced in the section "1.3.1 iLounge".

Data were collected through observations, pre- and post-study questionnaires, and ended with semi structured group interviews. The questionnaires have mainly helped us in the analysis of roles of the group members. Both the work sessions and the interviews were video taped. The recordings consist of four angles to cover the whole workspace (see Figure 2), and one channel for sound. Altogether the data material consists of 21, 5 hours of video data. As a tool for our analysis we have used Interaction Analysis [8], and more particularly certain foci for analysis, namely spatial organization of activity, participation structures, artefacts and documents, turn-taking, and trouble and repair.

Figure 2. The view of the video recordings with the four angles

3. Results

The results will focus on how the groups used the workspace, and how they came to a creative dialogue, and not the resulting multimedia guides. But a short description of the groups' work processes and the resulting multimedia guides, described in 3.1 will help to understand the excerpts and the discussion that follows.

3.1 Description of the groups' general work process and design product

The two groups of students worked rather differently. Group 1 was driven by the ideas they came up with during their work sessions. The group did not really consider different design proposals, instead they stuck to ideas that someone came up with, and in this way the design evolved. Already during the second work session the storyboard and features of the guide was close to the final solution. This is characteristic for the way they worked: very impulsively, and without thinking of involving the end user in the design process (although the teacher stressed the importance of involving the users in the design process many times). Group 2 on the other hand more strictly followed the instructions given at the beginning of the course and were thus more focussed in their work in coming up with different ideas. After three sessions they had eight design proposals, and after negotiation, they agreed upon one of them. They brought children to the exhibition at the museum, tested the design proposals on children before deciding upon which of their proposals that should be chosen, as well as made a user test of the final multimedia guide. During the design process they continuously documented their work and the process itself.

Group 1 designed a multimedia guide that described the evolution from Big bang to first life. They built a game called "Spaceflower", in which a woman (who is controlled by the user) finds a space rocket resembling a flower in her father's garage. When the user clicks on the space rocket the woman jumps into it, flies away, and gets lost in the universe. In finding her way back she is in contact with her father (who is a professor), and he helps her to get back by giving instructions. In order to get home the woman (user) has to solve different problems. Group 2 designed a game that teaches about the pre-historical mammals. When the game starts, the user meets a researcher in a library. The researcher has documents about pre-historical mammals sorted in piles in accordance with the era in which they lived. There is only one problem: the papers in the piles have become disorganized, and the task of the user is to get the piles in order again.

3.2 Use of Workspace

Most software resources in the environment are standard Microsoft© products which the teams have some familiarity with. In spite of this, the teams need to learn to navigate between different screens. This concerns both the general pointing devices and for sharing information, or rather sending information to different screens.

Figure 3. A student group discussing their design sketches made on the Smart boards

Most of the time the participants worked on one of the two Smart boards for making sketches, (as illustrated in figure 3), or for showing information found at the Internet to each other. While producing a sketch, one of the group members usually stood in front of the Smart board, and the other participants were sitting around the table. The person in charge of drawing the sketches alternated. For instance, one participant would be using the touch functionality of one of the Smart boards, another using the keyboard and mouse working on the same document, and the third using PointRight and iClipboard to insert a piece of text, and together they created a sketch. The transition between individual work and public presentation is often negotiated as illustrated in Excerpt 1.

Excerpt 1. Group 2, session 2. Transition between individual and public[3]

Time 0.12.55	Person	Transcript of interaction	Characteristic of action
1	#3	"We can also put some picture here [in the Notebook]".	Sits down. Looks at the right Smart board
2	#1	"You mean, when we draw the proposals we can do it with the Smart…"	Looks at #3 sitting next to #1.
3	#3	"Mmm, but we can draw now. We have written down some things about what we want. I don't know exactly what we are going to do now."	Looks at the right Smart board.
4	#1	"Mmm… We can do that."	Looks at #3.

In the post-survey, group members said that they had experienced that the work they had performed had been more effective than the group work they usually perform. One of the advantages they stressed was that everyone could check if the person in charge of writing or

[3] The transcriptions below are divided with resemblance to the work of [12]. But in our case "Characteristic of action" describes the actor's action, not the abstraction of the utterances.

drawing did that correctly. Also advantageous was the way the whole group could come to mutual agreements, which is next to impossible when a group works together in front of a desktop. At the same time a woman pointed out that it was frustrating to see another person making mistakes, without being able to change those, since only one person could work at a time. Excerpt 2, gives an example of the dissatisfaction of being the one that "goes public" and exposes ones creations.

Excerpt 2. Group 2. Direct continuation of excerpt 1. The embarrassment of going public with ones drawings.

Time 0.21.05	Person	Transcript of interaction	Characteristic of action
5	#3	"But if one draws something under here [shows with the pointer]. Or to make some more space.	Points with the pointer in the Notebook, on the right Smart board.
6	#4	"Hm..."	Looks at the right Smart board.
7	#3	"Some screens or something or... [refers to the design of the multimedia guide]"	Looks at the Notebook.
8	#4	"Yes. Is anybody good at this, to draw?"	Looks at #3.
9	#3	"I am very bad..."	Works with the Notebook.
10	#5	"So am I."	Looks at a Word document on the left Smart board.
11	#4	"There are others..."	Looks at #3.
12	#1	"On where? There? [points to the right Smart board] It is just to go there and draw with the hand."	Points at the right Smart board.
13	#4	"Yeah, right! If... Is there anybody with some talent of drawing?"	Looks at #3.
14	#5	"We don't care about how the animals looked."	Looks first at #3, then at the left Smart board. Talks simultaneously with #1, line 12.
15	#5	"What are we supposed to draw?"	Looks at #2 and #3. Talks simultaneously with #3, line 13.
16	#2	"Draw pictures of a screen with all the animals, maybe. It is just to make some dots."	Looks at #5.
17	#4	"Someone with some talent of drawing."	Talks at the same time as #2, line 16. Talks to #1.

Here is seems the Smart board is more inhibiting, than supporting, creativity. This seems to have more to do with the embarrassment of making drawings rather than the Smart boards affording something particular. The problem was resolved by ripping pictures from the Internet and by making simple symbols, as squares and circles, signifying animals. This was done using two smart boards in parallel, one for using the Internet and one for using the drawing program. This shows the interdependence of two seemingly independent processes, and the relation of how the workspace layout is supporting creative solutions and creative use of symbols in collaborative activities.

Only one of the groups used the corner space with one of the wall screens. The group used the corner when they wanted to divide the work and search for information on the Internet. The other group did not make use of the corner at all. They said that it would have felt like leaving the group. Both groups used the interactive table. Group 2 used it continuously for searching for information, and for reading documents. They found it annoying though, that they could not flip the view of the computer, since it always gives the person(s) sitting on one of the sides around the table a preferable view. Group 1 on the other hand used the table at one session for showing and discussing pictures, which worked as an inspiration for their design.

3.3 Roles of the Group Members

An interesting result is that the group members' roles seemed to change. In professional and standard projects there is often a dedicated project leader who is responsible for the project's progress towards the goal. In the pre-test questionnaire we asked the students if they usually when working in groups experienced that the group members take on and fulfil different roles, which they all agreed on. When we asked the same question regarding this particular group work in the follow-up questionnaire everyone but two disagreed[4]. This observation could point to that working in an interactive space can lead to a work process, that is less prone to support only certain people. Expressed differently, the interactive space is an environment where opportunities to come to different expressions are more available and also actualized to a larger extent. This may be the case since much of the work and discussions are made in the open, in front of all team members, which gives all team members an opportunity to contribute. An advantage with the interactive space is that it invites possibilities to work in different ways, and to create documents together. It was obvious when working with the sketches on the Smart boards that some of the participants preferred to do the work at the board directly using the pencils or the fingers for drawing and writing, while others preferred to sit down typing and inserting pictures, or looking for information at the web on one of the computers in the room. Figure 4 shows an example of the different ways of searching for information. This could also be seen as an indication of how the work equalises, and that everyone can contribute in a personally preferred manner.

Figure 4. Group members focusing on different activities

[4] The ones who agreed on the question explained that "the roles rotated [between the group members]", and the other commented the work rather than the roles by stating "I talked, but did not do so much practical".

This kind of work can have many advantages, but one disadvantage in this context is that it is harder to hold on to the project goals. Interactions around new information, new ideas are so creative that the goal and progress of the project is forgotten. New ideas tend to take over the team and inspire them into unforeseen directions.

3.4 Swapping Ideas by the Use of Smart boards

The Smart boards were mainly used in two different ways. The most common way was to present rudimentary sketches, often visual, to other team members. Individual sketches on paper sometimes preceded this. The other way to use the Smart boards was to present web pages from the Internet, in order to discuss the information that was found, design or other issues coupled to the project. In both cases the goal was to make information available to others in order to discuss (which makes it open for re-interpretation and contribution or to dispute the idea). In this way the team gets the "raw" information, rather than some pre-processed summary prepared by another team member. Excerpt 3 shows how the Smart board is used to present an idea. The excerpt is taken from an early part of session 3, where the group still neither has decided upon the design proposal, nor agreed on the concept of the multimedia guide. Before the excerpt below begins the members of the group have discussed what children would like to know, and how deeply they should go in to particular details. While other group members tried to solve some practical things, #1 stands up, and starts to make a sketch of a proposal of a game on the left Smart board. The theme is a competition, "like a boxing game", between animals.

Excerpt 3. Group 2, session 3. Presentation of ideas

Time 0.23.07	Person	Transcript of interaction	Characteristic of action
1	#2	"As one of the games, or...?	Sits down. Looks at #1.
2	#1	"Yes, but you can like this [pointing]... eh, I mean to eat or to be eaten, but you can choose, so you in one way or another, or maybe not like this. But you present the information about them, and then you can... or even if one might go here. But maybe also like this. "	Stands in front of the left Smart board. First looks and points at the sketch, then looks at the group around the table, and finally points at the sketch again.
3	#1	"You might go like this in the forest somewhere. Here you have..."	Opens a new page in the Notebook and starts to visualize how #1 thinks by drawing with the finger.
4	#3	"But if you think we are going to do this in a real way, then we need to know what they sound like, and how they use the body, and knock, and..."	Sits down. Looks at #1 and #5. #3 sits on the opposite side around the table.
5	#1	[Mumbles something inaudible]	Sketches in the Notebook. Nobody pays attention.
6	#5	"It is built upon research [inaudible]..."	Sits down. Looks at #3
7	#1	"Then you can have different animals."	Looks at the Smart board, and start to draw with the finger in the Notebook. Nobody listens.
8	#3	"Watch Jurassic Park [the movie]."	Looks at #5.
9	#1	[Mumbles something about "a cave"]	Sketches first, then turns around and looks at the group.
10	#5	"Mm..."	Looks at #3

As we can see the idea is forming as it is formulated. The team members are partly open to the idea, partly developing the idea but also tend to take the idea to a practical level of implementing it. As the discussion continues, the practicality of implementation becomes more focussed, illustrated in excerpt 4 below.

Excerpt 4. Group 2. Continuation of excerpt 3. Conceptual design crashes with implementation practicalities.

11	#3	"Some animals had such bone plates [shows at her own face], but of course, that were dinosaurs."	Looks at the sketch on the Smart board.
12	#1	"A cave and you can check who lived there, and, or you can also have such, as it was with the fox [?], that you have energy, and you have to eat, and you need to find someone to kill. And then you can have here [pointing at the sketch]. Walk a bit, and maybe there is [paints something in the sketch with the finger]."	Looks at the sketch, gesticulates, looks at the other group members, and finally continues to draw on the sketch.
13	#3	"Can you... How do you randomise things and such in Director, if you're going to do...?"	Looks at #1.
14	#1	"You can randomise things."	Looks at #3.
15	#3	"Can you?"	Looks at #1.
16	#1	"Yes, we did..."	Looks at #3.
17	#3	"Can you randomise any page, I mean any frame?"	Looks at #1.
18	#1	"Hm, we did somewhat... we randomised... we did it with a panda."	Looks at #3.
19	#3	"Hm..."	Looks at #1.
20	#1	"And then it randomised like... and was put... You have like a dictionary with different... and then it has to randomise."	Looks at #3.
21	#3	"Ok, so there is stuff."	Looks at #1.
22	#1	"Yes, in some way."	Looks at #3
23	#2	"But have we decided upon the game now, or? It feels a bit..."	Looks at #1 and #3, and at #1 again.
24	#1	"No, it's just a proposal."	Looks at the group.

The excerpt shows the way it is possible for any of the team members to form an idea or representation. However, at the same time it interrupts the whole team in trying to both listen to the person who thinks it is worthwhile showing something and reading, or at least glancing, through the information. This public presentation of information seems to generate creative discussions within the group. The person being in charge of a sketch has the power to be able to support a personal preferable idea, not supported by the others. This did not happen here, but it is clear that the #1 has a good tool for trying to convince the others, partly by standing in front of the others as having something to say, and partly by drawing at the same time as talking. In line 12, #1, wanted to tell the concept of the game, and did not care about the groups concern being much more practical.

3.5 Physical Space Matters

The following excerpts, excerpt 5-7, will illustrate how the use of the corner area and the main workspace led to creative dialogue. In the second session Group 1 works on sketching scenarios, making storyboards, and discussing design solutions. They have started to discuss their scientific knowledge about the "Big bang", when oxygen and water were formed, and the first life occurred. After about ten minutes at 1h 21min the woman suggests that they should search for information by their own now, instead of speculating about the theories, and be "a bit effective". They divide the topics between them, and search individually for information. #1 sits in the corner by herself, relatively isolated from the group.

Excerpt 5. Group 1, session 2. Using the backdoor in collaborative work.

Time 1.27.38	Person	Transcript of interaction	Characteristic of action
1	#1	[laughs] "[Inaudible] I found out what we need to have, we need to have this Dynamite Harry[5] when he says 'What a damn bang'".	Sits in the corner and searches for information
2	#2	[laughs and mumbles something inaudible]	Searches information on the right Smart board. Sits with the back towards #1 and looks at the screen.

Only #2 react clearly to #1s idea. It seems like the idea is found funny, but inappropriate, and left without notice except for #2s laughter. The woman who is still sitting in the corner tries once more to present the idea, now referring to Dynamite Harry as the main game character's father. Once again it is mainly #2 who reacts, and once again by laughter. Soon thereafter #3 responds, but not aimed towards #1 but rather towards the others around the interactive table. Now #4 responds.

Excerpt 6. Group 1. Continuation of excerpt 5. Using the backdoor in collaborative work.

Time 1.30.06	Person	Transcript of interaction	Characteristic of action
9	#3	"His father should be Einstein"	Searches information on the laptop.
10	#4	"Why?"	Reads a scientific magazine.
11	#3	"Who else could build a time machine?"	Searches information on the laptop.

The topic of Dynamite Harry fades and is left, and they individually continued to search for information. About 30 minutes later #1 joins the group around the interactive table. The others are discussing sketches that #4 is drawing. They discuss "Big Bang" and some wild ideas in order to make "Big Bang" interactive.

Excerpt 7. Group 1. Continuation of excerpts 5 and 6. Using the backdoor in collaborative work.

Time 2.07.25	Person	Transcript of interaction	Characteristic of action
22	#2	"Yeah, [Big bang] is not such an interactive concept"	Sits down. Looks at #1.
23	#1	"No. And since it didn't have anything to do with any dynamite men, while there were no dynamite men [inaudible]. No, but I kind of mean..."	Sits down. Looks at #2 and #4, back and forth.

[5] Dynamite Harry (*in Swedish:* Dynamit Harry) is a comedy character in Sweden that together with his two partners try to do coups. A typical Harry statement is "What a damn bang!" (*in Swedish:* "Vilken djävla smäll!").

24	#2	"But..."	Looks at #1.
25	#4	"I found the dynamite was pretty funny. I've found the dynamite pretty funny, in fact, personally, I have to say. It was a pretty funny thing. But exactly that... eh... eh... but I just thought if we can get a scenario..." [laughs]	Stands between the interactive table and the left Smart board, and looks at the group members.

Here, #1 rejects her own idea about Dynamite Harry. In the context of the discussion and the seriousness of the subject it may have felt a bit inappropriate. But now #4 is following up on the idea even though he did not respond to it before or in any other way tried to hang on to it since it was first mentioned. The discussions continue about the game, and it slowly moves to sketching the scenario. The final product, the "Spaceflower", has in some ways inherited aspects of the Dynamite Harry character, although transformed to a professor.

One important characteristic of the corner area is to provide with an area where one can be alone and concentrate on an idea that is only loosely dependent on the general work. At the same time, as experienced by the other group, there is a reluctance to sacrifice the possibility to be within the group. Physical space matters when it concerns getting ideas into the discussions immediately, but this does not mean that a great influence cannot be made in the joint group work. This kind of backdoor creativity is interesting as it shows how even peripheral, in a physical sense, team members are contributing to the teams overall creative work.

4. Discussion

Traditionally the concept of creativity has been regarded as a property of an individual mind. One point of departure in this paper was that instead of looking on the concept of creativity in this traditional sense it could be regarded as *"...a set of functional relations distributed across person and context, and through which the person-in-situation appears knowledgeably skilful"* [2, pp. 174]. It is therefore further suggested that an important goal for educators, designers, etc., should be to provide with environments and contexts through which talented and creative interactions can emerge.

Once again we can see that merely providing people with the appropriate technological tools is not enough in trying to reach this goal. Of course, artefacts of various kinds are part of the individual-environment transaction but the context is set by so much more. As exemplified by Barab [2], the experience from acting in particular socio-cultural contexts has natural consequences for being able to predict and understand what is expected in taking part in certain activities. This of course also concerns experience from interacting with and making use of artefacts of various kinds. Thus, the socio-cultural context, the physical space in which the work is carried out, artefacts and the task to be solved are all part of the individual-environment transaction and put natural restrictions on possible actions. With the concept of backdoor creativity we like to move beyond the traditional conception of individual creativity, as well as beyond creative negotiation between peers, to analyze the hap hazardous creativity of semi structured group collaboration. Backdoor creativity embrace the mundane forms of creativity were we get inspired by almost anything in our surroundings in order to make something new.

The interactive space is relatively unconstrained, and the design task the groups were assigned to is also relatively unconstrained. Although we can see some general pattern of how ideas are processed within the interactive space we will here try to present it in some phases connected to Shneiderman's genex [17]. The first phase included an unaided discussion between the team members. Ideas were swapped, criticized, negotiated until some general stance of the idea had been agreed upon. The next phase was when the team members worked by themselves. It seems as if this phase was very much based on individual preferences in choosing how to fulfil the idea. We have seen how some individuals sketched by themselves, others collected information through different information carriers, and sometimes peers who discussed the idea in a subgroup. The third phase consisted in interruption of individual, or sub-group, work; this might be seen as a kind of sub phase. It is constituted by that one individual presented the others with some found information more or less related to the first agreed upon idea. Sometimes these kinds of interruptions were presented as jokes. Regardless of whether the interruption was relevant for the task it was presented in a collective manner, either as speech or by sending the information to a public screen. The fourth phase was to present individual work to the group. This phase often started with presenting information on a public screen but then slowly got more unaided and finally became a general discussion. Then the cycle started all over again. The deeper the group got into a design frame the quicker the cycles and also the more focussed the comments. What we would like to see is some form of aid for collecting ideas and putting them up in a goal-tree or mind-map. Today as it is the users have to come up with some kind of idea and representation of how to collect and depict ideas and goals by themselves, some of these ideas have been discussed in Prante et al. [13].

The observations made in the study support the conclusion that the environment as it is designed today allow group members to work and express themselves and contribute to collaborative group work in different ways. We have tried to portray creativity in mundane teamwork where the task is to collaborate and make an innovative product and seen how people make use of each other for support, idea generation and criticism. We have called those practices of collaborative creativity backdoor creativity, as a way to metaphorically talk about creativity as an interactive effort between a group of designers and a peripheral team member. In this study we have seen that even as a peripheral group member, physically located at another place than the rest of the group, it is possible to influence the work. But not only is it still possible to contribute to the design process, this also provides a possibility to work with a stronger focus on own work without being excluded from the joint activity.

Even if the main entrance, in both concrete and metaphorical terms, is used for the elegant guests, the backdoor is much more often used for mundane and everyday situations, but also as an escape exit when one is trapped in ones own mind – just as creativity can be, and often is, a collaborative effort rather than exclusive for exclusive people. A future step to take is to conduct a more focussed and detailed analysis of the data with a focus on particular parts or artefacts in the environment. For instance, the use of the interactive wall displays, and the use of the backdoor, providing a possibility for creative contribution to the collaboration as a whole. Based on results from these analyses, aspects identified having the potential to support or strengthen creative interactions will be focussed and recommendations for system design will be made.

Acknowledgement

This work was in part sponsored by the Wallenberg Global Learning Network through the iSpaces Project (partners in the project are Royal Institute of Technology and Stanford University). The Wallenberg Foundation has financed the equipment in the interactive space. Finally we want to thank Maria Croné at DSV, who participated as systems designer and in conducting the study.

References

[1] Artman, H., Persson, M. (2000) Old Practices - new technology: Observations of how established practices meet new technology. In: R. Dieng, A. Gibson, L. Kersenty, G. De Michelis (eds.) *Designing Cooperative Systems*. p. 35-49. Amsterdam: Ios Press Ohmsha.

[2] Barab, S., & Plucker, J. A., (2002). *Smart People or Smart Contexts? Cognition, Ability, and Talent Development in an Age of Situated Approaches to Knowing and Learning*. Educational Psychologist, 37(3). Lawrence Earlbaum Associates, pp 165-182.

[3] Brown, J. S, Collins, A., & Duguid, P., (1989). *Situated cognition and the culture of learning*. Educational Researcher, 18 (1), pp. 32-42.

[4] Chaiklin, S., & Lave, J., (Eds.) (1993). *Understanding Practice: Perspectives on activity and context*. Cambridge, England: Cambridge University Press.

[5] Fischer, G. (2000). Shared Understanding, Informed Participation, and Social Creativity – Objectives for the Next Generation of Collaborative Systems. In: R. Dieng, A. Gibson, L. Kersenty, G. De Michelis (eds.) *Designing Cooperative Systems*. p. 3-16. Amsterdam: Ios Press Ohmsha.

[6] Hutchins, E., (1993). Learning to navigate. In: J. Lave & S. Chaiklin (Eds), *Understanding Practice: Perspectives on activity and context*. Cambridge, England: Cambridge University Press, pp.35-63.

[7] Johanson, B., Ponnekanti, S., Sengupta, C., Fox, A. (2001), "Multibrowsing: Moving Web Content Across Multiple Dis plays", In *Proceedings of Ubicomp 2001*, Atlanta, Georgia.

[8] Jordan, B. and Henderson A. (1995), Interaction Analysis: Foundations and Practice, *The Journal of the Learning Sciences* 4(1). 39-103. Lawrence Erlbaum Associates, Inc., 1995.

[9] Malone, T.W., Crowston, K. (1990), What is co-ordination theory and how can it help designco-operative work systems. In *Proceedings of Computer Supported Co-operative Work (CSCW90)*, pp. 357-370.

[10] Mark, G., Kobsa, A. and Gonzalez, V. (2002), "Do four eyes see better than two? Collaborative versus individual discovery in data visualization systems", in *Proceedings of IEEE Sixth International Conference on Information Visualization (IV'02)*, London, July 10-12, 2002. IEEE Press, pp. 249-255.

[11] Pea, R., (1993). Practices of distributed intelligence and designs for education. In: G. Salomon (Ed), *Distributed Cognitions: Psychological and Educational Considerations*. Cambridge, England: Cambridge University Press, pp. 47-87.

[12] Pomerantz, A. & Fehr, B.J. (1997) Conversation Analysis: An Approach to the Study of Social Action as Sense Making Practices. In van Dijk, T. A. (Ed) *Discourse as Social Interaction*. London: Sage Publications, pp. 64-91.

[13] Prante T., Magerkurth C., Streitz N., Developping CSCW tools for idea finding – Empirical results and implications for design, *Proceedings of CSCW'02*: New Orleans: Louisiana, USA, 2002, p. 106-115.

[14] Reddy, M. (1979), *The conduit metaphor*. In A. Ortony, (ed.). *Metaphor and thought*. Cambridge University Press. Cambridge, pp. 284-324.

[15] Salomon, G., (Ed.) (1993). *Distributed Cognitions: Psychological and educational considerations*. Cambridge, England: Cambridge University Press.

[16] Schmidt, K. & Bannon, L. (1992) Taking CSCW seriously. Supporting articulation work. In *Proceedings of Computer Supported Co-operative Work (CSCW99)*, 1, 7-47.

[17] Shneiderman, B. (2000), "Creating creativity: user interfaces for supporting innovation", *ACM Transactions on Computer-Human Interaction (TOCHI)*, Volume 7, Issue 1, March 2000.

[18] SMART Technologies: http://www.smarttech.com. URL last checked November 5th, 2003.

[19] Streitz, N.A., Geißler, J., Holmer, T., Konomi, S., Müller-Tomfelde, C., Reischl, W., Rexroth, P., Seitz, P., and Steinmetz, R. (1999), " i-LAND: An interactive Landscape for Creativitiy and Innovation", in *Proceedings of ACM Conference on Human Factors in Computing Systems (CHI '99)*, Pittsburgh, Pennsylvania, U.S.A., May 15-20, 1999. ACM Press, New York, 1999, pp. 120-127.

[20] Vass, M., Carroll, J. M., and Shaffer, C. A. (2002), "Supporting Creativity in Problem Solving Environments", in *Proceedings of the fourth conference on Creativity & cognition*, Loughborough, UK, October 13 - 16, 2002, pp. 31 – 37.

[21] Weiser, M. (1991), "The Computer for the 21st Century", *Scientific American*, vol. 265, pp. 94-104.

[22] Werle, P., Kilander, F., Jonsson, M., Lönnqvist, P. and Jansson, C. G. (2001), "A Ubiquitous Service Environment with Active Documents for Teamwork Support", in *Proceedings of Ubicomp 2001*, Atlanta, Georgia.

[23] Winograd, T. & Flores, F. (1986,) Understanding computers and cognition: A new foundation for design. Norwood, NJ: Ablex.

Cooperative Systems Design
M. Zacklad et al. (Eds.)
IOS Press, 2004

Regulating Prominence: A Design Pattern for Co-located Collaboration

Mattias ARVOLA and Anders LARSSON
Dept. of Computer and Information Science, Linköping University
SE-581 83 Linköping, Sweden
{matar, andla} @ida.liu.se

Abstract. Co-located people do things individually while participating in collaboration. It is, however, difficult for designers to foresee what they will do individually and what they will do jointly. Participants therefore need to be able to move any information object between private and public states, but that is cumbersome to do with objects confined to a traditional PC-based workstation. This paper describes a design pattern, which addresses the problem. Designers can resolve it by making a platform where users can regulate how prominent they want to make information for themselves and others. The pattern is based on field studies and design work in three different settings where desirable use qualities were identified, categorized and translated into forces in a design pattern. Conflicts between forces were noted as problems, and solutions were sought to establish a pattern. A multiple-device platform was finally derived from the pattern to provide an example of how it can be realized. It is concluded that use qualities from a qualitative analysis of technology usage can provide the empirical basis for a design pattern. This fits well with several traditions within HCI and CSCW such as ethnographically informed design, scenario-based design, and design space analysis.

Keywords: Design Patterns, Use Qualities, Co-located Collaboration, CSCW

1. Introduction

Users of technology need to move fluently between working in their individual ways and working collaboratively according to their communicative practices, but doing so may not be straightforward [1]. An example of one such situation is consultation meetings where clerks explain something and swivel their screen towards their customers [2, 3]. In human-computer interaction (HCI) and computer-supported cooperative work (CSCW), there has been a limited amount of research that has focused on systems that are *both* individually and jointly used [e.g. 2, 3, 4, 5]. This paper presents a design pattern for systems that are used within small face-to-face groups and often switch between individual and joint use. Not all individuals in such situations can be considered to be primary users all the time, but the presence of others influence the primary user's usage and the others are influenced in return.

There are several approaches to designing software for use in face-to-face situations. There are electronic meeting room systems that assist co-located collaboration. Examples include different kinds of electronic whiteboards [6], large shared displays [7, 8], and entire meeting rooms [4, 9, 10, 11]. There are also Single Display Groupwares, which enable shoulder-to-shoulder collaboration by means of simultaneous parallel input to a single shared display [12]. Most of the systems designed to support co-located groups have focused on joint use alone. With multiple-display solutions people have, however, the opportunity to work individually as well as jointly with the system. Such systems enable co-located users to work privately on an individual screen, such as a handheld computer, and they also allow them to share information on a public screen, and choose what to do on the big shared screen and what to do on the small private screen [13]. Interfaces for such software are distributed over several devices have been called distributed interfaces within the field of ubiquitous computing [14]. One such distributed interface is SHAREDNOTES, which is designed by Greenberg, Boyle and LaBerge [15]. They enforced a strict difference between public and private, where notes could be either completely private for individual use or completely public for joint use but nothing in between. It did not work very well and instead they recommend a design that allows users to fluidly shift between private and public work, including the many gradations in between. They ask for more research into the issue and the aim of this article is to make a clear statement of the important dimensions of the problem to allow designers to assess the impact on their specific design situation. This is achieved by presenting the results in the form of a design pattern for co-located cooperative systems. An additional aim is to illustrate how design patterns can be used for documenting design knowledge, hence contributing to a growing body of design patterns within CSCW [16, 17, 18]. This is accomplished by moving from studies of cooperative activities to actual design of a computer system through a design pattern.

2. Theoretical Background

During the seventies Alexander and his colleagues [19, 20] developed the concept of *design patterns* as a reaction against the kind of architecture that had been built within the modernist tradition. He felt that many of the immeasurable qualities of architecture had been lost. The Alexandrian patterns strive for making architecture come alive, and this, Alexander argues, happens when all the conflicts between different forces—wants, needs, and fears—that exist in a specific design situation are resolved. In this paper, forces are seen as potentially conflicting, but still desirable qualities in the usage of an artefact. These *use qualities* can be expressed in the form of adverbs, adjectives or descriptively used nouns like 'effectiveness', 'elegance' or 'integration' [21, 22, 23]. Each design solution can then be assessed in relation to these use qualities, for example as claims in scenario-based design [24].

Every design pattern describes a re-occurring problem, its context, the forces that are at play in the situation and a generic solution to the problem. The feature that solves the problem is written in a generic but concrete way, so that it can be designed in an infinite number of ways, but still is readily identifiable. Anyone should be able to see if a design solution has a particular feature or not. In a well-written pattern, every reader should also readily recognize the problem.

All patterns can be seen as working hypotheses; a pattern represents the current understanding of what the best arrangement is for solving a particular problem. For this reason, it is important that the pattern is clear, sharable, and debatable. Alexander and his team used an asterisk after the pattern name to indicate the degree of faith they had in the pattern. No asterisk meant that it was a tentative formulation of a pattern; one asterisk was that it was fairly stable; and two asterisks meant that it was very well supported.

Within HCI, a number of different formats for writing patterns have been suggested [e.g. 25, 26, 27], but we have, like Junestrand et al. [16], chosen to present the pattern in Alexander's original style, since his patterns are more alive and concrete than other patterns. We have, however, chosen to label the different parts of the pattern for clarity of reading. A more formal style would have provided more overview and ideally one would write patterns in two versions: one comprehensive for inspiration and evidence and one formal for overview and connection to other patters. A comprehensive version is presented in this paper. The descriptive form of patterns that Martin et al. [17, 18] advocate in their PoInter patterns, include vignettes that are real examples from their own and other's ethnographic fieldwork. We have instead chosen to extend the description of empirical material behind the identified the forces. The PoInter patterns do not provide the concrete solutions to concrete problems that interaction designers often seek for.

3. Method

The overarching research method is a qualitative collective case study [28] where three settings of co-present use of computers are compared: a professional setting (customer meetings at banks), an educational setting (interaction design education in a studio), and a leisure setting (home entertainment and information). The empirical work in these cases includes meeting all in all 49 informants during 41 observation and semi-structured interview sessions ranging from one to four hours, and 14 half-day workshops. The written up and transcribed field-notes were read and re-read by several researchers and expressions describing how it was or should be to use an artefact in that situation were marked (i.e. adjectives, adverbs and descriptive noun phrases). Descriptive qualities were transformed into prescriptive qualities (e.g. 'difficult to go between systems' turns into 'seamless tool integration'). The qualities were then categorized, and thematically organized into more abstract use qualities. Finally they were anchored in the empirical material to make sure that nothing had been lost in the abstraction. Conflicts between desirable use qualities were especially noted since they form a basis for the problem statement in design patterns in terms of conflicting forces. Finally, we tried to identify features of situations where the use qualities were not in conflict in order to find a solution to the problem. Two prototypes were built within the leisure case to elaborate the use qualities and patterns in interpretative iterations.

3.1 Procedure in the Professional Setting

The main focus of the studies conducted at the bank was to identify use quality requirements for a teller system, and to model and develop an online course in using the teller system (see [21] and [23] for other accounts of this study). In total, 35 to 40 hours of workshops, and 30 hours of observation and situated interviews were conducted.

The use of the teller system was modelled in 14 workshops at the bank. Several tentative models of use quality were developed and a new course in using the teller system was designed. The participants included two active researchers functioning as usability experts and interaction designers, a project leader at the bank, a bank employee who had developed a previous online course for the teller system, and a developer who had implemented that course. In addition, five clerks at four branches were tracked during two half-days at work. The researcher took part of their work, took notes, and asked questions. In total, 30 hours of observation let us learn more about their work and allowed us to ask probing questions about episodes that took place. Finally, interpretative workshops were conducted. A project team at the bank analyzed the transcribed field notes from the interviews and the observations during three 3-hour workshops. They were three learning developers and three in-house system developers that all had experience from bank work. One researcher facilitated the workshops while another researcher took notes and handled the video camera. Our own analysis was also informed by the interpretations made in these workshops.

3.2 Procedure in the Educational Setting

A focused field study in an interaction design studio at a Swedish university was conducted. The specific research focus was on events where students used resources individually and then jointly, and then back again to individual use. In an e-mail questionnaire, the students in the design studio were asked to answer when the work in the studio was most fun and when it was most tiresome and boring. The reason for this questionnaire was to get an idea about what the students cared about when they were in the studio. This set the frame for further observations. Five out of six students answered the questionnaire. During the course of one design assignment, a researcher worked in the studio by a desk, and did situated interviews as well as observation. Interviews were conducted as the opportunity arose in the observation and they were triggered by events that took place. A total amount of 20 hours was spent on observing the work of the six students and the two teachers, and field notes were continuously taken. The researcher investigating the studio had also taken classes in a similar studio a few years earlier and had also teaching experience from courses based on studio work.

3.3 Procedure in the Leisure Setting

Two interactive television (iTV) prototype systems have been developed (see [29, 30] for further details), and as part of that work, interviews have been conducted, both situated in actual homes and in simulated home environments after trials of the prototypes.

The situated interviews conducted in homes were made as technology tours [31], where people were asked to show and tell what technology they have and how they use it, or do not use it. In total, 56 hours of technology tours were made in eight homes. Field notes were taken during all interviews and most of them were audio recorded (some informants did not want to be recorded). Two informants were academics in their late twenties, three of them were middle aged with children who had left home, and four were elderly.

During tests of prototypes, 21 users were observed and interviewed afterwards about their experiences. All users were in their twenties. In total, 7–8 hours of observations and semi-structured interviews were made during these tests. They took place in environments that looked like somebody's home but apparently were not, since they were located in an office building. The first prototype was a quiz game and the second was an on-demand news service, which utilized two remote controls for simultaneous input. One initial session was also held with three participants that surfed online news with one remote control. Field notes were taken during all observations and interviews, and six of the ten sessions were audio or video recorded. The sessions lasted 30 minutes up to one hour.

4. The Professional Setting: Customer Meetings at Banks

In customer meetings at the bank, a consulting clerk and one or two customers met together in the clerk's personal office. The clerk used a PC with the screen turned away from the customers, and both customer and clerk utilized pen and paper. Their objectives were to get the customer's finances in order and perhaps make changes. The clerk also wanted to keep a good relation to the customer and make profit for the bank. A meeting was usually prepared in advance so that the clerk could guess what it would be about. The clerk printed out the forms, the information and the documents that probably would be necessary to go through together with the customer and placed them on the desk in full view for the customer. He or she often turned to the PC in order to get the latest information about interests and similar figures and sometimes the clerk would have to do extensive input to the system. The collaboration was to a high degree controlled by the clerk, but questions and requests from the customer usually led their cooperative activity in unanticipated directions. In order to be efficient and not keeping other customers waiting, the clerks often had parallel customers on-screen; preparing one customer while waiting for another. During meetings, clerks switched rapidly between different systems and tools.

5. The Educational Setting: Interaction Design Education in a Studio

Six to eight students worked together in the interaction design studio. They had their own PCs and their own desks, which were covered with sketches and personal items. Two design teachers were occasionally in the studio. The students could see and overhear each other and cooperate at the whiteboard, at the table, or at someone's desk. The whiteboard was also used for projection from a shared PC.

The students were there to design, deliver before the deadline and learn design by doing, reflecting and discussing. They also wanted to have fun and enjoy one another's company, while experiencing a flow of creativity in the group. Sometimes the students considered the studio to be too noisy. The teachers wanted to see every student's abilities and skill to find ways to strengthen the student, as well as facilitating a creative and friendly atmosphere.

Both students and teachers could easily see what others were working on by glancing at the sketches and the printed screen shots that the students had on their desks. This provided a ground for unplanned interaction (see also [32] and [4]). Students also presented their work for each other and for the teachers more formally at the end of each design assignment. During these "critique and focus sessions" the teachers and the students probed the rationale for the solution as well as the process. The objective of the sessions was peer learning.

6. The Leisure Setting: Home Entertainment and Information

People usually watched television seated on the couch in the living room, unless they only had it turned on in the background while doing other things. In general, 75–80% of the time in front of the television is spent together with others [33].

The television screen was a natural focus of attention. A single remote control was used for interacting with the television set and the set-top box, but in the technology tours it was noticed that that there usually were other remote controls lying on the table. Informants reported that they often conducted other activities in front of the television screen; for instance chatting, eating, drinking, knitting, reading, or even surfing the Internet on a laptop. They had three overarching motives for spending time on the couch: taking it easy, being together, and/or getting entertainment and information. In the technology tours, it was observed that the television usually was placed in front of a wall. There was a table a couple of metres away from the television screen and on the other side of that table there was usually a couch. On one or both sides of the couch there could be room for an armchair. The remote control was lying on the table where it was accessible for everybody, near a person in the couch, or in someone's hand. Some larger living rooms had different parts for different kinds of activities, for instance a large dinner table, a small coffee table, or perhaps a desk or a bureau. In smaller apartments there was a bed or a sleeping alcove in the same room. The exact arrangement of the living room depended on the architecture of the home, on the activities that were undertaken in the room and on the generation that the residents belonged to.

While testing the iTV-prototypes it was noted that the remote control owner often spoke out aloud about what he or she was doing. If he or she did not, the other people in the couch had trouble following the interaction. The others regularly lost interest in what was going on the screen, and the remote owner sometimes excused him- or herself for extensive surfing. Occasionally the others in the couch told the remote owner what to do. When the remote owner felt that he or she could not decide what to do, the remote was usually handed over to another person. Sometimes the other person asked for the remote control. When the remote was lying on the table it was considered to be free for anyone to access and manipulate, but only if that person was an equal participant: a guest in a household could hesitate to reach for the remote if not invited.

7. Design Pattern: Regulating Prominence *

The analysis of the three case settings revealed four use qualities as desirable for all three settings: participation, autonomy, extemporaneity and politeness. Conflicts between the qualities were also identified, and this formed the basis for the forces and the problem statement. The solution statement is based on analysis of situations where the forces are not in conflict, trying to find some feature that resolves the potential conflict.

7.1 Introduction to the Pattern

People in COLLABORATION IN SMALL GROUPS [17] work jointly, but also individually. It is therefore important for in such situations to be able to control the objects of work and fluently move them between private and public states, including gradations between [15], but so far no pattern has shown how to do so. This pattern can be used to figure out the digital details of work places provided by Alexander et al [19] in INTIMACY GRADIENT (127), SMALL WORK GROUPS (148), HALF-PRIVATE OFFICE (152), and ALCOVES (179). The pattern also complements the PRIVATE AND PUBLIC DIGITAL SPACES (127b) [18].

7.2 Problem Statement

People in small groups do things individually while participating in collaboration. Hindering people to do so or excluding them from the joint activity can be quite impolite. In addition, it is rather difficult to foresee what objects participants will use for individual actions and what objects they will use for joint actions. Therefore, people need to be able to move objects between private states and public states, including gradations between, but this is cumbersome to do with information objects confined to traditional PC-based workstation.

7.3 Problem body

Users of personal technologies often meet and co-use their devices [34] and occasionally there is some form of public display available that can be used for joint purposes (such as a television screen or a monitor swiveled towards a customer). Collaboration would be of better quality if users could then easily move information objects between their personal technologies as well as to the public screen and back again. In the home, all devices such as stereos, televisions, PCs, tablet computers, etc. could be interconnected, and whenever a conflict between personal interests arises the information object could be moved to another device. Consider a scenario where someone wants to watch a show on the television screen while someone else is in the living room listening to music, the music could be moved to the stereo in the bedroom and the other person could go there and listen instead, or perhaps they, by a simple operation, could move it to the personal handheld music device instead. Alternatively, if someone watches a movie on a small screen in a bedroom it could easily be moved to the large screen in the living room if anyone else also wants to watch. Four forces in this situation (participation, autonomy, extemporaneity and politeness) are described below by a short theoretical statement, which then is exemplified from the fieldwork.

Participation. People who are co-present in a situation of use have some projects that they do together. Sometimes the projects are small, like a greeting for instance, and sometimes they are bigger, like watching television together. The feeling of participation is also important for the individual participants and it is one strong incentive to participate. Below follows an excerpt from field-notes illustrating participation in the leisure case where two informants played a quiz game on the television screen.

Isabelle: Let's go for that category again. It was good.

Lisa: Yeah, *right*!

Isabelle: It's two or three. Let's say the window-sill. ((Gives incorrect answer. Hands over the remote control.))

Lisa: ((Hits the dice by pressing the OK-button, moves and gets a question.)) Oops, this is embarrassing. ((Gives incorrect answer.)) *No!* ((Hands over the remote control.))

Lisa pretended to be bitter when she said: "Yeah, right!" The participants playing the quiz game were involved in a joint pretence [35]. Throughout the game, players pretended to be angry and said insulting things to the other player, who recognized that it was not serious and played along. However, the design of the quiz game sometimes made it unnecessarily cumbersome for the players to create this joint pretence. Since they sat side-by-side their attention was directed towards the screen three meters away, rather than towards each other. This meant that it took more effort for them to attend the other person. If the players did not keep the attention partly directed towards each other they could not see when the other invited to a joint pretence. This was suggested not only by what was being said, but also what was being done in terms of posture, gestures, and facial expressions.

One important thing for the participants in the leisure case was to spend meaningful time together. In the bank case the participative aspects of using interactive artefacts in the customer meetings were disclosed in several different ways. Firstly, many of the activities that took place before an actual meeting aimed at creating common ground and a structure for coordination in order to have a smoothly running meeting in the end. Secondly, participative actions were directed at shared and public objects in the meeting. Thirdly, an awareness of the progress of the meeting as a whole was maintained by having the physical layout of documents on the desk in the peripheral.

In the interaction design studio, participation included getting help, inspiration, and serendipitous input from others. For doing so students needed to share objects and coordinate their activities. Awareness of what others were doing was obviously important for coordination purposes. It was be maintained by having others' objects of work in peripheral vision and by overhearing.

Joint projects have joint goals, shared objects and shared representations. In order to work on these shared objects, participants need to establish common ground and to maintain coordination [36]. This means that they have a shared view on what they mean by different terms, what they want to achieve and how to achieve it. For that to work, they need to devote some of their attention to the other participants and what they do. The usage of an interactive artefact is participative when the actions performed by means of it are oriented towards shared objects for a joint goal. In Heideggerian terms, whenever there are co-participants around even the most seemingly individual and practical action is partly oriented towards the others as part of being-with them.

Autonomy. Here follows an excerpt from the field-notes in the studio case where Jack and John worked on a group assignment:

> Jack rolls with his office chair to his desk when they have divided the work. Then they work in silence. After a while Jack leans back and stares up into the roof. He changes position, and continues to write.
>
> Jack: How is it going? I'm like done now.
>
> He walks over to John and they discuss.
>
> Jack: Ehm, we'll do it like this then?
>
> John: Yeah.
>
> Jack: Should they do that exactly?
>
> John: Ehm, But… I've changed some minor things.

In this episode Jack and John worked autonomously when they needed concentration and focus. They divided the work and when the different parts were completed they worked jointly again. Before this episode the sat by the shared table, sketching together on a large piece of paper and before that they worked individually, trying to figure out how to approach the problem. Their group assignment had large portions of autonomous work.

In the leisure case, the autonomous parts of the co-present setting showed themselves in many ways. The interests of one person in the living room could be completely different from another person, but they still wanted to spend time together. This meant that one person could surf on the Internet or play computer games while the partner was watching television. If there was no room for autonomous actions they had to take turns, otherwise the passive participant could leave the room to do something else. This is also probably why people excused themselves for extensive surfing; they did something not very interesting to the other participants.

In the customer meetings at the bank, clerks had many autonomous activities running in parallel with the joint activity that they had together with the customer. For instance they constantly kept track of what consequences changes in the customers financial behaviour could have for the profitability of the customer. They did this by keeping an eye on their computer screen. Occasionally they instead devoted all their attention to the computer and minimal attention to the customer. At these moments they excused themselves and blamed the computer and the routines for their inattention to the customer.

In more general terms, participants in the co-present setting have private agendas and activities as well as joint goals and activities [35]. They want to perform autonomous actions unimpeded. Individual work is performed in parallel with joint work and it is either stemming from a personal interest, from using objects as tools for one's own mind, or from private agendas. Attention must, however, still be partly oriented towards others individual work so that they are not disturbed. In addition, actions that normally would be characterized as participatory, often serve individual ends as well.

Extemporaneity. At the bank we could observe how extemporaneity affected the use of the computer systems. Take, for example, the following excerpt from an interview:

> "It should flow between the systems. You often have to get information from many different places, and suddenly you think: 'Where the hell do I find that information?' That cannot happen in the meeting with the customer. [...] It's about trust!" (Clerk)

To avoid this from happening clerks worked autonomously preparing the next meeting and finishing the last, at the same time as a new customer entered the office. The clerk needed to show and explain things to come to an agreement with the customer during the meeting. The clerk hesitated, however, to use the clerk's private screen as a shared reference, since it was full of confusing figures and codes, it showed secret information about the previous customer and it displayed the profitability of the current customer. The clerks regularly handled this by printing out information that could be shared, jointly accessed, and jointly manipulated in the meeting. This solution was, however, inefficient since unanticipated information could be needed. To share the new information with the customer they could choose between turning the screen to the customer, telling the customer what the information was, or making a new printout. Turning the screen led to the problem described above. Using only words to tell the customer and not being able to show was difficult. Making a printout took too much time, and again, if the clerks did not attend the customer they were impolite.

In the home we could observe how the appliances sometimes switched rapidly between being a media with content in focus, a tool for carrying out an autonomous action without concern of other participants, and a common resource that fed topics into the social interaction. The co-present activity could take any turn and the usage of the technology changed according to that (see also [23]).

In the design studio the extemporaneity disclosed itself in the following way. The students and the teachers could easily see what others were working on by glancing at the sketches and the printed screen shots on the desks. The possibility to see what the others were working on provided a ground for unplanned interaction and chat about their work. This created an opportunity for help and inspiration. After these shorter periods of group work it went back to individual work again as noted above under autonomy.

Whenever people meet in dialogue the outcome is somewhat unpredictable and spontaneous [35]. What previously was private may therefore, in a serendipitous interaction suddenly be needed for joint actions. Since individual and joint activities run in parallel and feed into each other an impulse that change the activity can come from any direction or source. A joint activity can spur an individual trail of thought and action, and what someone else does individually can also do so. In addition, what someone does for him- or herself can feed into a joint activity.

Politeness. At the bank, one of the most important goals for the clerk in a customer meeting was to manage the customer relationship. As noted earlier: It is about trust. The clerks wanted to be trustworthy, they did not want to lose face and they did not want the customer to lose face either:

> "The customer must never feel that their situation is abnormal, that would make the customer uncomfortable." (Clerk)

Sometimes, however, the systems at the bank made it more difficult for the clerk to create a good relation to the customer, since they sometimes drove the clerk to more or less ignore the customer, which was regarded as quite impolite. The clerk had to make excuses and apologize in order to keep the equity in the meeting.

Similar things could happen in front of the television. For example when someone monopolized an appliance, he or she occasionally apologized for doing so. Some users were very keen to make sure that the others got to see or read what they thought was interesting. Another way that politeness was shown was that guests in the household would not take control over an application if not invited.

Politeness in the studio included not looking in other students' drawers and not touching others' belongings. One should also state critique in a nice way, while also being able to take critique. Other things that reflect politeness was helping someone who asked for help, respecting others' concentration, and not peeking over someone's shoulder if not invited to do so. It is important not to build computer environments that disrupt these norms.

In theoretical terms, the participants in a co-present setting have a mutual wish to maintain each other's face [37, 38]. Every participant has a claim to autonomy and do not want his or her individual actions to be impeded by others. The co-participants recognize this autonomy and do not want to impede on it. They also respect and want respect for their self-image and self-worth. Not doing so would be impolite and face threatening. When the participants set up a joint project they have to make a commitment to get some work done. Any act taken within that commitment will affect not only the public perception of the actor's self-worth and autonomy, but also that of the co-participants'.

Summary. People do things autonomously while participating in collaboration. They also have others in mind while performing individual actions. Some of these are publicly displayed so that other participants can monitor the actions peripherally and through that create an awareness of what is going on. Hindering people to do their own things or shutting them out from a joint activity can be quite impolite. It is quite difficult to foresee what objects participants will use for individual actions and what objects they will use for joint actions because of the extemporaneity of face-to-face conversation.

In everyday life, our focus is constantly shifting between different objects while other objects are kept in the background. When working on physical objects it is easy to manage the shifts by for instance moving a piece of paper 20 cm or by swiveling our chair [39].

Managing a constantly shifting focus in the stream of everyday activities is hard to do on virtual information objects with our current technology, since they are confined to a rather small, stationary and inflexible physical surface.

Therefore:

7.4 Pattern Solution

As shown in Figure 1, provide participants with a platform where they can work in parallel on private information objects that are prominent only to them and also work together on joint objects that are prominent to others. Create a mechanism for easily making objects more and less prominent for oneself as well as for every other participant so that an object can be prominent for one person while peripheral to others.

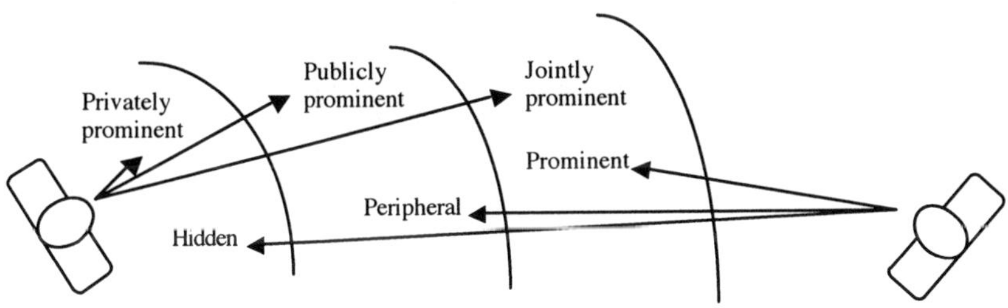

Figure 1. REGULATING PROMINENCE from the perspective of the left participant

7.5 Connections to Lower Level Patterns

It is likely that it takes several screens for the participants to run private activities in parallel. If privacy that is not necessary then a single big shared screen might work, but it would have to have a public area where all participants can work jointly on a prominent PUBLIC ARTIFACT [17], as well as a public area where they can work individually on objects that are prominent to them but peripheral to others, as with an ARTIFACT AS AUDIT TRAIL [17]. Such a division of the large screen can be made using TILED WORKING SURFACES [26]. A private surface on a otherwise shared screen would have to be hidden, for example behind tabs or a "hide-button" utilizing a STACK OF WORKING SURFACES [26], but that would not be a very elegant solution since a user have to turn the screen away, or ask the others to look away, in order to access that surface privately. This can be perceived as impolite to other participants.

8. Example of a Design Derived from the Pattern

REGULATING PROMINENCE can be realized in many different ways, but we wish to illustrate one way it can be implemented in a design. The LOCOMOTION system is a multimedia home platform derived directly from the pattern. It is based on two interconnected tablet computers and a PC with a large plasma screen, but other devices like mobile phones, handheld computers, personal video recorders and home-PCs can easily be integrated into the network. Users can move objects between the displays by a simple drag and drop. A user can tilt the tablet and make it peripherally public to the other in order not to not interrupt the other's activities. An object can be dropped on the drop-area for the plasma screen if a user wants to make an object prominent to the other. If one would want to make it really prominent to the other and also interrupt the others activity one can drop it on the other's tablet. Finally, if a user want to keep something hidden, the tablet can be tilted so that others cannot see the screen. In order to provide this, the system is built around a distributed event manager that allows the drop events to be transferred between different devices (see Figure 2).

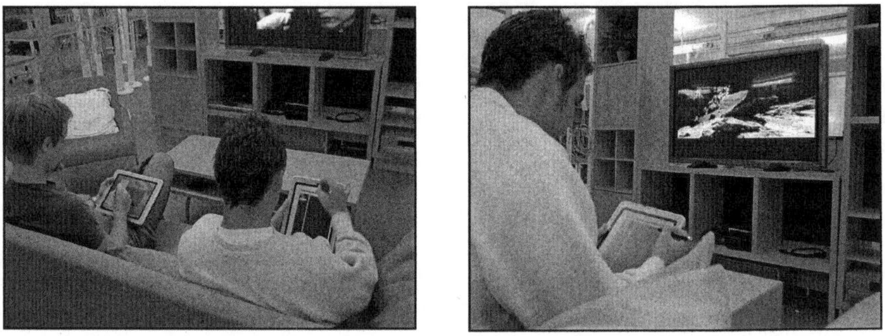

Figure 2: The current version of LOCOMOTION consists of two tablet computers and a PC with a plasma screen connected over the network.

LOCOMOTION is a distributed system consisting of two major sub-components; (1) a distributed event manager that allows system events to be transferred between devices over the network, and (2) a graphical system for representing the different devices connected together. It is built as a peer-to-peer system with no central server and this makes it easily adaptable to an ad-hoc network. It is implemented using the JAVA programming language, and the event manager uses a small protocol on top of TCP/IP. This approach allows the system to be language-independent in the graphical system, which in turn means that it is open to additional clients located on other types of device, such as PDA's or cell phones that do not support JAVA or high-level protocols.

9. Discussion

LOCOMOTION is an illustrative example of how one can implement a design solution based on the pattern REGULATING PROMINENCE. During the last five years several experimental systems have implicitly implemented, or have a potential to implement, the design pattern presented in this paper. One of them is the i-LAND environment, where different kinds of roomwares like the DYNAWALL, the COMMCHAIR, and the INTERACTABLE have been tested [11]. Another project which implements the pattern is the BLUESPACE workspace [40], which provides users with a number of different screens and display surfaces, including an EVERYWHERE DISPLAY projector, which allow users to display graphics on any surface of their choice. The DESIGN CONFERENCE ROOM, COLLABORATIVE CLASSROOM and RECONFIGURABLE COLLABORATION NETWORK [4] can also easily implement REGULATING PROMINENCE. Another way to implement it is to use occlusion on a digital table (see [41] for further discussion about digital tables). If the table knows where people are around it and where physical objects are on the table, it can display information so that one user can see it and not the other. One can also display information so that only people who know what to look for can see it [42].

There are, around us in our everyday life, different cooperative settings that implement this pattern to varying degrees. The counter in a shop is one such place where some parts of the desk belong to the shop assistant and some parts belong to the customer. The spatial properties of the desk provide natural surfaces for private, peripherally public and jointly public actions. We do, however, seldom meet computerized systems that work according to the pattern presented here. The ones that work include physical objects of work and not digital information objects. However, professional practices have overcome this limitation in cooperative process management like the underground line control [8, 43], and rescue management [44]. In these settings, the technical systems provide representations on both private and public work surfaces, and in order to make activities peripherally public the workers speak aloud and overhear each other.

The problem of information visibility and its control depicted in REGULATING PROMINENCE is applicable also to geographically distributed and partly to asynchronous collaboration, but the solution is not. Some kind of workspace is probably useful when trying to find a solution to the problem in distributed collaboration. In asynchronous work it would be advantageous to be able to leave information objects where you know others would find them, but since there is no immediate dialogue in such situations there is no extemporaneity and hence not the same need for fluid and seamless movement of objects.

Regarding the design methodology of design patterns, REGULATING PROMINENCE demonstrates that traditional qualitative analysis into categories of qualities-in-use of an artefact, can provide an empirical basis for forces in a CSCW or HCI design pattern. In the case of REGULATING PROMINENCE the forces are participation, autonomy, extemporaneity and politeness and these qualities have been grounded in empirical material. Conflicts between the use qualities were highlighted in a problem statement, and further analysis of situations that did not have the conflicts provided grounds for the solution statement of the pattern. This approach to documenting design knowledge fits well with current traditions in ethnographically informed design [45]. Use qualities as competing forces is not an entirely a new idea. One can trace it in the claims analysis of scenario-based design [24] as well as in the questions-options-criteria notation of design space analysis [46]. However, no previous research has made the explicit connection between desirable use qualities and design patterns.

A problem when generalizing over three very different cases to create a generic design pattern such as REGULATING PROMINENCE is that there is a risk to create a vague pattern since it becomes unspecific due to loss of detail. Design situations are unique situations and patterns should therefore be used with some care in a design process, contextual factors may have a very large impact on which design solutions that are appropriate. One should therefore read patterns as inspiration and reminders rather than as rules. Inexperienced designers will probably find them more rewarding to use than experienced designers will.

Several issues remain for future research. There is a large potential for scenarios to be used when describing forces in a design pattern to make the pattern and especially the conflicting forces come alive for a design team. In addition, it seems appropriate to relate the claims analysis in scenario-based design to the desirable use qualities in the situation, and hence to the forces in a design pattern. This is however only a working hypothesis at this time and future research on the issue is indeed welcome. Another direction for future research is to look into the efficacy of CSCW design patterns on actual design work in both educational and professional settings. One property of a well-written design pattern is that it is communicable and debatable and to be that it must be clearly stated. This should be empirically tested in practice.

9.1 Conclusions

The design pattern REGULATING PROMINENCE have demonstrated that the four forces participation, autonomy, politeness and extemporaneity can be in conflict with each other in co-located collaboration. The problem is that users need manage this conflict by moving objects between private states and public states, including gradations between. This can, however, be cumbersome to do with information objects confined to a traditional PC-based workstation. The solution is to provide users with a platform where they can regulate how prominent they want to make information for themselves and others. LOCOMOTION is one example among other systems that can implement this design pattern. A design methodological conclusion of this paper is that use qualities from a qualitative analysis of technology usage can provide the empirical basis for a design pattern. This fits well with several traditions within HCI and CSCW such as ethnographically informed design, scenario-based design, and design space analysis. Further research on exactly how to make the connection with scenario-based design is advocated.

Acknowledgements

We wish to thank others that have been involved in the work behind this paper: Stefan Holmlid, Magnus Rimbark and Patrik Ernfridsson. This research has been supported by The Graduate School for Human-Machine Interaction (HMI) and The Swedish Research Institute for Information Technology (SITI).

References

1. Baecker, R. M. (1993). The Future of Groupware for CSCW. In R. M. Baecker (Ed.), *Readings in Groupware and Computer-Supported Cooperative Work: Assisting Human-Human Collaboration.* San Mateo, CA.: Morgan Kaufmann Publishers, Inc.
2. Scaife, M., Halloran, J., & Rogers, Y. (2002). Let's work Together: Supporting Two-Party Collaborations with New Forms of Shared Interactive Representations. In M. Blay-Fornarino, A. M. Pinna-Dery, K. Schmidt, & P. Zaraté (Eds.), *Cooperative Systems Design: A Challenge of the Mobility Age.* Amsterdam, The Netherlands: IOS Press.
3. Rodden, T., Rogers, Y., Halloran, J., & Taylor, I. (2003). Designing Novel Interactional Workspaces to Support Face to Face Consultations. In *Proceedings of the CHI '03 conference on Human factors in computing systems.* April 2003, Ft. Lauderdale, Florida, USA.
4. Geisler, C., Rogers, E. H., & Tobin, J. (1999). Going Public: Collaborative Systems Design for Multidisciplinary Conversations. In *Proceedings of Cooperative Buildings: Integrating Information, Organizations and Architecture, CoBuild '99.* October 1–2, 1999, Pittsburgh, PA, USA.
5. Russel, D. M., Drews, C., & Sue, A. (2002). Social aspects of using large public interactive displays for collaboration. In *Proceedings of UbiComp 2002: Ubiquitous Computing. 4th International Conference.* September 29–October 1, 2002, Göteborg, Sweden.

6. Elrod, S., Bruce, R., Gold, R., Goldberg, D., Halasz, F., Janssen, W., Lee, D., McCall, K., Pedersen, E., Pier, K., Tang, J., & Welch, B. (1992). Liveboard: a large interactive display supporting group meetings, presentations, and remote collaboration. In *Proceedings of the CHI '92 conference on Human factors in computing systems: striking a balance*. May 3–7, 1992, Monterey, CA, USA.
7. Dourish. P., & Bellotti, V. (1992). Awareness and coordination in shared workspaces. In *Proceedings of Computer Supported Cooperative Work '92*. October 31 – November 4, 1992, Toronto, Ontario, Canada.
8. Garbis, C. (2002). Exploring the openness of cognitive artefacts in cooperative process management. *Cognition, Technology, and Work (2002) 4*, 9–21.
9. Stefik, M., Foster, G., Bobrow, D. G., Kahn, K., Lanning, S., & Suchman, L. (1987). Beyond the chalkboard: Computer support for collaboration and problem solving in meetings. *Communications of the ACM, 30 (1)*, 32–47.
10. Nunamaker, J. F., Dennis, A. R., Valacich, J. S., Vogel, D. R., & George, J. F. (1991). Electronic meeting rooms to support group work. *Communications of the ACM, 34 (7)*, 40–61.
11. Streitz, N. A., Geißler, J., Holmer, T., Konomi, S., Miiller-Tomfelde, C., Reischl, W., Rexroth, P., Seitz, P., & Steinmetz, R. (1999). i-LAND: An interactive landscape for creativity and innovation. In *Proceedings of the CHI '99 conference on Human factors in computing systems: the CHI is the limit*. May 15-20, 1999, Pittsburgh, PA, USA.
12. Stewart, J., Bederson, B. B., & Druin, A. (1999). Single-display groupware: A model for co-present collaboration. In *Proceedings of the CHI '99 conference on Human factors in computing systems: the CHI is the limit*. May 15–20, 1999, Pittsburgh PA, USA.
13. Myers, B. A. (2001). Using Handhelds and PCs Together. *Communications of the ACM, 44 (11)*, 34–41.
14. Bång, M., Berglund, E., & Larsson, A. (2002). A Paper-Based Ubiquitous Computing Healthcare Environment. Poster presented at *UbiComp 2002: Ubiquitous Computing. 4th International Conference*. September 29 – October 1, 2002, Göteborg, Sweden.
15. Greenberg, S., Boyle, M., & LaBerge, J. (1999). PDAs and shared public displays: Making personal information public, and public information personal. *Personal Technologies, 3(1)*, 54–64.
16. Innestrand, S., Keijer, U., & Tollmar, K. (2001). Private and public digital domestic spaces. *Int. J. Human-Computer Studies, 54*, 753–778.
17. Martin, D. Rodden, T., Sommerville, I., Rouncefield, M., Hughes, J. A. (2002) *PoInter: Patterns of Interaction: a Pattern Language for CSCW.* Available at http://www.comp.lancs.ac.uk/computing/research/cseg/projects/pointer/pointer.html (last accessed 2003.11.11).
18. Martin, D. Rodden, T., Sommerville, I., Rouncefield M., Viller, S. (2001). Finding Patterns in the Fieldwork. In *Proceedings of ECSCW 2001*. September 16–20, 2001, Bonn, Germany.
19. Alexander, C., Ishikawa, S., Silverstein, M., Jacobson M., Fiksdahl-King, I., & Angel, S. (1977). *A pattern language: towns, buildings, construction*. New York: Oxford University Press.
20. Alexander, C. (1979). *The timeless way of building*. New York: Oxford University Press.
21. Holmlid, S. (2002). *Adapting Users: Towards a Theory of Use Quality*. Linköping Studies in Science and Technology, Dissertation No. 765. Linköping, Sweden: Linköpings universitet.
22. Howard, M. V. (2002). Supporting design for quality-in-use through abstract usability objectives. In *Proceedings of APCHI 2002, 5th Asia Pacific Conference on Computer Human Interaction*. November 1-4, 2002, Beijing.
23. Arvola, M. (2003). The Interaction Character of Computers in Co-located Collaboration In *People and Computers XVII – Proceedings of HCI 2003*. September 2003, Bath, UK.
24. Rosson, M. B., & Carroll, J. M. (1995). Narrowing the Specification-Implementation Gap in Scenario-Based Design. In J. M. Carroll (Ed.), *Scenario-Based Design. Envisioning Work and Technology in System Development*. New York, NY: John Wiley & Sons, Inc.
25. Granlund, Å., & Lafrenière, D. (1999). A Pattern-Supported Approach to the User Interface Design Process. In *Workshop report of UPA'99 Usability Professionals Association Conference*. June 29 – July 2, 1999, Scottsdale, AZ.
26. Tidwell, J. (1999). *Common ground: A pattern language for human-computer interface design*. Available at http://www.mit.edu/~jtidwell/interaction_patterns.html (last accessed: 2003.11.11).

27. Erickson, T. (2000). Lingua francas for design: Sacred places and pattern languages*. In *Proceedings of Designing interactive systems: processes, practices, methods, and techniques (DIS 2000),* New York, NY, USA.
28. Stake, R. E. (1994) Case Studies. In N. Denzin and Y. Lincoln (Eds.), *Handbook of Qualitative Research.* Thousand Oaks, CA: Sage.
29. Arvola, M., & Holmlid, S. (2000). IT-artefacts for Socializing: Qualities-in-Use and Research Framework. In *Proceedings of IRIS 23: Doing IT Together*, August 12–15, 2000, Lingatan, Sweden.
30. Rimbark, M. (2002). *Do's and Dont's in Applications for Co-surfing News.* Master's thesis, Linköpings universitet. LiU-KOGVET-D--02/02--SE. Available at http://www.ep.liu.se/exjobb/ida/2002/002 (last accessed 2003.11.11).
31. Baille, L., Benyon, D., Macaulay, C., & Pederson, M. G. (2003). Investigating Design Issues in Household Environments. *Cognition, Technology & Work, 5(1)*, 33–43.
32. Bellotti, V., & Bly, S. (1996). Walking away from the desktop computer: Distributed collaboration and mobility in a product design team. In *Proceedings of Computer Supported Cooperative Work '96*, Cambridge, MA, USA.
33. Ellegård, K. (2001). *Lockropen ljuder: Komhem.* Working paper ISRN LiU-TEMA-TWP-230-SE, Department of Technology and Social Change, Linköpings universitet. ISSN 1101-1289. Available only in Swedish.
34. Weilenmann, A. (2001). Negotiating Use: Making Sense of Mobile Technology. *The Journal of Personal and Ubiquitous Computing, Special Issue on Mobile Communication and the Reformulation of Social Order, 5 (2),* 137–145.
35. Clark, H. H. (1996). *Using Language.* Cambridge, UK: Cambridge University Press.
36. Clark, H. H., & Brennan, S. A. (1991). Grounding in Communication. In L. B. Resnick, J. M. Levine, & S. D. Teasley (Eds.), *Perspectives on Socially Shared Cognition.* Washington, DC: APA Books.
37. Goffman, E. (1967). *Interaction Ritual: Essays on Face-to-Face Behavior.* Chicago, IL: Aldine.
38. Brown, P., & Levinson, S. (1987). *Politeness: Som Universals in Language Use.* Cambridge, UK: Cambridge University Press.
39. Luff, P., Heath, C., & Greatbatch, D. (1992). Tasks-in-Interaction: Paper and Screen Based Documantation in Collaborative Activity. In *Proceedings of the 1992 ACM conference on Computer supported cooperative work.* October 31 – November 4, 1992, Toronto, Ontario, Canada.
40. Lai, J., Levas, A., Chou, P., Pinhanez, C., & Viveros, M. (2002). BlueSpace: personalizing workspace through awareness and adaptability. *Int. J. Human-Computer Studies, 57*, 415–428.
41. Scott, S. D., Grant, K. D., & Mandryk, R. L. (2003). System Guidelines for Co-located Collaborative Work on a Tabletop Display. In *Proceedings of ECSCW '03.* September 14–18, 2003, Helsinki, Finland.
42. Intille, S. S. (2002). Change blind information display for ubiquitous computing environments. In *Proceedings of UbiComp 2002: Ubiquitous Computing. 4th International Conference.* Göteborg, Sweden, September 29 – October 1, 2002.
43. Heath, C., & Luff, P. (1992). Collaboration and control: Crisis management and multimedia technology in London underground line control rooms. *Computer Supported Cooperative Work (CSCW), 1*, 69–94.
44. Artman, H., & Wærn, Y. (1999) Distributed cognition in an emergency co-ordination center. *Cognition, Technology & Work, 1*, 237–246.
45. Hughes, J., King, V., Rodden, T., & Andersen, H. (1994). Moving out from the control room: ethnography in system design In *Proceedings of the 1994 ACM conference on Computer supported cooperative work*, October 1994, Chapel Hill, NC.
46. Maclean, A., & McKerlie, D. (1995). Design Space Analysis and Use Representation. In J. M. Carroll (Ed.), *Scenario-Based Design. Envisioning Work and Technology in System Development.* New York, NY: John Wiley & Sons, Inc.

Cooperative Systems Design
M. Zacklad et al. (Eds.)
IOS Press, 2004

From actions to suggestions: supporting the work of biologists through laboratory notebooks

Marcello Sarini*, Enrico Blanzieri**, Paolo Giorgini**, Claudio Moser***
*Dipartimento di Informatica, Sistemistica e Comunicazione
Università degli Studi di Milano-Bicocca
Via Bicocca degli Arcimboldi, 8 – 20126 MILANO-ITALY
**Dipartimento di Informatica e Telecomunicazioni
Università di Trento
Via Sommarive, 14 -38050, Povo, TRENTO-ITALY
***Istituto Agrario San Michele all'Adige,
Via E. Mach, 1-38010 San Michele a/Adige (TN)-ITALY
email: sarini@disco.unimib.it, {blanzier, pgiorgio}@dit.unitn.it, claudio.moser@mail.ismaa.it

Abstract. The paper presents an approach and a technology to support the work of biologists in their laboratories. By means of analysis of related literature, informal discussions with people working in laboratory, and experience of one the authors with laboratory work in genomic research, we identified different biologists' information needs and different strategies in order to satisfy them. A relevant part of biologists' work practice is about the continuous annotation of their work in their personal notebooks. We claim that observing notebooks can boost a technology which is a generalization of recommendation systems and provides biologists with suggestions concerning their work. These suggestions are generated by combining the observation of biologists performed actions in the past with actions patterns incorporating biologists' work practices that are discovered by the system out of the transcriptions of biologists' notebooks.

1 Introduction

Computer Supported Cooperative Work (CSCW) is the art of providing meaningful mediations between sociality of people and technological support in cooperative work. One of the main CSCW issues is to understand what collaboration is about. There are various forms of collaboration (e.g., coordination, use of common shared resources) and different social mechanisms people developed in order to let collaboration happen, such as artifacts [1], protocols [2], awareness of information [3], definition of conventions [4], and negotiation of meanings [5, 6]. However, depending on the situation, these mechanisms may be not effective enough and possibly technologies may play a supporting role [7].

Traditionally, Knowledge Management (KM) focuses on knowledge as something that can be separated from the people who produced it. This view overlooks the central role of people interactions that enable members of communities, ranging from small groups to large organizations, to create and exchange different forms of knowledge. Again, the use of these forms of knowledge can be supported by proper technologies, when needed [8].

In both areas CSCW and KM, the introduction and use of technologies taking into account the consolidated work practices is a major concern.

The aim of our work is to provide a technology that supports people in performing their work and acknowledges the value of their work practices. Following an approach developed in Artificial Intelligence [9] and applied to Information Retrieval [10, 11], the proposed technology generalizes the concepts of Recommendation Systems [12] to arbitrary complex scenarios where users receive suggestions concerning their work. The level of support provided by the system is limited by the possibility of observing users actions and by the capability of the system in generating meaningful suggestions. In this view, the proposed technology deals with two critical issues. First, to collect the work practices related to a certain domain in order to make them shared by the members of a community; second, to orient the workers towards the fulfillment of their goals, still leaving them free to behave according to their own work practices.

In this paper the technology is applied to support the work of biologists in their laboratories. We think this field could greatly benefit from this technology due to the tension between the often implicit nature of biologists' work practices and biologists' heavy information needs. In fact, in order to properly carry out their work, biologists have to apply specific protocols, handle reagents and instruments but often the related practices are just in the scientists' minds and rarely are shared among them. An important source of information in biological laboratories is the laboratory notebook where biologists register the actions they perform during their work. In Nonaka's terms [13], this behavior leads to the *externalization* of scientists' tacit knowledge concerning their work practices. The system collects single scientist work practices, combines these pieces of knowledge converting it into patterns of actions performed by the scientists and makes them available to all of them as a mean to satisfy their current information needs. The information provided by the system then helps biologists *internalize* what they experienced, thus enriching their tacit knowledge.

The paper is organized as follows. The next two sections describe biological work inside laboratories. In particular the first one focuses on the nature of biological work, while the second one identifies biologists information needs in order to complete their work and discusses how these needs may be satisfied. The remaining sections present the solution we propose in order to support biologists in accomplishing their work.

2 The nature of biological work in the laboratories

Let us now consider the nature of biological work inside laboratories. The following description is the result of direct interactions with people involved in university laboratories, the experience of one the authors with laboratory work in genomic research, and the reading of related literature (see for instance [14]).

During their work, scientists manage materials and instruments in order to conduct experiments. In managing materials they have to find them when needed: this is not always easy since materials can be in use by others laboratory members at the same time or can have been stored in an unknown location. A good laboratory practice is also to check in advance if there are enough materials for running a specific experiment. The use of laboratory instruments is often complex because it requires experience and their ad-hoc tuning. Therefore, experiments have to be planned in advance combining the information about the needed material, for the instruments tuning, and also for the procedure to follow. A typical example is represented by a PCR (Polymerase Chain Reaction) experiment. This is a very common enzymatic reaction that is used in biological and medical research in order to amplify a specific DNA fragment.

A fundamental resource supporting laboratory work is the scientist's notebook. An individual notebook contains the record of everything a scientist does [15].

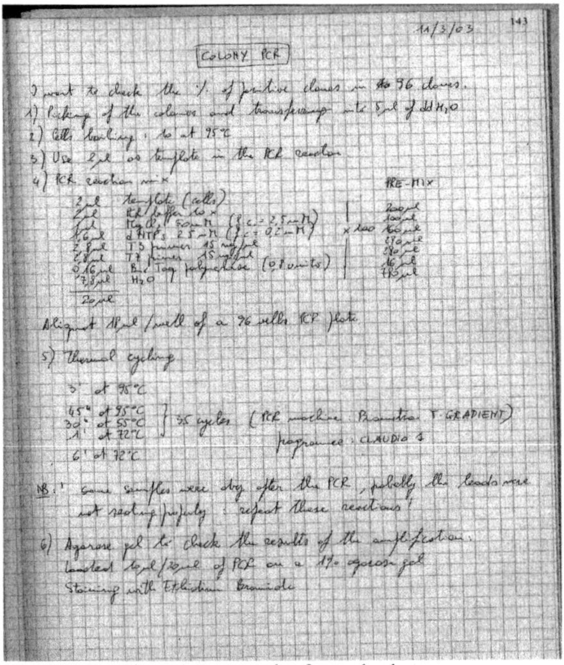

Figure 1: an example of a notebook page

Figure 1 shows an example of a laboratory notebook page reporting on a PCR experiment using a bacterial lysate (colony PCR). In the first row the main objective of the experiment is stated. Items 1 to 3 explain the procedure to prepare the bacterial lysate and specify how much of it has to be used in the PCR reaction. Item 4 lists all the components and the volume to be added in the PCR reaction mix specifying the concentration of each stock. Item 5 summarizes temperatures and times that will be used during the thermal cycling. This is the step where the amplification occurs. In item 5 is also reported an observation written after the thermal cycling was finished ("some samples were dry...") and a perspective for future work ("repeat those reactions"). Item 6 very briefly describes the analytical procedure used for checking the results of the PCR experiment.

Usually, scientists write on their notebooks the steps to go through in a detailed manner before to start the experiment which often is repeated several times introducing slight changes from one time to the other. A typical case is a PCR experiment performed for the development of molecular markers used in the construction of genetic linkage maps: several couples of primers are tested on the same or few types of genomic DNA templates. This implies that only the primers will vary among reactions while all the other reagents and also the actions to be performed will not change. According to this observation, the biologists designed a form (see Figure 2) which is an artifact reflecting the structure emerged in performing PCR experiments and which is used to organize biologists' work accordingly. This form, printed on a paper sheet, is filled according to the specific PCR experiment; it is then used like a recipe during the setting-up of the reactions and finally is attached in the lab-notebook.

Although notebooks are very personal they are consulted as a relevant support for the strict group of people who share the same interests. This is particularly true when an experiment is carried out involving different laboratory members in different times. In this case notebooks play the role of coordination artifacts [1] among the involved people, since they objectify the current state of the experiment and suggest the new actions to perform, according to the scientist's experience.

Progr.	
Taq. Pol.	
React. Vol.	
DNA Vol.	

Date	
Name	
Samples	

Primer		I	II	III	IV	V	VI	VII	VIII	IX	X	XI	XII
	1												
	2												
	3												
	4												
	5												
	6												
	7												
	8												

MIX :		
Rxs.	Single	Total
10XBuff.		
MgCl2		
dNTP		
P1		
P2		
Taq.		
water		

Comments

Figure 2: a form used by biologists for PCR experiments

3 Information needs in the laboratory scenario

The competence of one of the author in laboratory work allowed us to define a more precise scenario by focusing on scientist's information needs either to successfully complete her work or to understand why some performed experiments failed. These information needs are related to different aspects of ordinary working practices: *physical*, *scientific*, and *social*.

Physical aspects are about the use of materials which have to be found by the scientist while working in the laboratory. Different materials are stored in different places and it may be not easy for a scientist to find them at the right moment. As an example, consider that some reagents have to be stored in a freezer with a temperature of -80° C.

Scientific aspects are related to the knowledgeable practices of scientists in conducting their work: for instance, about successful and unsuccessful experiments, the proper tuning of instruments for specific experiments, and so on.

Social aspects concern the direct and indirect collaboration between people working in the laboratory. An example are the agreed upon conventions for keeping the laboratory notebooks making them easily consulted by other people.

Let us now consider different work situations in terms of information needs and in terms of required support to satisfy them.

Anna has just started working in the laboratory and she lacks experience in conducting her work. Since she needs some support, she looks for the experience accumulated by other scientists. She could ask her colleagues, but often they are either busy or out of the laboratory. She could also look in the notebooks of her colleagues, but there are two difficulties. The first one is to interpret the information found in the colleagues notebooks since they are organized according to their personal style and experience. The second one is to perform a "blind search" in the notebooks, without knowing a priori if the notebook may contain suggestions related to her current needs. To this aim, Anna needs an additional help since she could have not learned yet the conventions common to laboratory members for keeping their notebooks. However, due to her continuous presence in the lab, she is aware of the location of the materials she uses.

The situation is different for Paco, an experienced scientist, who is not always present in the laboratory but has a long experience of biological work. However, since he is not always present in the lab, he does not know where the materials he needs have been moved by other colleagues. Like in the case of Anna, it is sometimes problematic to ask other people also because he likes to attend the laboratory late in the evenings when nobody is there. To avoid wasting his time looking around in the shelves and fridges of the laboratory, Paco would like a support helping his search. On the other hand, due to his long working experience Paco could effectively help the other members of the laboratory by sharing the information reported in his notebook.

John attends the laboratory since a long time and usually he does not need any support. He is performing the same kinds of experiments since a long time, he knows where materials are, he has enough experience to perform his work, and he learned the conventions to compile the notebook. Due to his knowledge, he represents a useful source of information for the other colleagues. It is very important to recall here that although John does not need extra support to perform his work, nevertheless he actually provides information useful for the others. John's behavior, that might seem unrealistic (as it does not follow the logic of rewards [16]), is true in laboratory work, where the practice of compiling notebooks is part of the normal work. The reason is that laboratory work needs accountability, auditability and validability and these are achieved through the constant update of biologists' laboratory notebooks.

Summarizing the information issues in our scenario, scientists may need to get information about location of materials, action related to experiments, and sometimes about conventions for notebook compilation and use. There are different ways to collect this information either by asking colleagues or by consulting their notebooks. In the first case, problems may arise due to the different time schedules of the scientists in attending the laboratory. In the second case, either the searcher is not aware of the colleagues' notebooks contents or she is not able to interpret the collected information. The above considered problems are of the same nature: the need of collecting and sharing the valuable practices and the experiences of different scientists working in the lab. These problems may be solved in the same way by giving scientists the possibility to access this valuable knowledge and to get useful hints to complete successfully their experiments without waste of time and of personal budget.

4 Reading lab practices through Implicit Culture glasses

The concept of Implicit Culture [9] was introduced in Artificial Intelligence and in particular in the area of agents research. Implicit Culture is defined as the relation between two groups of agents such that the agents belonging to the second group behave consistently with the "culture" of the agents belonging to the first one. The technological counterpart of the Implicit Culture concept is a System for Implicit Culture Support (SICS) which is built upon collaborative filtering techniques. The system deals with arbitrary scenarios where users need suggestions concerning their work. In the scenario of biological work we considered, the system is used to support what is called in Nonaka's terms a *combination process* [13] to convert different bodies of explicit knowledge. In our proposal, this process concerns the reconfiguration of the knowledge the biologists embodied in their notebooks in terms of recurrent patterns of actions which the biologists performed during their work that the system discovers and makes available to biologists through the support it provides them.

Looking at the world with Implicit Culture glasses (and with SICS support) means that this world need to be observable, the actions need to be situated in a "computational" environment, along with the objects and the people involved in the actions.

Since our attention is focused on discovering the relation between actions performed by scientists in a laboratory and their information needs in order to support a biologist either to perform the next actions of an experiment or to better understand the causes determining the experiment failure, we adopt the same categorization we introduced above for the information needs, by distinguishing between *physical actions*, *scientific actions* and *social actions*.

According to the typology of considered action, different techniques may be used to observe and register the actions performed by biologists in the lab environment. Physical actions can be observed either tracking movements of objects in the lab with barcode like in the CyberFridge [17] or with surveillance technology using cameras along with object recognition techniques [18]. Scientific actions can be observed through the mediation of specific technology like Electronic Notebooks [19] or LIMS (Laboratory Informatics Management Systems) [20] which provide technologic frameworks where scientists can tune and control their experiments, but also of any technology supporting scientific production, like digital libraries and so on. Social actions are hardly observable from a technologic point of view except in particular cases where laboratory members are using a technology supporting collaboration and communication among them (like e-mail). However, usually biologists share the physical space of the lab and hence they rely on social mechanisms developed as a consequence of their co-presence.

5 The choice of notebooks as source of observation

There is a tradeoff between the ability to observe what happens in the laboratory and the richness of the support provided to scientists. Since notebooks are the main artifacts used by biologists to objectify work they perform in the laboratory, we focus on them in order to discover the relations among aspects that are relevant to scientists during their experiments. This information is then used to collect and make visible to biologists the practices encrusted in their notebooks. In this way, biologists are supported by the system during the conduction of their experiments maintaining a "peripheral awareness" [21] of their colleagues about performed actions and location of materials that would otherwise be invisible due to the implicit nature of their practices.

Protocols represent other kinds of artifacts that may be considered as biologists' reference for the practices related to the laboratory work. Biological protocols are written instructions that specify ingredients, equipments and sequence of steps for preparing and analyzing research materials [14]. Protocols may be either standardized procedures (in some cases sold by companies, in other cases provided as biological resources on the web [22] or collected in manuals) or hand-written procedures (codifying the experience accumulated by either a single scientist or inside a laboratory). Unlike [23], our focus is not on a technology designed to support workers in the execution of tasks associated to protocols. In fact as confirmed by observations of biologists' work in a laboratory and by related literature [14], usually actions reported in protocols are not slavishly executed by scientists but they are resources [24] which orient scientist in the completion of their work.

Instead, we focus on giving an indirect support to the scientists in deciding which actions to perform while "doing" the protocol [14]; actions may be suggested thanks to the visibility of laboratory practices. In fact, the latter may provide useful information about localization of materials, successful actions, and conventions to the scientists working in the same lab which may help scientists in performing actions.

We base our approach on the observation of notebooks and we argue this is feasible since notebooks are not totally unstructured due to the emerging of conventions related to their compilation as a consequence of the agreement among people working in the same laboratory. In the same vein Robinson et al in [21], base the reconstruction of processes related to work shifts in paper mill industries on diaries. The latter are artifacts and the reconstructed processes are artifact mediated processes.

The choice of notebooks as main source of observations implies requiring the scientists to do a technological shift from paper-based to electronic-based notebooks. In our opinion, this is not a critical issue for different reasons. First, experiments of PCR (like many others in a biological laboratory) are repeated several times introducing slight changes from one time to another and could therefore greatly take advantage from the use of electronic notebooks containing pre-defined working templates (as the one in Figure 2) and some kind of suggestions. Second, unlike the medical case where the shift from paper to electronic system becomes a critical issue due to the lack of a consolidated practice in compiling medical records as argued by Heath and Luff [25], in biological work the use of notebook is intrinsically related to the scientists' work practice. Accordingly, a wider set of Electronic Notebooks is proposed both commercially (see for instance The Gene Inspector by Textco Inc. [26] and E-Notebook by CambridgeSoft [27]) and in the research (see for instance [28]). A noticeable result of the research about electronic notebooks is represented by the Augmented laboratory notebook [29] which uses techniques of augmented reality to integrate the physical world of the biologists with a virtual one. Hence, the proposed notebook combines the flexibility of paper-based notebooks with the richness of computer supported information. In this way, the notebook is not disrupting the biologists' work practices due to its ability to correspond to its paper-based counterpart: for example it recognizes biologist's handwriting and adds the power of managing the biologists' information space at any place.

However, in our current research effort we did not choose any specific electronic notebook technology. From our point of view the choice of a specific technology is not a main concern. We advocate any technology allowing scientists to perform their work without disrupting their usual practices and leaving us the possibility to observe the biologists' transcriptions of the performed actions, including the related materials, machines used and people involved. Accordingly, we designed a first mock-up of the notebook interface focusing on the information which is possible to observe from transcriptions of biologists' work. This choice is motivated by the fact that we are interested in the information which is observable from the notebook and on how this information may be managed by the SICS technology to satisfy the biologists' information needs. In the next step, this initial mock-up will require further evaluation by the involved biologists and possibly a redesign by using other electronic notebook technologies as, for instance, the Augmented laboratory notebook described above.

6 Combining SICS with Electronic Notebooks

We consider two different scenarios of use of the proposed technology which are related to different phases of biologists' work. When a biologist is conducting an experiment, she has to perform actions in order to complete her work. When an experiment is completed it may result either in a success or in a failure according to the actions the biologists performed during the experiment. The support needed by the biologists changes according to these two different work situations. In the first case, during an experiment a biologist can not be able to perform the next action until a specific information need is satisfied. For instance before putting a reagent in the machine, the biologist has to know the reagent concentration or the temperature value to set. Or she needs to know how to proceed in her work, especially if she is a novice for the experiment she is running. The above situations require answers to the question "how can I proceed in completing the experiment?" and can be referred to in terms of "support for anticipation". In the second case, the scenario considers a biologist who completed an experiment. If the experiment failed she may like to know "why did it happen?". For instance she is interested in comparing her experience with the ones of other colleagues performing the same kind of experiment. What she needs is an "explanation of failure".

In the first situation the way to fulfill the current scientist's information need is to suggest a set of actions which, if performed, helps the biologist to answer the above questions. For instance, if the biologist finds a way know the needed concentration and the temperature value usually set for the procedure, she is able to continue her experiment. For what concerns the explanation of failure, the system helps the biologist in understanding the reasons of the failure. By suggesting the actions performed by colleagues in successful experiments of the same kind, the system allows the biologist to rethink her experiment by comparing the suggested actions with the ones she performed. Moreover, this learning process helps her to develop hypotheses about the failure of the experiment.

In this section we describe the architecture of a system that integrates Implicit Culture Support into an Electronic Notebooks (see Figure 3). The system takes into account the actions performed by the biologist in the physical space. Hence, the notebook of each biologist is the artifact which creates a link between the physical space where the biologists perform actions and the logical space where the system "observes" these actions. In order to simplify this flow of information, we designed a mock-up of the notebook interface which provides biologists with a semi-structure for keeping trace of the performed actions (see Figure 4). In the left part of the interface (see Figure 4), each action performed by the biologist is registered as a pair name of the action and set of parameters associated to it. Free text is then available for scientists in order to report personal annotations during the course of the experiment. Each action is then associated to a timestamp corresponding to the time of registration. In the right part of the interface (see Figure 4), the structure provided by the notebook makes it possible to register both the name of the scientist and the name of the experiments she runs. Moreover, since it is very important for a scientist to distinguish between successful and unsuccessful experiments, the notebook allows a biologist to register whether the experiment performed was successful or failed. The use of this semi-structure for registering scientific actions does not disrupt the biologists' practices of registering the performed actions in their notebooks since the semi-structure is flexible enough and reflects the structure of the performed actions that we observed in the paper-based notebook (see Figure 1). In fact, the considered semi-structure takes into account that each experiment has a performer, a name identifying it on the notebook pages, the date of execution, and that a biologist evaluates the results of the performed experiment also in terms of either success or failure. Moreover, it considers that a relevant part of the information reported on the notebook is about the actions she performed in order to complete an experiment with the associated values.

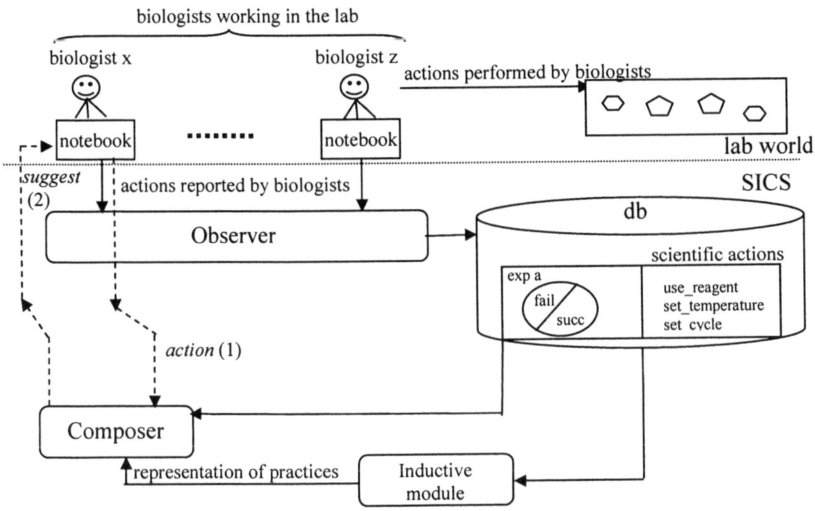

Figure 3: the SICS architecture in the laboratory scenario

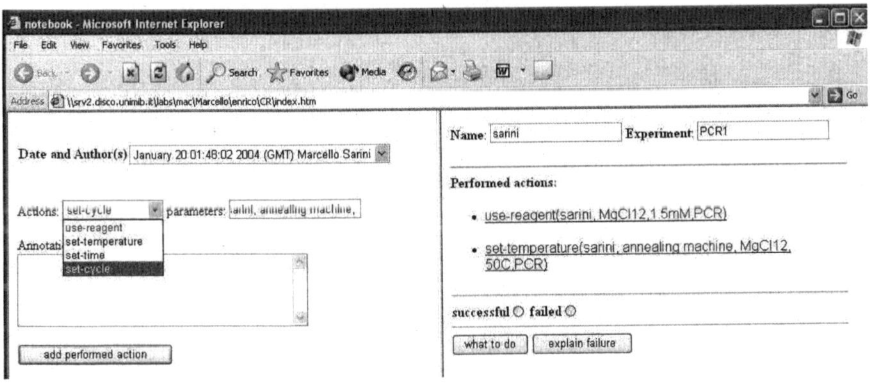

Figure 4: a mock-up of the notebook interface

As presented in [9], the architecture of a SICS is composed of three main modules (Figure 3): *Observer*, *Inductive*, and *Composer modules*.

6.1 The Observer module

The Observer observes the actions of biologists. We can distinguish two different typologies of actions to observe: (1) scientific actions performed by biologists during their work and that are written in their own notebooks; (2) actions that the biologists perform during the interaction with the electronic notebook, such as menu navigation or options choices. In this second case these actions could encompass the first ones as parameters. Since this second type strongly depends on the features of the designed interface of the electronic notebook we do not consider them at the present stage.

For what concerns scientific actions, we focused on a restricted set of meaningful actions which are a generalizations of the ones related to a PCR experiment (see for instance [22]). They refer to the percentage of reagent used in the current experiment; to the temperature the machine has been set during the reagent processing; to the time interval of reagent processing; to the number of cycle to be repeated in order to perform the experiment. This is in accordance with the concept of procedural abstraction advocated in the Labscape project (see [30]). In fact, according to the observations of work in a biological laboratory, the authors discovered that although laboratory work appears complex and tools and instruments are highly diverse, biologists perform only a few types of abstract operations, although in many different ways. More specifically, considering x a reference to the biologist performing an *experiment* by using a *machine* and a *reagent*, the actions are:

- *use-reagent(x, reagent, value, experiment)*, where *value* is the percentage used during the current experiment.
- *set-temperature(x, machine, reagent, value, experiment),* where *value* is the temperature set during the current experiment.
- *set-time(x, machine, reagent, value, experiment),* where *value* is the time interval the reagent is processed in the machine during the current experiment.
- *set-cycle(x, machine, reagent, value, experiment),* where *value* is the number of times the reagent is processed in the machine during the current experiment.

Then, the Observer module needs to collect together the scientific actions performed in a specific experiment and to distinguish between successful and unsuccessful instances of the same kind of experiment (see Figure 5). This is implemented by using a relational database where the scientific actions are stored and the needed views are created on the stored scientific actions. This way of organizing the information registered by biologists is then used by the system to relate the actions performed by biologists as described in the following.

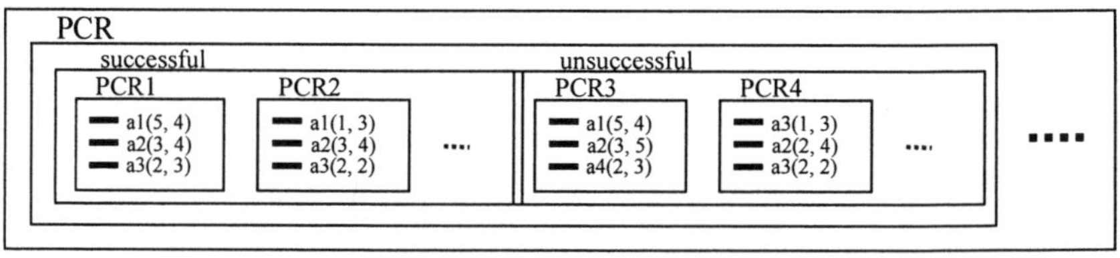

Figure 5: the views collecting scientific actions in the Observer database

6.2 The Inductive module

The Inductive module works on the scientific actions stored in the Observed module and discovers recurrent patterns which link them together. In this way the system supports the reconfiguration of the knowledge biologists externalized in their notebooks into patterns of actions in order to collect and make visible to biologists part of the implicit practices related to their work. The discovered patterns are expressed in terms of rules which have the following format:

$$A_1 \text{ and } A_2 \text{ and} \ldots \text{ and } A_n \rightarrow C \qquad (1)$$

where the antecedents of the rules are conjunctions of scientific actions and the consequent is a scientific action.

In order to discover patterns the Inductive module uses algorithms for mining association rules (like Apriori [31] in the WEKA implementation [32]).

We use two different strategies to discover rules which are of the first order. The choice of first-order rules is motivated by the fact that these rules have some parameters unspecified and hence they express more general patterns of association among scientific actions.

The first strategy uses the *Apriori* algorithm [31] to discover association rules involving actions which are grouped by the Observer module in the successful view. This is done by looking for actions whose parameters such as reagent, machine and temperature are frequently associated in the successful experiments. This algorithm is specifically designed to manage large amounts of data, typically for market analysis. The discovered association rules are propositional: this means that all their parameters have specified values. For instance consider that in successful experiments concerning PCR scientists consistently use the reagent MgCl2 with a concentration of 1.5mM, the annealing machine set with a temperature of 50°C running for 3 cycles. In this case, the Inductive module discovers and adds the following rule expressed where *x* is a generic scientist:

use-reagent(x, MgCl2, 1.5mM, PCR) and
set-temperature(x, annealing machine, MgCl2, 50 °C, PCR) →
set-cycle(x,annealing machine, MgCl2, 3, PCR) (2)

In order to generalize the rules mined by Apriori, our algorithm looks for actions with the same name and substitutes recurrent values of parameters with unspecified parameters. For instance consider that in successful experiments about PCR scientists used the reagent MgCl2 with a concentration ranging from 1.5mM to 3mM, with machines set with a temperature ranging from 50°C to 70°C and a variable number of cycles ranging fro 3 to 5, then the Inductive module discovers and adds the following rule:

use-reagent(x, MgCl2, c mM, PCR) and
set-temperature(x, m, MgCl2, t °C, PCR) →
set-cycle(x, m, MgCl2, N, PCR) (3)

where *c* represents the concentration of the reagent *MgCl2*, *m* the machine used by the biologist set with a temperature *t* and *N* represents the parametric value for the number of cycles; all these parametric values will be provided by the Composer module as described in the following.

The second strategy is used if the number of observed actions is limited; in this case it is possible to use mining algorithms such as *FOIL* [33] which directly obtains first-order rules like for instance:

use-reagent(x, MgCl2, c mM, PCR) →
set-temperature(x, annealing machine, MgCl2, t °C, PCR) (3bis)

where *c* represents a parametric value for the concentration which will be unified by the system with a value taken from an action performed by a biologist, while *t* representing a parametric value for the temperature will be provided by the Composer module as described in the following. The above rule simply says that biologists that uses a reagent for a PCR has to set the temperature of the annealing machine.

6.3 The Composer module

The Composer module is the core of the system, since it uses the information collected by both the Observer and the Inductive modules in order to propose a biologist the information which either satisfies her needs or helps her to understand why the experiment she performed failed. To illustrate how it happens (see dashed arrows in Figure 3) let us consider the flow of interaction inside the SICS system which starts from considering the need of a biologist up to providing the latter with the needed information. In step 1 an action performed by the biologist on the notebook triggers the Observer module to store it and starts the Composer module to select among the rules discovered by the Inductive module the ones whose left side is satisfied by the considered action. Then by using the selected rules, the Composer takes into account the previous biologists' experiences and proposes a suggestion to the biologist which should satisfy her information needs.
In particular this module consists of two main sub-modules:

- the Cultural Action Finder (CAF)
- the Scene Producer (SP)

6.3.1 *The Cultural Action Finder (CAF)*

Aim of the CAF module is to implement step 1 (see dashed arrow (1) in Figure 3) of the flow of interaction described above. Again, we have to consider the two different identified scenarios. During "support for anticipation" if a biologist wants to receive a suggestion from the system on the next action to perform, she requests it by asking through the notebook interface what to do next (see bottom right part of Figure 4). This request triggers the CAF to retrieve the last scientific action registered in the notebook of the biologist and hence stored by the Observer module. If the support provided by the system is related to "explanation of failure", when the biologist reports on her notebook interface the failure of an experiment, then if she wants to have some explanation for failure she may request it through the notebook interface (see bottom right part of Figure 4). This request triggers the CAF to iteratively retrieve all the scientific actions she performed in the failed experiment as registered in her notebook and stored by the Observer module.

Then, the CAF starts to consider the last action performed by the biologist as reported in her notebook. As a first step, the CAF has to select from the rules discovered by the Inductive module the one most suitable considering both the current action and the previous ones performed by the biologist during the same experiment. To do this selection the CAF tries to match the action executed by the involved biologist with the atoms belonging to the antecedents of the rules discovered by the Inductive module. This works by using a matching function which returns true when the names and parameters of the two actions match. Since it is possible that more rules may be selected, the algorithm sorts the rules by considering the number of atoms in the antecedent parts.

The algorithm then starts from the rules with the greatest number of atoms up to the ones with the lowest number and tries to select a rule which matches both the current scientific action and the actions the biologist performed in the same instance of the experiment. In this way the algorithm takes into account the current action, but also the previous history of the biologist who performed the considered actions and her experience in completing an experiment.

Once a rule is selected, the CAF looks whether there exists actions performed in successful instances of the same kind of experiment which satisfy the left part of the considered rule. This is done by looking in the Observer module. Hence, the actions belonging to the same successful experiment are collected together as single elements (a tuple) of a set if and only if each of them satisfies one of the atoms (representing an action) constituting the left part of the selected rule.

Then, the CAF returns as many actions as the cardinality of the set. Each action is the same reported in the right part of the selected rule but with different values of its variables. In fact, for each element of the set the variables of the action are unified with the corresponding values of the actions belonging to the considered element of the set. When there are no corresponding values for the parameters of the action, they are left unspecified.

In this way the system retrieves the past experience of the biologists dealing with a specific situation codified by a rule. The returned actions are called in Implicit Culture terms as *cultural actions* since in performing them a biologist behaves according to the culture of the others. In addition, these actions if performed by the biologist should satisfy her current information needs, in coherence both with the patterns previously discovered by the Inductive module and with the past actions performed by biologists.

Let us consider this situation: if during the analysis of the actions performed by a biologist in an unsuccessful experiment the action currently considered is *set-temperature(x, annealing machine, MgCl2, 50 °C, PCR)*, the CAF in the first step selects rule (3) since it is satisfied by the considered action. Then the CAF looks for successful past actions performed by other biologists satisfying the left part of the selected rule: for instance *use-reagent(x, MgCl2, 1.5mM, PCR)*. Hence, the CAF returns as cultural action the action *set-cycle(x, annealing machine, MgCl , N, PCR)* which is the result of the unification of the variables of the action in the right part of rule (3) with the corresponding values of the collected actions satisfying the left part of the rule. If the cultural action is specified in each of its parameters, for instance *set-cycle(x, annealing machine, MgCl, 3, PCR)*, the system can try to satisfy the biologist's current information needs by simply suggesting the considered action. Otherwise, if the cultural action has one or more of its parameters not specified, as *set-cycle(x, annealing machine, MgCl, N, PCR),* the role of the system is to suggest effective values for these parameters, in this case the number of cycles *N* to run the machine. In this last situation the job of the Scene Producer module is more complex since it has to find suitable values which better specify the selected cultural action among the actions stored by the Observer module.

6.3.2 The Scene Producer (SP)

The cultural actions determined by the CAF algorithm are then passed as input to the Scene Producer module which implements step 2 (see dashed arrow (2) in Figure 3) of the above described flow of interaction. In particular, for a given cultural action the SP generates on the biologist's notebook interface a suggestion such as it is maximized the probability that the biologist will perform next the cultural action proposed by the CAF. In case the cultural action is completely specified, the SP simply proposes it as suggestion to the biologists. In the other cases, the SP generates the suggestion for the biologist through an algorithm working in three steps.

1) *For each cultural action found by the CAF module, find the group of biologists which performed actions similar to the considered cultural action.* Again, computation of similarity is performed by looking in the Observer repository and by using a similarity function which works on the scientific actions. Here, scientific actions are similar to the considered cultural action if they belong to the same view, names match and the related parameters matches without considering the ones in the cultural action still with unspecified values. For instance if *use-reagent(x, MgCl2, c mM, PCR))* is the considered cultural action, *use-reagent (y, MgCl2, 3mM, PCR))* and *use-reagent(z, MgCl2, 4mM, PCR))* are similar to it if both of them belong to the same view which groups scientific actions performed in successful PCR experiments. Then *y* and *z* are references of the biologists returned by the sub-module in the first step of computation. At this point the SP has to use a strategy to select which action to consider as a relevant suggestion. This is done in the next step by looking for the biologists who are most similar to the one under concerns.

2) *Select among the biologists collected during step 1 a subset of biologists which are the most similar to the biologist who asked for suggestion.* Since biologists are working in the same laboratory and sharing common work practices, we could consider all of them similar. However, we want to consider here another form of similarity among biologists. In fact, in order to assess the similarity between the biologists we define a similarity function expressed as a sum of the similarities of the actions they performed stored by the Observer module. Namely, two biologists are similar if they reported in the notebooks similar actions. This form of similarity is used since we argue that similarity of biologists based on the performed actions is a reasonable way to relate the action to be suggested with the real needs of the considered biologist. A more fine grained similarity function which has still to be investigated could rank the biologists most similar to the one under concerns privileging the ones more experienced. In order to measure experience among biologists we consider for each of them the number of successful experiments versus the total number of completed experiments. In case all the identified scientific actions in the previous step were performed by the same biologist then the subset contains only the considered biologist which is obviously the most similar to the one under concerns. In this situation we provide as suggestion all the identified scientific actions.

3) *Once collected the actions similar to a cultural action performed by the most similar biologists, generate the suitable suggestions to the biologist in order to satisfy her needs.* This is done by generating a suitable clue on the biologist's notebook interface (for instance a pop up with the text of the suggestion). If the actions similar to the cultural action are too many it is possible to use a filtering technique that generalizes collaborative filtering [10]. Consider the case of explanation of failure, when considering an action *use-reagent(x, MgCl2, 2mM, PCR))* performed by the biologist *x* in a failed experiment. If the cultural action selected by the system is *set-cycle(x, annealing machine, MgCl2, 3, PCR))* then the related biologist *x* receiving it as a suggestion may compare the actions she performed in the experiment with the one proposed by the system. In this way the biologist is supported in rethinking the experiment she performed and in understanding, if possible, why it failed comparing her experience with the knowledge of her colleagues collected and proposed by the system.

7 Conclusions and future works

In this paper we proposed an approach and a technology to provide biologists with the support needed to complete their work. By observing the nature of laboratory work in the laboratories we identified situations where biologists have various information needs to be satisfied. Often biologists do not have the information they need at the right time and sometimes they lack the way of satisfying their needs. This because it may happen that colleagues which are a suitable source of information are busy or not present in the lab. Moreover, the scientific information they have access through common repository is hardly usable to satisfy a need in a specific situation.

We observed that a relevant work practice of biologists concerns the registration on their own notebooks of everything they do in a laboratory. Even though this information is freely available to people working in the same laboratory, often its interpretation is hard due to different personal organization of work and different levels of expertise. Hence, even if notebooks are artifacts where the tacit knowledge of biologists related to their experiences and practices is externalized, this knowledge is often not exploited by other biologists.

Adopting the Implicit Culture approach and the SICS technology our system tries to make the knowledge maintained by the notebooks more usable. In this way the SICS observing the transcriptions of the notebooks converts this knowledge in recurrent patterns of actions performed by biologists during experiments. By using these patterns expressed in terms of first-order rules the system is able to support the work of biologists by satisfying their needs. In particular, we identified two modalities of use of the system according to the biologists' needs: the support for anticipation and support for explanation of failure.

In the first case, it may happen that while performing an experiment a biologist may not be able to perform the next action until a specific information need is not satisfied. This is associated to an interactive use of the system: the system considers the last action performed by the biologist and suggests an action which if executed is coherent with the patterns of actions discovered by the system considering the successful experiments of the same kind. In this case, since the system suggests to the biologist an action to perform next, it may also be possible to observe on her notebooks if the suggested action is really performed by the biologist. Then this observation could be stored as an *accept()* action in the database. The use of this additional information of indirect feedback provided by biologists may be considered in a future extension of the system. In this way it may be possible to tune the support the system provides to the biologists taking into account the level of usefulness of the suggestion it proposed with respect to experience and preferences of the biologists working in the same lab.

In the second case, when the system is used to support the "explanation of failure" for an experiment, a biologist who performed an unsuccessful experiment would like to have some information in order to understand why it failed. In this situation the system works in "batch mode" that is considering all the actions performed by the biologist in the considered experiment. Then for each of them the system suggests the biologist the actions other colleagues performed in successful experiments of the same kind. Again, these actions are proposed by the system by considering the patterns of action discovered from the transcriptions of the notebooks.

There are several directions of future work. One direction is the investigation of techniques to discover more complicated patterns of actions, taking into account also sequence of actions. In fact our patterns, represented as first-order rules with conjunction of actions, do not express whether an action is performed before of another one.

A second direction will address other information needs. Though in this paper we focused on scientific needs, that is needs related to the scientific actions performed by biologists during an experiment and registered in their notebooks, we argue that the system can be extended to support biologists to satisfy other needs. In particular we want to focus our future work on physical needs: that is, to have some suggestions about the location of a reagent by considering the transcriptions of the notebooks in the database of scientific actions. In fact, since this database stores scientific actions, it can answer queries like "which is the last action performed by using a specific reagent?". Hence, the answer contains references either to the scientist who performed the action or to the machine used during the considered action. In this way, the system integrating the notebooks with the database of scientific actions indirectly provides the biologists with hints about the location of a reagent according to the scientific actions performed. In addition, since the system is able to observe actions performed by biologists on their notebooks, it is possible to register in the Observer module the queries performed by biologists to request for a reagent. Then these actions may be used by the Composer module to suggest a biologist, querying for a reagent, to contact the biologists who asked for it previously. This represents an extension of the system towards the suggestion of social actions to satisfy biologists' information needs.

Acknowledgements

Many thanks to Carla Simone for strong support, encouragements, and suggestions; to Michele Telaro and Jasminko Novak for useful discussions.

References

[1] K. Schmidt and C. Simone, "Coordination Mechanisms: Towards a conceptual foundation for CSCW systems design," *Computer Supported Cooperative Work, The Journal of Collaborative Computing*, vol. 5, pp. 155-200, 1996.

[2] M. Klein (editor), "Special Issue on Adaptive Workflow Systems," *Computer Supported Cooperative Work, The Journal of Collaborative Computing*, vol. 9, 2000.

[3] K. Schmidt (eds), C. Heath, and T. Rodden, "Special Issue on Awareness in CSCW," *Computer Supported Cooperative Work, The Journal of Collaborative Computing*, vol. 11, 2002.

[4] G. Mark, "Conventions and Commitments in Distributed CSCW Groups," *Computer Supported Cooperative Work, The Journal of Collaborative Computing*, vol. 11, pp. 349-387, 2002.

[5] L. Bannon and S. Bodker, "Constructing Common Information Space," ECSCW'97, Lancaster (UK), 1997.

[6] M. Sarini and C. Simone, "Recursive Articulation work in Ariadne: the alignment of meanings," COOP2002, Saint Raphael, France, 2002.

[7] U. M. Borghoff and J. H. Schlichter, *Computer-Supported Cooperative Work: Introduction to Distributed Applications*: Springer Verlag, 2000.
[8] A. D. Marwick, "Knowledge management technology," *IBM SYSTEMS JOURNAL special issue on Knowledge Management*, vol. 40, 2001.
[9] E. Blanzieri and P. Giorgini, "From Collaborating Filtering to Implicit Culture: a general agent-based framework," Workshop on Agent-Based Recommender Systems (WARS) in Autonomous Agents (Agents2000), Barcelona, Spain, 2000.
[10] E. Blanzieri, P. Giorgini, P. Massa, and S. Recla, "Information access in Implicit Culture framework," Tenth ACM International Conference on Information and Knowledge Management (CIKM 2001), Atlanta, Georgia, 2001.
[11] E. Blanzieri, P. Giorgini, F. Giunchiglia, and C. Zanoni, "Personal Agents for Implicit Culture Support," AAAI Spring Symposium on Agent-Mediated Knowledge Management (AMKM-03), Stanford CA, 2003.
[12] P. Resnick and H. R. Varian, "Recommender Systems," *Communication of the ACM*, vol. 40, pp. 56-58, 1997.
[13] I. Nonaka and H. Takeuchi, *The Knowledge Creating Company*. Oxford, UK: Oxford University Press, 1995.
[14] M. Lynch, "Protocols, practices, and the reproduction of technique in molecular biology," *British Journal of Sociology*, vol. 53, pp. 203-220, 2002.
[15] Lab Notebook Description in BioSci 1510, at http://www.pitt.edu/~biohome/Dept/docs/syllabi/1510_031.pdf Fall Term 2002.
[16] J. Grudin, "Why CSCW Applications Fail: Problems In The Design And Evalutation Of Organizational Interfaces," Proceedings CSCW'88, Portland, Oregon, USA, 1988.
[17] J. Mankoff, J. Somers, and G. D. Abowd, "Bringing people and places together with Dual Augmentation," Proceedings of the 1998 Spring AAAI Symposium on Intelligent Environments, 1998.
[18] G. Andolfi, M. Aste, M. Boninsegna, R. Cattoni, A. Potrich, and B. Caprile, "The Advanced Visual Monitoring Project at IRST," in *Advanced Video-Based Surveillance Systems*: Kluver Academic Publisher, 1998.
[19] Collaborative Electronic Notebook System Association (CENSA), at www.censa.org.
[20] LIMS Guide on Online Journal Scientific Computing and Instrumentation, at http://www.scimag.com/Scripts/lims.asp?SECTYPE=LIMS 2003.
[21] M. Kovalainen, M. Robinson, and E. Auramaki, "Diaries at Work," Proceedings CSCW'98, Seattle Washington, 1998.
[22] bioProtocol. a Bio Online Site, at http://bioprotocol.bio.com 2003.
[23] B. Katzenberg, F. Pickard, and J. McDermott, "Computer Support for Clinical Practice: Embedding and Evolving Protocols of Care," Proceedings CSCW'96, Cambridge MA, 1996.
[24] L. A. Suchman, *Plans and situated actions. The problem of human-machine communication*. Cambridge: Cambridge University Press, 1987.
[25] C. Heath and P. Luff, "Documents and Professional Practice: 'bad' organisational reasons for 'good' clinical records," Proceedings CSCW'96, Cambridge MA, 1996.
[26] Gene Inspector, at http://www.textco.com/products/gene_inspector.html.
[27] P. Minoofar, "E-Notebook A Digital Alternative to the Mighty Lab Notebook," *ChemNews.com; http://chemnews.cambridgesoft.com/art.cfm?S=275*.
[28] The ORNL Electronic Notebook Project, at http://www.csm.ornl.gov/~geist/java/applets/enote/.
[29] W. E. Mackay, G. Pothier, C. Letondal, K. Boegh, and H. E. Sorensen, "The missing link: augmenting biology laboratory notebooks," Proceedings of UIST'02, Paris, France, 2002.
[30] L. Arnstein, C. Hung, Q. H. Zhou, G. Borriello, S. Consolvo, and J. Su, "Labscape: A Smart Environment for the Cell Biology Laboratory," *IEEE Pervasive Computing*, vol. 1, pp. 13-21, 2002.
[31] A. Rakesh and S. Ramakrishnan, "Fast Algorithms for Mining Association Rules," Proc. 20th Int. Conf. Very Large Data Bases (VLDB), 1994.
[32] Weka 3 - Data Mining with Open Source Machine Learning Software in Java, at http://www.cs.waikato.ac.nz/ml/weka/.
[33] J. R. Quinlan, "Determinate Literals in Inductive Logic Programming," Proceedings 12th International Joint Conference on Artificial Intelligence, 1991.

Cooperative Systems Design
M. Zacklad et al. (Eds.)
IOS Press, 2004

Finding Partners in the Coordination of Loose Inter-Organizational Workflow

Eric ANDONOFF, Lotfi BOUZGUENDA,
Chihab HANACHI, Christophe SIBERTIN-BLANC
IRIT-UT1, Université Toulouse 1,
Place Anatole France, 31042 Toulouse Cedex
{andonoff, lotfi.bouzguenda, hanachi, sibertin}@univ-tlse1.fr

Abstract. This work deals with coordination in the context of loose Inter-Organizational Workflow (IOW). Loose IOW refers to occasional cooperation, free of structural constraints, where the partners involved and their number are not pre-defined. We discuss three possible abstract architectures for the design and development of IOW and highlight the one that matches the requirements of loose IOW.

Afterwards, we detail the selected architecture according to an agent-group-role based approach, which is in addition compliant with the WfMC reference architecture.

Finally, we give an overview of our implementation limited, for the moment, to a matchmaker finding workflow partners.

Keywords. Workflow, Agent, Coordination, Organizational Model.

Introduction

Inter-Organizational Workflow (IOW for short) aims at supporting cooperation between business processes running in different organizations. When several organizations gather to cooperate, they put in common resources and combine their respective skills to reach a common goal. Business processes are key resources providing services, and their combination could provide a new-added value service. The objective of IOW is to support the automation and the coordination of such distributed and heterogeneous business processes ([1] ,[2]) in order to provide a global service.

Expanding the use of IOW needs to extend the capabilities of existing workflow systems in order to meet the requirements that are emerging from the new working conditions such as the distribution and the heterogeneity of processes. The availability of low-level tools easing distributed objects interoperability (e.g. Corba, Federated Databases) and of Internet provides a basic communication infrastructure. However, many of the problems encountered in this new working context cannot be solved at this level and questions are still asking for an answer. In fact, semantic interoperability at a workflow and business level is still a challenge ([3], [4]) and current Workflow Management Systems (WfMS) are too rigid to deal with the diversity of contexts due to the presence of heterogeneity at different levels: processes, policies, objectives, authorities, local and global commitments, security. Regarding the analysis and synthesis of pre-existing processes, *how to execute and coordinate them?* how to reuse them? how to control them? Regarding the control and visibility of the whole process, should we build an IOW and its control from scratch, by merging pre-existing workflows or by federating several WfMS?

Roughly speaking, IOW coordination can be investigated in the context of the two following distinctive scenarios [5]: loose IOW and tight IOW. *Loose Inter-Organizational Workflow* refers to occasional and opportunist cooperations, free of structural constraints, where the partners involved and their number are not pre-defined. *Tight Inter-Organizational Workflow* refers to a structural cooperation among organizations. A structural cooperation means a cooperation based on a well-established infrastructure among pre-defined partners. In this case, the organizations involved are engaged in a long-term cooperation and their workflows (business processes) are interdependent.

In this paper, we concentrate on loose IOW. In such an open and dynamic context, - where partners (workflow service requesters, workflow service providers) are numerous, leaving and joining the global system freely, ignoring one another a priori -, it is highly desirable to have middle resources that help to select and locate partners, and ease interoperation between them. At the local level, each node needs to be provided with specific models for negotiating and sharing information and activity with middle resources and partners. These requirements impact the workflow description language, the WfMS architecture and the execution model.

Regarding the execution of IOW, two approaches have been proposed in the literature [6]. The first is a centralized technique where a unique WfMS synchronizes processes executed in different organizations. This technique is obviously inappropriate in the context of loose IOW. The other technique is a decentralized one, where each organisation has its own WfMS, and a "Middleware" software (also called mediator) supports their coordination. This Middleware enables the component applications to post events and to react to events published by other components. Events correspond to call for partners, exchange of information or results, ... Examples of such mediators [6] are "message brokers", "transactional queue managers", and "publish/subscribe" mechanisms. This technique is more appropriate to Loose IOW.

However, IOW coordination issues remain insufficiently addressed, since there are only isolated proposals which are not situated in an engineering perspective that aims at designing, specifying and implementing IOW systems. Moreover, the compliance with the WfMC reference architecture [7] is most of the time not discussed.

Giving that, the problem being addressed in this paper is "*how to coordinate workflow components in the context of loose IOW, with an engineering perspective and within a coherent framework of reference*?". The coordination in loose IOW raises several precise sub-problems such as the location and selection of partners, the negotiation of the workflow service quality, and the definition and selection of the interaction protocol to deploy during the workflow execution in order to manage and follow the workflow execution which may be a long-term transaction. This paper also addresses the first sub-problem i.e. *the location and the selection of partners*.

Our approach is based on the following principles:

- *The use of Agent Technology,* which provides relevant high-level features to design and implement IOW. Indeed, Agent technology provides *natural abstractions* to deal with autonomy, distribution, heterogeneity and cooperation which are inherent to IOW.
- *An organizational oriented coordination model.* A good coordination model among loose IOW components requires an organizational model which attributes roles to each component and constraints their interactions.

This paper is organized as follows. Section 1 presents three abstract architectures for the design and development of IOW and identifies the one that matches the need of loose IOW. Section 2 details an agent-based architecture to support loose IOW. Section 3 proposes an organizational model structuring the coordination of loose IOW and a capacity description language for partners finding. Section 4 shows how the organizational model has been implemented with the Madkit platform (http://www.madkit.org).

1. Three abstract architectures for the design of IOW

The purpose of this section is to present possible software architectures for the design and the development of IOW, and identify the one that better fits the needs of loose IOW.

First, let us give some definitions. *A Workflow* is an automation of a business process. A workflow defines a set of component tasks, their coordination, and the information and performers involved in each task. As an example of process, we can consider the reviewing process of a conference (paper distribution, parallel reviewing or sub-contracted reviewing, selection, notification, ...) which uses papers, produces review sheets, and involves authors, reviewers and PC members. The dynamic control structure of a workflow is described by using a language such as Petri Nets, State Charts or Active Rules. A WfMS is a software system that allows an organization to define, analyse, execute and monitor workflow processes. An *IOW* is composed of several individual workflows that are defined and executed in different organizations. We call an individual workflow within an IOW a *Component Workflow*. A *Global Process* is the process corresponding to an IOW and a *Local Process* is the one deployed by a Component Workflow.

If we consider again the review process, we can base it on volunteer referees (as it is the case for the ACM Special Track on Coordination for example). In this condition, the referee process is deployed in the context of a *Loose IOW* since it involves actors (PC members and referees) from different organizations (universities, laboratories, industries) without special agreements between them, and the referees involved and their number are not pre-defined but are dynamically recruited. Our implementation presented in section 4 develops this scenario.

We view an IOW architecture through four dimensions:

- The global process which can be predefined or dynamically built.
- The control of the global process which can be centralized, hierarchical or distributed.
- The component workflow coordination. It can be inexistent if the global process is predefined and deployed as a process. The coordination is static if the interaction of Workflow components is predefined, and dynamic if neither the workflow components nor the structure of their interactions are known in advance.
- As a result, the context of application is either a Loose IOW or a Tight *IOW*.

As shown in table 1, we have identified three relevant abstract architectures which are detailed below.

Table 1. Three abstract architectures for IOW

	Definition of the global process	***Control of the Global Process***	***Coordination of Component Workflows***	***Type of IOW***
Architecture 1	Predefined	Centralized	No	Tight
Architecture 2	Predefined	Hierarchical	Static	Tight
Architecture 3	Dynamic	Distributed	Dynamic	Loose

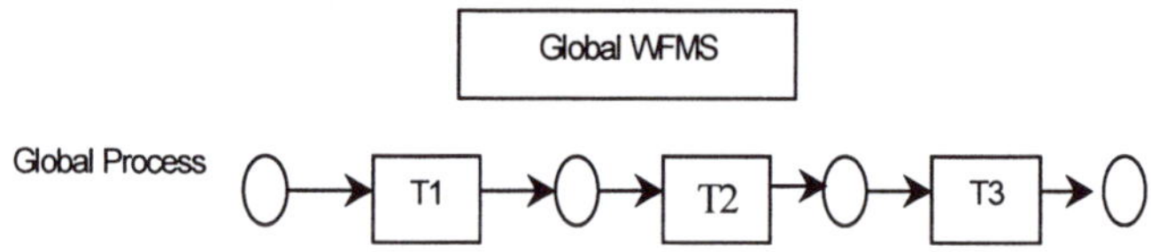

Figure 1. Architecture 1

Architecture 1 (see Figure 1) corresponds to a scenario where partners agree on a global process (described by a Petri Net in the example), and a unique WfMS supervises its execution, involving the resources and actors of the different organizations. In this case, the global process is predefined, there is a centralised control even if the execution is distributed over the different partners. This scenario is possible only in the case of Tight IOW since it requires preliminary agreements between partners.

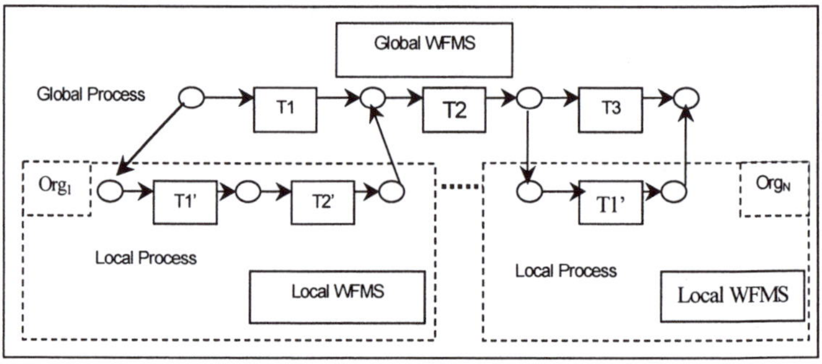

Figure 2. Architecture 2

Architecture 2 (see Figure 2) corresponds to a scenario where there is an agreement on how the component workflows must interact. This agreement is concretized by a Global Process (T1-T2-T3 in figure 2) that specifies how to synchronize the component workflows that run in org_1, ...org_N. However, each organization keeps the control on its own local workflow: It can decide by itself i) how to deploy its local process ii) to modify it or not iii) to make it public or private. In this scenario, the control is hierarchical (from global to component Workflows), the execution is distributed over each organization, and the coordination of component workflows is static since the identities of partners are known and the interaction among component workflows is predefined. This scenario assumes a tight IOW since it requires preliminary agreements between partners.

Architecture 3 (see Figure 3) corresponds to a situation where an organization (org_1 in figure 3) initiates a workflow process where some tasks are local and others are to be sub-contracted to partners unknown a priori. In this case, a Mediator is useful to connect a requester workflow to a provider one. Once a partner is selected, the requester engages a cooperation with the provider (org_N in figure 3). In this scenario, the global workflow process is not predefined but dynamically built as one goes along, because the identities of partners and their processes are not known. The control and the execution of the global workflow process are obviously distributed. The coordination of component workflows is dynamic since the identity of partners and their interaction protocols are not known and could change from an execution to another, even if the API to communicate is well established through interface 4[1].

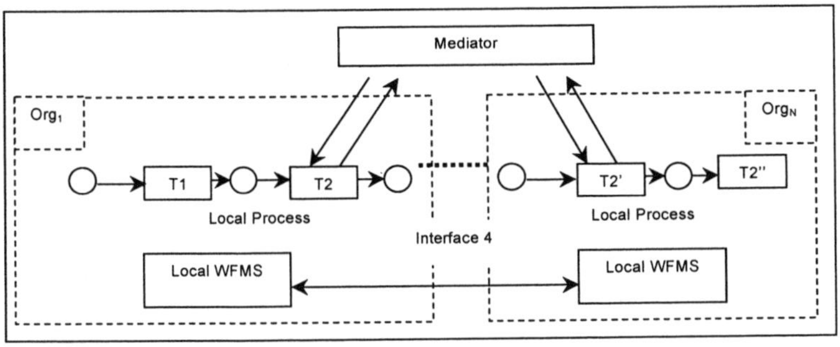

Figure 3. Architecture 3

2. An Agent-based (Reference) Architecture to Support Loose IOW

In order to favor syntactic interoperability between WfMSs and communication between workflows, the Workflow Management Coalition has defined a *reference architecture* [7] for WfMSs. According to this architecture (see Figure 4), a WfMS includes a *Workflow Enactment Service* that manages the execution of workflow processes and supports the following well-defined interfaces:

- Interface 1 with the Process Definition Tools,
- Interface 2 with Workflow Client Applications,
- Interface 3 with Invoked Applications,
- Interface 4 with Other Workflow Enactment Services,
- Interface 5 with Administration and Monitoring Tools.

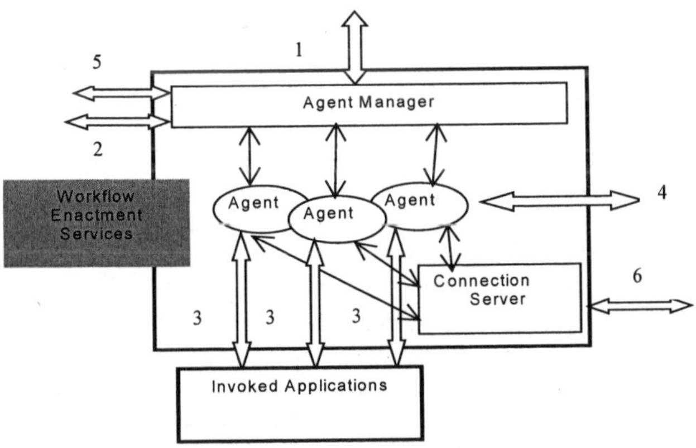

Figure 4. An agent-based architecture for the Workflow Enactment Service

[1] The interfaces supporting the communication between the different components of a WfMS are being unified and standardized by the WfM Coalition under the term WAPI for Workflow API. Interface 4 connects two WfMSs.

Conforming with this reference architecture allows WfMSs to exchange data while avoiding the syntactic communication problems, even when they are implemented in different organizations. Thus, we fulfil this conformance, which is highly appropriate when dealing with IOW.

This reference architecture concerns only the interfaces to be supported by a Workflow Enactment Service (WES) and imposes no constraints upon its internal structure. So, Figure 4 presents an agent-based architecture for the WES: it includes as many agents as the number of Workflow process instances being currently in progress, an Agent Manager (AM) in charge of these agents, and a Connection Server (CS) that helps agents to extend their acquaintances according to their needs.

The key idea is to implement each Workflow process instance as a software process, and to encapsulate this process within an active agent. Such a *workflow agent* includes a Workflow Engine that, as and when the Workflow process instance progresses, reads the workflow definition and triggers the action(s) to be done according to its current state. This definition can be expressed using a high level Petri net formalism such as CoOperative Objects [8], [5]. This agent supports Interface 3 with the applications that are to be used to perform pieces of work associated to process' *tasks*.

The *Agent Manager* controls and monitors the running of Workflow agents:

- Upon a request for a new instance of a Workflow process, it creates a new instance of the corresponding agent type, initializes its parameters according to the context, and launches the running of its workflow engine.
- It ensures the persistency of agents that execute long-term business processes extending for a long time in which task performances are interleaved with periods of inactivity.
- It coordinates agents in their use of the local shared resources.
- It assumes Interfaces 1, 2 and 5 of the WfMS with the environment.

In a loose IOW context, workflow agents need to find external workflow agents running in other organizations and able to contribute to the achievement of their goal. However, as the capacities, the availability or even the presence of such partners is not steady. Finding them requires searching capacities and maintaining knowledge about resources in the environment. The role of the *Connection Server* (**CS**) is to manage this knowledge and to help agents to find the partners they need. To do this, the CS interacts with Matchmaker agents, which are specialized in finding agents and WfMSs able to fulfill a requested need. This requires a new interface, *Interface 6*, that allows the CS of different Workflow Enactment Services to interact with each other.

The AM and the CS relieve workflow agents of technical tasks concerning relations with their internal and external environments. Each agent being in charge of a single one Workflow process instances, it can adapt to specific requirements of this process, that is it can more easily features the *flexibility* known as being one of the most challenging issues in WfMS. Indeed, each instance of a business process is a specific case featuring distinctive characteristics with regard to its objectives, constraints and environment. These differences arise both in a diachronic perspective –considering successive instances of a business process that evolves according to business requirements–, and in a synchronic perspective –considering the exceptions encountered by contemporaneous instances of a business process. Beyond the common generic facilities for supporting flexibility, the workflow agents we are considering are provided with two additional capabilities. First, each agent includes its own definition of the process –what is to be performed is specific to the agent– and second, it includes its own engine for interpreting this definition –how to perform is also specific. Moreover, tailoring an agent to the distinctive features of its Workflow process takes place at the time of its instantiation, but it may also occur dynamically as the agent is running.

3. Agent-Based Organizational Model for Finding Partners in Loose IOW

In this section, we will detail Interface 6 and show how a Connection Server of a Workflow Enactment Service proceeds to find functional resources – and especially workflow processes of other organizations – on the behalf of its workflow agents

3.1 Organizational perspective

To this end, we adopt an organizational view that provides appropriate concepts to describe the macro-level dimension [9] of the cooperation among WfMSs in terms of externally observable behaviour, independent of the internal features of each participating component. More precisely, this view makes possible the inheritance of natural, powerful and experimented concepts, such as, for example, roles, groups, teams, interactions, commitments, responsibilities, or permissions. These abstractions are conceptual tools that ease the capture and modelling of the structure and the behaviour of the systems under consideration.

The Agent, Group and Role (AGR) meta-model [10] is one of the frameworks proposed to define the organizational dimension of a multiagent system, and it is well appropriate to the IOW context. According to this model, the organisation of a system is defined as a set of related groups, agents and roles.

A *group* is a set of *agents* that also determines an interaction space: an agent may communicate with another agent only if they belong to the same group. The cohesion of the whole system is maintained by the fact that agents may belong to any number of groups, so that the communication between two groups may be done by agents that belong to both. Each group also define a set of *roles*, and the *group manager* is the specific role fulfilled by the agent that initiates the group. The membership of an agent to a group requires that the group manager authorises this agent to play some role, and each role determines how the agents playing that role may interact with other agents. So the whole behaviour of the system is framed by the structure of the groups that may be created and by the behaviours allowed to agents by the roles. On the other hand, the AGR model agrees with any kind of agents since it imposes no constraint on their internal structure.

3.2 An Agent-Role-Group model for loose IOW

Our organization model (see figure 5) is organised around the following components:

- *Four types of groups* represented by ellipses: Search Contract, Requesters, Providers, Contract (described below). In this figure, we have two Search Contract Groups;
- *Three types of agents* represented by candles: Connection Server, Workflow Agent and Matchmaker Agent;
- And *ten roles* since each agent plays a specific role in two groups. The communication between agents within a group follows standard Workflow API (interfaces 6 and 4) as shown in figure 5.

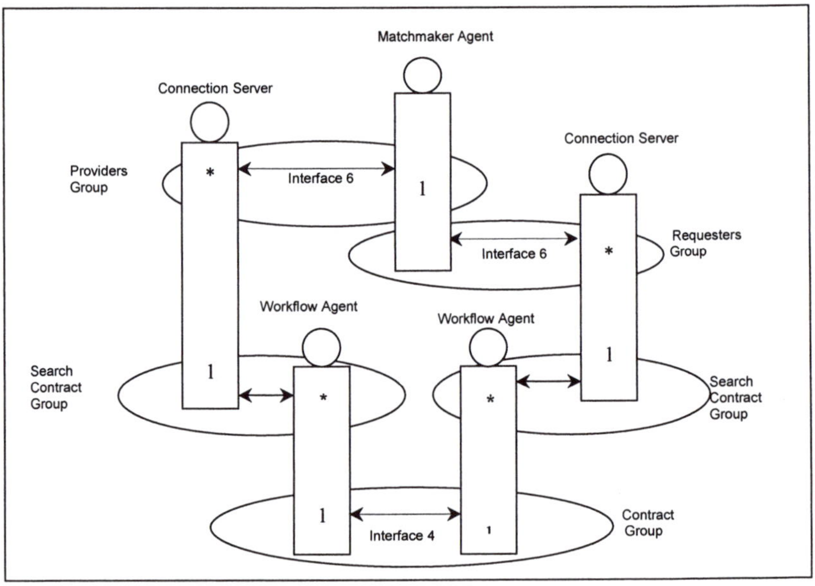

Figure 5. Findings workflow partners using matchmaker

Let us detail how does each group operate.

The Search Contract Group enables one or several Workflow Agents (the multiplicity is represented by a star inside the role) to enter in connection with their Connection Server to which the search of a partner (a provider or a requester) will be delegated.

The Providers Group is an interaction space enabling each Connection Server to advertise the services, offered by the agent it represents, to a matchmaker. The role of the matchmaker in this group is to register the capabilities of Workflow Agents which play the role of providers.

The Requesters Group enables i) each Connection Server to submit a request for a service and ii) the Matchmaker to return to this Connection Server the identity of a Provider Agent that has advertised that service. Once the Connection Server has the identity of a provider, it informs its Requester Agent (within the Search Contract Group), and this latter creates *a Contract Group* within which the cooperation will take place.

The Contract Group is an interaction space created by a Requester Agent to cooperate with a Provider Agent. For each cooperation commitment a Contract Group is created; it involves only those two agents.

3.3 A Capacity Description Language for Partners Finding

To interact, agents need an *Agent Communication Language (ACL)* that will be used for exchanging information, intentions or goals. In our context, we propose the use of the Standard *KQML (**K**nowledge **Q**uery and **M**anipulation **L**anguage)* [11] which is both *a language* composed of a set of performatives and *a set of associated protocols* that specify how to react after sending or receiving a message. As shown in table 2, a KQML performative is composed of several parameters among which the ontology and the language in which the content of a message is written. The ontology specifies the common vocabulary of the domain being considered, which partners must share, at least during their cooperation.

Table 2. Combining KQML and LARKS

(KQML - Performative

: Sender < parameter > //* Address of a sender of the message

: Receiver < parameter > //* Address(es) of a receiver(s) of the message

: Language < parameter > //* in LARKS

: Ontology< parameter > //* The ontology of the domain being considered

: Content < parameter > // *Communicated information compliant with Larks and using the term of the ontology)

Regarding the content language, and since our purpose is to ease the finding of partners, we have chosen LARKS [12] ***(L**anguage for **A**dvertisement and **R**equest for **K**nowledge **S**haring)* that enables the description of both advertisement and request of agent capabilities. Besides Larks supports inferences allowing the matchmaker to deduce from the request, the capacities an agent must feature to answer this request. Using these deductions, the matchmaker is able to select the best partner for a given request. The structure of LARKS specification is given in Table 3.

Table 3. Specification in LARKS [12]

Context	Sub-domain of the ontology considered
Type	This field is optional. It describes the types of additional data (that are not present in the ontology) used in this specification.
Input	List of input variables.
Output	List of output variables.
InConstraints	Constraints on input variables (pre conditions).
OutConstraints	Constraints on output variables (post conditions).
ConcDescriptions	Optional description of the meaning of additional data used in the specification.
TextDescription	This field is optional. It is a textual description of the specification.

Table 4 and Table 5 show respectively an advertisement and a request of agent capabilities. Table 4 corresponds to an advertisement published by a provider workflow agent. It advertises its capability to review paper in the groupware area, it precises its availability period, the limit number of pages accepted, and it guarantees to fill the review sheet before the deadline review. Table 5 corresponds to a request submitted by a requester workflow agent. The advertisement and the request have the same format, but they are supposed to be sent by two different performatives that give the way they must be interpreted.

Table 4. Example of an advertisement of agent capabilities.

Context:	Reviewing papers, Conference.
Input:	DateStartReview,DeadlineReview, Topic, Paper, PaperLength, ReviewSheet
Output:	ReviewSheet, DateReview
InConstraints:	(DeadlineReview-DateStartReview >=1month) and (ReviewSheet is empty) and (PaperLength <= 20) and (Topic ="Groupware")
OutConstraints:	(ReviewSheet is filled) and (DateReview <= DeadlineReview)

Table 5. Example of a request of agent capabilities.

Context:	Reviewing papers, Conference
Input:	DateStartReview,DeadlineReview, Topic, Paper, PaperLength, ReviewSheet
Output:	ReviewSheet, DateReview
InConstraints:	(DateStartReview ="15/01/2004")and (DeadlineReview="20/02/2004")and (Topic = "Workflow")and (PaperLength<=15)
OutConstraints:	(ReviewSheet is filled) and (DateReview <= DeadlineReview)

Naturally the request does not need to match exactly the advertisement. An advertisement is eligible if it subsumes the request. For example, the groupware domain is supposed to subsume the workflow one.

4. Overview of the Implementation

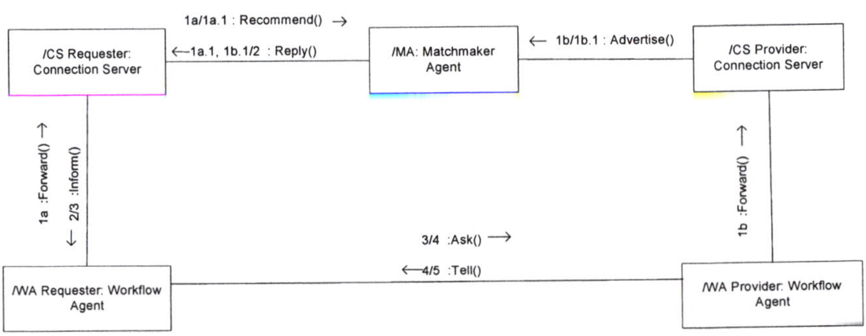

Figure 6. Collaboration diagram between the different types of agents

In order to validate our organizational model, we have implemented a simulator called "MatchFlow" for the "partners finding" aspect. Naturally, we have used the Madkit platform, which integrates the AGR meta-model. We have tested the case study mentioned in section 2: "the reviewing process of a conference". Figure 6 gives an UML collaboration diagram presenting the different agents involved in our simulator and how they interact.

Since our system is a simulator, we have implemented a user interface to supervise the execution even if in fact no interaction with the user is needed. Figure 7 shows several windows of this simulator and particularly:

- Windows 1 informs of the availability of the *matchmaker*;
- Windows 2 and 4 present respectively a provider and requester connection server. This interface enables the user to order the entrance or the departure of the corresponding agent from a group. The role of the connection server is either to submit the requested service or to advertise the offered service to a matchmaker.
- Windows 3 enables a provider connection server to precise its ontology (For example in our context: "Conference"). This ontology is used to select the most appropriate *Matchmaker* (only one is available in our system).
- Windows 5 and 6 present respectively *a provider workflow agent* and *a requester workflow agent*. Interface 5 enables the user to enter in connection with its connection server, to describe advertisements, to contact or interacts with requesters. Windows 6 enables the user to enter in contact with its connection server to visualise offers, to know the identity of a partner, and contact a provider in order to request a service.
- Windows 7 shows an advertisement of an agent capabilities.
- Windows 8 is a debugging window presenting all the groups (the requesters group, providers group, search contract groups and the contract group) and the roles attributed to each agent.

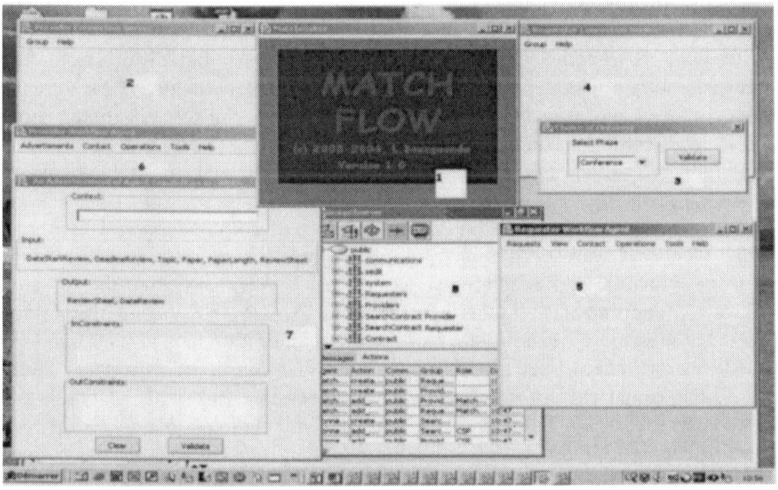

Figure 7. An overview of the simulator

5. Related Works

Workflow systems first differ one from the other according to *the core technology* they exploit: email, database, web, or more recently Agent technology. The first class uses *electronic mail* for the routing and presentation of work to users. An example of this class of systems is given by MILANO [13]. The second class is based on *database technology*, generally for storing routing and status information. Examples of workflows of this type are Wide and Pantha Rei [14]. Lately, a number of workflow systems have started adopting *the web* as technical infrastructure, focusing on distribution and accessibility. Examples of such systems are WebFlow [15], WebWork [16] and DartFlow [17]. The particularity of Webwork is to be entirely implemented with the web technology (Web browsers, Web servers, HTML, java script and CGI). Recently, web services have been adopted as a mean to make computational tasks available in an interoperable format, and approaches have been proposed to compose them according to workflow schema in order to provide added value services ([23], [26]). Finally, Agent technology has been adopted for providing flexibility and high-level interactions in dynamic and cooperative environments ([18] , [25], [23]).

Considering the *Agent technology*, there are two broad approaches to investigate and implement workflow :

- *Agent-enhanced Workflow* aims at adding value to WfMS by providing an agent layer in charge of social facilities (e.g. filtering messages or signaling pending commitements). For example, in the workflow system MILANO [13] agents are used for the elaboration of messages and for keeping the overall status of the on-going processes.
- *Agent-based Workflow* ([19], [18]) renews the way of considering workflow systems by fully rethinking the design and the development of the system in terms of agents. Among the different systems we can mention ABACO [20] and ADEPT [21].

Our work is directly related to this second approach but differs from the existing systems on four points : our architecture is compliant with the WfMC architecture, it adresses inter-organizational workflow, it fully exploits the Organizational dimension of Agent technology to abstract and structure the interaction space, and finally it focuses on the partner mediation aspect which has not been treated through agent technology elsewhere.

Finally, we should mention recent works that combine several technologies and notably agent and web-services ([25], [26]). Agent technology provides a framework to support coordination and adaptativity, while web services constitute the ressources to be coordinated (coordinable). In this context, [25] explains how agent technology can be exploited to give more flexibility to Workflow-like definition languages such as BPEL4WS [27] (Business Process Execution Language for Web Services). Our paper contributes to this effort inasmuh as our matchmaker and its possible link with an ontology are both useful to enact workflow in the web environment. In that direction, and in order to ease web service selection, [24] proposes a semantic matching process making the correspondance between offers and requests expressed with the DAML-S language. Our implementation could be rethought with that language with very few modifications.

Regarding IOW coordination, we must mention the works of [1] and [4] that define interaction patterns to deal with semantic interoperability within IOW. These patterns have inspired the abstracted architecture previously defined. The closest work to ours is the one of [22], developped in the context of the CrossFlow European Project, which proposes a market place to find partners and then contract-based protocols to support the collaboration.

However, the differences with our work are numerous : [22] has not been adressed with an agent perpective, it corresponds to a tight rather than loose IOW scenario since it is deployed in the context of Virtual Entreprise, and finally our work defines an explicit component (a matchmaker) to support the finding partner process.

6. Conclusion

In this paper, we have presented three possible abstract architectures for the design and development of IOW in order to support business processes that span across multiple organisations. They have been discussed according to four dimensions (1) the *global process* which can be *predefined* or *dynamically built* (2) the *control of the global process* which can be *centralized, hierarchical* or *distributed* (3) the *component workflow coordination* which can be static or dynamic, and (4) The resulting type of IOW which can be *Loose* or a *Tight*.

Then, we have identified the architecture that fits the need of loose Inter-Organizational Workflow and refined it in terms of Agent technology, according to an organizational perspective while remaining within a coherent framework of reference (the WfMC architecture).

An important idea applied in this paper is that organizational perspective plays a key role in the semantic interoperability between workflow systems. On the one hand, an organizational perspective eases the capture and the modelling of the coordination dimension of the systems under consideration. On the other hand, it eases a modular design and implementation by separating drastically the macro-level (coordination) from the micro-level (agent level). For example, using the Agent-Group-Role meta model [10], the internal architecture of the agents may be thought and then implemented independently from their coordination.

As future work, we plan to integrate the Quality of Service in the Capability Description Language.

7. References

[1] W.M.P. Van der Aalst
"Inter organizational Workflows: An Approach based on Message Sequence Charts and Petri Nets". Systems Analysis Modelling Simulation, 34(3): 335--367, 1999.

[2] F. Casati and A. Discenza
"Supporting Workflow Cooperation within and across Organizations". International Symposium on Applied Computing, Como, Italy, March 2000.

[3] M. P. Papazoglou and W. Van Den Heuvel
"From Business Processes to Cooperative Information Systems". An information Agents Perspective. In M. Klusch, editor, Intelligent Information Agents. Springer, Berlin, Germany, 1999.

[4] F. Casati
"Semantic Interoperability in inter organizational workflows". In WACC workshop on cross-organizational workflows, San Francisco, CA, February 1999.

[5] M. Divitini, C. Hanachi and C. Sibertin-Blanc
"Inter organizational Workflows for Enterprise Coordination". chapter 15 of Coordination of Internet Agents. In A. Omicini, F. Zambonelli, M. Klusch, R. Tolksdorf, editors, Springer, Berlin, Germany 2001.

[6] U. Dayal, M. Hsu and R. Ladin
"Business Process Coordination: State of the Art, Trends and Open Issues". The VLDB Journal, 2001.

[7] WfMC
"Reference Model-The Workflow Reference Model". Technical Report WFMC-TC-1003, Workflow Management Coalition, November 1994.

[8] C. Sibertin-Blanc
"CoOperative Objects: Principles, Use and Implementation". In Concurrent Object-Oriented Programming and Petri Nets, G. Agha & F. De Cindio (Eds.), LNCS 2001, Springer-Verlag 2000, (p. 210-241).

[9] A. Artikis and J. Pitt
"A Formal Model of Open Agent Societies". In Proceedings of Autonomous Agents, Montreal, 2001, pp. 192-193.

[10] J. Ferber and O. Gutknecht
"A Meta-Model for the Analysis and Design of Organizations in Multi-Agent Systems". In proceeding of the 3rd International Conference on Multi-Agents Systems(ICMAS'98). IEEE CS Press, June 1998.

[11] "Specification of the KQML Agent-Communication Language".
http://www.csee.umbc.edu/kqmlspec/spec.html.

[12] k. Sycara, S. Widoff, M. Klusch and J. Lu
"LARKS: Dynamic Matchmaking Among Heterogeneous Software Agents in Cyberspace". Autonomous Agents and MultiAgents Systems, 5, 173-203, 2002.

[13] A. Agostini, G. De Michelis and M. A. Grasso
"Rethinking CSCW systems: the Architecture of Milano". In Johan A.Hughes, Wolfgang Prinz, Tom Rodden, and Kajeld Schmidt, editors, Proceeding of the Fifth European Conference on Computer Supported Cooperative Work, ECSCW'97, Lancaster, U.K., pages33-48, Dordrecht, August 1997. Kluwer Academic Publishers.

[14] J. Eder, H. Groiss and W. Liebhart
"The Workflow Management System Panta Rhei". In Asuman Dogaç, Leonid Kalinichenko, M.Tamer özsu, and Amit Sheth, editors, Workflow Management Systems and Interoperability, NATO ASI Series. Springer, Berlin, 1998.

[15] A. Grasso, J. L. Meunier, D. Pagani and R. Pareschi
"Distributed Coordination and Workflow on the World Wide Web". Computer Suported Cooperative Work: the Journal of Collaborative Computing, 6(2-3):175-200, 1997.

[16] J. Miller, D. Palaniswami, A. Sheth, K. Kochut and H. Singh
"WebWork: METEOR2'S Web-Based Workflow Management System". In Journal of Intelligent Information Systems- Special Issue: Workflow Management Systems, pages 185-215, March-April 1998.

[17] T. Cai, P. Gloor and S. Nog
"DartFlow: A Workflow Management System on the Web using transportable agents". Technical report, Dartmouth College,1997.

[18] P. Singh Munindar and N. Huhns Michael
"Multi-agent Systems for Workflow". Draft Sep 1998. based on a talk given at IJCAI Worksop on Business Applications of Artificial Intelligence, Nagoya, Japan, 1997.

[19] N. R. Jennings, P. Faratin, M. J. Johnson, T. J. Norman, P. O'Brien and M. E Wiegand
"Agent Based business process management". International Journal of Cooperative Information Systems,5(2&3):105-130, 1996.

[20] C. Simone, M. Divitini and Ariadne
"Supporting Coordination Through a Flexible Use of Process Knowledge". In Information Technology for Knowledge Management, ed. U.M. Borghoff and R. Pareschi. Berlin- Heidelberg: Springer, pp. 121-148, 1998.

[21] M. Reichert and P. Dadam
"ADEPT flex Supporting Dynamic Changes of Workflows Without Loosing Control". In Journal of Intelligent Information Systems, Vol 10, N° 2, pages 93-129, 1998.

[22] H. Ludwig and Y. Hoffner
"Contract-based Cross-Organizational Workflows". The CrossFlow Project. In P. Grefen, C. Bussler, H. Ludwig, M.-C. Shan (eds): Proceedings of the WACC Workshop on Cross-Organisational Workflow Management and Co-Ordination, San Francisco, February 22, 1999.

[23] M. P. Papazoglou
"Web Services and Business Transactions". Technical Report DIT-03-014, Informaticae Telecomunicazioni, University of Trento, 10 April 2003.

[24] M. Paolucci, T. Kawamura, T. R. Payne and K. Sycara
"Semantic Matching of Web Services Capabilities". In First International Semantic Web Conference (ISWC), 2002

[25] P. A. Buhler, J. M. Vidal and H. Verhagen
"Adaptive Workflow = Web Services + Agents". In Proceedings of the International Conference on Web Services, ICWS '03, June 23 - 26, 2003, Las Vegas, Nevada, USA.

[26] M. P. Singh
"Distributed Enactment of MultiAgent Workflows: Temporal Logic For Web Service Compostion, International Conference on Autonomous Agents and MultiAgent Systems (AAMAS'03), July 14-18, 2003, Melbourne, Australia.

[27] T. Andrews, F. Curbera, H. D. Y. Goland, J. Klein, F. Leymann, K. Liu, D. Roller, D. Smith, S. Thatte, I. Trickovic, and S. Weerawarna
"Business Process Execution Language for Web Services", Version 1.1 BEA, IBM, Microsoft, Siebel, Mar. 2003.

The Role Concept as a Basis for Designing Community Systems

Thomas Herrmann, Isa Jahnke, Kai-Uwe Loser
Informatics & Society, University of Dortmund, Germany
{thomas.herrmann; isa.jahnke; kai-uwe.loser}@uni-dortmund.de

Abstract. This paper describes the sociological concept of roles as a basis for designing computer-supported community systems (CSCS). The goal is the systematic analysis of roles and role-development from a sociological point of view to enhance socio-technical community-systems. In system theory social structures are expectational structures and roles identify these expectations [22]. Roles explain how actors interact, collaborate and work together to cultivate knowledge exchange. The role concept in social science assumes that people interact with respect to their social roles and take certain roles as a basis for their social interaction and communication. Persons' activities and interaction is shaped by roles and vice versa. In contrast, the role concept of computer science focuses on the management of access rights and access control models, and should be clearly differentiated from the sociological understanding.

This paper presents the sociological perspective of the term "role" and explores it in more detail. Then, we present an explorative study of role-development in a web-based learning environment. We conclude by giving examples and making proposals for the technical support of roles. We pay special attention to role-taking, role-making, assigning roles, defining roles and changing roles.

Keywords: Communities, Community Systems, Roles, Sociology

1. Introduction

The experience gained in case studies and experiments with a prototype of the web-based collaborative learning environment KOLUMBUS [12] revealed that a successful usage required the possibility to be able to structure the communication process. This is the result of a detailed experiment and 10 case studies in the area of knowledge management [13]. They did show that the participants (of web-based collaborative learning processes) attempted to take different roles and tried to change their roles dynamically in being able to structure their communication. For instance, on one occasion they discussed rules and forms of annotations (e.g. the position to upload) and another occasion they contributed on content. They distinguished between organizational contributions and content. (Details of the explorative study are presented in section 3.) In addition, results of Strijbos' et al. experiment in 2003 [34] emphasised that roles appear to increase participants' awareness of interaction and efficiency through cohesion and responsibility[1]. This applies to small groups as well as social systems in general.

We presume that this also concerns computer-supported cooperative work and groupware as well as computer-supported community systems (CSCS). Further evidence can be

[1] Their study involved 57 persons, separated in ten groups. Five groups "were instructed to use roles" and the other five were "instructed to rely on their intuition and previous experiences" [34].

found in the literature (e.g. [11], [42]), which refers to a multitude of different views on roles. If we support role-development in social systems, which use computer-mediated communication, we also have to design the technical system. Often technical systems do not permit role-development, e.g. role-taking and role-changing. The establishment of social systems depends on the construction of social processes (communication processes), which are based on behavioral expectations and the differentiation between roles. In particular, the participants should be supported in selecting different types of roles, role-taking, role-assignment and role-changes. However, in the literature, roles are usually considered as having a secondary importance. Therefore, a systematic analysis is missing, which could help to find a differentiation of roles and present possibilities to support role-development and role-taking. The paper's aim is to present a systematic approach of the analysis of roles and supporting community systems. Furthermore, it is not made clear as to how the term "role" is used, in both, sociological theory and computer science. However when supporting socio-technical systems like web-based communities it is indispensable to understand the differences.

In computer science the term "role" is used in different areas, such as computer-supported collaborative learning (CSCL, e.g. [23]) or in the context of workflow-management systems (WMS). The understanding is related to roles, which are usually characterized by a set of access rights. Users in technical environments have certain opportunities of doing something if they are authorized to use them. This authorization determines the kind of access to data or the selection of functions, which can be activated (e.g. [30]) – such as deleting a persons file or creating a new folder. This WMS-oriented type of technical support for roles is not sufficient in the context of knowledge management systems, web-based learning environments and community systems. For instance, users have no opportunity of indicating role-change (colloquially: *putting on another hat*). This can be observed in face-to-face situations (with verbal and nonverbal behavior), but is missing in virtual settings. In face-to-face workshops, person A answers as a participant. A few minutes later she can stand up and give instructions as a facilitator to structure the discussion. Our explorative study also shows existing role differentiation in the logged dialogues in a learning environment, and we think supporting role-development more actively may result in a more effective social interaction, communication and knowledge transfer.

Furthermore, it would be useful, if contributions, which are entered into a technical system, were labelled differently in accordance with their communicative purposes in relationship to the role of the contributor. For example, for retrospection on a web-based discussion it could be helpful to differentiate between content and organisational contributions and to allow the users to extract exclusively the content parts. So far, approaches which are inspired by a sociological understanding of roles to achieve an elaborated support for handling roles in computer-supported cooperative learning systems are hard to find. WMS, for example, are limited to predefined roles and to the assignment of tasks to a selected range of possible roles. In computer-supported virtual communities, it is not sufficient to offer pre-defined roles which are temporarily taken during a session and which can not be flexibly changed. Thus, the CSCL literature often suggests arranging certain roles with specific tasks, for example facilitator, expert and tutor (see [9], [2]). However, these suggestions neglect the possibility for dynamically creating new roles and flexible redefinitions.

From our point of view, one reason for this neglect is that the handling of social roles usually takes place implicitly for the whole group, although it is individuals that are consciously reflecting this. During the social interaction, roles are developed, assigned, or taken over, usually without a conscious decision. Exceptions are team-building processes in business enterprises where tasks and roles are assigned explicitly to persons. In terms of sociological theory, structuring is a process based on social interaction [6] which reduces complexity [22]. This is an essential part of our "life" and also an indispensable requirement for social structuring in web-based communities, to enable them to develop. Roles are a special kind of structure – which emerges by the observations of observable interactions and behaviour, which can be understood as patterns – which can be referred to in social interaction processes. This support of forming social processes facilitates work and communication and makes them more efficient. The roles which are gradually developed can be referred to explicitly by giving them names. For example, business enterprises employ this phenomenon and specify positions and roles (e.g. organizational structure, with formal organization charts). However, the aspect of dynamical change of role-development is often neglected (e.g. adaptation of task functions to an established role and the creation of new roles).

We start with the presentation of theoretical considerations which reflect the sociological term of role in respect to communities (section 2). Thus, providing the theoretical background for section 3 where we describe selected aspects of an explorative study. The study will present examples to show that participants in computer-mediated community systems attempted to structure their social interaction, and communication processes based on role-mechanisms like role-taking and role-assignment. The exploration shows the relevance of the term role in socio-technical environments and reveals some deficits. We found examples where it is hardly comprehensible to other participants, who plays which roles at any given time and who changes their role. The study will not and can not derive the definite set of features of role-design and role-development for technical systems. However, these examples point out the necessity for technical support of role-assignment and role-taking in web-based learning environments. Finally theoretical analysis of role-mechanisms provides a structure to present some simple technical options to support social role-development in computer-supported community systems. This is systematically explored in section 4.

2. Communities, Roles and Role-Mechanisms

Sociological theories distinguish between societies (organizations and groups) and communities: the distinction reflects the difference between a formal systemic integration and an informal social integration of people into social systems. The first term is based on functional differentiation which includes the development of organizations and groups, assignment of duties and delegation of functions. The second term emphasizes social relations to neighbours, friends and kin relationship. We understand the concept of a social community as social relations and social networks, in which rules and conventions, as well as concrete membership develop dynamically. They are different from formally organised social systems (organisational systems based on mainly formal roles) or from well established small groups. Their participants are informally or loosely coupled and not formally bound e.g. by a work contract (e.g. project-groups give specific tasks to their participants). Although role development is more dynamical in communities, role development is also observable in groups and organisations. If for example a small group starts using a web-based communication platform, they have already established a role structure and they are heavily influenced by knowledge and expectations they already have about each other. These characteristics are related to their size and the opportunities provided for face-to-face communication. In contrast, communities, especially web-based communities, can be very large. Memberships can vary and they exist in non-virtual as well as in virtual communities. Memberships are investigated by research using both aspects. Under these conditions of new information technologies there are many different types of communities on the web, e.g. *discussion forums about a certain topic*, *news forums*, SLASHDOT.ORG or EBAY. These type of communities are characterized by attributes such as *online*, *virtual* or *computer-supported communities.*

2.1. The term "Community"

Tönnies work on community (German: Gemeinschaft) and society was first published at the beginning of the 19th century (first edition 1887 [35]). As examples of communities families were used. Following Tönnies, communities are characterized by traditional behavior patterns (community of the blood: Kinship; Community of the place: Neighbourhood; Community of the spirit: Friendship). In 1979, Barry Wellman began a new discussion about communities [38], and later he extended his work to virtual communities. His works emphasise six aspects in analysing virtual communities: "density, boundedness, range, exclusivity, social control and strength of relationship" ([39], pp. 185). Another approach is called communities-of-practice: in the beginning of the 1990's, the term community was related to Communities of Practice by Lave & Wenger [19][17]. They assume that coherence of a community is based on common activities[2]. Wenger [38] called it „joint enterprise": not the interest of the participants makes a community but common actions and procedures. Wenger distinguishes it clearly from Communities of Interests, which do not need to have a shared practice. Jean Lave and Etienne Wenger [19] analysed the different forms of learning processes, by which a beginner becomes a full member of a community. It is important to realise, that a community of practice is not mainly characterised by the presence of participants common goals as is roughly the case with a homogeneous community of interest. Furthermore, the building of boundaries against other communities is not based on formal organisational rules. (In contrast to other authors who extend the term *community* by emphasising the aspect of common interests; e.g. [4], [20], [32]).

Both, Wellman and Wenger show how the analysis of virtual communities might be useful in understanding how persons relate to each other using web-based learning environments. Their thesis is based on constructivism, theory of action and social network analysis. The current support of role-based interaction provided by computer science is not reflecting these insights on the characteristics of communities in an appropriate way. In the computer science literature, sociological role concepts and research on communities is only partially taken into account. There is a gap between theories in social science and the design of community systems. We propose to carefully look into possibilities to support the dynamical development of roles to enable flexible development of communities. Thus, we will try to derive possible technical support mechanisms for community systems directly from the sociological role concept.

From a sociological point of view there are three different analytic levels which can be applied to the phenomenon of communities: aspects of system, action and structure (e.g. [17]). Thus, the following three characteristics are relevant for the **definition and analysis of communities**:

(1) Communities develop a shared social identity and social unity [40] based on communication processes. The elements of such an entity consists of relationships (network) of communication which refer to role-expectations (Luhmann [22]). That means communities build a boundary against their environment by processes of selection (systems-theoretical aspect, [22]). In this sense communities are a kind of social system.

(2) In distinction from organizations such as enterprises, communities build themselves (informal character) by mutual engagement, commitment and activities. Cultivating shared, social values and norms based on behaviour-expectations (action aspect). Roles are based on behavior expectations which are extended to patterns of behaviour-expectations (see section 2.2). It is an ongoing process of interaction and social negotia-

[2] In 2003, an experiment of Strijbos and his colleagues shows that roles are an important aspect for supporting coherence [34].

tion. The exchange of ideas, knowledge and beliefs as well as collaboration, mutual support and shared understanding are central for communities [40]. Communities exchange knowledge about a domain to develop individual capabilities. They foster interactions and social relations "involving the heart as well as the head" ([41], p. 29).

(3) To maintain their capability of action, communities develop specific roles. Roles find expression in behaviour-expectations of a role-actor. Following Luhmann, expectational structures are social structures [22] (structure aspect).

Another distinction of communities concerns the size (e.g. small groups). For instance, Wellman distinguishes communities between "dense, bounded groups" and "sparse, unbounded networks" [39]. Furthermore on-line (virtual) communities are characterised by the fact that their communication processes are computer-mediated (by information technology). In contrast local communities regularly meet face-to-face [17].

If we analyse collaborative learning, knowledge exchange and interaction in virtual communities, we have to ask for the kind of expectations persons have towards the behaviour of each other in informal social relations. These expectations refer to the analysis of roles. Roles are a necessary element in supporting cooperative activity and learning. The forming of communities, which share interests, values and a practice of learning, are positively influenced by social roles: they have a structuring, coordinative and supportive function for the communities. The network of a communities' social relations can be considered as a web of interactions, and communication acts between participants playing their roles. In section 3.1, the first example of the empirical study shows that the participants discuss about expectations. Nevertheless before presenting the empirical study we describe the term role.

2.2. The term "Role" and Role-Mechanisms

The development of social roles in community systems is hardly systematically analysed and intentionally supported. Social roles in communities refer to social interaction: the individual participant (ego) realises himself and his counterpart (alter ego) in roles. *Ego* expects a specific behaviour of *Alter*. Ego tries to anticipate how *alter ego* might behave. Therefore, the analysis of roles is necessary for two reasons. On the one hand, social systems create and change themselves by reciprocal expectations towards behaviour (this is also presented by Luhmann's social system theory; [22]). These expectations are related to social roles. On the other hand, informal social relations and communities can only develop and build up, if the participants accept the conditions under which they can interact and the scope of options which determine their activities.

The term "role" has a long tradition. At first it could be found in the work of Mead [24] who was a protagonist of a role concept in the context of symbolic interaction (further contributions by [8], [18]). Mead assumed that society is composed of interactions. These interactions develop role structures. In contrast the functionalistic perspective (e.g. [21], [28]; [5]) is characterised by the idea that society determines roles, which are defined by a set of normative expectations and sanctions. Both paradigms try to explain the relationship between individual and society or between person and system. The functionalistic approach suggests the existence of objective structures which determine the individuals' behaviour. In contrast, the symbolic interaction approach emphasises that roles are formed on the subjective will of the actors. The role theory was criticised especially in the 1950's - 1970's as not being fully able to explain the complexity of social systems. Thus, role theory was no longer considered as a complete sociological theory, but the term role was integrated as a basic term in contemporary social science. A more detailed description of the sociological and social-psychological role theory can be found in Biddle & Thomas [3][1]. Contemporary social systems theory, especially Luhmann' s theory, included "role" as a basic term [22] as well as other role transitions in recent contributions e.g. Ashforth in 2001 [1] and Montgomery (1998 [26]; 2000 [27]).

Roles are often defined as sets of activities performed by individuals [7]. "A role is a set of prescriptions defining what the behaviour of a position member should be" ([1] p. 29). But this is not enough to understand role behaviour in community systems. To put it roughly, a role is the sum of all behaviour expectations of a social system towards a concrete role actor. The role actor is in a certain position, which is linked to tasks and functions. From our point of view, a **role** has the following **four characteristics**:

(1) Position: A role always includes a position, which is linked to functions and tasks. Originally, the term "position" refers to a social stratum in a society or to the hierarchy level in a business enterprise (e.g. organisational chart). The position of a role also indicates the social position. Positions have relations to other relevant positions in a social system (static aspect of structure [37]). Thus, the matrix of positions mirrors the structure of the social system. (This is also valid for informal, emerging roles. The only distinction is the level of consciousness and awareness i.e. level of explicit integration of position, tasks and functions. The turn to formal roles is gradual.)
In the empirical study (section 3) all participants had the same positions as persons who have to negotiate an interesting topic for the whole community. There is no specific designation (name) for this position. The position also includes the task, i.e. what to do.

(2) Function/Tasks: The position implies special functions and tasks, usually in the form of explicit and documented expectations, rights and obligations, which are addressed to the role actor by the social system (e.g. job descriptions and task assignment).
If we examine virtual communities we find the same phenomenon: There are persons on certain positions like administrator, authors, lurker and contributor (persons who discuss something). The name of the position often includes what to do (task and function of the position). Often, virtual communities have a website, a kind of document, that describes the uses of the different positions: the administrator has another access right as the normal contributor. For instance, the administrator can delete files or can change other persons contributions. Contributors do not have this right.

Both aspects – 1 and 2 – are used by the computer science view. Software engineers use roles to administrate and manage access rights for persons in technical systems. For instance, Sandhu et al. [30] created a role-based access control model (RBAC) for a better support of the administration of technical systems. However that is not enough to understand role behaviour. A role is a more complex phenomenon than a task/job because it develops in a network of social expectations and possibilities for positive or negative sanctions. "Roles exist in the minds of people", because "expectations are beliefs or cognitions held by individuals" [14]. The work of Ilgen and Hollenbeck (1991) distinguish between jobs and roles as structure of an organisation. "Jobs are viewed as a set of established task elements" that are objective, bureaucratic and quasi static [14]. Roles also include informal implicit expectations based on social interaction (follow aspects 3 and 4).

(3) Behaviour-Expectations: The role concept covers more than only the formal job description. There are also expectations which are not explicit. It includes informal notions and agreements [10].
If you contribute to a discussion in a virtual platform you should acknowledge certain rules, e.g. how to contribute without nonverbal behaviour, what is on-topic or not, how to formulate politly, what are "emoticons" etc. Virtual communities assume that these

facts are known. It is mostly an informal agreement and commitment. If participants do not keep to this agreement, they can expect to somehow become excluded. This is called negative sanction.

(4) *Social Interaction*: Within certain limits the role actor can actively form a role he or she has taken. However, this forming depends on the interaction with other participants in the social system. Roles are the result of a negotiation between the role actor and those with whom he or she interacts, face-to-face or virtual. The role actor *transforms* the role expectations into concrete behaviour (aspects of role-making; see below). Each participant will fill out the same role (slightly) differently [31].

The stability of a formally established organisation is based on explicit formal roles and less on informal, emerging, implicitly developing roles. The role-development for these roles is not as dynamical as roles in communities. Communities have only few formal roles but a lot of dynamically developing informal roles. Both, formal or informal roles require a kind of role-development. Formal roles can be handled more easily, because they can be considered quasi as static. Web-based systems require a different support: a socio-technical solution which enables role-development in computer-mediated communication. The term role-development consists of several mechanisms. The description of these mechanisms is the basis for the technical options (section 4).

Roles are gradually developed in social systems by perceiving the repetition of social interaction patterns based on patterns of expectations. Repeated and anticipated behaviour leads to expectations which characterise a role. The development of roles is accompanied by the shaping of interaction patterns for role-taking and role-making etc. These patterns can metaphorically be described as *role-mechanisms*. The following differentiation of **role-mechanisms** is derived from the role concept (see above):

(A) *Role-assignment*: There are two types of role-assignment: active and passive. A person assigns a concrete role to another person (active role-assignment). A person takes a concrete role and other participants agree more or less explicitly (passive role-assignment). In section 3 we give an example of a role-assignment. A community-participant has specific expectations of another participant: "Please, provide more information about structure." The expectations can be explicitly or indirectly conveyed with an expression and they may be positively or negatively sanctioned.

(B) *Role-taking*: For a person acting in respect to the expectations of a specific role, we use the term role-taking. "Role taking (...) is a process of looking at or anticipating another's behaviour by viewing it in the context of a role imputed to that other", Turner ([36], p. 316). Role taking is related to expectations which can be potentially enforced by sanctions being imposed on the role actor. A person can decide to take a role. She has the opportunity of accepting the role or not[3]. She can also develop a personal attitude towards the expectations of a role – even if she has already taken the role. This so-called role-distance means a critical distance to the role someone has taken [7]. The role distance includes a competent, critical, evaluative attitude towards the expectations, which specify a role. This attitude does not imply a fundamental refusal of the role or a behaviour which does not comply with the role [37].
Furthermore, the distinction between class – an abstract role, which may be taken by various persons – and instance – role being taken by a concrete person (role actor) – is to be considered. In virtual communities the existence of a role "facilitator" can be gen-

[3] It is not possible to freely decide every type of role taking, e.g. taking socio-biological roles (such as father or mother) can be considered as mandatory.

erally accepted on the level of the class. Nevertheless, not every person is allowed to take this role, e.g. persons who are newcomers at a discussion platform.

(C) To allow someone's role-taking: Persons can take roles, without doing this as a response to expectations of others. Someone can claim to take a role, which already exists (e.g. expert in virtual communities to a certain topic) or can introduce a new role (e.g. conflict-mediator). If those, who have the right to assign certain roles, do admit or support someone to take this role, the role-taking is approved or an assenting/passive assignment has taken place. New roles can be developed by persons who take this role.

(D) Role-change: A person can in principle hold various different roles (role-set, [25]). For example, she can be a *scaffolder* in a virtual community and structures the discussion. The next time she is a regular contributor. Other persons can be taken by surprise if she on the one hand structures and on the other hand does not, although it would be necessary. Thus, it is important for participants to comprehend the role-change.

(E) Role-making: It characterises how a person *lives* (plays) a role, and how she transforms the expectations into concrete behaviour. Role-making is embedded in social interaction: Role-making refers to two or more participants, which negotiate the expectations being significant for a role [7]. The problem (from the community's point of view) is that the role actor has a certain attitude to the role (role-distance) and this attitude can differ from what the original expectations have intended [8] (*intra-role-conflict*).

(F) Role-definition: If some expectations are addressed more frequently than others and are accepted, a new role results from this repetition. The process of the role-definition is supported particularly if the processes of role-assignment and role-taking are reflected and articulated. The role-definition becomes a part of the self description of a community. For example if it is specified explicitly that a virtual community wants to have a function *gate-keeper*, a specified form of the role facilitator, who deletes spam or other disagreeable information, then the tasks of the role facilitator are extended.

(G) Inter-role-conflict: If a person takes more than one role, a conflict between the roles can occur. For the participants of a community it is important to understand the potential inter-role-conflicts [25]. These result from different demands on different roles. For example, a person takes the two roles such as facilitator and participant at the same time. In the first situation, she structures the participants' discussion and therefore should take a neutral standpoint. In the second role she provides her own content and argues for her own opinion. Thus, there is a conflict in the person' different interests.

The analysis of roles should make the role-mechanisms conscious to participants to help and support to fulfil, or change expectations as well as making role-development comprehensible. According to the results of Strijbos et al. experiment [34], roles increase participants' awareness of interaction and efficiency through cohesion and responsibility. Thus, roles also support knowledge exchange and collaborative learning. In section 3, we analyse an experiment to show that roles are visible, and show how roles develop in computer-mediated community systems.

3. Explorative Study: how to find roles in web-based community systems

3.1. Description

In an empirical study we analysed the logged (text-based) dialogues of the communication during an explorative study with the web-based learning environment KOLUMBUS ([12], [15], [16]). The study of communication sequences intended to analyse roles and role-mechanism such as role-taking and role-assignment. The design of the learning platform

KOLUMBUS was based on communication theory, and requirements for collaborative learning and knowledge exchange. The aim was to use this learning system to initiate communication processes to enable mutual learning and shared understanding. For the evaluation of the functionality of this system, case studies and experiments were accomplished. In the context of an experiment (period 14 days), four small groups (3-5 persons each) had the task of identifying interesting topics and agreeing upon which one of them would be the main topic of a workshop for the whole group (12 persons). The discussion had to take place within the web-based computer-supported learning environment exclusively without any further communication outside the learning-system. The participants should settle the following:

- The participants should put forward three of their own ideas.
- The next step was to discuss others ideas.
- Finally they should vote on proposed ideas to find the most agreeable idea or contribution.

In order to analyse the material, i.e. logged dialogues, the first methodical step was to identify the communication dialogues and interaction sequences in the web-based system which were related to role expectations. Our first step was to expose social interaction patterns. On the basis of the methodology of Strauss & Corbins' grounded theory (text-analysis) [33] we selected those contributions which were not directly related to content and analysed their relevance to the development of roles. In a second step we analysed the role-mechanisms. We are therefore looking for types of behaviour (communication) patterns which establish roles, and we are looking for communications which contain expressions of expectation and activity. There are different types of being involved from the speakers point of view: On the one hand, the roles which are taken and/or claimed by the speaker himself (e.g. "I" or "my" etc.); on the other hand, the role, which is assigned by the speaker to somebody else. We found there were situations, where it had to be clarified as to who assigns roles (role-assignment), who takes which role actively/passively (role-taking) and whether or not the role-taking is accepted and/or confirmed (see examples 1 and 2).

First example: Active role-taking (1)

In the dialogue example 1 (figure 1), it is obvious that person A requests more structuring of the discussion several times. Thus, person A takes the role of a *scaffolder*. Person B agrees after some time and thereby she approves of her role as *scaffolder*. The expectations of person A are verified, as person B agrees. (With the term "we" she even speaks from the others point of view.) In this short section we cannot so far speak of a newly established role. It is the beginning of a process which establishes a new role by the repeated interaction pattern, which includes the participants confirmation.

Person A:	„Procedural remark: Please, directly annotate a contribution."
Person A:	„ Always, include your annotation on top, please. "
Person B:	„Okay"
Person A:	„Please, provide more information about structure: Titles, author, publisher and so on!"
Person B:	„Okay, your are right. But we are still exercising ;-)"

Figure 1: Active role-taking

Second example: Active role-assignment (2)

Person B suggests creating a new folder within the web-based learning environment but did not specify, who should do it (see figure 2). With "Let us create a folder" she addresses the group. This request is an attempt of assigning other group members a role. Person C supports this idea and claims the role of an author of a new proposal: "Let us create a single proposal". She already limits the possible action to person B and to herself (and does not address the whole group). Eventually, person A addresses C as the person who should create the folder. She assigns the role of an author to person C. Finally, person C accepts the role and carries out the activity. Thereby she implicitly accepts the role which person A assigns to herself (which can be called a *decision initiator*).

Person B:	„Well, it seems we're all interested in discussing PP. Let us create a folder to collect everything about this topic."
Person C:	„I agree. Let us create a single proposal."
Person A:	„Yes, of course, you (person c) should create a proposal and start a voting about it"
Person C:	„Okay."

Figure 2: Active role-assignment

3.2. Results and Conclusions of our empirical study

The empirical analysis of the role-related dialogues gives concrete indications as to how social roles can develop in web-based learning environments and community systems: This happened during processes of discussion and negotiation. By analysing the interaction patterns, it became clear that the *participants* had specific behaviour expectations of others – such as *author* (to add content and contributions) or *conclusion-maker*. Other roles are related to learning processes (*promoter of the procedure* and *decision-initiator*), others refer to technical problems (*technical-supporter*) or support the development of appropriate structures to cooperate (*scaffolder*). Furthermore the common situation of learning needs support so as to create and think about organisational conventions (*organisational-supporter*) and personal conflicts have to be solved (*conflict-mediator*). We presume that the support of flexible role-taking and role-assignment improves knowledge exchange, mutual learning and the development of shared understanding. The result of our analysis is an enumeration of nine possible roles, which can be derived from the text-analysis and rudimentarily be described on the basis of the observed behaviour (see table 1 below).

As the period of this particular explorative study was relatively short, it cannot be concluded that new roles were established. However it gives first clues as to the starting points for the development of roles in communities when using web-based communication. Due to the team structure which had already existed before the experiment started, the already existing roles were partially reproduced. Structures, which were completely new, have not been developed. However, some dialogues revealed, that the existing role structure might change if the observed interaction patterns were repeated more often in the web-based learning environment. New roles were then possible such as conflict-mediator and structure-giver. It has to be emphasised that we did not determine and assign any specific role for the experiment. Role taking and role assignment happened spontaneously – partially regarding the existing structure and partially regarding the specific requirements of the experimental tasks.

Role	Description	Examples from exploration (*original in german*)	Specific tasks during empirical study
1. Author (Editor)	Contributes content, communicates own ideas by writing short statements	Suggestion/Contribution/ Ideas; "thought-provoking impulse of Person A."	Add own contributions and ideas
2. Guest (only lurking)	Visitor, only interested in getting an orientation without making own contributions	„Good idea, seems relevant for our group, too."	Reads others contributions (gets inspiration for other groups)
3. Conclusion-Maker	Adds comments (conclusions) to the process of communication	„From my point of view, the conclusion looks like ...."	Has an essential influence on the content discussion
4. Promoter of the procedure	Makes the current procedure more transparent, supports task completion	„Have you all fallen asleep? You should either agree to this proposal or enter new proposals.	Promotes (accelerate) the voting process
5. Decision-initiator	Combines diverging contributions by relating them to a summarising statement	„Are we sharing this view of the problem?"	If divergent discussion, he/she initiates a concrete voting to reach a decision
6. Scaffolder	Support to cultivate cooperation	„Please, always include annotations on top."	Support common rules for holding discussion together
7. Organisational-supporter	Coach; helps to give another view of the activities (top-level)	„What about opening a kind of meta-discourse to discuss the procedure and negotiate our conventions?"	Support to think about organisational conventions (e.g. how to vote)
8. Technical-supporter	Solves technical problems	[Person B doesn't know, where the items are; the technical-supporter helps] „the items are stored and sorted automatically."	Explains the use of the technical system (e.g. where are the annotations stored?)
9. Conflict-mediator (CoM)	Acts as mediator in emotional conflicts	[2 persons have a dispute] „Right, second is similar to the first. I integrated both suggestions into one."	Intervention at emotional discussions (to enable the discussion to continue)

Table 1: Roles during the empirical Study

Table 2 (see below, next page) lists roles of our explorative study and those we found in the literature of computer-supported collaborative learning (CSCL) and knowledge management (the rows are not linked, it is only an enumeration). The three columns contain roles which are similar or have overlapping characteristics. However, some roles, which were at least suggested as a possibility in our empirical study, are different and cannot be derived from the literature. We take this as a clear hint that it is not sufficient to introduce and support predefined roles in community systems which have already been identified from existing case studies. It seems to be sensible to offer a flexible role-design which enables the development of new or the redefinition of existing roles.

To derive a definite set of features of role-design and role-development for technical systems was not the aim of our study. But it points out the necessity for supporting roles and role-mechanisms such as role-assignment and role-taking in web-based learning environments. In addition, the theoretical considerations of virtual communities referring to empirical results encourages us to continue our research in supporting socio-technical role-development. From this point of view we derive requirements for the technical support of community systems (see section 4).

Empirical Analysis KOLUMBUS Explorative Study	Literature Learning Processes, e.g. CSCL	Literature Knowledge Management
Author	Teacher	Editor
Guest	Lurker	Co-Author
Conclusion-maker	Moderator, Gate-keeper	Leader KM
Promotor to the procedure	Tutor	Process Owner
Decision-initiator	Initiator	Chief Knowledge Officer
Scaffolder	Expert	Expert
Technical-supporter	Student	Administrator
Organisational-supporter	Mentor	Content Steward
Conflict-mediator	Reviewer, Enquirer	Cooperator

Table 2: Roles from the empirical study and literature

4. Supporting role-development in computer-supported community systems

In this section we discuss technical options (see table 3), which could support interaction based on roles and support their flexible development in computer-supported community systems (CSCS). Technical support may facilitate processes in communities, but they may also be problematic. In social science the role term is basically an analytical concept, but programmed functionality of roles in software systems creates a manifestation of the role concept, where the options and restrictions for action within a role are enforced at a certain level. These problems are similar to the problems that were discussed when Winograd and Flores [43][41] used Speech Act Theory as a foundation for the system COORDINATOR. The system required that users actively classify messages as speech acts. During normal communication the speech acts are implicit, and it is unusual that an expression is explicitly classified. Consequently, the system was not used as intended (e.g. [29]). In contrast, assigning roles to persons is usually more interactive and leaves more explicit traces in communication processes than the categorisation of speech acts. (Furthermore the term role is used in everyday life, e.g. at work, conferences, sessions; at theatre and cinema, role-games at internet, etc.) So if we derive technical role-support we would not foster static formal roles but dynamically use role-mechanism to support social interaction and make it more flexible.

To derive technical functionality we especially focussed on the mentioned activities and constellations in the context of role-taking and role-assignment. We assume that in most cases it is not possible to know in advance which roles will develop. Therefore the goal is to support the development of roles as flexibly as possible. The social interaction patterns described in section 2 (role-taking, inter-role-conflict etc.) are metaphorically understood as role-mechanisms, and for these mechanisms technical support may be useful. To make clear that a support can refer to an abstract role on the one hand and a role in concrete situations on the other hand, for example when a specific person takes a role, we distinguish between classes and instances. In table 3 we propose several possible support functionalities, which are not intended as a complete enumeration, but as a starting point. The descriptions should also be understood as limiting the possible actions within a role and the possible definitions of attributes of roles.

This depends on the domain, the specifics of a role and its context. We emphasise that it is not either reasonable or possible to develop a single cooperative system with all the shown aspects of technical support of role-mechanisms nor to install them altogether and test them empirically. This would overwhelm users with an overload of functionality.

Role-Mechanisms	Class level	Level of instantiation
Role assignment	Defined roles are made available and can be assigned by drag und drop. A role-assignment is suggested as a possible action, with an appropriate display.	It is displayed which user has an authorisation for a role. The attempt of a role-assignment to another person is indicated.
Role taking	Preconditions can be defined, for example if only one person or several can take the role or if a role-owner can take more than one role. Contributions connected to a role are indicated automatically (selectable or predefined). Available roles are displayed permanently. A role can be taken by drag und drop (*to take a hat*). Participants receive an awareness display if someone tries to take a role or release a role.	The involved participants have to agree. Preconditions are verified automatically to a concrete role-owner. The number of available functions and options are adapted to the individual role-owner (in dependence of other roles). Unavailable roles are greyed out. An attempt at taking a concrete role is indicated to everybody.
To allow role taking	A support for negotiating role-taking can be helpful: Per class of roles the modes of voting are specified (Veto or not; anonymous voting etc.). It is possible to specify restrictions Conditions to release a role are defined (e.g. temporal).	A negotiation is initiated. Each participant can specify conditions. The voting is evaluated.
Role change	Conditions given to a role-change are transparent. Determining, which role-changes have to be announced in advance.	Concrete role-changes are indicated. Concrete role-changes are announced in advance.
Role making	A participant who takes a role or assigns a role is allowed to change parameters or examples, which describe the role.	The role-owner is allowed to choose between effects of a role-taking (e.g. special indication of contributions). It is possible to change the conditions/requirements of a specific role.
Role definition	Repeatable interaction patterns are made transparent (e.g. by recording und mapping) There is a list of parameters to describe roles (free annotations are possible) Examples of dialogues are collected, which show the expected behaviour of a role.	A simple click can be used to encourage repetitive behaviour of a nearby defined role, including role taking.
Inter role conflict	Interrelations between roles are illustrated in a graphical form.	The current roles of the participants are visible. Conflicts are made transparent, e.g. in preparation of a voting.

Table 3: Role-Mechanisms and technical support

Furthermore it must be considered that useful role support should be context- and domain-specific: enterprises, where knowledge management is used, need different role support than CSCL systems or CSCS, because an enterprise includes more formal roles, or the redefinition of roles needs different kind of approval.

How can this functionality (table 3) help in the context of the empirical case study (section 3.1)? How would interaction during the case study be changed with a system with some of the proposed functionality?

For the case study (section 3) the groups themselves had not been organised in advance. All participants were able to create content and help to organise the discussion. But during the case study a moderator (facilitator) developed only in some groups, in others all were equally contributing as moderators. Given the new functionality, in a group with moderator the interaction may have looked like this: The participants contributed content, but were not relating to each others contributions. One participant – named moderator – proposes some rules and uses functionality to mark her contributions as "organisational". Other participants are easily able to agree on the proposals and to encourage the moderator to provide organisational comments, by clicking on specific symbols next to the entered item (role definition). This simple pattern of one participant proposing guidelines to organise the group-process and others agreeing on them happens several times. Finally the moderator proposes to reorganise the content. The functionality enabling this to be done is usually not activated, so as to avoid incomprehensible manipulation of the shared workspace by one participant. With an organisational contribution, the moderator requests permission to reorganise the workspace (role taking). This needs other participants approval. With the approval the participants can then select between: deny, grant permission for a certain period of time, grant permission generally, or create a role with the right to reorganise the content and to connect this role with the moderator (allow role-taking and role definition). A name for this newly created role can also be entered.

With this mechanism of granting, permission of use of critical functionality can be given to those participants with an outstanding position in the community, and binding these to a role can also help others to be aware of the problems with some functionality (like reorganising the content), as well as giving the group themselves a chance to perform certain changes in their work-space. At the moment, this critical functionality is only available to technical administrators. It is not usually open to the group itself. An even more concrete example can be found in the interaction: "Let us create a single proposal" (see empirical study section 3.1). Creating a new integrating proposal is only necessary, if earlier contributions cannot be changed. A copy operation within the system, which allows users to change their contribution afterwards, should usually be avoided so as to keep authorship clear and distinguishable, but in this interaction it is socially approved that one has the right to perform some integrating action on the content. This may also result in a general permission being given to a certain person to carry out these kinds of changes.

It should be made clear, that different community systems have to support different role-mechanisms, based on their primary functionality. For example EBAY.COM, to purchase by auction, has a different kind of interactions, than a news forum or discussion forum to solve technical problems of a certain software-product. The empirical experience described in section 3 gives some hints for plausible scenarios, where several of the listed mechanisms may function hand in hand. E.g. it seems possible on the basis of the behaviour of the members that a discussion forum suggests the introduction of the roles of editor and facilitator. It also seems plausible that it is necessary to support social interaction processes such as role-assignment, role-taking and role change and that it is possible to assure compliance with the social "rules" technically. The differentiation between the roles may be documented within the system for further development. Solutions are specific to the domain and system. We suggest that in different community systems parts of the mentioned functionality should be integrated and tested empirically in a concrete context.

5. Conclusion

This paper presented the term "role" from a sociological point of view as a foundation for building and supporting socio-technical community systems. The community building process (stages of development, e.g.[41]) differentiates social structures where roles are central. The result is a set of dynamically developed roles – informal or (maybe later) formal roles. This development can be observed in any social community. We used an empirical explorative case study to show the relevance of the term role and role-development (section 3). In current technical systems roles are not actively and systematically supported. We think, that considering role-mechanisms (role-assignment, role-taking etc.) as a foundation for developing supportive functionality will help members to communicate more effectively and to exchange knowledge and to learn mutually. Obviously there is currently a gap between the role terms in computer science and social science. On the one hand, computer science assigns roles to persons as formal rights. Primarily access controls (authorizations) and assignments of tasks are controlled by static roles. This notion is present in today's co-operative computer-systems, like WMS, CSCL, knowledge management and community systems. On the other hand there is the sociological role concept: roles are a dynamic social interaction phenomenon. Participants interact on the basis of social roles and take a role for a certain period of time, to act and to get in contact with others. As an example the roles from an exploration with a CSCL-application were presented. In available technical systems no attention is paid to the dynamic development of roles in the sociological understanding.

We started with a detailed analysis of the sociological role concepts, and discussed its relevance for communities. From theory we have derived certain role-related actions (role-mechanism), e.g. role-taking and, role-assignment. This analysis leads to new options for supporting roles in community systems as well as collaborative software-systems.

References

[1] Ashforth, B. E. (2001): Role transitions in organizational life, an identity-based perspective. Mahwah, NJ: Lawrence Erlbaum Associates (LEA).

[2] Berge, Z. L.; Collins, M. P. (2000): Perceptions of E-Moderators about their roles and functions in moderating electronic mailing lists. In: Distance Education: International Journal, Vol. 21, No. 1. pp. 81-100.

[3] Biddle, B. J.; Thomas, E. J. (1966): Role Theory: Concepts and Research. New York: John Wiley.

[4] Brown, J. S.; Grey, E. S. (1995): The people are the company. In: Fast Company, 1, pp. 78-82.

[5] Dahrendorf, R. (1958): Homo Sociologicus. (1. Aufl.) Opladen: Westdeutscher Verlag.

[6] Giddens, A. (1984): The Constitution of Society. Cambridge: Polity Press.

[7] Goffman, E. (1959): The Presentation of Self in Everyday Life. Doubleday: Garden City, New York.

[8] Goffman, E. (1972): Encounters: Two Studies in the Sociology of Interaction. London: Allen Lane, pp 85-132.

[9] Harasim, L. (1995). Collaborating in Cyberspace: Using Computer Conferences as a Group Learning Environment. Interactive Learning Environment, 3 (2), pp. 119-130.

[10] Harrison, R. (1972): Role Negotiation - A Tough Minded Approach to Team Development. In: W. Warner Burke & Harvey A. Hornstein (Eds.): The Social Technology of Organization Development. Fairfax, VA: NTL Learning Resources Corp., pp. 84-96.

[11] Hedestig, U.; Kaptelinin, V. (2003): Facilitator's invisible expertise and supra-situational activities in a telelearning environment. In: Proceedings of the 36th Hawaii on System Sciences. Online.

[12] Herrmann, Th.; Kienle, A. (2003): KOLUMBUS: Context-oriented communication support in a collaborative learning environment In: van Weert, T.J.; Munro,R.K. (eds.): Informatics and the Digital Society. Social, Ethical and Cognitive Issues. Boston et al.: Kluwer. pp. 251-260.

[13] Herrmann, Th.; Mambrey, P.; Shire, K. (2003): Wissensgenese, Wissensteilung und Wissensorganisation in der Arbeitspraxis. Opladen: Westdeutscher Verlag.

[14] Ilgen, D. R.; Hollenbeck, J. R. (1991): The Structure of work. Job Design and Roles. In: Dunette, M. D.; Hough, L. M. (Eds.): Handbook of Industrial and Organizational Psychology. Vol. 2 Paolo Alto, California: Consulting Psychologists Press, p. 165-207.

[15] Kienle, A. (2003): Integration von Wissensmanagement und kollaborativem Lernen durch technisch unterstützte Kommunikationsprozesse. Köln: Eul-Verlag.

[16] Kienle, A.; Herrmann, Th. (2003): Integration of communication, coordination and learning material – a guide for the functionality of collaborative learning environments. In: Proceedings of the Thirty-Sixth Annual Hawaii International Conference on System Sciences.

[17] Koch, M. (2002): Interoperable Community Platforms and Identity Management in the University Domain. In: International Journal on Media Management, Vol. 4, No. 1, pp. 21-30.

[18] Krappmann, L. (1973): Soziologische Dimensionen der Identität, Stuttgart: Klett-Verlag.

[19] Lave, J.; Wenger, E. (1991): Situated learning. Legitimate Peripheral Participation. Cambridge: University Press.

[20] Lesser, E.; Prusak, L. (1999): Communities of Practice, Social Capital and Organizational Knowledge In: Information Systems Review 1, No. 1, 3-9.

[21] Linton, R. (1936): The Study of Man. New York: Appleton-Century-Crofts.

[22] Luhmann, N. (1995). Social systems. Stanford CA: Stanford University Press.

[23] Matthes, F. (2002): Softwarearchitekturen für CSCL-Lösungen. In: Proceedings des Workshops CSCL und kooperatives E-Learning der GI-Jahrestagung 2002.

[24] Mead, G. H. (1934): Mind, Self and Society. London: University of Chicago Press, 1967.

[25] Merton, R. K. (1949): Social theory and social structure. Glencoe, Ill., London: Free Press/Macmillan.

[26] Montgomery, J. (1998): Toward a role-theoretic conception of Embeddedness. In: American Journal of Sociology, 104, p. 92-125.

[27] Montgomery, J. (2000): The Logic of Role Theory. In: Work in progress, available online.

[28] Parsons, T. (1951): The social system. London: Routledge & Paul.

[29] Robinson, M. (1991): Double-Level Languages and Co-Operative Working. In: AI & Society 5 (1) pp. 34-60.

[30] Sandhu R.; Coyne, E.; Feinstein, H.; Youman, C. (1996): Role-based access control models. In: IEEE Computer, Vol. 29, pp. 38-47.

[31] Sievers, B.; Auer-Hunzinger, V. (1991): Organisatorische Rollenanalyse und –beratung: Ein Beitrag zur Aktionsforschung. In: Gruppendynamik, 22. Jahrg., Heft 1, S. 33-46.

[32] Stewart, T. A. (1996): The invisible key to success. Shadow groups called communities of practice. In: Fortune Magazine, 1996, Aug. 5th, pp. 173-176.

[33] Strauss, A.; Corbin, J. (1990): Basics of Qualitative Research: Grounded Theory Procedures and Techniques. Newbury Park, CA: Sage Publications.

[34] Strijbos, J.-W.; Martens, R.; Jochems, W. (2003): The Effect of Roles on Group Efficiency. In: Wasson, B.; Baggetun, R.; Hoppe, U.; Ludvigsen, S. (Eds.) International Conference on Computer Support for Collaborative Learning 2003. Bergen: Intermedia

[35] Tönnies, F. (1887): Gemeinschaft und Gesellschaft. Berlin: Curtius, 3. Aufl. 1935.

[36] Turner, R. H. (1956): Role taking, role standpoint, and reference-group behavior. In: American Journal of Sociology, 61, pp. 316-328.

[37] Ullrich, O; Claessens, D. (1981): Soziale Rolle. Der Rollenbegriff und seine empirischen Anwendungen. Fernuniversität Hagen.

[38] Wellman, B. (1979): The community question. In: American Journal of Sociology, 84, p. 1201-1231.

[39] Wellman, B. (1997): An Electronic Group is Virtually a Social Network. In: Kiesler, S. B. (Ed.): Cultures of the internet. Hillsdale, NJ: Lawrence Erlbaum, p. 179-205.

[40] Wenger, E. (1998): Communities of Practice. Learning as a social system. In: Systems Thinker, 6/1998.

[41] Wenger, E.; McDermott, R. & Snyder, W. M. (2002): Cultivating Communities of Practice. A guide to managing knowledge. Boston, Massachusetts: Harvard Business School Press.

[42] Wessner, M.; Pfister, H.; Miao, Y. (1999): Umgebungen für computer-unterstütztes kooperatives Lernen in der Schule. In: Schwill, A. (Hrsg.): Informatik und Schule. Berlin: Springer.

[43] Winograd, T. (1988): A Language/Action Perspective on the Design of Cooperative Work. In: Greif, I. (1988): Computer-Supported Cooperative Work: A Book of Readings. San Mateo, California: Morgan K. Publishers. pp. 623-653.

Cooperative Systems Design
M. Zacklad et al. (Eds.)
IOS Press, 2004

Model Checking Groupware Protocols

Maurice H. ter Beek Mieke Massink Diego Latella Stefania Gnesi
Istituto di Scienza e Tecnologie dell'Informazione, CNR
Area della Ricerca di Pisa, Via G. Moruzzi 1, 56124 Pisa, Italy
{terbeek,massink,latella,gnesi}@isti.cnr.it

Abstract. The enormous improvements in the efficiency of model-checking techniques in recent years facilitates their application to ever more complex systems of concurrent and distributed nature. Many of the protocols underlying groupware systems need to deal with those aspects as well, which makes them notoriously hard to analyse on paper or by traditional means such as testing and simulation. Model checking allows for the automatic analysis of correctness and liveness properties in an exhaustive and time-efficient way, generating counterexamples in case certain properties are found not to be satisfied. In this paper we show how model checking can be used for the verification of protocols underlying groupware systems. To this aim, we present a case study of those protocols underlying the Clock toolkit [1, 2] that are responsible for its network communication, concurrency control, and distributed notification aspects. In particular, we address key issues related to concurrency control, data consistency, view consistency, and absence of (user) starvation. As a result, we contribute to the verification of Clock's underlying groupware protocols, which was attempted in [3] with very limited success.

Keywords: groupware protocols, model checking, Clock toolkit, concurrency control, distributed notification

1 Introduction

Computer Supported Cooperative Work (CSCW for short) is concerned with understanding how people work together, and the ways in which computer technology can assist this cooperation [4]. By the nature of the field, this technology mostly consists of multi-user computer systems called groupware (systems) [5]. Our focus is on groupware allowing real-time collaboration, which is also called synchronous groupware. Examples include video conferencing, collaborative writing, and multi-user games. Synchronous groupware is inherently distributed in nature and the design of its underlying protocols thus needs to address the intricated behaviour based on network communication, concurrency control, and distributed notification. This has led to the development of groupware toolkits that aid groupware developers with a series of programming abstractions aimed at simplifying the development of groupware applications. Examples include Rendezvous [6], GroupKit [7], and Clock [1, 2].

In this paper we look at the Clock toolkit, mainly because its underlying protocols have been formally specified in [3]. Clock has been used to develop a number of groupware applications, such as a multi-user video annotation tool [8], the multi-user GroupScape HTML browser [9], a multi-user design rationale editor [10], and the ScenicVista user interface design tool [11]. We analyse several of Clock's underlying groupware protocols, among which those concerned with its concurrency control and distributed notification aspects. The analyses of the correctness and performance of these protocols with traditional techniques, such as testing and simulation, may not reveal all possible problems and are usually very time consuming. We thus propose the use of model checking, which has recently become mature enough to address problems of industrial size. Model checking is an automated technique for verifying whether a logical property holds for a finite-state model of a distributed system. In [3], an attempt was made to use model checking for verifying the correctness of Clock's protocols. Due to the level of detail of that specification and the capabilities of model-checking tools at that time, the state space was too large to handle and the attempt thus had very limited success. We revisit this work by developing a more abstract specification (model) of the concurrency control and distributed notification aspects of Clock that nevertheless covers faithfully many issues of interest. We show that this model is very well amenable to model checking by addressing the formalisation and verification of several issues specifically of interest for the correctness of groupware protocols in general, i.e. not limited to those underlying Clock. We focus on key issues related to concurrency control, data consistency, view consistency, and absence of (user) starvation. As a result we thus contribute to the verification of Clock's protocols.

In a broader context, our work shows that with relatively simple models one can verify highly relevant properties of groupware protocols with currently freely available verification tools, such as the model checker Spin [12]. The properties we verify are mostly formalised as formulae of a Linear Temporal Logic (LTL for short) [13], reflecting properties of typical—desired or undesired—behaviour (or uses) of the groupware system. Our future aim is to extend the models developed in this paper in order to cover also session management, various forms of replication and caching, and other concurrency control mechanisms.

Although time-performance issues are very important in groupware systems [14], the correctness of many of their underlying protocols is not critically depending on real time. In other words, the groupware protocols need to function correctly under whatever time assumptions are being made. This is mainly so because these groupware systems have often been designed for being used over the Internet, where the time performance that can be guaranteed is usually of the type 'best effort'. This means that much of the correctness of the groupware protocols can be analysed also with models that do not include real-time aspects. Of course this does not mean that real-time and performance aspects are not relevant to the design of groupware systems, to the contrary, but they need not necessarily be addressed in the same models as those being appropriate to verify correctness issues. In fact, abstracting from real-time and performance issues at first may make the difference between models that are computationally tractable and those that cannot be analysed with the help of automatised tools.

We begin this paper with a brief description of the Clock toolkit and its underlying Clock protocol. We continue with an overview of the basic concepts of model checking and the model checker Spin, followed by a discussion of the specifications in Spin's input language Promela of some of Clock's groupware protocols. Subsequently we verify a number of core issues of the Clock protocol. Finally, we conclude with a discussion of future work.

2 The Clock Toolkit

In this section we present an overview of the Clock toolkit and its underlying protocols. For more information or to obtain Clock, cf. `www.cs.queensu.ca/~graham/clock.htm`.

The Clock toolkit is a high-level groupware toolkit that is supported by the visual Clock-Works [15] programming environment and which has a design level architecture based on the Model-View-Controller (MVC for short) paradigm of [16]. According to this paradigm, an architecture organising interactive applications is partitioned into three separate parts: the Model implementing the application's data state and semantics, the View computing the graphical output of the application, and the Controller interpreting the inputs from the users. In Figure 1, the MVC architecture is depicted together with its communication protocol.

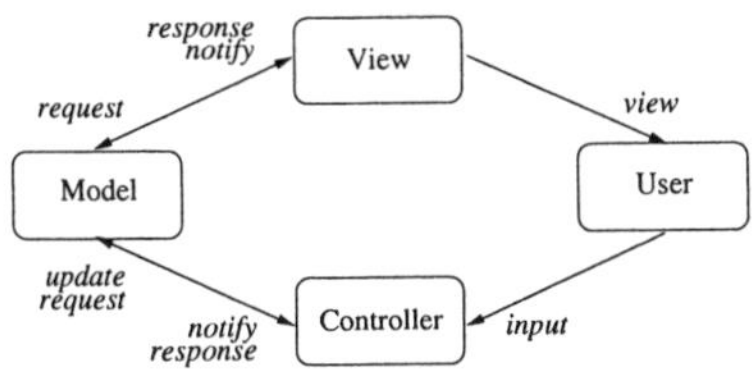

Figure 1: The MVC architecture and its communication protocol.

The Controller transforms an *input* from the User into an *update*, which it sends to the Model. In order to do so, it may need to obtain data from the Model by communicating via *request* and *response*. Upon receiving an *update*, the Model changes its data state and sends a *notify* to both the Controller and the View. The latter, upon receiving this *notify*, recomputes the display—for which it may need to obtain the new data state from the Model by communicating again via *request* and *response*—and eventually sends a *view* to the User.

In Clock's design-level architecture, the Model is situated on the server, while the View and the Controller are integrated and situated on each of the clients. The communication between the server and the clients is defined by a set of (communication) protocols, together called the Clock protocol. In [3], a version of this protocol capturing its behavioural aspects but leaving out many implementation details was formalised in the specification language Promela and an attempt was made to verify it with the model checker Spin [12]. Partly due to insufficient computing resources, however, it was impossible to verify the entire protocol. Consequently, an attempt was made to verify only a part of the protocol still large enough to be relevant, viz. the part relevant to concurrency control and distributed notification. Unfortunately also this attempt was largely unsuccessful as only 2% of the total state space was covered. We make some further abstractions in order to obtain a Promela specification that is amenable to model checking, but which still models the core issues of the concurrency control and distributed notification aspects of the Clock protocol. Since these issues are present in many groupware systems, we aim at providing a sort of reference specification that can be used as starting point for the specification of variants of the protocols considered here.

2.1 The Clock Protocol

The functioning of the Clock protocol depends on the way it communicates with its environment. As depicted in Figure 2, its environment consists of a Session Manager communicating with the server and a set of Users communicating with the clients.

The Clock protocol consists of four protocols, viz. the MVC, the Cache, the Concurrency Control (CC for short), and the Replication protocol. Based on the MVC paradigm, the MVC protocol implements multi-user communication between the server and its clients. The Cache

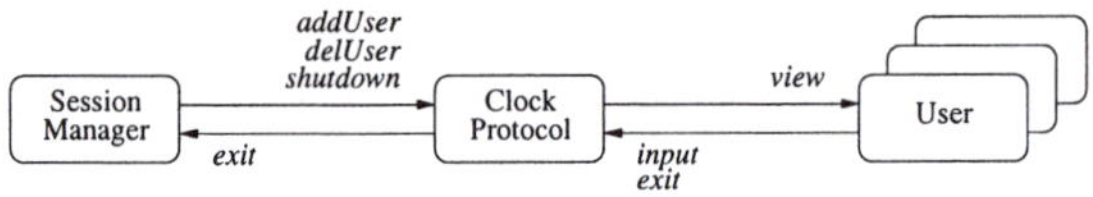

Figure 2: The Clock protocol embedded in its environment.

protocol controls caches at the server and its clients in an attempt to reduce the time needed to access shared data. The CC protocol implements synchronisation of concurrent updates and controls the processing of user input and view recomputation. The Replication protocol, finally, controls local copies of selected shared data.

Due to the size of the full Clock protocol, we abstract from it and focus on those protocols that are fundamental to that aspect of the Clock that we want to verify. Since in this paper we are interested in its concurrency control and distributed notification aspects rather than in its data aspects, we thus focus on the MVC and the CC protocol. All protocols constituting the Clock protocol are implemented by one component on the server and one on each of the clients. In case of the MVC protocol this results in a Model component on the server and an integrated View/Controller (VC for short) component on each of the clients, while in case of the CC protocol this results in a Concurrency Controller (CC for short) component on the server and an Updater component on each of the clients.

In [3], two different mechanisms implementing the CC protocol are studied: the locking mechanism and the eager mechanism. The locking mechanism uses a single, system-wide lock that a client must acquire before it can process inputs and apply updates, thus guaranteeing a sequential application of updates. Moreover, no updates are allowed during view recomputation, i.e. the locking mechanism is more involving than only providing mutual exclusion. The eager mechanism, on the other hand, allows concurrent updates and update coalescing. To this aim, all updates that are in conflict with other concurrent updates are aborted and subsequently regenerated until they are handled. In this paper we focus on the locking mechanism, leaving the eager mechanism for future work.

Summarising, we thus address the MVC and the CC protocol, and we assume that the latter is implemented by the locking mechanism. Hence we consider the part of the Clock protocol and its environment as depicted in Figure 3.

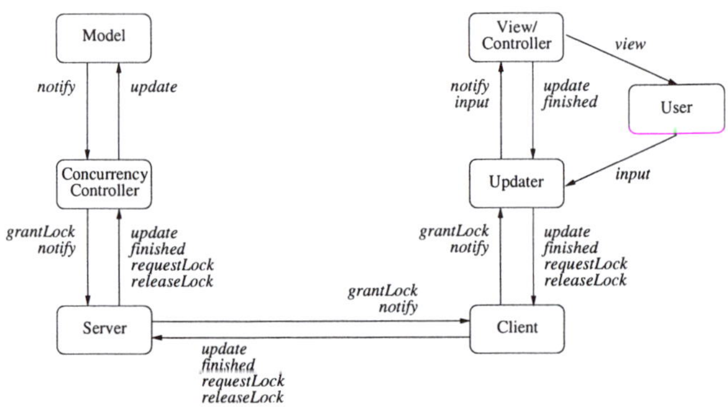

Figure 3: The part of the Clock protocol and its environment relevant to the locking mechanism.

From now on we shall refer to this part of the Clock protocol and its environment as the Model-View-Concurrency-Control (MVCC for short) protocol. A typical series of actions that can take place in the MVCC protocol is the following. Upon receiving *input* from the User, the Updater tries to obtain the system-wide lock by sending a *requestLock* to the CC. The CC handles such lock requests in their order of arrival by sending a *grantLock* back to the Updater. Only upon receiving a *grantLock*, the Updater is able to forward the original *input* to the VC. The VC transforms the *input* into an *update* and returns it to the Updater. The latter returns the lock by attaching a *releaseLock* to the *update* and sending this back to the CC. The CC forwards the *update* to the Model, acknowledges the *releaseLock*, and is only now ready to handle the next lock request. Upon receiving an *update*, the Model changes its data state and sends a *notify* back to each of the VC. Each VC, upon receiving a *notify*, recomputes the display, sends a *view* to its associated User, and sends *finished* back to the CC.

3 Model Checking the MVCC protocol

In this section we present the basic concepts of model checking and of the model checker Spin, followed by an overview of the abstractions we have applied to the specification of [3].

Model checking is an automated technique for verifying whether a logical property holds for a finite-state model of a distributed system [17]. Such verifications are moreover exhaustive, i.e. all possible input combinations and states are taken into account—a task that is impossible to undertake by hand. This makes model checking ideally suited for verifying whether a system design satisfies its specifications. To avoid to run out of memory due to a state-space explosion—which would make an exhaustive verification impossible—usually a model of the system is used that abstracts as much as possible from implementation details, while still capturing the essence of the behavioural aspects of the system.

One of the best known and most successful model checkers is Spin, which was developed at Bell Labs during the last two decades [12]. It offers a spectrum of verification techniques, ranging from partial to exhaustive verification. It is freely available through `spinroot.com` and it is very well documented. Apart from these obvious advantages we have chosen to use Spin in this paper also because of the aforementioned earlier attempt at verifying a version of the Clock protocol with Spin in [3], which moreover contains a specification of it in Spin's input language Promela.

Promela is a non-deterministic C-like specification language for modelling finite-state systems communicating through channels [12]. Formally, specifications in Promela are built from processes, data objects, and message channels. Processes are the components of the system, while the data objects are its local and global variables. The message channels, finally, are used to transmit data between processes. Such channels can be local or global and they can be FIFO buffered—for modelling asynchronous communication—or handshake (a.k.a. rendezvous)—for modelling synchronous communication. Assume that processes A and B are connected by a channel aToB. Then A can send a message *m* to B over this channel by executing the statement `aToB!m`. If aToB is a buffered channel and its buffer is not full, then *m* is stored in the buffer until B executes `aToB?m` and thereby receives *m* from A over this channel. This is an example of asynchronous communication between A and B. If, on the other hand, aToB is a handshake channel, then the above two executions must be synchronised, i.e. aToB can pass but not store messages. This is an example of synchronous communication. For more detailed information on Promela, we refer the reader to [12].

Promela specifications can be fed to Spin, together with a request to verify certain correctness properties. Spin then converts the Promela processes into finite-state automata and on-the-fly creates and traverses the state space of a product automaton over these finite-state automata, in order to verify the specified correctness properties. Spin is able to verify both safety and liveness properties. Safety properties are those that the system under scrutiny may not violate, whereas liveness properties are those that it must satisfy. Such properties either formalise whether certain states are reachable, or whether certain executions can occur. A typical safety property one usually desires is the absence of deadlock states, i.e. states from which there is no possibility to continue the execution that led to these states.

There are several ways of formalising correctness properties in Promela, the following two of which we shall use in this paper. First, we may add *basic assertions* to a Promela specification. Subsequently, we can verify their validity by running Spin. As an example, consider that we want to be sure that no lock has been granted the moment in which we are to grant a lock request. Consider moreover that there is a boolean variable `writeLock`, which is set to `true` every time a lock request is granted. Then we can add the basic assertion `assert(writeLock == false)` to the specification just before a lock is granted and let Spin verify whether there are any assertion violations. If Spin concludes that this assertion may be violated, then it also presents a counterexample showing the model's undesired behaviour. Otherwise it simply reports that there are no assertion violations, meaning that the property is satisfied by the model.

Secondly, we may add *labels* to the Promela specification, which mark a specific point in the specification. Subsequently, we can use such labels to formulate an LTL property and test its validity by running Spin. LTL is an extension of predicate logic allowing one to express assertions about behaviour in time, without explicitly modelling time. Spin accepts formulae in LTL that are constructed on the basis of atomic propositions (including `true` and `false`), the Boolean connectives $!$ (negation), $\&\&$ (and), $||$ (or), $->$ (implication), and $<->$ (equivalence), and the temporal operators $[]$ (always), $<>$ (eventually), and `U` (until). A system computation is modelled by a sequence of states and the *behaviour* of a system is the set of all such sequences. Given a sequence σ of states from the behaviour of a system, the formula $[]\,p$ is `true` if the property p always remains `true` in every state of σ, the formula $<>\ p$ is `true` if the property p eventually becomes `true` in at least one state of σ, and the formula $p\,\mathtt{U}\,q$ is `true` if the property p remains `true` in the states of σ until the property q becomes `true` in a state of σ. A system (Promela model) satisfies a formula if and only if the formula is `true` for all sequences of its behaviour. For more detailed information on LTL, we refer the reader to [13].

As an example, consider that we want to guarantee that the Promela specification of the MVCC protocol excludes starvation of its users, i.e. we want to know whether a user can always eventually provide input. The User process is specified as follows in Promela.

```
proctype User(byte id)
{
  do
  :: userToUpdater[id]!input;
  :: vcToUser[id]?view;
  od
}
```

It consists of a do-loop with two statements that can be chosen non-deterministically every time the loop is entered. The first models the user sending an *input* to the Updater, while the second models the user receiving a *view* update from the VC. Here `id` identifies the entry of the userToUpdater and vcToUser arrays of (buffered) channels. Imagine that we add the label `doneInput` to this specification directly following a user input, i.e. just after the statement `userToUpdater[id]!input`. Then we can formulate the LTL formulae

$$[\,]\ <>\ \text{User[pid]@doneInput},$$

where pid is the *process instantiation number* of the User process about which we want to know whether every sequence of states from the behaviour of the specification of the MVCC protocol contains a state in which this user's state is the label `doneInput`. Starting with 0, Spin assigns—in order of creation—a unique pid to each process it creates, which can be used in LTL formulae for process identification. Finally, we can verify the validity of the above LTL formulae (one for each user) by running Spin. Again, if Spin concludes that this statement is not valid, then it also presents a counterexample showing a computation of the system during which the particular user is never able to perform an *input*. Otherwise it simply reports that the statement is valid.

3.1 The Promela Specification

In this section we discuss the Promela specification of the MVCC protocol of which we intend to validate a number of properties in the next section. Our starting point is the Promela specification of the aforementioned simplified Clock protocol as given in [3]. The source code of this specification was generously provided by the author himself.

Recall that our focus on concurrency control and distributed notification aspects of Clock has led to the MVCC protocol as an abstraction of the Clock protocol. From the Promela specification given in [3] we have thus omitted the parts concerning session management, various forms of replication and caching, and the eager concurrency control mechanism. Since none of these parts interfered with either the concurrency control algorithm underlying the CC protocol or the distributed notification algorithm underlying the MVC protocol, their removal does not alter the behaviour of these algorithms. These changes led to a reduction of the total number of processes, data objects, and message channels, and thus to a reduction of the state space and thereby the risk to run out of memory during verification.

Subsequently we have worked on a further reduction of the state vector. The state vector is used by Spin to uniquely identify a system state and contains information on the global variables, the channel contents, and for each process its local variables and its process counter. Minimising its size thus results in fewer bytes that Spin needs to store for each system state.

Finally, in [12] it is noted that next to the total number of processes, data objects, and message channels in a Promela specification, the most common reason for running out of memory is the buffersize of buffered channels. The most important further modifications that we have performed on the Promela specification of the MVCC protocol are the following.

1. We have reduced the number of processes and channels by integrating the Server and Client processes into the CC and Updater processes, respectively. In Figure 3 we can see that this is a valid abstraction, since the Server and Client processes are nothing more than message-passing processes. Therefore, integrating them with the CC and Updater processes does not alter the meaning of the specification. This obviously reduces both the size of the state space and that of the state vector.

2. We have reduced the number of buffered channels by replacing them as much as possible by handshake channels. This reduces the number of interleaving steps and thus the size of the state space. It moreover reduces the channel contents and thus the state vector.

3. We have further reduced the number of interleaving steps by grouping assignments into atomic blocks where possible. More precisely, all administrative statements (e.g. updating bits or booleans) have been grouped into `d_steps`. These are then treated as one deterministic sequence of code that is executed indivisibly, i.e. as if it were one statement. This thus reduces the size of the state space, where all interleaving executions are considered.

The resulting Promela specification has a 160 byte state vector, whereas that of [3] has a 332 byte state vector. The abstractions that we have applied have thus reduced the state vector with more than a factor 2. Summarising, we thus consider the modified MVCC protocol as depicted in Figure 4 in case of two users, where buffered (handshake) channels are depicted as dashed (solid) arrows. It is important to note the buffered channel that is shared by the two Updaters and which connects them to the CC, as it regulates FIFO scheduling of the lock requests from the two Users. The blocks connected by arrows labelled with messages represent processes communicating by sending variables through channels in the complete Promela specification, which can be found in [18].

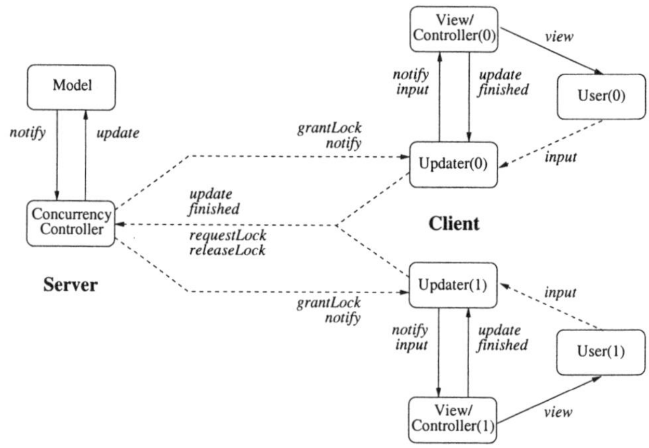

Figure 4: The modified MVCC protocol in case of two users.

4 Validation with Spin

In this section we show that the abstractions which we have applied to the Promela specification of [3] are sufficient for verifying a number of core issues of the MVCC protocol with Spin. All verifications have been performed by running Spin Version 4.0.4 on a SUN® Netra™ X1 workstation with 1 Gigabyte of available physical memory.

First we have let Spin perform a full state-space search for invalid endstates, which is Spin's formalisation of deadlock states. It took Spin just two seconds to conclude that there are no deadlocks, which is an enormous reduction compared to the hour it took in [3] to cover only 2% of the total state space. From this we gain a lot of confidence w.r.t. the verifiability of future extensions of our Promela specification, e.g. by adding the protocols concerning session management, various forms of replication and caching, or concurrency control based on the eager mechanism. To begin with, however, we want to assure that the MVCC protocol satisfies some core properties of concurrency control based on the locking mechanism.

4.1 Correctness Properties

In [3], several correctness criteria that the CC protocol must satisfy have been formulated, covering both safety and liveness properties. Since these properties should also be satisfied by the MVCC protocol, we now briefly recall them.

Data consistency. The server's shared data state must be kept consistent. Any user input that is processed by a client must thus lead to a complete update of the shared data state, which in its turn must result in a notification of this update to all clients.

View consistency. No updates are allowed during view recomputation. Any user's view recomputation must have finished before another update of the shared data state takes place.

Absence of starvation. Every user input must eventually be responded to. Any user's input must thus result in a lock request, which eventually should be granted.

We also add several core properties of concurrency control based on the locking mechanism.

Concurrency control. Every lock request must eventually be granted; only one user at a time may be in the possession of a lock; every obtained lock must eventually be released.

In the subsequent sections we verify all the above properties for the modified MVCC protocol in case of two users by using Spin, the Promela specification given in [18], and an extension of the latter which we will discuss shortly. This shows that verifications of the optimised Promela specification of the MVCC protocol are very well feasible with the current state of the art of available model checking tools such as Spin. This gives us more confidence on the correct design of the MVCC protocol than, e.g., traditional analysis techniques such testing and (symbolic) simulation, which usually cover only a part of the reachable state space.

4.2 Concurrency Control

In this section we verify three core properties of locking-based concurrency control.

First it must be the case that every lock request is eventually granted. To verify this we have added the label `doneRequestLock` to the specification of the Updater at the point where it sends a *requestLock*, accompanied by the `id` of the user requesting it, to the CC (`updaterToCC!requestLock,id`) and the label `doneGrantLock` at the point where it receives a *grantlock* from the CC (`ccToUpdater[id]?grantLock`). Consequently, we have let Spin run verifications of the LTL formulae

[] (Updater[pid]@doneRequestLock -> <> Updater[pid]@doneGrantLock),

where pid is 3 (for Updater(0)) or 6 (for Updater(1)). We thus verify whether it is always the case that whenever an updater has requested a lock on behalf of a user, it eventually grants this user a lock. It takes Spin just a few minutes to conclude that these formulae are valid.

Secondly, it must be the case that the CC may have granted only one lock at a time. Therefore, the basic assertion `assert(writeLock == false)` was added to the CC's specification there where it sends the Updater a *grantLock* (`ccToUpdater[id]!grantLock`) and then we have let Spin run a verification on assertion violations. We thus verify whether it is always the case that the boolean variable `writeLock` is false (indicating that no user currently has a lock in its possession) the moment in which the CC is about to grant a user a lock by sending *grantLock* to the updater associated to this user. Note that `writelock` is set to true by the CC directly after it has sent this *grantLock*. Again, in just a few seconds Spin concludes that the above basic assertion is never violated.

Thirdly, it must be the case that every obtained lock is eventually released. To verify this we have added the label `doneReleaseLock` to the specification of the Updater at the point where it sends the CC a *releaseLock* (`updaterToCC!releaseLock,id`) and then we have let Spin run verifications of the LTL formulae

$$[\,]\,(\text{Updater[pid]@doneGrantLock} \;{-}{>}\; {<}{>}\; \text{Updater[pid]@doneReleaseLock}),$$

where pid is 3 (for Updater(0)) or 6 (for Updater(1)). We thus verify whether it is always the case that whenever an updater has obtained a lock on a user's behalf, then it eventually releases this lock. It takes Spin a few minutes to conclude that also these formulae are valid.

The verifications performed in this section show that the concurrency control aspects of the MVCC protocol are well designed. They moreover satisfy the core properties of concurrency control based on the locking mechanism, as specified in the previous section.

4.3 Data Consistency

In this section we verify data consistency, which is an important property of groupware systems in general and the MVCC protocol in particular. Data consistency not only requires the server's data state to be kept consistent, but each update of the shared data state should moreover be communicated to all clients through distributed notification. Any user input processed by a client must thus lead to a complete update of the shared data state, which in its turn must result in a notification of this update to all clients.

Unfortunately, the specification used so far does not contain enough information to verify data consistency. This is due to the fact that adding a label `doneUpdate` to the specification of the Model there where it receives an *update* from the CC (`ccToModel?update,_`, where _ matches any value) would not have allowed us to conclude which user's input caused this update. To nevertheless verify data consistency, we have extended our specification only for verification purposes with a user ID. This ID identifies the user that has *caused* an update and is sent along with all actions involved in the resulting distributed notification of this update, i.e. *update*, *notify*, and *finished*. The complete Promela specification extended with this user ID is given in [18]. We have added the labels `doneUpdate0` and `doneUpdate1` to the extended specification of the Model just after the statement `ccToModel?update,ID` in the form of an `if`-statement, guaranteeing that `doneInput0` is passed if the `ID` in `ccToModel?update,ID` equals 0 (for User(0)), whereas `doneInput1` is passed if it equals 1 (for User(1)). Likewise, we have added the labels `doneNotify0` and `doneNotify1` to the extended specification of the Updater at the point where it receives a *notify* from the CC (`ccToUpdater[id]?notify,ID`) in the form of an `if`-statement which guarantees that `doneNotify0` is passed if the `ID` in the statement `ccToUpdater[id]?notify,ID` equals 0 (for User(0)), whereas `doneNotify1` is passed if it equals 1 (for User(1)).

Subsequently, in order to verify that any user input that is processed by a client must lead to a complete update of the shared data state, we have added the label `doneInput` to the extended specification of the Updater at the point where it receives an *input* from the User (`userToUpdater[id]?input`) and then we have let Spin verify the LTL formulae

$$[\,]\,(\text{Updater[pid]@doneInput} \;{-}{>}\; {<}{>}\;\text{Model[1]@doneUpdateX}),$$

where pid is 3 and X is 0 (for Updater(0) corresponding to User(0)) or pid is 6 and X is 1 (for Updater(1) corresponding to User(1)), while 1 is the pid of the Model. We thus verify whether it is always the case that whenever an updater processes a user input, then the Model eventually updates the shared data state. It takes Spin several minutes to conclude that the above LTL formulae are valid.

Finally, to verify that any update of the shared data state in its turn results in a notification of this update to all clients, we have let Spin run verifications of the LTL formulae

$$[\,]\,(\text{Model[1]@doneUpdateX} \;{-}{>}\; (({<}{>}\;\text{Updater[3]@doneNotifyX})\;\&\&\;({<}{>}\;\text{Updater[6]@doneNotifyX}))),$$

where 1 is the pid of the Model, 3 is the pid of Updater(0), and 6 is the pid of Updater(1), while X is 0 (for Updater(0)) or 1 (for Updater(1)). We thus verify whether it is always the case that whenever the Model updates the shared data state on behalf of one of the users, then all updaters eventually receive a notification of the update for that user. It takes Spin about a quarter of an hour to conclude that also the above LTL formulae are valid.

The verifications performed in this section show that the distributed notification aspects of the MVCC protocol are well designed and that data consistency is guaranteed.

4.4 View Consistency

In this section we verify view consistency rather than data consistency as another important property of groupware systems in general and the MVCC protocol in particular. These two properties are related, but the focus now lies on what a user sees on his or her screen. In [3], view consistency is defined as excluding updates during view recomputation. Hence any user's view recomputation must have finished before another update of the shared data state occurs (and triggers a new view recomputation). However, a user's input is based on what he or she sees on his or her screen. Therefore, we believe it to be equally important for groupware systems in general and the MVCC protocol in particular that input should not be based on an outdated view. Hence any user's view recomputation based on an earlier input should have finished before this user can provide further input.

Initially, we verify that any user's view recomputation must have finished before any further update of the shared data state can take place. To do so, we have used the temporal operator `U` (until) to prohibit the CC to forward an *update* to the Model for the second time before both user's views have been recomputed as a result of the first time it has forwarded an *update* to the Model. We thus needed to distinguish the label indicating that the CC *has* in fact forwarded an *update* from the one indicating that it *does not do so again* until it has received a *finished* from the VCs of both users. Therefore we have added to the extended specification of the CC the labels `doneInputY` and `doneInputY2`, where `Y` is 0 (for an *update* from Updater(0)) or 1 (for an *update* from Updater(1)), in this order at the point where the CC sends an *update* to the Model (`ccToModel!update,id`) and the labels `doneFinishedXY`, where `X` is 0 (for a *finished* from Updater(0)) or 1 (for a *finished* from Updater(1)) and `Y` is 0 (for a *finished* resulting from an *update* from Updater(0)) or 1 (for a *finished* resulting from an *update* from Updater(1)), to the extended specification of the Updater at the point where it sends a *finished* to the CC (`updaterToCC!finished,id,ID`). Consequently, we have let Spin run verifications of the LTL formulae

```
[] (CC[2]@doneUpdateY2 ->
        (((!CC[2]@doneUpdateY) U CC[2]@doneFinished0Y) &&
                ((!CC[2]@doneUpdateY) U CC[2]@doneFinished1Y))),
```

where 1 is the pid of the CC and Y is 0 (for an *update* from Updater(0)) or 1 (for an *update* from Updater(1)). It takes Spin almost an hour to conclude that these LTL formulae are valid.

Next we verify that any user's view recomputation based on an earlier input must have finished before this user can provide further input. To do so, we have again used the temporal operator `U`, this time however to prohibit a user to provide input (i.e. pass the `doneInput` label) before both user's views have been recomputed (i.e. both have passed the `doneView` label). We thus needed to distinguish the label indicating that a user *has* in fact provided input from the one indicating that it *does not do so again* until both users have passed the `doneView` label. Therefore we have added the label `doneInput2` to the Promela specification of the User just after the label `doneInput` and then we have let Spin run verifications of the LTL formulae

```
[] (User[pid]@doneInput2 -> ((!User[5]@doneInput) && (!User[8]@doneInput)) U
                (User[5]@doneView && User[8]@doneView)),
```

where pid is 5 (for User(0)) or 8 (for User(1)), while 5 and 8 are the pids of User(0) and User(1), respectively. It takes Spin just a few seconds to conclude that these formulae are not valid! It in fact presents counterexamples, one of which we have sketched in Figure 5.

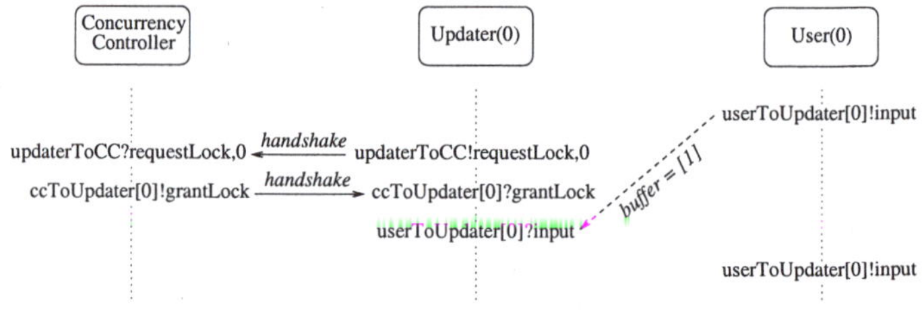

Figure 5: The message sequence chart of a counterexample for view consistency.

This message sequence chart describes the following problem. At a certain moment in time, User(0) provides an input by storing an *input* message in the buffered channel (with buffersize 1) connecting User(0) with its associated Updater(0). This Updater(0) consequently participates in two handshakes with the CC, the first one to request the lock and the second one to obtain the lock. Now that Updater(0) has obtained the lock, it reads the *input* message from the aforementioned buffered channel, thereby emptying its buffer. At this moment,

User(0) may thus fill the buffer again with an *input* message, which is by definition based on a view that has not been updated w.r.t. User(0)'s own input.

The verifications performed in this section show that view consistency is guaranteed when it is understood as the prohibition of updates during view recomputation. However, a user's input may be based on an outdated view.

4.5 Absence of Starvation

A further desirable property of any groupware system in general and the MVCC protocol in particular is that none of its users can be excluded forever, i.e. every user input must eventually be responded to. In this section we verify this absence of (user) starvation and the fact that any user's input must result in a lock request, which eventually should be granted.

The main question is thus whether each user can infinitely often provide input if it wishes to do so. To verify this, we have let Spin run verifications of the LTL formulae

$$[]\ <>\ \text{User[pid]@doneInput},$$

where pid is 5 (for User(0)) or 8 (for User(1)). We thus verify whether it is always the case that a user always eventually sends *input* to its associated Updater. Unfortunately, in just a split second Spin concludes that the above LTL formulae are not valid. It moreover presents counterexamples. More precisely, it finds cyclic behaviour in which one of the user processes can never again send *input* to its associated updater, after having done so just once in the very beginning. Even if we use Spin's weak fairness notion, defined below, then the above formulae are not valid. It can still be the case that a user is continuously busy updating its view through the statement `vcToUser[id]?view` rather than performing an input through the statement `userToUpdater[id]!input`. We come back to this issue in the next section.

We now verify that any user's input must result in a lock request, which eventually should be granted. We already know that every lock request is eventually granted. To verify that a user input eventually results in a lock request, we have let Spin verify the LTL formulae

$$[]\,(\text{User[pid1]@doneInput} \;{-}{>}\; <>\ \text{Updater[pid2]@doneRequestLock}),$$

where pid1 is 5 and pid2 is 3 (for User(0) and Updater(0)) or pid1 is 8 and pid2 is 6 (for User(1) and Updater(1)). We thus verify whether it is always the case that whenever a user provides input, then its associated updater eventually requests a lock. It takes Spin just several seconds to conclude that the above LTL formulae are not valid. This does not come as a surprise, because the cyclic behaviour in the above counterexample in fact is such that the updater that is associated to the user that can never again send *input* after having done so once in the beginning, is continuously busy with operations related to the updating of its associated user's view (that are the result of the other user's continuous stream of *inputs*).

The verifications performed in this section show that a user input need not be responded to. As a result, we were not able to guarantee the absence of user starvation and thus neither the fact that any user's input should lead to a lock request. In the next section we show that under a proper condition, absence of user starvation can however be guaranteed.

4.6 Spin and Fairness

In the previous section we have seen that, given the specification of the MVCC protocol in [18], Spin does not allow one to conclude that a user can always provide input in the

MVCC protocol, not even when using weak fairness. Instead, Spin can continuously favour the execution of the statement `vcToUser[id]?view` updating a user's view over that of the statement `userToUpdater[id]!input` performing a user's input (recall the specification of the User process from Section 3). The reason for this is the way fairness is implemented in Spin, viz. at the process rather than at the statement level. Consequently, a computation is said to be weakly fair if every process that is continuously enabled from a particular point in time will eventually be executed after that point. Note that this does not guarantee that every (infinitely often) enabled statement of such a process will eventually be executed after that point. This is due to the fact that such a process may contain more than one statement that is continuously enabled from a particular point in time and in order for this process to be weakly fair it suffices that one of these statements will eventually be executed after that point. In this section we discuss one possible solution to overcome this problem and thus enforce fairness on the statement level.

In [12] it is suggested to enforce weak fairness by specifying the desired fairness constraint c as an LTL formula and consequently verifying whether a specification satisfies a property p under the condition that it satisfies c. Rather than verifying p one thus verifies $c \mathrel{-}> p$. LTL is sufficiently expressive for specifying fairness constraints of this type.

To overcome the problem encountered above, we had to specify a constraint guaranteeing that both users are equally given the possibility to perform input. Therefore we have added the label `checkInput` to the specification of the VC there where it receives an *input* from the Updater (`updaterToVC[id]?input`) and the label `checkNotify` there where it receives a *notify* from the Updater (`updaterToVC[id]?notify`). Then we have let Spin run verifications of the LTL formulae

$$(([]\ <>\ \text{VC[pid1]@checkNotify}) \mathrel{-}> \ []\ <>\ \text{VC[pid1]@checkInput}) \mathrel{-}> \\ []\ <>\ \text{User[pid2]@doneInput},$$

where pid1 is 4 and pid2 is 5 (for VC(0) and User(0)) or pid1 is 7 and pid2 is 8 (for VC(1) and User(1)). We thus verify whether a user can always provide input under the condition that its VC checks for update notifications and user input in a fair way, i.e. whenever it checks for a *notify* from an updater, then it always eventually also checks for an *input* from the corresponding user. It takes Spin just over three quarters of an hour to conclude that the above LTL formulae are valid.

The verifications performed in this section show that absence of user starvation can be guaranteed by adding a proper constraint as a preamble to the LTL formula expressing the absence of user starvation. Such a constraint could reflect a possible implementation strategy guaranteeing fair treatment of enabled options.

5 Conclusion

In this paper we have shown that model checking can be used for the verification of protocols underlying groupware systems. More precisely, we have presented a case study on the formalisation and verification of those protocols underlying the Clock toolkit that are responsible for its concurrency control and distributed notification aspects. The correctness properties that we have verified in this paper are related to important groupware issues such as concurrency control, data consistency, view consistency, and absence of (user) starvation. As a result, we contribute to the verification of some of Clock's underlying groupware protocols, which was attempted earlier in [3] with very limited success.

In the future we plan to prove other interesting properties after extending the model developed in this paper in order to cover also session management, various forms of replication and caching, and other concurrency control mechanisms. Regarding the Clock toolkit this can be achieved by incorporating some of its components that we have abstracted from in this paper, i.e. the Cache and the Replication protocol from the Clock protocol, the part of the CC protocol regarding the eager mechanism, and the Session Manager from Clock's environment. For the development of such extensions of the specification we moreover plan to take into consideration other modelling techniques, in particular compositional ones like process algebras and team automata. The combination of compositionality and powerful abstraction notions supported by a sound algebraic theory (e.g. congruences and equational laws) not only makes process algebras well suited for protocol modelling, but also gives opportunities for effectively tackling the complexity of the analysis. Furthermore, nowadays several model checkers are available for process algebras (e.g. JACK [19], CADP [20], and CWB-NC [21]). Team automata were introduced explicitly for the description and analysis of groupware systems and their interconnections [22] and were shown to be useful in a variety of groupware settings [23]. A key feature of team automata is the intrinsic flexibility of their synchronisation operators. In [24] it was shown that constructing team automata according to certain natural types of synchronisation guarantees compositionality. Moreover, in [25] some preliminary work on model checking team automata using Spin was carried out.

Finally, an important component of groupware analysis has to do with performance and real-time issues. Consequently we plan to carry out experimentation with quantitative extensions of modelling frameworks (e.g. timed, probabilistic, and stochastic automata), related specification languages (e.g. stochastic process algebras), and proper support tools for verification and formal dependability assessment (e.g. stochastic model checking [26]).

Acknowledgements

Maurice ter Beek has been partially supported by an ERCIM postdoctoral fellowship. Moreover, all four authors have been partially funded by the Italian Ministery MIUR "Special Fund for the Development of Strategic Research" under CNR project "Instruments, Environments and Innovative Applications for the Information Society", subproject "Software Architecture for High Quality Services for Global Computing on Cooperative Wide Area Networks".

The authors are grateful to Tore Urnes for sharing the source code of his Promela specification of part of the Clock protocol.

References

[1] T.C.N. Graham, T. Urnes, and R. Nejabi, Efficient Distributed Implementation of Semi-Replicated Synchronous Groupware, Proceedings UIST'96, ACM Press, New York, NY (1996) 1–10.

[2] T. Urnes and T.C.N. Graham, Flexibly Mapping Synchronous Groupware Architectures to Distributed Implementations, Proceedings DSVIS'99, Springer-Verlag, Wien (1999) 133–148.

[3] T. Urnes, Efficiently Implementing Synchronous Groupware, Ph.D. thesis, Department of Computer Science, York University, Toronto (1998).

[4] J. Grudin, CSCW: History and Focus, IEEE Computer **27, 5** (1994) 19–26.

[5] C.A. Ellis, S.J. Gibbs, and G.L. Rein, Groupware: Some Issues and Experiences, Communications of the ACM **34, 1** (1991) 38–58.

[6] R.D. Hill, T. Brinck, S.L. Rohall, J.F. Patterson, and W. Wilner, The Rendezvous Architecture and Language for Constructing Multi-User Applications, ACM Transactions on Computer-Human Interaction **1, 2** (1994) 81–125.

[7] M. Roseman and S. Greenberg, Building Real Time Groupware with GroupKit, A Groupware Toolkit, ACM Transactions on Computer-Human Interaction **3, 1** (1996) 66–106.

[8] T.C.N. Graham and T. Urnes, Integrating Support for Temporal Media into an Architecture for Graphical User Interfaces, Proceedings ICSE'97, ACM Press (1997) 172–182.

[9] T.C.N. Graham, GroupScape: Integrating Synchronous Groupware and the World Wide Web, Proceedings INTERACT'97, Chapman & Hall, London (1997) 547–554.

[10] M. Sage and Ch. Johnson, Pragmatic Formal Design: A Case Study in Integrating Formal Methods into the HCI Development Cycle, Proceedings DSVIS'98, Springer-Verlag, New York (1998) 134–155.

[11] J. Brown and S. Marshall, Sharing Human-Computer Interaction and Software Engineering Design Artifacts, Proceedings OzCHI'98, IEEE Computer Society Press (1998) 53–60.

[12] G.J. Holzmann, The SPIN Model Checker: Primer and Reference Manual, Addison Wesley Publishers, Reading, MA (2003).

[13] Z. Manna and A. Pnueli, The Temporal Logic of Reactive and Concurrent Systems—Specification, Springer-Verlag, Berlin (1992).

[14] C. Papadopoulos, An Extended Temporal Logic for CSCW, The Computer Journal **45, 4** (2002) 453–472.

[15] T.C.N. Graham, C.A. Morton, and T. Urnes, ClockWorks: Visual Programming of Component-Based Software Architectures, Journal of Visual Languages and Computing **7, 2** (1996) 175–196.

[16] G.E. Krasner and S.T. Pope, A Cookbook for Using the Model-View-Controller User Interface Paradigm in Smalltalk-80, Journal of Object-Oriented Programming **1, 3** (1988) 26–49.

[17] E.M. Clarke Jr., O. Grumberg, and D.A. Peled, Model Checking, MIT Press, Cambridge, MA (1999).

[18] M.H. ter Beek, M. Massink, D. Latella, and S. Gnesi, Model Checking Groupware Protocols. Technical Report 2003-TR-61, Istituto di Scienza e Tecnologie dell'Informazione, Consiglio Nazionale delle Ricerche, 2003. Available through `fmt.isti.cnr.it`

[19] A. Bouali, S. Gnesi, and S. Larosa. The Integration Project for the JACK Environment. Bulletin of the EATCS **54** (1994) 207–223. Cf. also `fmt.isti.cnr.it/jack/`

[20] J.-C. Fernandez, H. Garavel, A. Kerbrat, L. Mounier, R. Mateescu, and M. Sighireanu, CADP: A Protocol Validation and Verification Toolbox, Proceedings CAV'96, LNCS **1102**, Springer-Verlag, Berlin (1996) 437–440. Cf. also `www.inrialpes.fr/vasy/cadp/`

[21] R. Cleaveland and S. Sims, The NCSU Concurrency Workbench, Proceedings CAV'96, LNCS **1102**, Springer-Verlag, Berlin (1996) 394–397. Cf. also `www.cs.sunysb.edu/~cwb/`

[22] M.H. ter Beek, C.A. Ellis, J. Kleijn, and G. Rozenberg, Synchronizations in Team Automata for Groupware Systems, Computer Supported Cooperative Work—The Journal of Collaborative Computing **12, 1** (2003) 21–69.

[23] M.H. ter Beek, C.A. Ellis, J. Kleijn, and G. Rozenberg, Team Automata for Spatial Access Control, Proceedings ECSCW 2001, Kluwer Academic Publishers, Dordrecht (2001) 59–77.

[24] M.H. ter Beek and J. Kleijn, Team Automata Satisfying Compositionality, Proceedings FME 2003, LNCS **2805**, Springer-Verlag, Berlin (2003) 381–400.

[25] M.H. ter Beek and R.P. Bloem, Model Checking Team Automata for Access Control. Unpublished manuscript, 2003.

[26] C. Baier, B.R. Haverkort, H. Hermanns, and J.-P. Katoen, Automated Performance and Dependability Evaluation Using Model Checking, Performance Evaluation of Complex Systems: Techniques and Tools—Performance 2002 Tutorial Lectures, LNCS **2459**, Springer-Verlag, Berlin (2002) 261–289.

Cooperative Systems Design
M. Zacklad et al. (Eds.)
IOS Press, 2004

Designing Mixed Media Artefacts for Public Settings

Gustav TAXÉN, John BOWERS, Sten-Olof HELLSTRÖM, and Helena TOBIASSON
Centre for User-Oriented IT Design, Royal Institute of Technology (KTH), 100 44 Stockholm, SWEDEN

Abstract. This paper describes how principles which are emerging from social scientific studies of people's interaction with mixed media artefacts in public places have been used to support the development of two installations, the second of which is a long term museum exhibit. Our principles highlight the design of 'emergent collaborative value', 'layers of noticeability' and 'structures of motivation' to create an 'ecology of participation' in installations. We describe how our first installation was used as a 'research vehicle' that guided and shaped the design of the museum installation. We also provide an account of how people interact with our installations and how this analysis has shaped their design. The paper closes with some general remarks about the challenges there are for the design of collaborative installations and the extent to which we have met them.

1. Introduction

In recent years, research in Computer Supported Cooperative Work (CSCW) has begun to include topics and settings which add to its traditional concern for the world of work and the information technologies to be found there. For example, Craven et al. [8] describe applications of collaborative virtual environments which have clear leisure and entertainment uses. While these authors speculate that the methods they have used for organising participation in game-like or story-telling environments might have applications in more traditional areas of CSCW (e.g. the coordination of contributions to a shared work task), this is not their primary concern. Mynatt et al. [19] discuss a community computing initiative called SeniorNet in which people who are or who are about to become retired from employment are supported in their use of networked computing technologies. Brown et al. [5] describe a system for music sharing (Music Buddy) which embeds this activity in social interaction and collaborative exchange. Again, the concern is to examine a phenomenon not normally associated with activity at the workplace to "learn lessons for more conventional CSCW applications" (p.180). All three of these examples demonstrate a growing tendency to broaden the remit of CSCW beyond workplace settings, systems and applications, even if an ultimate reference back to them is intended.

Another tendency in recent CSCW contributions is to examine the use of technology by a broad population of users. The Craven et al. research just mentioned is concerned to enable members of the public to participate in 'on-line experiences' of an entertaining kind. SeniorNet and Music Buddy are similarly broad in their conception as to who count as users of them (the over 50s, music fans). This stands in contrast to much traditional CSCW which trades on a strong conception of users or workers as engaged with particular work tasks and, through analysis of that work, offers design ideas or systems intended to mesh with those work settings. Rather, we see CSCW coming to engage with notions of 'the citizen' or 'the public'.

Indeed, some researchers have begun to examine people's encounters with technologies in public places such as museums and art galleries. Büscher et al. [6] describe a media art exhibition space and characterise the ways in which people move between the pieces contained therein, learn about them and cooperate with each other in making sense of them. On the basis of these observations, the authors make proposals for organising of large scale, interconnected multi-user virtual environments and enhancing their intelligibility. In recent work, Heath et al. [12] describe how people engaged, largely within small groups of friends, with an interactive visual installation so as to draw each others' attention to interesting features while cooperating on the joint operation of the piece. In particular, these authors are concerned with how co-participants shape each others' perception and appreciation of the installation, and how passers-by maintain a peripheral awareness of the activities of those directly engaged with it, perhaps learning from them when they in turn initiate interaction.

1.1 Social Scientific Design Sensitivities

The work we report in this paper is an extension of this emerging concern for engagement and collaborative interaction with technologies in public places in general and museums in particular. The paper centres on the design of two installations. The first, ToneTable, acted as a prototype and 'research vehicle' where we explored a number of interaction principles derived from social scientific design sensitivities. This research was then used to shape the design of a long-term installation, The Well of Inventions, at the Museum of Science and Technology in Stockholm, Sweden. Our work, in many respects, instantiates a design response to the social scientific precepts we gain from the work of Heath et al. and Büscher et al. and their studies of behaviour in public places with respect to artistic and museum pieces. In particular, we itemise two areas of concern we wish to be sensitive to in design.

- *Multiple forms of participation.* People manifest many different orientations towards artefacts, installations and exhibitions. There is a range of forms of engagement–central or peripheral, active or passive, overhearer/overseer etc.–which need to be taken account of. Visitors who are alone, and those who come with others, need equally to be accounted for. If possible, one should design so as to support the simultaneous coexistence of these multiple forms of participation in an 'ecology of participation' (Heath et al. [12]).
- *Interaction and co-participation.* Interaction should not refer to just the interaction of a single 'user' with an exhibit but should address the multiple ways in which people engage with each other in, around and through the artefact. This may involve providing "enhanced or variable functionality when participants interact with each other in and through the exhibit" (Heath, et al. [12]).

2. ToneTable

ToneTable is a multi-participatory, mixed media installation which embodies a number of systematic strategies for combining sonic and computer graphical materials in ways which support multi-participant interaction. The installation consists of a table-top graphical projection situated in the middle of a multi-speaker sound environment. We publicly exhibited ToneTable a number of times and continually refined its design in the light of experience, which allowed us to illustrate a number of interesting design principles in action in real practical settings. As we shall see, we have worked with some specific design concepts to respond to the social scientific sensitivities outlined above. As such, we hope our work shows how social scientific work in CSCW can be responded to methodically yet creatively.

2.1 Related Technologies

A number of table-top interaction devices with an embedded graphical display have been reported in the CSCW, HCI (human computer interaction) and allied literatures. For example, the InteracTable developed at GMD (http://www.darmstadt.gmd.de/ambiente/activities/interactable.html) uses a large projection onto a table top with information manipulation being supported by pen and finger-touch based interaction at a touch sensitive surface. Local infra-red networking allows other devices to be brought to the table for interaction purposes. Interactive sound has been incorporated into InteracTable to provide feedback to user gesture, in some cases through the physical modeling of dragging and writing sounds.

A further development of this concept is to combine the manipulation of specially designed physical objects on the surface with a projection of a computer graphical world onto the surface. For example, DigitalDesk [22] and phicons [16] are both concerned with the combination of computational media with a physical device or display surface.

Hoch et al. [14] describe The RoundTable in which a visualisation is projected up onto a table surface. On the table surface, a small number of phicons can be placed, which can have a variety of effects on the visualisation. The phicon positions, orientations and identities are extracted from video which is captured by a camera positioned above the table. Hoch et al. describe an application in which movements of the phicons control, amongst other things, the deployment and movements of virtual cameras in an on-line collaborative virtual environment, the table top visualisation providing a map-view of the overall environment. In an extension of this work, Bowers et al. [3] describe an application of The RoundTable in which the positioning of objects on the table surface mixes sound sources, a kind of 'mixed reality mixer desk'. The position, orientation and identity of objects in the visualisation denote sound sources, while the position et cetera of phicons placed on the surface denote virtual microphones with the mix at a selected virtual microphone being computed and rendered on a stereo loudspeaker system.

In our current work with ToneTable and The Well of Inventions, we decided to simplify the interaction methods to concentrate on design principles for supporting multiple participants working with sound and graphics. Accordingly, we chose to work with simple trackball based interaction (rather than the phicons and video processing of The RoundTable). This simplification enabled us to explore more satisfying inter-media relations than our earlier mixed reality mixer desk. Our installations support multi-user interaction with real-time sound synthesis, as well as sound file playback and processing, both in relation to the behaviour of a computer graphical animation.

2.2 Introducing ToneTable

ToneTable is a sound and computer graphics installation which enables up to four people to collaborate to explore a set of dynamical relationships between different forms of media [4]. We envisioned a scenario in which visitors would encounter a table within a room-sized environment which also contained a multi-speaker sound system. A visualisation of a real-time updated physical model of a fluid surface would be projected onto the table from above (Figure 1). The 'virtual fluid' would have its own autonomous flowing behaviour, as well as being influenced by the activity of the visitors. A small number of virtual objects would be floating on the surface, and these would move around the display in response to the dynamics of the modeled fluid surface. By using the trackballs, our visitors would be able to move sources of virtual 'wavefronts' around the display, which in turn would enable the visitors to 'push' the floating objects. If the local force upon a floating object exceeded a certain threshold, the object would suddenly exhibit a radically different behaviour. In our realisation of ToneTable, we chose to let this new behaviour consist of an orbiting motion around the display, which would gradually come to rest and resume the more gentle meandering behaviour characteristic of the objects moving as a result of the flowing surface alone.

Figure 1. The graphical projection of ToneTable. Each of the four 'wavefronts' is associated with the motion of a trackball. The 'stars' are the visual representation of the spatialised sound textures.

To achieve a mixed media installation, our scenario involved a number of correlations between the interactive computer graphics and the sound. Each floating object would have a specific sound texture associated with it. By carefully arranging a set of four speakers in the vicinity of the table, we would create a soundfield within which these sound textures could be heard. Furthermore, the sounds would be spatialised so that their visual representation on the table was spatially consistent with their heard-location in the soundfield.

2.3 Design Principles and Scenarios

ToneTable can be seen as an exploration of a number of principles for the design of interaction in mixed media artefacts, principles that are responsive to the design sensitivities emerging from the social scientific work touched on above. These principles include (from [4]):

Layers of Noticeability, Varieties of Behaviour, and Structures of Motivation. Our ToneTable scenario involved a variety of sonic and graphical behaviours which would be progressively revealed through visitor interaction (both individually and collectively) with the trackballs. This would give a 'structure of motivation' to the installation. That is, we intended to provide an 'in-built' incentive to explore the table and its varied behaviours and image-sound relations. Indeed, the dynamical behaviours of ToneTable were defined and calibrated with various non-linearities. Our intention here was to make the exploration of ToneTable an open-ended affair with some of the behaviours it is capable of being 'emergent' and not necessarily known to the designers in advance. As such, we were hoping that ToneTable would make for a contrast with interactive installations where there is a 'key' or hidden, underlying principle that needs discovery and, once discovered, exhausts the interest of the piece. Finally, by 'layering noticeability and interaction' in the manner we have described, we wanted to create an artefact which could be explored over various timescales. While there would be an immediate responsivity to its use, additional behaviours would be revealed with more extended engagement. In this way, ToneTable is intended to give value no matter how long visitors engage with it.

Interaction Through a Shared Virtual Medium and Emergent Collaborative Value. Our ToneTable scenario was developed to support interaction between visitors through a shared virtual medium. By coordinating their activity in that medium, visitors can engender 'added values'; behaviours of ToneTable which a person acting alone can not so easily obtain. However, the resting state of ToneTable would not be without interest and variety: it would have a variety of behaviours available to visitors acting alone. The intention here was to design an artefact which permits variable forms of engagement, both individual and collaborative, both 'hands-on' and spectating. In addition, by coordinating activity through a common virtual medium, we hoped that participants could gracefully move between one form of engagement and another. They could work individually or in close coordination with others through the use of the same devices and repertoire of gestures. Thus, collaboration would not require a switch of 'interface mode' over individual activity (cf. the proposals for 'encouraging collaboration' in [1]).

Variable Image-Sound-Activity Associations. ToneTable relates image, sound and participant-activity in a variety of ways. Sound is associated with individual graphic objects. Sound is also associated with individual device-usage. This variety of strategies was intended to enable an approach to the mixing of media which is rich and more satisfying for participants than if just one technique had been employed. It has the consequence that a single gesture may well produce multiple sonic effects.

Abstract, Yet Suggestive Content. ToneTable was developed in cooperation with the Museum of Science and Technology in Stockholm, a cooperation which carried over into the development The Well of Inventions. The museum allowed us autonomy in the design of content for The Well of Inventions, which enabled us to regard ToneTable as a 'research vehicle' for exploring various inter-media design strategies and approaches to collaborative interaction. These strategies and approaches then became the foundation from which the design of The Well of Inventions was built. The content of both installations is 'abstract, yet suggestive'. That is, neither installation attempts to compete with any of the museum's substantive exhibits. They both suggest the domain of fluid dynamics and could be related to other interactive exhibits whose treatment of physics is more 'correct' than our approximations. They do not directly attempt to teach fluid dynamics but could provide an occasion for a teacher or the museum staff to do so. By dealing with content in this way, we hoped to produce exhibits of a playful sort that could be incorporated alongside more pedagogical exhibits or be treated as just fun.

2.4 Observations of ToneTable in Use

ToneTable has been presented to the public on a number of occasions, and feedback from the public enabled us to refine its design (cf. [4] for details). In addition, we also collected video-based material at one of the public events where ToneTable was displayed. Although this material was not optimal for detailed interaction analysis (sound quality was poor, for example), we were able to use it to draw a number of conclusions that assisted in shaping the design of The Well of Inventions.

Our treatment of the data collected (video-recordings and field notes) draws upon principles of ethnographic research as established in CSCW by authors such as Hughes and his colleagues (e.g., [2]) while being sensitive to interactional phenomena of the sort documented by Heath et al. [12]. This social scientific tradition of research emphasises detailed descriptions of the data (here concerning interaction and gesture in relationship to a mixed media artefact) rather than a hypothesis testing approach.

In general, most of our visitors appeared to endorse the quality of sound and graphics in ToneTable, together with the existence of different behaviours which could be progressively uncovered. Some visitors, however, were less tolerant of something 'abstract, yet suggestive' and found ToneTable lacking in real content (an issue which we shall return to in section 4). However, amongst those who were willing to enter in a more playful spirit, we were able to see many examples of careful collaborative interaction between participants at the table as, on a number of occasions, people coordinated their gestures to jointly elicit the orbiting behaviour and other effects.

Gestural Variety. Although ToneTable used conventional trackball input devices, it should not be thought that there is necessarily anything lacking in them with respect to their usefulness in this setting. Indeed, we observed a great variety of different gesture types being performed on the trackballs, with correspondingly a variety of different behaviours being achievable in the virtual environment projected on the table and in the soundfield.

Some of the gesture types we have noted include the following.

- *Tickles.* By gently and in turn moving the fingers over the trackball a slow, continual, yet interruptible, trajectory of the wavefront across the table can be sustained.
- *Tremors.* By quickly moving a finger or the palm backwards and forwards or from side to side, the wavefront can 'shudder' on the display.
- *Rubbings.* By rolling the palm across the trackball, a large displacement of the wavefront on the table can be achieved. Such gestures have a characteristic acceleration and deceleration and a start-move-stop 'envelope'. They are often followed by a rubbing in the reverse direction as large oscillations across the display and the soundfield are accomplished.
- *Circular rubbings.* By rolling the palm around the trackball, a large continuous circular path can be inscribed on the display, perhaps pushing sound objects around the soundfield along the way.
- *Single finger rub.* A single finger, commonly the index, might be used to accurately and delicately position the wavefront at a particular locus in the display so as to interact with, for example, a single object/sound.
- *Flickings.* A single finger, again commonly the index, is withdrawn under the base of the thumb and out of contact with the trackball, it is then suddenly released, hitting the ball which turns freely and then decelerates while the flicking finger follows through. This produces a trajectory on the table with sudden onset and rapid movement, and a corresponding sudden change in the soundfield.

Coordinating Gestures. Our video recordings revealed a number of examples of co-participants closely coordinating the kinds of gestures they perform and their temporal patterning. For example, at one moment, Y initiates a rubbing gesture to perturb one 'corner' of the graphical display. Immediately following this, M moves his wavefront to the same corner and performs the same gesture type. After a couple of seconds of this joint activity, they both simultaneously 'expand' the rubbing behaviour so as to take in more of the display in their wavefront movements with a highly noticeable increase in intensity of the activity sonification accompanying their gestural expansion.

Figure 2. Coordinated gestures at the table.

Figure 2 shows three people at ToneTable. The two to the right of the picture are both jointly engaged in rubbing gestures, one with the middle and ring fingers in contact with the ball, one with the thumb. They are jointly achieving an extensive perturbation of the virtual surface at the corner between them. For her part, H with her back to the camera and to the left of the picture is rubbing the trackball vigorously with the palm of her hand, producing large movements of her wavefront over the rest of the display. At this moment, then, a pair of participants are coordinating their gestures with each other in close interaction, while a third person employs a gestural type which will enable her to make a big effect but without disturbing them. Importantly, then, the table is able to support the coexistence of a variety of gestural types and activities. It does not enforce all participants to collaborate with one another and is tolerant of variable groupings and foci for activity.

Gestures in Physical Space. So far we have discussed some of the different gestures which we have observed being made with respect to the trackballs and the different effects in the graphical and sonic environment they produce. We have also noted how participants coordinate their different gestures with each other. We will now consider some other kinds of gestures, in particular, those not made on or with the trackball. For example, at one moment, K points to a region of the display just adjacent to where L and M are making their wavefront movements, and he is using the shadow of his hand in the projection to precisely pick out a graphical object he would like his co-participants to try to perturb.

Gestures of this sort are often precisely timed so as to accomplish a kind of 'commentary' or 'suggestion' with respect to what is going on within the display, without disrupting it. Equally, activity on the table often accommodates such gestural commentaries and suggestions as they are being offered.

In Figure 3, H is making a large circular gesture with her right hand to draw attention to the orbiting of a sound around the room's soundfield. In this way, she picks out a particular consequence of her activity at the table and draws attention to the relationship between sound and graphics. This occurs just after the moment depicted in Figure 2 where H was dramatising the effect of large gestures. The table and her gestural activity with respect to it is enabling H to 'instruct' visitors to the installation in the graphical-sonic relationships it contains for her. Throughout all this, two other participants continue to explore the table with smaller gestures.

Figure 3. Gesturally 'animating' the moving sounds.

Coming and Going. Throughout our work on ToneTable, we have been designing not just for hands-on use of the devices at the table but for a participant's trajectory through the installation. Our design is very flexible in how it allows for 'comings and goings'. A single person can explore the table, as can a pair both working together or separately. While up to four people can be accommodated hands-on, they can pattern their activity very flexibly. Equally, there is space allowed for others to peripherally participate, perhaps waiting their turn while watching, or allowing a friend to have their turn.

The simplicity of the trackball as an interaction device and the fact that it requires no special 'tooling up' or instruction allows comings and goings at the table to be elegantly managed. A visitor can peripherally monitor the action at the table standing close to one of the participants. When that participant gives way, the new person can take over probably having already worked out the associations of particular trackballs to particular wavefronts and having observed a variety of behaviours and gestural types. Our design makes it easy for a newcomer to 'pick things up' where an earlier participant 'left off' and either extend the earlier person's explorations or try something new.

Collaboration and Emergent Effects. In several groups of participants we were able to observe a repeatable pattern of coordination which tended to elicit the orbiting behaviour of the graphical objects and their associated sounds. If two or more participants approach one of the floating objects together following approximately the same trajectory with their wavefronts passing over the object at approximately the same time, then the object is highly likely to start orbiting. By jointly pursuing the orbiting object, the participants are likely to get the object to orbit again once it stops. This strategy of 'co-chasing' one or more objects is likely to systematically elicit the orbiting behaviour and maintain it, if not continuously, then at least prominently. A number of groups of participants realised this and organised themselves to achieve this outcome. In particular, one pair of participants returned to ToneTable on a further occasion with an extra friend so as to more effectively chase the computer graphical objects around the projected display, and make the sounds move around the room.

3. The Well of Inventions

At the initiative of the Museum of Science and Technology in Stockholm, we evolved the design of ToneTable into a long-term, unattended museum installation–The Well of Inventions–which opened in May 2002 and is currently still on display. Let us now describe how the design sensitivities upon which ToneTable was developed have been carried over into the new installation.

Layers of Noticeability, Varieties of Behaviour, and Structures of Motivation. It is well established within museum research that visitors' prior motivation and expectations together with their current knowledge, beliefs and interests shape and influence the outcome of their visit (e.g., [7], [13], [15], [11]). Choice and control, and whether such choice is governed by intrinsic or extrinsic factors have also been shown to be important factors. For specific interactive activities, characteristics like clear goals, immediate unambiguous feedback, and levels of difficulty that are in balance with the visitor's abilities have been shown to be important features of successful exhibit designs [9].

With ToneTable and The Well of Inventions, we have attempted to be sensitive to this research by providing visitors with artefacts that can be used in multiple ways, and where new features are progressively revealed through extended use. At the same time, uncovering all of these layered features is not essential to the quality of the visitors' experience. Furthermore, our ToneTable observations suggested that the use of trackballs might be particularly suitable for The Well of Inventions; while they were straightforward to use for most visitors, they also afforded a large range of expressive and creative types of interaction. Indeed, many museum installations make use of trackballs, albeit more often as a replacement for on-screen cursor positioning devices like mice than as an integrated part of an exhibit.

Interaction Through a Shared Virtual Medium and Emergent Collaborative Value. Recent museum learning research suggests that the social circumstances and how people interact with each other at exhibits directly influence the success of their museum visit [11]. Thus, many museums are now showing an increasing sensitivity towards designing exhibitions that encourage discussion and collaboration between visitors and between visitors and staff. However, the physical design of many interactive exhibits still neglects to explicitly support multiple co-present visitors, and this is especially true for computer-based exhibits (e.g., [11], p. 191, [10], [18]).

The interaction principles embodied in ToneTable thus seemed particularly suitable for the museum setting. By supporting simultaneous input from multiple co-present users, ToneTable enabled–and indeed seemed to encourage–collaborative behaviour. By projecting onto a table, other forms of participation were made possible, ranging from passive observation to pointing and gesturing. The physical design of ToneTable also allowed for graceful turn taking.

Variable Image-Sound-Activity Associations. Different forms of multimedia have been used in museum exhibitions for a long time. Such technologies are typically straightforward in their use of inter-media connections, e.g., CD-ROM-based catalogues, kiosks and listening booths. At the same time, museums are currently facing fierce competition from other entertainment providers such as theme parks and movie complexes, which has resulted in an increasing interest in state-of-the-art technologies (ranging from IMAX-like theatres with interactive elements to personal, portable digital assistants). However, non-trivial forms of associations between image, sound and visitor activity in interactive museum exhibits are still relatively rare. Thus, in addition to acting as a 'research vehicle' for the exploration of a number of interaction principles as described above, ToneTable also embodied a number of design principles that have previously received limited attention within the museum domain – principles we sought to extend in The Well of Inventions.

3.1 The Design of The Well of Inventions

From our observations of ToneTable, we concluded that while its basic design supports and extends important features of the modern museum experience, its content, aesthetics and physical features would have to be further developed before it was suitable as a unsupervised long-term exhibition. Furthermore, the number of visitors to the Museum of Science and Technology can be very large at times. Therefore, our new installation had to support larger groups of co-present users than ToneTable. As a result, we envisioned a configuration of the architectural space that would make it possible to walk through the installation area without interrupting the activities at the table. The space would also contain a spectator platform from which it would be possible to overlook the installation, and a number of movable stools would allow visitors to sit down at the table. Figure 4 shows the ensuing layout of the installation.

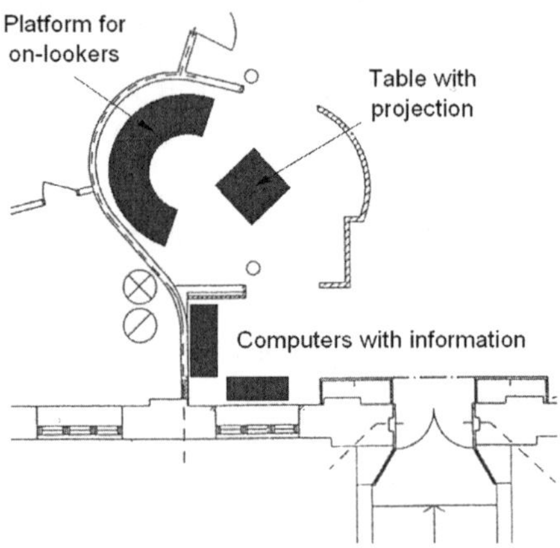

Figure 4. The layout of The Well of Inventions.

The Well of Inventions would be situated in the museum's Science Centre gallery where most exhibits are of a concrete, pedagogically oriented, experimental nature. Thus, we felt that a more explicit content for our installation would be less disruptive and fit better with the general theme of the gallery. At the same time, we wanted to retain the overall 'abstract, yet suggestive' feel of ToneTable. The Museum of Science and Technology contains many artefacts that are associated with machinery and dynamics in different ways, and this provided us with a suitable theme for the installation. Thus, our scenario for The Well of Inventions involved replacing the abstract star-like floating objects of ToneTable with depictions of museum artefacts like propellers and turbines. The object sound textures were also modified to be suggestive of these depictions.

Our scenario also allowed the objects to be situated both above and beneath the fluid surface, and replaced the empirically developed equations that governed their motion in ToneTable with rigid body mechanics (Figure 5). We also extended the range of motion behaviours by replacing the original fluid-like animation of ToneTable with a two-dimensional fluid flow simulation beneath the water surface and an airflow simulation above the surface. As a result, trackball motion would 'stir' the water by injecting virtual forces into the simulation. Such 'stirring' would move the objects along the local velocity of the fluid flow. In addition, by correlating the buoyancy of the objects to their velocity, it would be possible to 'push' the objects through the water surface. Above the surface, the motion of the objects would be governed by the airflow simulation, which would allow them to move in a radically different manner. This feature would replace the original 'orbiting' behaviour in ToneTable. In our scenario, the trackball positions would also act as wind vortices that create turbulence in their vicinity. Thus, by coordinating their activities at the table, visitors would be able to collaborate to more readily push the objects through the water surface or cause the objects to 'hover' above the surface.

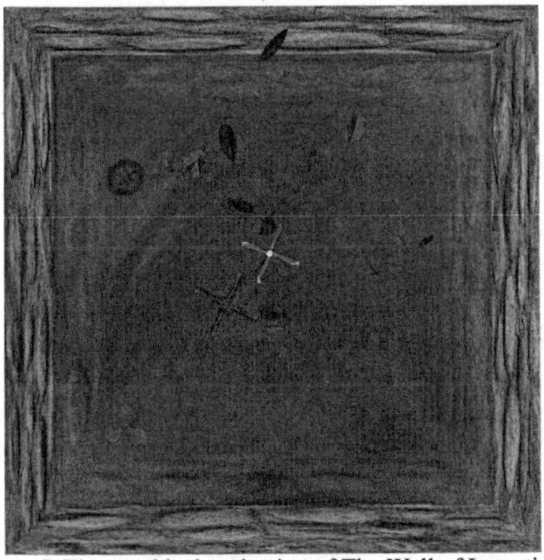

Figure 5. The graphical projection of The Well of Inventions.

While we acknowledged the need to provide visitors with background information concerning the purpose and goals of the exhibition, we did not want to introduce such texts into the main installation area. Thus, the installation was to be accompanied by an 'antechamber' that would contain a number of computer monitors. These monitors would display a set of different slideshows containing the background information.

Our scenario also introduced additional layers of noticeability, including ghostly reflections in the water and 'sticky' water. The reflections are images of machinery in which propellers and turbines are used, and constitute the inventions referred to by the title of the installation. 'Sticky' water is achieved by successively increasing the apparent viscosity of the fluid locally around two or more cursors when they are in close proximity for an extended period of time. When the cursors are brought apart, the viscosity gently relaxes back to its default value. In this way, the behaviour of the installation can subtly change depending on how visitors coordinate their movements and positions in the shared virtual medium. Further details concerning The Well of Inventions can be found in [20] and [21].

3.2 Observations of The Well of Inventions in Use

We have observed visitors interacting with The Well of Inventions for a total of approximately twelve hours, spread across multiple days. As with ToneTable, most of our visitors appeared to endorse the quality of sound and graphics present in the installation. Although our data indicate that visitors interacted with The Well of Inventions in ways that were similar to how visitors interacted with ToneTable, a number of interesting differences are also present.

Larger Variations in Dwell Times. Typical dwell times at The Well of Inventions varied from a few seconds to roughly ten minutes. The longest dwell time we observed was close to thirty minutes. Often, visitors would stay for at least a minute if they 'got hooked', which is considerably longer than with ToneTable.

Opportunities for Rest and Relaxation. The Well of Inventions appears to provide many visitors with an opportunity for relaxation and rest. On many occasions, we have observed visitors who approach the installation at a high pace and initiate their interaction with it through quick and aggressive trackball gestures, and then successively relax down into a slower pace and more intricate and careful trackball movements. Our observations also include other types of visitor body postures that are typical of restful environments, such as relaxation and lowering of shoulders, sighs, leaning forward towards the table, and using the table to support arms and body weight. The environment also seems to afford a more quiet verbal intercourse than other parts of the Science Centre.

Layers of Noticeability Were Challenging to Discover. Of those that interacted with the exhibition, about one in five discovered that it is possible to push the underwater objects through the water surface, while almost all ToneTable visitors were able to produce the orbiting behaviour. Most visitors that interacted with the exhibition were able to discover the association between trackballs and cursors (and reliably produce the splashing sound associated with high trackball activity). Those visitors that did manage to push objects through the surface frequently co-operated with others to keep them in the air. Only a small number of visitor groups discovered that the water surface has the ability to become 'sticky'.

Age Group Differences. As with ToneTable, it was common for one visitor to discover a feature and demonstrate to other visitors how to use it. However, our ToneTable visitors were almost exclusively adults, while visitors to the Museum of Science and Technology are a substantially less homogenous group, both with respect to age and demographic background. With ToneTable, visitors would sometimes leave to bring back friends, and this behaviour occurred at The Well of Inventions as well, especially among children. Young children were often fascinated by the graphical animation of the water surface and would put their fingers onto the display to 'feel' the water. Children in the approximate age-range of ten to thirteen seemed to be more interested in the exhibition than other age groups. These children typically viewed the exhibition as a game: they often (quite enthusiastically) referred to the transformation of objects moving through the water surface as 'a kill'. However, adults expressed less interest in the installation, and would often encourage their children to leave while they were still engaged at the table.

Interaction with Other Visitors. Many of the visitors that entered the space as a group discussed the purpose of the installation and the nature of the interaction. They also verbally negotiated the meaning and underlying rules of the motion of the objects. The issue of legibility was of limited concern with ToneTable since a member of the design team was always present within the installation to explain its background and purpose. With The Well of Inventions, the computer screens in the antechamber provide this information. During our observations, however, very few visitors read the text on the screens. Many adult visitors also expressed puzzlement with respect to the educational goals of the installation, which may account for the fact that many adults encouraged their children to turn to other exhibits in the Science Centre.

Figure 6. Interaction at The Well of Inventions, as seen from the antechamber. Note the person quietly observing the activities at the table from the platform in the background.

The Design of the Environment. Apart from the fact that a few visitors found it difficult to spot the trackballs that are built into the table, the environmental design of The Well of Inventions appears to be largely successful. Most visitors that enter the Science Centre gallery approach or walk through the installation, and it is able to support both observation and active participation simultaneously (Figure 6). Larger groups of visitors also make use of the platform for on-lookers (when space runs out at the table) and older children often spend extended amounts of time exploring the physical features of the room, such as determining the source of the graphical projection or searching for a hidden 'control room'.

4. Conclusions: Designing Mixed Media for Public Settings

In this paper, we have presented two installations which combine, in a number of different ways, high quality computer graphical and sonic materials in room-sized environments. We have exhibited these installations on numerous occasions, ranging from short demonstrations to long-term unsupervised display. We have adopted a design strategy of incremental improvement in the light of experience, while being guided by some substantive design principles and concepts. These have been proposed as responses to social scientific sensitivities emerging from studies of interaction with and around artefacts within public places. Overall, we believe that we have developed artefacts which support collaboration and which are tolerant of multiple coexisting forms of participation. This enables people to explore a variety of gestures and concomitant behaviours of graphical and sonic objects. The installations have been exhibited with systematic regard for the trajectories people follow as they participate in relation to the artefacts at different times and in varied relationship to other people. Furthermore, we believe that we have produced two engaging mixed media installations which are sensorially rich without being overwhelming, and which repay repeated visits.

However a number of challenges endure.

- *Educational issues.* Neither ToneTable nor The Well of Inventions has any elaborate high-level educational goals in themselves (although, as we have pointed out, they could be used by museum staff or teachers as tools in an educational context). However, our observations of The Well of Inventions indicate that some adult visitors encourage their children to leave the installation. We believe that one important reason for this is that the installation is situated in a Science Centre, where adult visitors can expect exhibits to feature a straightforward pedagogical 'opening' from which educational interactions with their children could be built. Because few visitors make use of the information available in the antechamber, this 'opening' is not readily apparent in The Well of Inventions. Thus, we are currently experimenting with different ways of subtly suggesting such 'openings' within the main installation area itself.

- *'True' collaborative emergence.* While we have referred to 'emergent collaborative value' as a strategy for giving motivation to collaboration, it is questionable whether our installations truly manifests 'emergence' in the stricter senses one often encounters in the literature on complexity and non-linear dynamics. To obtain a greater likelihood of novel and unexpected behaviour as participants interrelate their conduct, we simply introduced thresholds in the underlying dynamics. This has the virtue of the dynamics being manually 'tuneable': the threshold can be set to taste with ease. A more thought-through non-linear dynamics could allow for a greater variety of behaviours emerging with different constellations of participants. In addition, a time-varying dynamics (e.g. possibly through the mutation of the underlying dynamical equations or a drift in their parameterisation) would allow for yet further behaviours to be encountered on re-visiting. Such dynamical systems would require a kind of 'in-line' calibration of their equations to user-input. This is a difficult, yet fascinating challenge.
- *Object-sound associations.* Some of the sounds in play in ToneTable and The Well of Inventions stand in a one-to-one relationship with particular graphical objects. However, even with a small number of sound-object pairings (currently four), we do not have evidence of participants commonly 'decoding' the relationships so that they can, say, 'map' the rattling sound to the brown aircraft propeller. It has to be noted that participants were not set this as any kind of 'task' to perform but neither did these particular object-sound relations form part of their spontaneous discourse at the table. Other sound-image-interaction relations were clear as intended, however. For example, the sonification of activity at the table was clearly notable in both ToneTable and The Well of Inventions and, even, 'performable/playable'. A number of visitors have compared the installations to, or could imagine an extension of them, as collaborative musical instruments.

Let us finish this account by drawing out some lessons of general interest from our design work and our studies of people interacting with ToneTable and The Well of Inventions.

When interactive artefacts are deployed in public settings, it is noticeable that people take very varied orientations to interaction with them. An important challenge is to think how these multiple and varied participation formats can be designed for in an integrated fashion when developing an artefact (installation, exhibit or whatever) for a public setting. This is a much more complex question than those traditionally discussed in HCI research under the rubric of 'usability', and points beyond 'interface design' narrowly considered to the careful design of all environmental elements: computational, architectural and social. In our development of ToneTable and The Well of Inventions, we have tried a number of design strategies for addressing such settings. We have explored notions of 'collaboration through a virtual medium', 'emergent collaborative value', 'layers of noticeability', and 'structures of motivation'. Other important issues concern ergonomic aspects, social interaction, age group differences and affordances of the overall physical environment. These are all concepts and sensitivities intended to suggest ways for orienting the design of mixed media artefacts to support variable participation in public settings.

Acknowledgements

Initial steps developing ToneTable were taken during a 'constructional workshop' of the EU's IST project SHAPE (http://www.shape-dc.org), part of the Disappearing Computer initiative. We thank all our SHAPE colleagues for their participation at that workshop and support in the subsequent development and study of ToneTable. We would also like to thank the Museum of Science and Technology for hosting The Well of Inventions and for the helpful participation of the museum's staff. The support of Clavia DMI is also acknowledged.

References

[1] Benford, S. and 13 others. Designing Storytelling Technologies to Encourage Collaboration Between Young Children. Proceedings of CHI 2000. ACM Press, 556-563.
[2] Bentley, R., Hughes, J. A., Randall D., Rodden, T., Sawyer P., Shapiro, D. and Sommerville, I. Ethnographically-informed systems design for air traffic control. Proceedings of the 1992 ACM conference on Computer-supported cooperative work, Toronto, Canada, November 1992.
[3] Bowers, J., Jää-Aro, K.-M., Hellström, S.-O., Hoch, M. and Witfield, G. Production Support Tools for Electronic Arenas: Using Tangible Interfaces for Media Editing. In Bowers, J. M. (editor) Deliverable D4.5 of the ESPRIT eRENA project, KTH, Stockholm, 2000.
[4] Bowers, J. TONETABLE: A Multi-User, Mixed-Media, Interactive Installation. Proceedings of the COST G-6 Conference on Digital Audio Effects, Limerick, Ireland, December 2001.
[5] Brown, B., Sellen, A. and Geelhoed, E. Music sharing as a computer supported collaborative application. Proceedings of ECSCW2001, September 2001, Bonn, Germany.
[6] Büscher, M., Hughes, J., Trevor, J., Rodden, R., O'Brien, J. Supporting cooperation across shared virtual environments. Proceedings of the international ACM SIGGROUP conference on Supporting groupwork November 1999.
[7] Caulton, T. Hands-on Exhibitions. Managing Interactive Museums and Science Centres. London: Routledge, 1996.
[8] Craven, M., Benford, S., Greenhalgh, C., Wyver, J., Brazier, C., Oldroyd, A. and Regan, T. Ages of Avatar: Community building for inhabited television. ACM CVE2000, San Fransisco, September 2000.
[9] Csikszentmihalyi, M. and Hermanson, K. Intrinsic motivation in museums: why does one want to learn? In [14], pp. 146-160.
[10] Dean, D. Museum Exhibition. Theory and Practice. London: Routledge, 1994.
[11] Falk, J. H. and Dierking, L. D. Learning from Museums: Visitor Experiences and the Making of Meaning. Walnut Creek: AltaMira Press, 2000.
[12] Heath, C., Luff, P., vom Lehn, D., Hindmarsh, J. and J. Cleverly. Crafting Participation: Designing ecologies, configuring experience. Visual Communication, 1(1), 2002, 9-34.
[13] Hein, G. E. Learning in the Museum. London: Routledge, 1998.
[14] Hoch, M., Jää-Aro, K.-M. and Bowers, J. The Round Table: A Tangible Interface for Virtual Camera Control. In Bowers, J. M. et al. (editors) Deliverable D4.3/4.4 of the ESPRIT eRENA project, KTH, Stockholm, 1999.
[15] Hooper-Greenhill, E. (Ed.) The Educational Role of the Musuem. 2nd ed. London: Routledge, 1994.
[16] Ishii,H. and Ullmer, B. Tangible Bits: Towards Seamless Interfaces between People, Bits and Atoms. In Proceedings of CHI '97. ACM Press, 234-241.
[17] vom Lehn, D. and Heath, C. Displacing the object: mobile technologies and interpretive resources. Proceedings of the 7th International Cultural Heritage Informatics Meeting (ICHIM 2003), Paris, September 2003.
[18] Lord, B. and Lord, G. D. The Manual of Museum Exhibitions. Walnut Creek: AltaMira Press, 2002.
[19] Mynatt, E., Adler, A., Ito, M., Linde, C. and O'Day, V. The network communities of SeniorNet. Proceedings of ECSCW1999, September 1999, Copenhagen, Denmark.
[20] Taxén, G., Hellström, S.-O., Tobiasson, H., Back, M. and Bowers, J. The Well of Inventions - Learning, Interaction and Participatory Design in Museum Installations. Proceedings of the 7th International Cultural Heritage Informatics Meeting (ICHIM 2003), Paris, September 2003.

[21] Taxén, G. Towards Living Exhibitions. Licentiate thesis in human-computer interaction. TRITA-NA-0311, Department of Numerical Analysis and Computing Science, The Royal Institute of Technology, Stockholm, May 2003.

[22] Wellner, P. Interacting with Paper on the DigitalDesk. Communications of the ACM 36(7), 1993, 87-96.

Cooperative Systems Design
M. Zacklad et al. (Eds.)
IOS Press, 2004

Shared displays for promoting informal cooperation: an exploratory study

Monica DIVITINI* & Babak A. FARSHCHIAN•
* *Dpt. Information and Computer Science, NTNU, Trondheim, (N)*
•*Telenor R&D, Trondheim (N)*
Monica.Divitini@idi.ntnu.no; Babak.Farshchian@telenor.com

ABSTRACT: In this paper we present KOALA, a system realizing shared displays for promoting informal cooperation. We report the results from an exploratory study of real world usage of KOALA that we have conducted to understand how shared display systems are used and how their usage patterns might differ from their paper-based counterparts. This study was conducted with the aim of informing the design of ambient displays to be used in office settings. A number of lessons learned from the experimentation are outlined.

1 Introduction

Shared displays, i.e. large shared interactive screens containing public or community information, have been recently advocated as a novel technology for supporting collaboration [12]. As pointed out in [9], a combination of shared displays and mobile devices can be used to support different degrees of mobility and a smooth switch from individual to collaborative activities, from public to shared information. Shared displays can also facilitate socialization, as suggested in [3].

The growing interest in these devices comes from the popularity of conventional bulletin boards and similar paper-based artifacts. Bulletin boards play a variety of roles in any space inhabited by a group, a family, or a community. Electronic counterparts of these artifacts are developed with the hope to overcome their limitations, such as limited interactivity and no support for remote access.

In this paper we report on the development and experimental usage of the KOALA shared display system. KOALA (KOmmunity Awareness with Large Artifacts) is developed with the main aim of promoting informal cooperation and presence in a community of people sharing physical spaces in their office setting. As discussed in [6], paper based artifacts are in fact widely used for similar purposes. Figure 1 shows the type of paper-based artifact that has guided the development of KOALA. The photo (taken from Telenor R&D's premises) shows three different displays used in a coordinated manner. To the left there is a traditional corkboard with various printouts that can be of interest for the community. In the middle there is a whiteboard where people can mark their availability during the two coming weeks (middle-term availability). To the right there is a printout of a table with the holiday schedule (long-term availability). This simple snapshot clearly points out three ways in which displays promote social presence and informal cooperation in a community. First they provide *traces of community life*. A glance at the corkboard is enough to see whether there is any news that one should be aware of, what information is relevant for the specific community, who is expected to do what, and so on. Second, these artifacts act as a *community concierge*, proving information on who is in, who is out, and where each person is. Third, as already pointed out in [2], shared displays can play the role of *community memory*. In all these cases displays are mainly supporting asynchronous cooperation by providing information that might be needed by different community members.

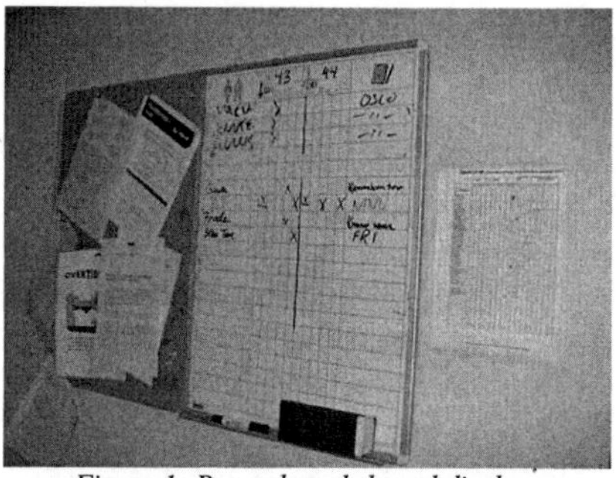

Figure 1: Paper-based shared displays

The described usage of these artifacts has many similarities with the usage of displays in the home environment reported in [4]. There the authors introduce the category of coordinate displays, i.e. displays that are introduced “for the express purposes of collaborative actions” and that are ecologically distributed and interconnected.

The paper is organized as follows. In Section 2 we briefly present KOALA and its functionality. In Section 3 we present the results from the usage of the system for one month in the premises of Telenor R&D. In Section 4 we discuss the results and draw some lessons learned that can be useful for the development and deployment of technology of this type. We believe that despite the growing number of research published in the topic there is still a need for experiences like the one that we are reporting here of actual usage of such systems. Empirical investigation is in fact essential to understand how these new applications can be used in different settings and for informing their design [1]. In this perspective, our experimentation is not aiming at evaluating the system, but it is rather an exploratory study of how this type of novel technology is actually used in real world settings.

2 The KOALA system

KOALA is a distributed shared display system designed to provide functionalities similar to the ones described in the Introduction for paper-based displays. Our goal when developing KOALA has been to design a bulletin board like system that is easy to contribute to (by end-users), is interactive, supports geographically distributed users, supports different interaction modalities, and is extensible [6]. KOALA central component is the *shared display*, i.e. a physical public screen where information posted by the user community is displayed (Figure 2). Users can use KOALA's client applications, called *interaction clients*, to post information to the shared display from their desktop PCs, PDAs, or mobile phones. In order to support geographically distributed communities, KOALA allows multiple shared displays to be located in several physical locations. Access to all shared displays in a KOALA installation is coordinated by a central server. All connected displays can share the information content on the server, but each shared display will in addition have its own specific information to display.

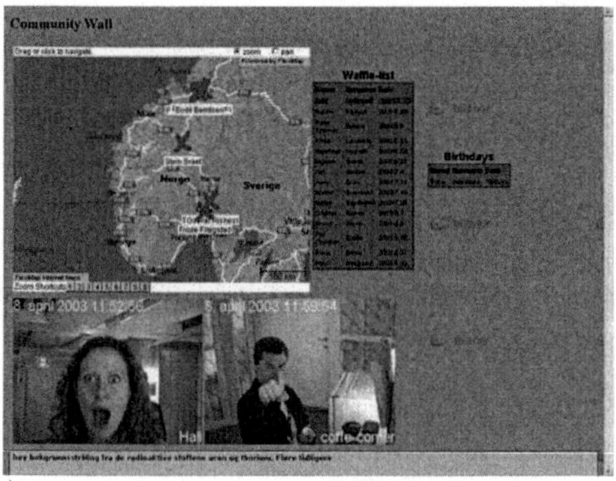

Figure 2: A KOALA shared display

KOALA's current users are the employees at Telenor R&D in Trondheim, Norway. KOALA was developed through an iterative process strongly influenced and informed by its users. The first version of KOALA consisted of a screen showing a map of Norway with the current locations of the employees marked on the map. Telenor R&D is distributed across several cities in Norway. This map screen (hanging on a wall in the coffee corner) was seen as a valuable service, allowing people to see who is traveling and who is in Trondheim. We decided to extend this map service with informal information and increased interactivity through mobile devices, to make it function more as a digital bulletin board. Two consequent versions of KOALA were developed before we did the study of its usage that is reported in this paper. One version added a number of information services to the screen. After this version was installed, we distributed a questionnaire where we asked the users about what mobile devices they used, how they use them, and based on the example services provide in the current version, which type of services they were more interested in seeing on the shared display. The third version added interactivity, allowing people post information to the shared display from their mobile devices.

2.1 KOALA services

KOALA is designed to be extensible, allowing easy addition of services that are relevant for its specific usage context. This extensibility is implemented into the system by using open standards and a component-based architecture (see Section 2.2). In the following we describe the specific KOALA services that we have used during our experiment. Technically, the services fall into one of three categories. *Proprietary services* are those that are implemented specifically for KOALA and use KOALA's database for storing their information. *Proxy services* are services that format and display continuously updated information from the Internet. *Messaging services* allow users to send different types of messages to one or several KOALA displays.

2.1.1 Proprietary services

Proprietary services are made specifically for KOALA. Their information is stored in the KOALA database, and their visualization on the screen is completely decided by KOALA.

In the installation used in our experiment proprietary services include the birthday service (displaying upcoming birthdays of Telenor R&D employees), the waffle service (displaying who is in charge of preparing the Friday waffle for the group's waffle party), upcoming events service (showing events that are relevant for the users).

2.1.2 Proxy services

Proxy services visualize external information, i.e. information not contained within KOALA database but collected from somewhere on the internet. Proxy services provide a convenient means for displaying information from the internet on a KOALA display. Implemented proxy services include the map service (Telenor R&D's initial Norway map showing employee locations), Dilbert strip service (showing the Dilbert comic strip of the day), weather service (showing daily weather forecast for Trondheim) and the news ticker service (providing local and international news from a selected news source).
Another technically more advanced proxy service is the snapshot service. The snapshot service can show a continuously updated image on a shared display (the image is downloaded from any given URL as frequently as every 5 seconds). Each of the shared displays used in our experiment has a web camera located close to it. Images from these cameras are available to KOALA users as snapshot services visualized within the shared displays. This gives the illusion of an almost-live video stream from one display's location to the other (see Figure 2). In addition to providing a synchronous communication link, we used the images taken by the web cameras for our analysis of system usage (see Section 3).

2.1.3 Messaging services

Messaging services allow a user to post messages to KOALA displays. Posted messages are displayed as post-it notes on the shared display. Messages can be sent to all shared displays or a specific display in a KOALA installation. Interaction clients are used for posting messages, where each user has to log on prior to posting a message. A web-based interaction client is developed in addition to a SMS interface for posting text messages. (Currently no support for multimedia messages is provided.) The web-based client is designed specifically for PDA screens, but can also be used on desktop browsers. For each message the sender can specify the period the message should be displayed. For example, if a person is late at work, she can inform the entire group about this by sending a single message that will last for a couple of hours. Unfortunately due to technical problems the SMS interface for posting messages was not available during our experiment.

2.2 System architecture

Figure 3 shows KOALA's overall architecture, which is explained very briefly in this section. An important goal when developing KOALA has been to make its architecture scalable and flexible. KOALA's architecture makes it easy to install new shared displays, add new services to each display, and customize the contents of each display in a very flexible way.

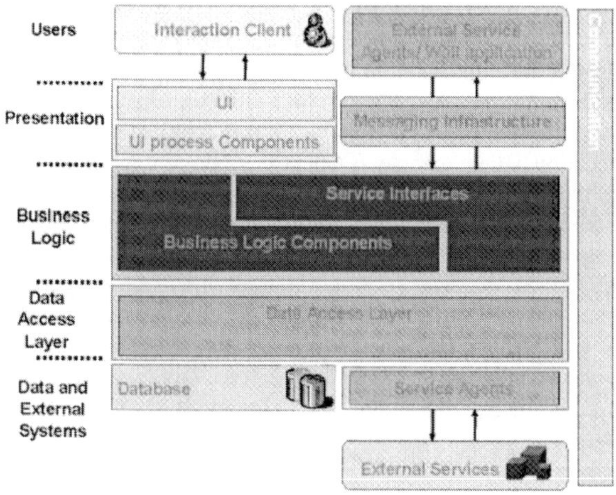

Figure 3: KOALA's overall architecture

Figure 3 shows the main components of KOALA's architecture. Interaction clients (top layer) are operated by users when posting messages to the shared displays. The clients consist of dynamic web pages created by UI process components. Wall application implements the client running on each shared display, and updates its content using KOALA's messaging infrastructure. Business logic components consist of all the utility libraries and servlets used for extracting and representing information for each KOALA service. Access to the database is done through the data access layer. Data for proxy services is not stored in the KOALA database but is fetched from external services using service agents.

Flexibility and scalability is guaranteed by using open standards and a modular architecture. Web services standard is used for all communication among KOALA modules. This allows for loose coupling among services and easy addition of new services. The least flexible part of the architecture is the rendering of shared display user interfaces. For each new service that is added to KOALA, the algorithm for displaying the new and the already existing services has to be modified. This is an area where we expect improvements in future versions of KOALA.

3 The setting for the experiment

KOALA has been installed in the premises of Telenor R&D and its usage has been logged for the first 2 months of adoption. The employees of Telenor R&D consist of 32 persons, and represent our user community. The installation has two shared displays, one in the entrance and one in the coffee corner (respectively X and Y in the map shown in Figure 4). Figure 5 shows the two locations and the shared displays. The offices to the left of the entrance (in the map of Figure 4) belong to a different company whose employees have not taken part in this research study. The displays are located fairly close to each other, but they are out of sight and located in different settings. The first display (marked as X in Figure 4) is hanging on a wall in the entrance to Telenor R&D premises (Figure 5, b). This is a passage point for people arriving at work or leaving. Nothing was hanging on the wall before we placed the display. Any activity in front of the display is therefore likely to be caused by the presence of KOALA. On the entrance display we installed birthday service, weather service, Dilbert service, message service, news service and a snapshot service showing both display locations each in its own window. The second display (marked as Y in Figure 4) is hanging in the coffee corner. In this location there are two sofas, a refrigerator, and the coffee machine. The location is frequently used by people during the day and is a location where people frequently gather for informal encounters. At this location, before the experimentation started, there was a screen displaying the location service and a number of paper notes tacked to the wall, displaying cartoons, newspaper clippings etc (Figure 5, a). On coffee corner display we installed birthday service, waffle service, location service, message service, news service and the same snapshot service as the entrance display. In this way the two displays were connected through an image link.

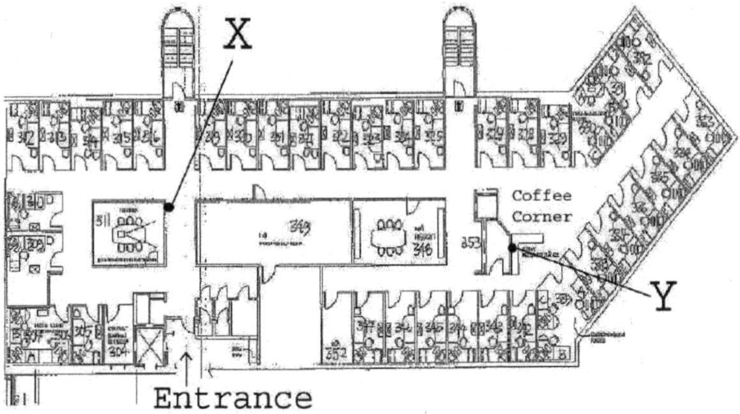

Figure 4: An office map of Telenor R&D with the two displays marked as X and Y

(a) *(b)*

Figure 5: The two displays in the coffee corner (a) an the entrance (b)

To call the attention of the users on the system and to inform them of the possibility to use it interactively, all members of the test group received an e-mail describing the system. We also posted user documentation for how to log on to KOALA next to each display.
To collect data on system adoption we have used several data gathering techniques. During the whole experimentation we have logged the interactions of users with the system. In addition, we have used the recording from two web cameras that are part of the system and mounted close to the two displays. We have also distributed a questionnaire to get a better understanding of people perception of the system.

4 Results

4.1 Different usage patterns

From our observations we have identified four different patterns by which the users use KOALA. The first pattern is represented by *glancing*. With glancing we mean a single user passing by the display and giving it a look before passing by. This use ranges from a passing glance to stopping and studying the display's content. Figure 6 illustrates some occurrences of passers-by.

Figure 6: Glancing at a shared display

The second pattern of usage is represented by *people gathering* around the display. With this we indicate people making conversation induced by KOALA or some KOALA-related topic. The rationale behind the design of KOALA is that shared displays can promote informal communication by creating opportunities for informal talking. The system does this in two ways: by supplying content that can be discussed and by creating a focal point around which users gather. Figure 7 shows one occurrence of people gathering in front of the display. The first frame shows two members of the test group approaching the display, discussing some of its content. As they stand there discussing, several members of the group drop by and attend the discussion.

Figure 7: Example of people gathering at the display

The third form of usage is *remote communication*, indicating interaction between people at the different displays (using the snapshot service). In Figure 2 it is possible to see a case of interaction between two persons at the two locations. In this case the persons at the different displays have stopped to view some content on the display at the same time. They notice the person standing at the other display, and starts interacting through the web cameras. We observed remote communication even though the displays are located not far from each other.

The last pattern of usage is represented by *active interaction*. This type of interaction occurs mainly when users want to send messages to either a specific display or all the installed displays. Figure 8 shows an occurrence of system-user interaction where we see a member of the test group logging in to the system for posting a message to the display. As he is doing so, others stop by to watch how the display is being used.

Figure 8: Example of interactive use

4.2 User observations

In this section we summarize the data obtained from user observations, as collected from the snapshots taken by the web cameras. (For detailed data see [7].) During the 30 days in the test period we observed 621 usages of the system in one of the categories described in the previous section. After the experimentation period we analyzed 30 days of video recording. We have analyzed only the recordings relating to working hours and weekdays. Moreover, due to technical problems web cameras have been out of usage in some short periods.

Figure 9 depicts the average number of observations per hour for the different usage patterns. Most of the interactions are belong to the glance pattern, with or without stopping. It is however worth to note that there has also been a considerable number of gatherings around the displays. There is a gathering around one of the displays about once every second hour. Remote communication between the two displays happened instead very rarely. Given that the displays are in close proximity and that the communication is only through still images this was expected. Direct interaction is not discussed here since it is better understood looking at the system logging. However, from the analysis of the video we can see that all direct interactions with the displays (in front of the displays) resulted in people gathering, as illustrated in Figure 8.

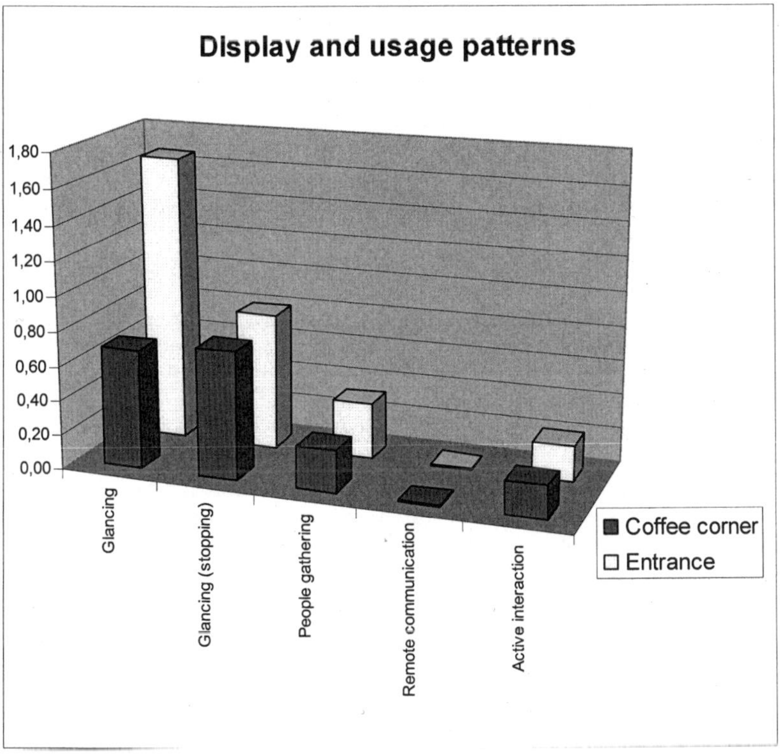

Figure 9: Usage patterns in the experiment

Looking at usage distribution during a workday, we can identify three periods of the day where the use of the displays intensifies. The first of these peaks is at the very start of the day. People are coming to work, passing by the entrance display and entering the office, and making their first cup of coffee at the coffee corner. The next peak is around lunchtime. The third peak is when people go home. This last peak is represented by glancing, with a very low number of gatherings. There are however some differences in the patterns of usage during the day. During lunchtime there is little activity at the hall display, probably signifying that people are at lunch. Since the coffee corner is in an area used for lunch by some employees, this display has a peak during lunch. The entrance display however has peaks just before and after lunch, due to traffic to and from the cafeteria. The number of gatherings around the entrance display decreases dramatically after lunch. Both displays have a small increase shortly after the workday ends. The results seem to yield no major differences between the weekdays, except small peaks at Monday, Wednesday, and Friday with a higher number of gatherings. (On Wednesdays Telenor R&D has regularly scheduled presentations and on Fridays employees gather for waffle party.)

As discussed in Section 3, the two displays have rather different profiles. It is therefore important to understand if this impacts the way they are used. Our observations show that the entrance display has been used as much, in some categories even more, than the coffee corner display. The coffee corner, being the established meeting place at Telenor R&D, was expected to draw more attention than the entrance display. More than half of the recorded gatherings took place at the entrance display. It is here important to mention that if we had counted gatherings that were not related to the displays (i.e. people standing around talking without any connection to the KOALA) the results would yield more gatherings around the coffee corner.

4.3 System logging

In this section we present the results from the logging of users' interactions with KOALA through an interaction client. In general, the possibility to interact with the system has not been used much. This is partly in line with the indications collected during the design of the system when in potential users ranked very low the need for interactive services.
It was evident from early in the project that some people were more interested in KOALA. This fact is clearly reflected in the logs. Out of a total number of 32 users, 17 logged in one or more times, two of these used the displays considerably more than others. If we look at the number of logins we can clearly identify a peak following a message that was sent to the user community informing about the system. It should be noted that just after the period of observation ended some people have "rediscovered" the possibility to use KOALA interactively and started sending messages. However, we have no data for explaining what triggered this new usage.
When we look at the device through which users logged on, we get 55% of the login made via a PDA, and 45% via the PC. No log in was done via mobile phones, despite many employees have mobile phones allowing it. During the experimentation users have mainly logged in for changing their profile. There has been however very little usage of the possibility to send messages.

4.4 Questionnaire

After the period of observation we have distributed a questionnaire for understanding the perception of the system that users developed during the period. In the questionnaire we asked users their opinion e.g., about the placement of physical displays, their location, and suggestions. Out of the 32 distributed questionnaires, we have received 20 filled-in questionnaires.

4.4.1 System usage

A first set of questions aimed at clarifying the perceived usage and problems encountered during the experimentation. Users have been asked to rate how often they were using the system in the different categories identified in Section 4.1. The results are in line with the results from the observations and logging. However, there are some discrepancies around how often users perceived they have been gathering around the display and the usage of web cameras, with perceived usage much higher than the recorded one. A possible explanation for the higher perceived frequency of gathering is that users tend to consider all gatherings around the display, independently by the fact that they were in some way directly triggered by the presence of the display. The discrepancies in the usage of web cameras is that the video recording only reveals usage when it is visible that users are in fact using the cameras. If a person is looking at a display it is difficult to say if the focus is on the image of the other site or on some other piece of information. Considering the feedback from users we tend to believe that usage of video cameras is more relevant than appearing from the initial observations, even if this might have not resulted in actual communication between the two locations.
One of the many reasons for creating KOALA is that it should foster informal cooperation by gathering people together and creating occasions for informal communication. With the questionnaire we tried to understand the reasons behind the gatherings that we have

observed were taking place relatively frequently. From the questionnaire it emerges that 44% of the times people perceive that their gatherings around the displays were due to content displayed at the display. In 39% of the cases, it was due to the display and KOALA. Only 17% of the gatherings were not related to the display at all.

4.4.2 Interactivity and ease of use

As evident from the observations and the logging, the usage of interactive services has been very low. This is in line with the low interest for interactive services expressed during the design of the system. However, during the experimentation we felt that the interactive services, in particular messaging, should have been used more.
We have therefore asked users to express their impression of how easy it was to use the system. The respondents did not find the non-interactive part of the system difficult to use, while the interactive part proved more challenging. This is surprising since the test group consists of persons with a good familiarity with novel technology. However this result must be read together with the difficulties that users have identified as a reason for not using the interactive part of the system. (The questionnaire was asking to select from a list of statements the one that was more in line with the motivations of the user.) All the respondents were aware of the possibility to log in to the system. 20% did not log in because they thought it was not providing any added value. 20% could not take advantage of this possibility because they were lacking the necessary equipment, 10% found the web logon difficult. For 50% of the respondents the lack of interactive usage was due to technical problems. These problems mostly relate to the existing infrastructure at Telenor R&D such as firewalls.
Given the low usage of interactive possibilities, we have asked users if they had any suggestion for alternative means of interaction, asking them to rank the suitability of different tools. In general, users seem to be open to different interaction devices, with a slight preference for touch screens, which would allow users to interact directly with the system. Users also ranked as well suited RFID[1]. By equipping each display with an RFID-transceiver and embedding an RF tag into, e.g., the access card that all the employees already carry, users could log on to KOALA automatically just passing by. This approach was used in the "Active Badge" system [13]. One member of the group proposed a system with RFID for identification and login (which would then become a passive event) and touch screen for simple interaction with the display. As he said "It must be easy there-and-then to communicate with the system."

4.4.3 The physical displays

95% of the test group found the placement of the display in the coffee corner to be good and 5% neutral. In contrast, only 35% of the users found the placement of the entrance display good and 10% bad. These answers suggest that the test group prefers to have the displays placed on sites that are already used for gathering and socializing. In the words of a user: "Coffee corner is an established meeting place. The entrance is not." This is an interesting result when compared to Figure 9, which shows that the entrance display is used at least as much as than the coffee corner display.
When selecting the actual device to use as KOALA display during the experimentation, we anticipated that the size of the displays would be of paramount importance, but we chose to use relatively small displays, 15" LCD displays with a resolution of 1024x768 pixels,

---

[1] Radio Frequency IDentification is a system based around a small RF-tag programmed with unique identification.

mainly for economical reasons. When we asked about the size of the screens however, 65% of the test group found the display size to be adequate, only 35% finding it to be too small.

4.4.4 Added value

We asked the users how they rated the overall impact of KOALA on their working environment. None of the group members felt that KOALA had a negative impact and most of the users declared that KOALA provided "some benefit". From the answers it is also clear that they felt that the system was more helpful for social and entertainment purposes, rather than as a source of information. This can be partly explained with the type of available services.

During the study period we experienced some technical problems that limited the availability of the system. We asked the test group whether they noticed that the displays were out of order and how much they missed them on these occasions. Just about everybody in the test group noticed the displays being out of order. How much the system was missed varies. Almost a third of the test group did not miss the displays at all, whereas the rest missed them to a certain degree. This of course might depend on many factors, including e.g. the down time and the type of problems. For example, at times the system has been working correctly apart from the web cameras that were not updating the still-image on the display.

5 Discussion: implications for design and deployment

Our experience shows that computer-based systems can be used to provide services similar to the ones illustrated in the introduction and currently provided by paper-based displays in the workplace. However, our results also show differences in the pattern of usage and important factors that need to be taken into account for the wide adoption of this type of systems.

As it is emerging from the results presented in the previous section, KOALA has been used on a regular basis throughout the test period. The data also points out that the two displays have been used in slightly different ways, coinciding to some degree with the profile of each display. The entrance display, being in a transit area, has many people just glancing at it, and the usage peaks are at slightly different times of the day than what is the case for the display in the coffee corner. However, we need to point out that during our experimentation KOALA was used mainly as a background service with only a few episodes of interactive usage.

LL1: Displays can become community places. There is a striking difference between the usage of traditional paper-based displays that we experience every day in the workplace and the one that we observed for KOALA, namely the number of gatherings that are trigged by the display, in our case a gathering almost every second hour. According to the feedbacks that we have collected from the questionnaire, this was mainly due to the content of the display, followed by the display as a phenomenon, and only 17% of the respondents related the gatherings to reasons external to the display. This was a surprising result also considering the limited content available. The gatherings cannot be explained by the novelty effect of the technology since they continued to happen for a rather long period of time (two months) without any large variations. We believe that this can be explained by the dynamic nature of the content. During the experimentation we have seen displays become appreciated not only as devices, but also as places for people to meet. This is for

example witnessed by the high number of gatherings around the display in the hall, location were previously people were just in transit.
This lesson learned has important implications for the design as well as the deployment of shared displays. From the design point of view it means that the system must be designed so to support a "virtuous cycle":

- It must be possible to easily add relevant information, even for users who are remotely located, e.g. for an external meeting. This helps to keep the interest for the system high by increasing relevance of the content and dynamicity and consequently provides occasions for gatherings.
- It must support an easy transition from informal communication to focused cooperation, possibly producing new relevant information, more integration of the display system in the local practices, and more occasions for encounters. For example, the system could give the possibility to the people that are gathering to access and visualize documents that they need to discuss and work on. KOALA was not able to support this transition, but after this experience we believe that this could provide a key advantage when moving from paper-based to computer-based displays. In this way chance encounters would not be only a moment for socialization and knowledge sharing, but could trigger contextualized and focused cooperation "on the flight".

From the deployment perspective, this lesson learned implies that displays need to be put in places where they are highly visible and where people can gather around. There need to be people passing by the display in order for people to stop at it, and people need to have the space to stop and gather in order to facilitate conversation opportunities.

LL2. Display systems are highly visible and they get adopted quickly. Our results show that the KOALA displays have been used regularly during the experimental period. Also, according to the results from our questionnaire, 95% of respondents declared they noticed when the system was down (even though the displays were used in an ambient manner). This shows the potentiality of this type of systems that are easily adopted and highly visible. We also observed that some people have taken more ownership of the application than other users and have at several occasions started the system if needed, rather than waiting for the responsible to do it. Though we cannot expect in all the settings users with the willingness to take care of the system from a technical point of you, we believe that the emergence of "super-users" can be a general phenomenon. The system should therefore be designed so to promote the involvement of super-users, possibly supporting the tailoring of the systems to the specific context of usage [11]. At the deployment level, this implies that tailoring should be promoted and rewarded.

LL3. Content plays a key role in the adoption of the system and it is related to the place where it is made available. The content on the display plays a significant role in determining system usage. This is for example witnessed by the differences in usage of the hall display that we observed among people belonging to the test group and the ones not belonging to it. Based on the results from the video recording people external to the test group rarely stopped or gathered in front of the displays and when they did it was for shorter periods of time. These results are in line with the findings in [10] which state that personalized and customized content on public displays help to create conversation opportunities. The relevance of the content strongly depends on where the display is positioned and how its users use that space. If the content on the display is focused towards the situation in which the display is placed and the audience it addresses, people are more

likely to stop and for a longer period of time than they would without directed content. Furthermore it seems the content has a profound effect on the way in which people use the displays, e.g. in terms of their tendency to gather. Data on the usage of the two displays during the working day help support the conclusion of a spontaneous and opportunistic use of the displays and to identify clear profiles of use.
From a design point of view this lesson learned points to the need to design flexible systems that are be easily tailored to the expected needs of the community. At the deployment level, it suggests that for each display it is necessary to identify its profile. This is not depending only from the physical position of the display, as we assumed when we started the experiment, but also, and possibly more important, by the work practices that characterize the specific location. The differences in profile must then be taken into account when choosing the content of the display. For a location where users are mainly on transit, one can place content that "catches the eye", such as a comic strip. In places where users are more prone to slow down, more complex content like news and messages, which is less noticeable and takes a bit longer to read can be placed. This however needs to be carefully tuned to the work practices and can vary for example during working hours. It is also important to take into account the emergence of patters of usage different than expected and be ready to adapt consequently. For example, during the adoption of KOALA people found subjectively the coffee corner display more important and one could have expected it to trigger a higher numbers of gatherings, but this was not actually the case.

LL4. Interactivity is problematic. One of our initial assumptions, shared also by other researchers in the field, is that a higher level of interactivity can represent the added value of computer-based displays on paper-based ones. However, during our initial investigations we noticed a low interest of users in interactive services. At the same time, interactive services such as sending messages have been seldom used during our period of observations. There are two factors that, in combination, we can use to explain these results. First, interactivity is not always part of the mental models that users have of a display, that is normally seen as a source of information to be used mainly passively, at least in the workplace. This means that starting to use the system interactively requires understanding and embracing the system more thoroughly that to use if for simply reading the information that is available on it. Second, interact with the system can be technically demanding and this creates an additional barrier to the interactive usage of the system. We therefore agree with [8] that easiness of interaction is a key success factor for these systems. This however has to be understood not only in terms of usability of the interactive services, but also in terms of, e.g., compliance of the system to the mental models of its users, support for interactivity via different devices, easy integration of the system in the existing network. Easiness of access to and usage of interactive services have to be carefully taken into account during the design of the system, but it has also implications on its deployment since it is necessary to promote the interactive components among users.

LL5. Functional and technical flexibility. Since the very beginning of the project it was evident the need of developing a system that is scalable, flexible, extendable, and easy to integrate with a range of different technologies. Our results strengthened this assumption and showed the need to have flexibility as one of the requirements strongly influencing the design of these systems, starting from the technical infrastructure on which they are developed. In fact these systems must be able to grow with their community, both in terms of the new services that might be needed and in terms of new technical possibilities, for example, for promoting interaction by using new mobile devices.

6 Conclusions

In this paper we have presented KOALA, a system for promoting presence and informal cooperation by using shared displays enriching the support offered by paper-based displays common in any workplace. In the paper we have also presented the results from the initial adoption of the system in the organization of one of the co-author. During the experimentation both displays have been used on a regular basis. The data points out that the two displays have been used in slightly different ways. Patterns of usage are directly affected by the placement of the display as well as by the working and social practices of the user group. The system was mainly used as a background service, not taking advantage of the possibility to use it interactively, i.e. for sending messages to other users. The results of this experimentation allowed us to point out some strengths and weaknesses of this type of systems, and a set of empirically grounded lessons learned for their development and deployment. We are fully aware of the limitations of our experimentation. It has involved a limited number of people and is limited to one specific system and one specific social setting. However, we believe that some of the implications from our results are fairly general and can be used to design better systems that can be tried out in more complex contexts.

Our work is proceeding mainly in two directions. First, we want to improve the flexibility of KOALA, both at the functional and technical level. With this aim we are integrating KOALA into a ubiquitous platform that we are developing [5]. Second we want to make available through KOALA services for supporting a smooth transition between informal and formal cooperation, for example, by temporally tailoring a display to be used for supporting a local meeting by accessing shared workspaces.

Acknowledgements

We thank Christopher Pharo Glaserud and Torstein Hoem for their help with the development of the system and the experimentation. We are also grateful to the people at Telenor R&D that used the system and that provided us with valuable comments throughout the whole process.

References

1. Abowd, G.D., Mynatt, E.D. and Rodden., T. The Human Experience. *IEEE Pervasive Computing, 1* (1). 48-57.
2. Ackerman, M. and Halverson, C. Considering an Organization's Memory. in *Proceedings of the ACM 1998 Conference on Computer Supported Cooperative Work - Seattle, WA, November 14-18,1998*, ACM Press, 1998, 39-48.
3. Agostini, A., De Michelis, G., Divitini, M., Grasso, M.A. and Snowdon, D. Design and Deployment of Community Systems: Reflections on the Campiello Experience. *Interacting with computers, 14* (6). 689-712.
4. Crabtree, A., Hemmings, T. and Rodden, T. Social construction of displays: ecological networks and coordinate displays. in O'Hara, K., Perry, M., Churchill, E. and Russell, D. eds. *Public and Situated Displays: Social and Interactional Aspects of Shared Display Technologies*, Kluwer Academic Publishers, 2003.
5. Divitini, M., Farshchian, B. and Samset, H., Ubiquitous access to group information. in *ACM SAC2004*, (Nicosia, Cyprus, 2004), ACM Press, (to appear).

6. Divitini, M. and Farshchian, B.A., Shared visual displays to increase social presence. in *HCI International 2003,*, (Crete, Greece, 2003), Lawrence Erlbaum Associates.
7. Glaserud, C.P. and Hoem, T. Community Wall - Prototype and Usage, IDI, NTNU, Trondheim, Norway, 2003.
8. Lank, E., Designing a perceptive smart room interface. in *Workshop on Collaboration with Interactive Walls and Tables, held in conjunction with UbiComp 2002*, (2002).
9. Luff, P. and Heath, C., Mobility in collaboration. in *Computer Supported Cooperative Work*, (1998), ACM, 305--314.
10. McCarthy, J., Using public displays to create conversation opportunities. in *Workshop on Public, Community and Situated Displays, held in conjunction with ACM CSCW2002*, (2002).
11. Morch, A. and Mehandjiev, N. Tailoring as collaboration: The mediating role of multiple representations and application units. *Computer Supported Cooperative Work*, *9* (1). 75-100.
12. O'Hara, K., Perry, M., Churchill, E. and Russell, D. (eds.). *Public and Situated Displays - Social and Interactional Aspects of Shared Display Technologies*. Kluwer Academic Publisher, 2003.
13. Want, R., Hopper, A., Falcao, V. and Gibbons, J. The active badge location system. *ACM Transactions on Information Systems (TOIS)*, *10* (1). 91-102.

Configuring the Ubiquitous Home

Tom RODDEN,[1] Andy CRABTREE,[1] Terry HEMMINGS,[1] Boriana KOLEVA,[1] Jan HUMBLE,[2] Karl-Petter ÅKESSON,[2] and Pär HANSSON [2]

[1] *School of Computer Science & IT, University of Nottingham, Jubilee Campus, Wollaton Road, Nottingham, NG8 1BB, UK.*

[2] *Swedish Institute of Computer Science, Box 1623, SE-164 29 Kista, Sweden.*

Abstract. This paper presents the development of a lightweight component model that allows user to manage the introduction and arrangement of new interactive services and devices in the home. Interaction techniques developed through user-participation enable household members – rather than designers – to configure and reconfigure interactive devices and services to meet local needs. As part of this we have developed a tablet-based editor that discovers available ubiquitous components and presents these to users as jigsaw pieces that can be dynamically recombined. We conclude by considering the broad implications for the design of interactive domestic environments suggested by our approach.

1. Introduction

Developing ubiquitous technologies for the home has become a growing focus for many HCI researchers. New technologies have been suggested ranging from novel forms of interactive device [2] to a wide range of information appliances [1]. Many of these developments have been supported by purpose built domestic environments. These range from the development of domestic spaces [4] to the construction of purpose built homes [14]. These environments have tended to be used as "living labs" to support the development new interactive devices and explore how these can be placed within a domestic setting. The construction of these spaces has been complemented by an empirical exploration of domestic spaces where researchers seek to understand the everyday nature of the homes we inhabit. A number of different research approaches are being used to seek to understand the domestic. These include ethnographic studies [15, 17], the development of technology models [22], the use of cultural probes [10], and patterns [5]. Despite the diversity of these studies one common and important issue emerges: namely, that the home is open to continual reconfiguration by those who inhabit it.

More recently, researchers have started to develop domestic technologies "in the wild" by constructing and placing technologies within domestic settings in partnership with users. This includes 'technology probes' [13] where development takes place in partnership with a number of distributed families and the development and placement of lightweight media space technologies [11]. Not only has this work highlighted the importance of the inhabitants becoming involved in the design process it has confirmed the need for technology to be open to reconfiguration within the home. Similarly, architectural historians, such as Brand [3], have highlighted the importance of change to allow inhabitants to appropriate and adapt domestic spaces to meet their evolving needs. Researchers have extended this work to consider ubiquitous computing and domestic technologies [18]. A key feature is the relationship between the technologies within the home and the underlying services needed to support them. This paper builds upon this previous work by considering how inhabitants can reason about supporting services and dynamically reconfigure technology in the home.

We explore the potential to support reconfiguration through the development of a lightweight component model that allows household members to manage the introduction and arrangement of interactive devices. Part of this has involved the development of an inhabitant's editor to allow the reconfiguration of interactive devices that has been briefly reported elsewhere [12]. In this paper we focus on how the development was directed by a series of focused user studies that exploited a paper-based 'mock up' approach [9] married to 'situated evaluation' [21]. This provided a means of engaging domestic inhabitants with ubiquitous computing at their own level of complexity. We were able to develop the component model in partnership with users and allow them to be involved in the identification of new components that made sense from their perspective.

2. Making the Infrastructure Available

A central issue in supporting the reconfiguration of innovative ubiquitous devices for the home is the relationship between devices and the supporting infrastructure. Essentially users must be able to easily place devices in the home, understand this placement and rapidly reconfigure devices. Furthermore, as Edwards and Grinter point out the networked home of the future will not be custom designed from the start but "it seems more likely that new technologies will be brought piecemeal into the home" [7]. As ubiquitous devices enter the home in the 'piecemeal' way predicted, they need to be made part of the broader infrastructure of the home. Consequently, the underlying supporting infrastructure needs to become increasingly prominent and available to users. In fact, we would argue that this underlying infrastructure needs to become sufficiently visible to users to make it part and parcel of their everyday practical reasoning about the nature of their home. Consequently, we need to develop a flexible infrastructure that reduces the cost of introducing new devices and allows users to control and evolve their use within the home.

To allow digital devices to be treated as 'everyday stuff' [20] we need to open up access to the supporting infrastructure that connects devices and provide users with a simple model that allows them to mange the introduction and arrangement of new interactive devices. While existing infrastructures such as Jini [23], UpnP,[1] and the Cooltown infrastructure,[2] among others provide services and component based abstractions for ubiquitous computing. However, few researchers have explored the rapid composition of applications through the dynamic configuration of these components. Two notable examples are the Speakeasy system [8], which has adopted a composition model based on typed data streams and services, and iStuff [2] that knits together a number of ubiquitous devices via a state based event-heap. Both tend to focus on the *developer* rather than the eventual *inhabitant* of a ubiquitous environment. As in the case of iStuff we allow a number of different devices to be composed within a ubiquitous environment. However, our challenge is to allow users to view these compositions and rapidly reconfigure them to meet their changing needs. Below we present a simple user-oriented component model to allow the rapid composition of devices to support the everyday interactive arrangement of the home.

---

[1] Universal Plug and Play - http://www.upnp.org

[2] Cooltown - http://cooltown.hp.com/cooltownhome/

2.1 A Compositional Approach to Home Environments

Our starting point has been the development of a component model for ubiquitous devices in home environments suitable for further elaboration by inhabitants. The basis of our component model is the notion of a shadow digital space that acts as a 'digital' representation of the physical environment. Devices can use this shared digital dataspace to become aware of their context and represent this contextual information to other devices and to make this manifest in the physical world. The aim of devices within the physical environment is either to make information from the physical available within the digital or to make digital information have a corresponding physical manifestation. The fundamental aim of components in our arrangement is to ensure the convergence of the physical and the digital environment. There are three main classes of components.

- ***Physical to Digital Transformers*** take physical effects and transform them into digital effects.
- ***Digital to Physical Transformers*** make digital information physically manifest in the real world.
- ***Digital Transformers*** act upon digital information and effect digital information.

In the associated toolkit the different transformers are realized as JavaBeans which exposes the properties they wishes to share through a distributed dataspace. This model is analogous to the one proposed within iStuff which provides developers with a set of discrete devices that can be assembled through publication of state information within a dataspace called the event-heap. This paper further extends this approach by focusing on how components such as the devices in iStuff and the ways in which they are configured might be exposed to inhabitants for them to reason about. Consequently, our emphasis is on the development of user-oriented techniques that allow the dynamic assembly of devices.

2.2 Components and Jigsaw Pieces

The first issue we had to address concerned how we might present underlying device configurations to users. A number of candidate representations to support practical reasoning within the domestic environment were already available, including variants of electronic wiring diagrams and plumbing schematics currently in use. However, our initial explorations suggested that these were heavily loaded with existing interpretations and their use required a significant degree of technical competence. Consequently, we sought a more neutral approach based on the notion of assembling simple *jigsaw-like* pieces. Our choice is based on the everyday familiarity of the 'jigsaw piece' and the intuitive suggestion of assembly through connection. Essentially, we wanted to allow users to connect components and so compose various arrangements through a series of left-to-right couplings of pieces. The 'jigsaw' provides a *recognizable interaction mechanism* for connecting services together (Figure 1). It is worth stressing that within this approach we are constraining the potential for development. For example, we do not have the richness of programming expression allowed by iCap [19]. However, the benefit to be accrued from reducing complexity of assembly is that inhabitants might more readily understand the environment. Our exploration of the applicability of this jigsaw-based approach to reconfiguration was undertaken using a user-oriented approach. Through a series of focused user studies we sought to:

- ***Understand*** the intuitive availability and efficacy of the jigsaw-based approach from inhabitant's point of view.

- ***Uncover*** inhabitants understanding of abstraction in order that we might keep the level of complexity in reach of the practical reasoning of inhabitants.
- ***Develop*** insights into what sorts of devices might fit into real home environments and so inform continued development of new devices and components.

Figure 1. The physical jigsaw editor

In order to undertake these studies we exploited a paper-based 'mock up' approach [9] married to 'situated evaluation' [21] where a series of physical jigsaw pieces were made available to users practical considerations. These session where recorded on videotape to promote a later in-depth analysis. We also presented users with a set of initial seed scenarios elaborating various transformers and their potential arrangement. These reflect different levels of abstraction and provide a starting point allowing users to reason about the complexity of configuration, and the nature of ubiquitous computing in the context of their everyday lives. The seed scenarios were drawn from earlier ethnographic studies [5], and some initial prototype development within a lab based domestic environment [12].

3. Learning from Potential Users

In order to bring users' expertise to bear on development – both to establish the veracity of our technological concepts and to elaborate future avenues of technical work - we undertook a series of mockup exercises. Mockups are early expressions of potential technological futures and they are essentially incomplete, thereby providing an opportunity to engage end-users early on in the design process in a formative process of *mutual learning*. Mockups enable users to get 'hands on' experience of potential technological futures, providing a tangible basis for users to reason about and elaborate technological possibilities. The mockups are embedded in seed scenarios, which furnish a context for users' reasoning, sensitizing them to design concepts and visions. These scenarios are not specifications to be assessed by users but 'triggers' designed to engage them in an open-ended design dialogue. They provide a concrete entry point for users and designers to work out what the future might amount to in detail, prompting reflections on and, importantly, projections of technological possibilities which in turn drive development work. We marry mocking-it-up with situated evaluation, which exploits ethnographic study to support the learning exercise and identify salient issues to design. The focus of the study is the designers and users talk, specifically the conversational formulations triggered by the seed scenarios which articulate technological possibilities [6]. When analysing the mockup sessions and presenting findings we do so in terms of designers and users talk and in relation to a number of relevant development criteria [16].

- ***Seeing the Sense of the Technology.*** On encountering a novel technology, users can rarely see the sense of it. It is not, at first glance, intelligible to them and its potential use must therefore be explained. This involves guiding users through technological functionality and may be accomplished via mockups, prototypes or both. Whatever the medium, the first question is, given that course of explanatory work, will users see the sense of the technology or will it remain unfathomable?
- ***Recognising the Relevance of the Technology.*** That users may come to see the sense of the proposed technology does not mean that they will recognize it as relevant to their everyday activities. If users are to engage in any meaningful analysis of the technology's potential utility, and further elaborate functional demands that may be placed on it, then they need to be able to recognize the relevance of the technology to their everyday lives. The question is, will users recognise the relevance of the proposed technology and, if so, in what ways?
- ***Appropriating the Technology.*** That a new technology may be recognized as relevant by potential users does not necessarily mean that they wish to appropriate that technology. Naturally there are many reasons for this, though in the early stages of development concerns are likely to expressed about the available range of functionality. The question is in what ways, if any, will users conceive of appropriating the technology and what will those conceptions be concerned with?

Six mockup sessions were conducted with eight participants aged from their early twenties to late fifties in six homes. The length of the sessions varied between one and four hours. Below we present a series of vignettes to convey a flavour of the main issues to emerge from the mockup exercise in relation to the criteria laid out above.

3.1 Seeing the Sense of the Technology

Even at this early stage in design it was possible for participants to see the sense of the technology. Although the specific details of participation changed from case to case, the following vignette nevertheless illustrates the way in which our participants generally came to achieve this outcome. We can be sure that participants see the sense of the technology when, as in this case, they make the imaginative leap beyond our initial scenarios to incorporate new elements into the design dialogue. Thus, and by way of example, the vignette shows Sean makes an imaginative leap from Jack's (one of designers) working of the mock-up, making sense of the technology in the context of his own unique domestic arrangements. Accordingly, Sean speaks of preparing and sending a shopping list to his partner, arriving at concrete sense of the technology by envisioning how it can be incorporated into and tailored to support his life and personal relationships. All our participants came to see the sense of the technology and all did so in similar ways by making the technology relevant to the practical circumstances of *their* everyday lives. This is of the utmost importance as it in turn moves beyond particular design visions, and the sense others might see in them, to consider ways in which potential users recognise the relevance of the technology to their practical concerns.

Vignette #1

Jack, a member of the design team, is sat at the kitchen table with one of our participants, Sean. The jigsaw pieces are spread out on the table in front of them and Jack is working through the seed scenarios with Sean.

Jack: OK, so each one of these pieces when they are put together would set up a series of connections (Jack assembles the pieces involved in Seed Scenario #1). So this piece (points to **GroceryAlarm**) connects to this (**AddToList**) and this (**AddToList**) to this (**SMSSend**) and that would then send a message to you, OK?

Figure 2. Assembling seed scenario #1

Sean: So this (pointing to the pieces Jack has connected) is configuring it here?

Jack: Yeah.

Sean: So the computer's in the background somewhere?

Jack: Yeah. Alternatively, you might want a list to be generated and sent to the kitchen table (points to KitchenTable jigsaw piece). There could be a display in this table (runs his hand over the table they are sat at) and you could then transfer the list from the table to, say, your PDA. Or you might decide that you want each family member to have an icon (takes an identity card out of his wallet and places on the table). This is you, it's your Identity icon. You could be the administrator for the household - so each person in the house has an Identity icon and they have certain privileges - so you might want to put that down first (puts Identity icon down on table) and that (connects GroceryAlarm piece to Identity icon) goes there and that (connects AddToList to series) goes there and then a list is sent to

Sean: Me.

Jack: Yeah, this is your list.

Figure 3. Sean's assembled list

Sean: Right, OK. Or you could send it to somebody else, say Charlotte, and make sure she does the shopping instead of me if I'm late home from work.

Jack: Exactly.

3.2 Recognising the Relevance of the Technology

Recognition of the relevance of the technology follows from the understanding developed of the basic working of the technology – of the assembly of various pieces to produce particular outcomes – and the embedding of that understanding in the participants' practical circumstances. As this vignette makes visible, participants come to recognize and articulate the potential relevance of the technology by continued working of the pieces to meet specific needs, such as the paying of household bills. The vignette, like many others, also instructs us in the participant's grasp of complexity and their ability to handle abstraction, where they take over the assembly of pieces to produce outcomes that are greater than the individual functions of the pieces making up any particular assembly. In other words, in recognizing the relevance of the technology, participants demonstrate the efficacy of the jigsaw metaphor and that reasoning about complexity in this manner is readily intelligible to them. At the same time, and reflexively, in making their own assemblies of pieces, participants articulate areas of activity that they see the technology as being relevant to: paying bills, doing the shopping, organizing the collection of children from school, managing appointments and schedules, monitoring the children, controlling domestic services and appliances, making the home more secure, etc., etc., etc. Participants come to recognise the relevance of the technology by getting their hands on the mock-ups and tailoring their use to address salient issues in their own lives.

Vignette #2

Jack has worked through the seed scenarios with Sam and she is getting increasingly more curious and articulate about the jigsaw pieces and their potential use. Indeed, like our other participants, she is starting to 'run' with the ideas articulated by Jack, as the following vignette shows:

Sam: What's that? (Points to a piece on the table).

Jack: This is the bubble tower. Say someone's accessed your website – it could be indicated in the water tower with a change in the bubbles or changes of colour.

Sam: Hmmm.

Jack: You can decide what sort information is communicated. So this could be in the corner of the room and its Sunday and

Sam: Actually that's quite a good idea. Let's says you were at work. I know we're talking about home right now but lets say you were at work. Rather than having something like Outlook, you have say a task manager with a list of things (points to the **AddToList** piece then moves her finger, motioning across and down as if to indicate rows and columns). Then say at home, you have bills on your list and you want to be reminded to pay them. So you could have a little sort of nudge in your house, you know, you could see the bubble tower constantly in the corner of the room and you could also be reminded by SMS to your mobile to pay the gas bill or pick the kids up from school.

Sam: By the same token you could have your lamp change to blue after that list has been prepared. Effectively you can have your lamp change from amber say to blue when you run out of X number of items of food (connects **GroceryAlarm** to **AddToList** to **BubbleTower**). Like that you see.

Figure 4. Making relevant *ad hoc* assemblies

Jack: Right. Yeah, that's great.

3.3 Appropriating the Technology

In the course of recognizing the potential relevance of the technology participants begin to articulate ways in which the technology might be appropriated. As the sessions unfold, users become more and more familiar with the technological possibilities to-hand and users begin to *project* the technology into their everyday lives and configure it to meet their particular requirements. These projections go beyond existing design conceptions and engage users and designers in a creative dialogue that conveys participants' practical concerns and reflexively articulates future avenues of work that provide direction for a continued and iterative course of development. User projections elaborated a wide range of practical concerns including being able to survey visitors to the home both from inside and outside the environment, of being connected to family and friends through a variety of devices, of accessing and controlling devices in the home from outside the home. These and a host of other practical concerns elaborate the design domain and real user needs, paramount of which is the ability to configure ubiquitous computing to meet the *local, contingent and unique* needs of potential users, several of which are articulated in the following vignettes.

Vignette #3. The Doorbell

In this segment of conversation we see a specific suggestion emerge that requires the addition of a new component (a doorbell), which the user then exploits to assemble an arrangement of devices to monitor access to the home.

Bill: I might want to see who's coming to the house during the day while I'm at work. So I might want to have this (picks up a blank jigsaw piece) as a doorbell, yes?

Jack: Yes (sketches a **Doorbell** icon on the blank piece). And when the doorbell is activated it links to?

Bill: A video camera or webcam or something like that.

Jack: Yes a camera, good idea (takes another blank paper jigsaw piece and sketches a **Webcam** icon).

Bill: Even better. If we have that (points to the newly sketched **Webcam** icon) and the doorbell rings, OK? Then the image from the webcam goes to

Jack: A web page? (Jack places jigsaw piece showing **WebToText** icon next to jigsaw pieces bearing sketches of **Doorbell** and **Webcam**).

Bill: Or even a picture text message. I suppose you could have a picture flashed up on my mobile (points to his Sony Eriksson T300 and then replaces the **WebToText** piece with the **SMSRecieve** piece) and that shows me just who's at the door!

Figure 5. Bill's doorbell assembly

Jack: So you'd have an image of who and how many people have been to your home.

Bill: Yeah.

Vignette #4.The Office

This segment of conversation suggests the need for more abstracted concepts (in this case the office) to be reflected in the set of components available and for these to be linked with other components to build an arrangement for monitoring the home.

Kate: Let's say you were interested in whose calling at night, as a security measure. If you were in, it could be displayed on your TV screen

Jack: So it goes to your TV at home?

Kate: Yes, or in a little TV monitor that flashes up on your TV, or that's waiting on your TV when you come in from work.

Jack: So you capture pictures with the webcam which sends them to a TV display (sketches a **TVDisplay** icon on a blank jigsaw piece and connects it to the **Webcam** icon).

Kate: You could see the display when you're at home and if you don't want to answer the door you can ignore it. It could come up with a picture of the person at the door automatically in a little insert screen in the corner of the screen while your watching. Or when you come in and turn on your TV you might have a list - a 'rogues gallery' of people who have come to your house during the day or night. So when someone says, "I've been and I've tried to deliver this ..."

Jack: Yeah, that's a good idea.

Kate: Could you have it sent to work?

Jack: (Sketches an **Office** icon and then connects the pieces together).

Figure 6. Kate's home office assembly

Kate: Yeah, that's it.

Vignette #5. Main Access Point

In this final segment the user requests a main point of access to allow her to edit and manipulate the assembly of components.

Jo: Anyway, I don't want to play with your bits anymore (pushes jigsaw pieces away and laughs).

Jack: That's all right.

Jo: You know, my dream is to have one screen which you can access everything through.

Jack: Yeah.

Jo: It's like your main access point - you can access everything through it. That's my thing and I don't think you have a picture of it here?

4. Responding to User Projections

Users' projections do not furnish requirements for design – there is not a necessary one-to-one correspondence between users' visions and future design work. Rather, users' projections provide inspiration for design. The point might be more readily appreciated if we consider the notion of a 'main access point', for example. While intelligible, that notion does not tell us what a main access point might look like, it does not tell us what to build. What it does do is provide a grounded form of inspiration for design that is intimately connected to the development of specific technological concepts through direct user participation. Design work is directed towards developing, in this instance, a single, coherent interface where users can access the technological environment and configure the components therein to meet their particular needs. Thus, we have developed an electronic jigsaw editor and a range of other devices in response to users projections.

4.1 The Jigsaw Editor Tablet

Responding to the request for a point of access we constructed the Jigsaw Editor Tablet [12]. The Jigsaw editor is made available to users using a tablet PC that uses 802.11 to talk to the dataspace (Figure 7). The editor discovers the dataspace and is notified of the components available within the dataspace. The editor is composed of two distinct panels, a list of available components (shown as jigsaw pieces) and an editing canvas. Jigsaw pieces can be dragged and dropped into the editing canvas or workspace. The editing canvas serves as the work area for connecting pieces together and visualizing their activities.[3]

Figure 7. The tablet editor and the editor screen

[3] Commercial partners in the ACCORD project have also developed a paper jigsaw editor, which utilizes paper-based identification technology. Each component is represented in the same way as on the graphical editor (Figure 7) as a jigsaw piece but this time it is a physical jigsaw piece. Users can create services by connecting physical pieces together in a left-to-right order. Unfortunately we are constrained by the commercial sensitivity of the underlying technology and so can say little more about this particular development here.

4.2 Adding Simple Sensors: The Doorbell

Responding to the doorbell projection, we extended the set of components to provide a simple touch sensitive component. This component utilizes the Smart-Its toolkit,[4] a general-purpose hardware toolkit for ubiquitous devices. A component acts as a proxy for the sensor device allowing it to expose the state information in the dataspace. Once made available to the dataspace it appears on the jigsaw editor and users can connect the sensor device to other components (Figure 8). For example, the sensor can be used to drive larger scale devices connected to the dataspace. Two such devices are the web camera and a portable display.

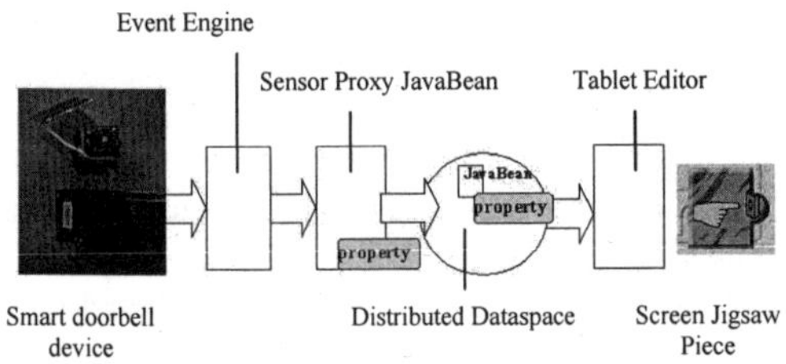

Figure 8. Making lightweight sensors available

4.3 Integrating Larger Devices: The Webcam and Display

The arrangement used to add larger devices to the system is similar to the approach for lightweight sensors. Essentially the device is 'wrapped' as a component allowing the associated property to be shared across the dataspace. This means that the device can be combined with the inputs provided by the lightweight sensors. For example, the arrangement shown in Figure 9 shows the pushbutton being used to signal a webcam to take a picture. Linking the webcam jigsaw piece to a portable display means that this picture is then directed to that display. In this case the display is a driver that sends the image to a mobile phone using MMS.

Figure 9. The doorbell, the webcam and the portable display

4.4 Exploiting Applications: The Weblog

Responding to the office projection suggested by users requires us to consider how to ingrate the sensors and devices with more abstract entities. In this case the user suggested that they wanted to be able to monitor the home while at the office.

[4] Smart-Its - http://smart-its.teco.edu.

a) The sensor

b) The jigsaw assembly

c) The weblog page

Figure 10. Combining a lightweight sensor, a device and an application to monitor a space

We address this issue by exporting the properties representing larger applications. This allows users to combine these with lightweight sensors and devices. In order to address the link between the home and the office we see a combination of jigsaw pieces (Figure 10b) that results in a lightweight sensor (a Smart-It motion sensor (Figure 10a) triggering a device (a webcam) and making the output from the device available to an application (a weblog – Figure 10c). This configuration means that whenever motion is detected within a space this is used to take a picture that is then automatically added to the weblog. Users away from the home can access the weblog (www.accord.blog) and view the image realising the remote monitoring envisioned by users during the mockup sessions.

5. Reflections and Conclusions

In this paper we have presented the evolution of a simple component model in partnership with users. The model supports user configuration of ubiquitous computing environments. The use of jigsaw pieces allows users to develop functions through a process of left to right assembly. A formative user-centred approach has underpinned the elaboration of the component model. A key element of our approach has been the use of mock up sessions with users that have highlighted that:

- Users can readily understand components as jigsaw pieces and understand the concepts involved in building assemblies of devices
- Users can reason about simple interconnections of devices and handle the complexities involved in building simple connections
- Users can make assemblies of components to meet their local needs and can suggest additional devices that can fit into the overall framework and metaphor.

In addition to confirming the overall veracity of our approach and allowing users to engage in the development of our component model these studies have also highlighted some broader lessons in designing technologies for domestic settings.

5.1 Reasoning with Diverse Elements

It is worth reflecting on the diversity of the components users wished to connect together. It was not unusual to see users develop assemblies that combined lightweight sensors with more traditional computer devices and larger applications and services. For example, users would link something as small as a doorbell with something as complex and varied as "the office". This form of reasoning is somewhat in contrast to how developers might normally consider components where they would seek to understand elements at similar levels of abstraction. It appears from our exploration that inhabitants are less concerned with the variability of the complexity of these components than they are with the interactions between them. We have addressed the need to interconnect components of varying complexity by allowing components to make properties available to a distributed dataspace. This arrangement allows different types of component to offer a very simple state based interface, which can be presented to users to allow them to construct assemblies to meet their particular needs.

5.2 Inhabitants as Designers and Developers

A key feature of our exploration is that once user became familiar with the broad approach they sought to compose assemblies that met their needs and desires. Essentially, they wished to further refine our existing seed suggestions to interleave with the practicalities of their everyday lives. For example, users would seek to redirect output to more appropriate devices or even suggest new classes of input and output device. Shifting to consider how we might design for appropriation suggests an interesting relationship between those who seek to design technologies for the home and the inhabitants. Rather than consider design as a problem solving exercise where designers seek to develop a technology to meet a particular need our aim has been to furnish inhabitants with the tools of design. We wish to help users design and develop their own arrangements of technologies just as they design many aspects of their home. We have sought to do this through the provision of a simple editor to allow the direct composition of device assembles.

5.3 Interleaving the New and the Old

One of the most notable aspects of our sessions with inhabitants was the desire to interleave new devices and facilities with older more established devices and services. For example, users would wish to direct output to their TV or to their mobile phone. Similarly, users would wish to take output from web pages and display this on a local display or to link with their existing alarm systems. Although providing difficult technical challenges links of this form are essential if devices are to be interleaved into the everyday activities of the home. In fact many of our assemblies provided just this function with new sensors and cameras being connected to older devices such as mobile phones or placing material on the World Wide Web.

5.3 Linking Outside the Home

While the home offers new challenges for designers and developers and suggest new values for design, such as playfulness [10], our explorations also stress that the domestic is interleaved with many activities outside the home. Indeed, these confirm the importance of communication suggested by the Interliving project [13] and by Hindus et al on Casablanca [11]. Many of the assemblies of devices developed by inhabitants sought to access the outside world from the home or to make the home more accessible from outside. For example, inhabitants sought to send messages to the office or to household members away from the home. We have also sought to support these through the development of communication facilities including the weblog application.

5.4 Future Work

The process of user-based development is ongoing, with each iteration leading to the further refinement of the technical infrastructure and toolkit of devices, software and applications that embed ubiquitous computing in the domestic environment to meet real user needs. We are currently in the process of placing the toolkit in a number of users' domestic environments for prolonged assessment and continued elaboration. We envisage these trials raising significant issues of collaborative access and control as the toolkit is exploited cooperatively by families to meet their day-to-day needs.

6. Acknowledgement

This research was funded by the EU Disappearing Computer Initiative, IST-2000-26364 ACCORD. The current version of the toolkit, including the jigsaw editor, is publicly available and may be downloaded from the project's website: www.sics.se/accord

7. References

1. Abowd, G. and Mynatt, E. (2000) "Charting past, present, and future research in ubiquitous computing", *ACM Transactions on Computer-Human Interaction*, vol. 7, (1), pp. 29-58.
2. Ballagas, R., Ringel, M., Stone, M. and Borchers, J. (2003) "iStuff", *Proceedings of the 2003 CHI Conference on Human Factors in Computing Systems*, pp. 537-544, Florida: ACM Press.
3. Brand, S. (1994) *How Buildings Learn*, New York: Viking.
4. Brumitt, B., Meyers, B., Krumm, J., Kern, A. and Shafer, S. (2000) "EasyLiving: technologies for intelligent environments", *Proceedings of the 2nd International Symposium on Handheld and Ubiquitous Computing*, pp. 12-29, Bristol: Springer.
5. Crabtree, A., Hemmings, T. and Rodden, T. (2002) "Pattern-based support for interactive design in domestic settings", *Proceedings of the 2002 Symposium on Designing Interactive Systems*, pp. 265-276, London: ACM Press.
6. Crabtree, A. (2003) *Designing Collaborative Systems: A Practical Guide to Ethnography*, London: Springer.
7. Edwards, K. and Grinter, R. (2001) "At home with ubiquitous computing: seven challenges" *Proceedings of the 3rd International Conference on Ubiquitous Computing*, pp. 256-272, Atlanta, Georgia: Springer.
8. Edwards, K., Newman, M., Sedivy, J. and Izadi, S. (2002) "Recombinant computing and the speakeasy approach", *Proceedings of the 8th Annual International Conference on Mobile Computing and Networking*, pp. 279-286, Atlanta: ACM Press.
9. Ehn, P. and Kyng, M. (1991) "Cardboard computers: mocking-it-up or hands-on the future", *Design at Work: Cooperative Design of Computer Systems* (eds. Greenbaum, J, and Kyng, M.), pp. 169-195, Hillsdale, New Jersey: Lawrence Erlbaum Associates.
10. Gaver, W., Dunne, A. and Pacenti, E. (1999) "Design: cultural probes", *Interactions*, vol. 6 (1), pp. 21-29.
11. Hindus, D., Mainwaring, S.D., Leduc, N., Hagström, A.E. and Bayley, O. (2001) "Casablanca: designing social communication devices for the home", *Proceedings of the 2001 CHI Conference on Human Factors in Computing Systems*, pp. 325-332, Seattle: ACM Press.

12. Humble, J., Crabtree, A., Hemmings, T., Åkesson, K-P, Koleva, B., Rodden, T. and Pär Hansson (2003) "'Playing with your bits': user-composition of ubiquitous domestic environments", *Proceedings of the 5th International Conference on Ubiquitous Computing*, October 12th-15th, Seattle: Springer.

13. Hutchinson, H., Mackay, W., Westerlund, B., Bederson, B.B, Druin, A., Plaisant, C., Beaudouin-Lafon, M., Conversy, S., Evans, H., Hansen, H., Roussel, N. and Eiderbäck, B. (2003) "Technology probes: inspiring design for and with families", *Proceedings of the 2003 CHI Conference on Human Factors in Computing Systems*, pp. 17-24, Florida: ACM Press.

14. Kidd, C.D., Orr, R.J., Abowd, G.D., Atkeson, C.G., Essa, I.A., MacIntyre, B., Mynatt, E., Starner, T.E. and Newstetter, W. (1999) "The aware home: a living laboratory for ubiquitous computing research", *Proceedings of the 2nd International Workshop on Cooperative Buildings*, pp. 191-198, Pittsburgh: Springer.

15. Mateas, M., Salvador, T., Scholtz, J. and Sorensen, D. (1996) "Engineering ethnography in the home", *Proceedings of the 1996 CHI Conference on Human Factors in Computing Systems*, pp. 283-284, Vancouver: ACM Press.

16. Mogensen, P. (1994) *Challenging Practice*, DAIMI PB 465, Dept. of Computer Science, Århus University.

17. O'Brien, J., Rodden, T., Rouncefield, M. and Hughes, J.A., (1999) "At home with the technology", *ACM Transactions on Computer-Human Interaction*, vol. 6 (3), pp. 282-308.

18. Rodden, T. and Benford, S. (2003) "The evolution of buildings and implications for the design of ubiquitous domestic environments", *Proceedings of the 2003 CHI Conference on Human Factors in Computing Systems*, pp. 9-16, Florida: ACM Press.

19. Sohn, T. and Dey, A. (2003) "iCAP", Interactive Poster, *Proceedings of the 2003 CHI Conference on Human Factors in Computing*, pp. 974-975, Florida: ACM Press.

20. Tolmie, P., Pycock, J., Diggins, T., Maclean, A. and Karsenty, A. (2002) "Unremarkable computing", *Proceedings of the 2002 Conference on Human Factors in Computing Systems*, pp. 399-406, Minneapolis: ACM Press.

21. Twidale, M., Randall, D. and Bentley, R. (1994) "Situated evaluation for cooperative systems", *Proceedings of the 1994 ACM Conference on Computer Supported Cooperative Work*, pp. 441-452, Chapel Hill, North Carolina: ACM Press.

22. Venkatesh, A. (1985) "A conceptualization of household-technology interaction", *Advances in Consumer Research*, vol. 12, pp. 189-194.

23. Waldo, J. (1999) "The Jini architecture for network-centric computing", *Communications of the ACM*, pp. 76-82, vol. 42 (7), pp. 76-82.

Cooperative Systems Design
M. Zacklad et al. (Eds.)
IOS Press, 2004

The Participative Framework as a Design Model for Newsgroups: PartRoOM

Myriam LEWKOWICZ, Michel MARCOCCIA
Université de Technologie de Troyes, Laboratoire Tech-CICO, 12 rue Marie Curie, BP 2060, 10010 TROYES Cedex - FRANCE
{firstname.lastname}@utt.fr

Abstract. The main objective of this paper is to show that a participative-role oriented model (PartRoOM) could be a guideline for designing an innovative kind of newsgroup. We adopt the Participative Framework Model, in which audience roles are distinguished and ranked, according to whether or not the participants are known, ratified or addressed by the speaker. We firstly present here our model (described with UML), then a proposition of implementation of this model in a system. This system permits a user to choose the primary or secondary recipients of his/her message, and to choose if he(she) wants to let his message visible to the ones which are not addressed, or in contrary if he/she wants to have a real private conversation. We also define a profiled interface which permits users to visualize threads sorted by his/her participative role. We finally describe how PartRoOM could fill the lacks of existing newsgroup, and improve discussion management and organizational dynamics.

1. Methodological statements

Several studies have already described communication problems with existing newsgroups (we propose a synthesis in section 2). Contrary to some authors who claim that writing bridles communication, we will focus our attention on the communicational model out of which these newsgroups are designed. In fact, our hypothesis is that existing newsgroups are based on a communicational model which is too far from face-to-face model, and which only allows speaking to no one in particular. In order to validate this hypothesis, we propose in this paper a participative-role oriented model, which could be a guideline for designing a new kind of newsgroup. We assume that this type of newsgroup could afford advantage mainly for group communication (and indirectly for collective problem solving or decision taking), especially in intra-organizational context. This thought processes is in accordance with the abstract approach as defined by [7]. These authors identified three different approaches for designing Computer Mediated Communication systems which take care of social cues:

- The realistic one, in which the system is designed to overcome lacks of communication due to a limited mutual perception. Face-to-face situations, as for example conversations in small groups ([26]), are simulated.
- The mimetic one, in which the hypothesis is that the human-computer interaction would be improved if the computer simulates a human, as, for example, the recent study on the impact of the use of avatars in ([9]).
- The abstract one, in which it is admitted that text conveys social cues that are described by a model or a graphical description.

  In this abstract approach, we can find studies with different goals:

- On one hand, some authors aim at structuring conversations, by typing posts regarding to model's categories. The difference between these studies is the origin of the categories; some are based on speech acts ([28], [18]), and others on Problem-Solving strategies ([20]).
- On the other hand, some authors aim at helping the conversations' reader by presenting the messages and/or the threads sorted by actors' behaviour or conversational activity. This sort can be visualized graphically, as in Chat Circles or Loom ([6]), or not, as in ([8]), where important members in a newsgroup are put forward, their importance being based both on objective metrics and subjective ones (peers evaluation).

We present here another way to follow the abstract approach: we consider that the design of a newsgroup has to be based on a coherent theory of multi-party conversation. In that sense, it seems necessary to take advantage of the theories of multi-party discourses proposed by several researchers, in the field of conversation and discourse analysis (for example [30], [17], [3], [12], [16]).

The analysis of multi-party (or polylogal) conversations challenges the postulate that any speech (or utterance) has a specific identifiable function in conversation, whereas a great number of conversational models used for designing discussion tools are based on this postulate. Indeed, in a polylogue, a message could have a specific conversational function for a particular recipient and other functions for the other participants. For example, the same utterance could perform two different illocutionary acts addressed to two different recipients. "*Close this window*" is at the same time a directive act for the target recipient and an assertion for another participant, who is a mere member of the audience.

In fact, analysing the dynamics of multi-party discussion requires the adoption of a model, based on the Participative Framework. In this model, audience roles are distinguished and ranked, according to whether or not the participants are known, ratified (acknowledged but not necessarily addressed), or addressed by the speaker. This model was developed as a tool for conversation analysis by [1], [19], [4] or [5], for example. Fundamentally, it is based on the interactionist micro-sociological concept of production and reception format elaborated by Goffman ([10]). According to him, four categories of potential recipients of a message can be theoretically differentiated:

- Ratified recipients: they are the "official" recipients of a message. Two types of ratified participants can be distinguished: direct (addressed) and indirect (unaddressed) recipients. A direct recipient is regarded by the speaker as his main partner in the discursive exchange. In principle, a direct recipient of an utterance is identifiable owing to certain discursive marks, as explicit addressing marks (for example [15]: 86-101).
- Bystanders: they compose the audience of a discussion from which they are theoretically excluded. Within this category, an overhearer can be distinguished from an eavesdropper. A speaker is aware of the former's presence, even if this presence is fortuitous, whereas the latter is an intruder, who listens to a speech without the speaker's knowledge.

These categories and the classifying criteria they obey are summarized in the following table 1, from the most to the less addressed participants.

Table 1. Reception roles of a message

	Known	Ratified	Addressed
Addressed recipient: addressee	+	+	+
Non-addressed recipient: auditor	+	+	-
Overhearer	+	-	-
Eavesdropper	-	-	-

We make the assumption that designing a newsgroup based on this hierarchical participative model will permit to elaborate a tool for written communication which will be near a face-to-face conversation abstract model. It will be a profiled newsgroup, in the sense that the interface of the system will be structured depending on the participative role of the recipient. In other words, each member of the conversations will visualize them in a different way. We will then be able to represent the fact that the perception of a conversation depends on the participative role of the actor who perceives it.

This participative role model can be seen as a conceptual (and sometimes physical, in face-to-face conversation) representation of the distance between a speaker and the other participants. Thus, the concept of participative role designates the position occupied by a participant in the reception format of a message, and not a type of interactional activity (like host or joker, for example). However, there can be a connection between a participative role and an interactional activity. For example, we assume that the host of discussion is always a ratified recipient ([23]).

The model of Participative Framework is at odds with a linear (or telegraphic) model of communication and allows understanding the way participants manage a polylogal discussion. For example, the way a participant identifies his/her reception role determines the turn-taking system and the next speaker selection. Generally, the definition of its recipient(s) is a necessary condition for analysing a message, its content, its illocutionary or argumentative force, its function in discussion dynamics, etc.

Participative Framework has been already used by several previous studies for comparing face-to-face with computer-mediated discussions (for instance [29]) or for analysing the importance of different participative roles (main or peripheral) and the mobility from a role to another, like [24] and [25], for example. In these papers, the concept of Participative Framework is useful for understanding in a subtle way interaction situations and conversational phenomena. Some principles of design for mediated-discussion tools are then inferred from this analysis: supporting the management of parallel discussions, monitoring of turn-taking, and integration of peripheral participants by giving them access to the system and ensuring them some visibility in comparison with main participants.

Our approach comes within the scope of these papers but can be distinguished by the operationalization of the Participative Framework. In our mind, Participative Framework is not only a useful concept for preliminary analysis of communicative interactions, but it can constitute by itself an implementable model for designing computer-supported discussion tools.

2. Communicational problems of existing newsgroups

The usual newsgroups (for example the Usenet newsgroups) structure the multi-party discussions according to heterogeneous criteria: date (the discussion is a chronological list which reproduces the temporal dynamics of the conversation), sender (an alphabetical list), subject (a list which is hierarchically organized into sequences). This kind of structure and the asynchronicity of the discussion lead to several problems.

2.1. The Participative Framework

Some papers deal with the question of Participative Framework in computer-mediated communication, by electronic mail [27] or newsgroups [23]. The conversational analysis of usual newsgroups (like Usenet newsgroups) brings to the fore that the Participative Framework of such a discussion tool is incomplete and "rigid" (in comparison with a face-to-face polylogal discussion) insofar as it only defines two types of recipients and these types constitute the only way of organizing reception into a hierarchy ([23]).

In face-to-face conversation, the selection of the addressee is based on verbal and non verbal signs (pronouns, terms of address, content of the message, body orientation, eye-contact). In newsgroups, participants have less means for selecting a recipient; the content of the message, terms of address and the position of the message in the conversation structure.

By default, when a participant posts a message which initiates a thread, he cannot select a recipient and is constrained by the system to address no one in particular. When a participant sends a responding message, he selects a unique addressed recipient because the newsgroups system requires the users to choose the message they answer. But, even if the message has an addressed recipient, it remains readable by any person connected to the system.

In fact, the usual newsgroups impose users a poor and simplistic selection of the recipients of their messages. Besides, the distinction between ratified participants and bystanders becomes less meaningful, because messages sent to usual newsgroups can be read at any moment by anyone who is connected to the system. In other terms, it is impossible to know who belongs to the conversational group at any moment. When a participant sends a message, he has no way of knowing who will read it but can only hope that, if he is addressing a specific recipient, this one will be the one to answer.

Furthermore, the way the discussions are structured in usual newsgroups does not take into account the particular participative and interactional role of the host ([22]).

2.2. Topical coherence

Several studies, like [13], [14] or [23] show that computer-mediated discussions are often confused and have a low level of interactional and topical coherence, because of the "proliferation" of discussion threads and parallel conversations.

Thematic digression is a very frequent phenomenon in newsgroups: the various discussion threads could deal with topics which are very distant and, within one discussion thread, the thematic development resulting from the sequence of messages could be similar to a real "topic decay" ([13]).

To a large extent, this thematic incoherence is the consequence of some difficulty for the users in having a global reading of the messages sent to the newsgroup, which would be a necessary condition for identifying which topic is off the subject ([14]: 82-83). Thus, the considerable number of discussion threads and irrelevant messages prevents a user from knowing if the message he reads and he wants to answer creates or not a "topic decay". At last, the possibility of joining in various parallel discussions does not invite the participants to maintain a high thematic coherence.

2.3. *Readability of the sequential structure*

Messages are sometimes inaccurately positioned in the sequential structure of the conversation, and, even if it is not the case, the discussion structure is sometimes misunderstood by the newsgroup users. For example, its content could signify that a message is an answer whereas it initiates a new discussion thread ([23]).

2.4. *Exchanges length*

In a usual newsgroup, exchanges of messages are often truncated. When exchanges are not truncated, the conversational sequences are generally very short. ([23]).

2.5. *Conversational history*

Moreover, in a usual newsgroup, it is impossible to know the extent of the participants' knowledge of the discussion in which they are taking part. Golopentja ([11]) has described the important function of "conversational history" for the collective management of discussion, which means the participants' capacity to have a shared knowledge of the previous communicative exchanges within the group. In actual newsgroups, no participant can know the other participants' knowledge of the discussion.

3. PartRoOM: a Participative-Role Oriented Model for designing a profiled newsgroup

As we already expressed, our hypothesis is on the one hand that the limits which we listed above come from the non appropriateness of the underlying communicational model, and on the other hand, that a newsgroup based on a model which takes in account the Participative Framework might bypass this limits.

According to the Participative Framework (cf. section 1), the identification of the recipient(s) of a message is an essential point to interpret its content, its pragmatic or argumentative value, its role in the exchanges' dynamic, etc. Thus, our proposition to improve newsgroups' interfaces in order to fulfil the existing limits consists firstly in allowing a user to differentiate the ratified member(s) from the audience of the conversation.

Consequently, the system will have to permit a user to choose the recipients of his/her message, and more precisely, the major or secondary recipients, to choose if he/she wants to let his/her message visible to the ones which are not ratified, or in contrary if he/she wants to have a *real* private conversation. Secondly, we want to define an interface which allows the user to visualize threads sorted by his/her participative role, which can change depending on the messages; in fact, a user could be an addressee (major recipient) of a message, then be an auditor (secondary recipient) of one of the answers, and then be excluded of a small conversation taking place between other participants of this thread.

In order to take into account these conditions, we propose a model, named PartRoOM (Participative Role Oriented Model). Contrary to existing tools based on semi-structured messages ([21]), a PartRoOM-based newsgroup will not force a user to type his/her message according to a content category, or to follow a selected format, but it will impose to select explicitly the recipients of the message.

After explaining the organizational metaphor which a PartRoOM-based newsgroup takes into account (table 2), and the interface that could display the conversations (table 3), we will then describe PartRoOM with the UML language ([2]), showing two state-charts diagrams, the first on thread management (figure 1), and the second one on the dynamics of a conversation (figure 2). Finally, we will illustrate the use of a PartRoOM-based newsgroup with a use cases diagram (figure 3).

3.1. Organizational face-to-face conversations metaphor supported by PartRoOM-based newsgroups

According to the fact that PartRoOM is an implementation of a face-to-face conversational model, our metaphor for the system that we plan to design is the one of face-to-face conversations in an organization. We have identified six main categories of these conversations:

- An event is announced to the entire organization, or to a part of it, but without addressing someone(s) in particular.
- Someone questions someone else, or a group of people in the organization, and the others know about this question.
- The members of a near meeting are notified
- During a meeting:
    - Someone is speaking to the whole meeting,
    - Someone has a private conversation with a part of the meeting, but the others could hear him/her
    - Someone chooses to whisper during a private conversation, which means that the others are not able to hear him/her.

The mapping between these face-to-face conversations in an organization, and communications mediated by a PartRoOM-based newsgroup is described in table 2.

Table 2. Conversation situations taken in account in PartRoOM

Organization metaphor		PartRoOM translation
Announcement		Non ratified, public message
Questioning		Addressed, public message
Meeting start		Message to ratified recipients
Meeting progress	Speaking to everyone	Message to the (ratified) members of the meeting (a kind of "reply all")
	Have a private conversation	Message to a sub-group of the meeting members
	Whisper	Message to a sub-group of the meeting members, "whisper" box checked

3.2. Interface structure of a PartRoOM-based newsgroup

The users will visualize the threads in an interface made of four tabs, as shown in table 3. In order to propose an understandable vision of conversations, we have chosen to not separate the messages of a thread; so, for example, when there is at least a message in a thread where a user is a principal recipient, the system considers that the user will see this thread in the principal tab. We will show in the next section the benefits of this solution, in term of Participative Framework dynamics.

Table 3. Structure of user interface, depending on conversational role of the reader

	Type of tab		Criteria to show a thread in the tab	Name of the tab in the interface
Live conversations	Ratified	Major	at least one message has the reader in the "To" field	TO: username
		Secondary	the user is never a principal recipient and at least one message has the reader in the" CC" field	CC: username
	Bystander		the reader is never addressed and at least a message is public	Public Conversations
Past conversations			Archived Thread	Past conversations

We propose also a new function which does not come from the implementation of the Participative Framework, but from the analysis of one of the exposed limits in section 2. This function consists in distributing the management of the conversation threads, by giving the responsibility of the thread to its launcher. That means that the author of the first message of a thread (his/her launcher) will be able to decide when to close, to archive, or to delete it. These actions of closing, archiving or deleting threads, represented in the state-chart diagram on figure 1, will be available in a particular tab named "Management of my threads", where only the title of the threads will be displayed. By default, the whole thread will be seen by his/her launcher in the "major recipient" tab, even if there are no messages except the first one.

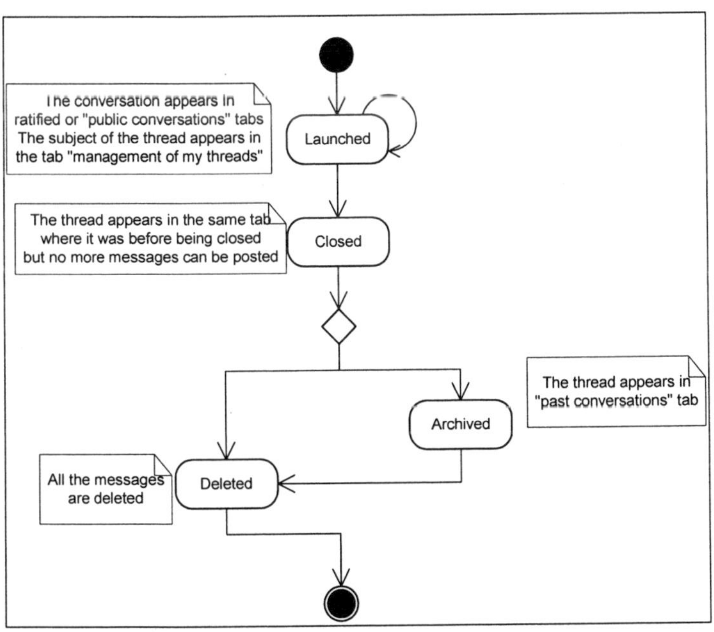

Figure 1. State-chart diagram representing thread management by his/her launcher

3.3. Rules of displaying conversations in the interface

As we have seen in table 3, the principle of PartRoOM is to display the threads in different tabs, depending on the participative role of the reader. Because of our choice to not separate the messages of a thread, and to consider that when there is at least a message in a thread where a user is a principal recipient, the system displays it in the principal tab, we have to take into account all the kinds of messages, the possible flows between messages in a conversation, and their consequences on the visualization of the thread. This description of the dynamics of a conversation is illustrated in the state-chart diagram on figure 2 below.

From the less to the most private, a message can be non addressed (public, by default), posted to a list of members (named Li in the diagram of the figure 2) *and* public, or simply posted to a list of members; Li is then a list of ratified recipients (addressed or non addressed in the Goffman sense). When someone replies to a message, the fact that he/she decides to make a private conversation, to whisper, or the fact that at least a message of the thread was public have consequences on the way of the thread will be displayed. Concerning the private conversations and the whispering, when one of the members replies to message, he/she can make a private conversation by restricting the list of recipients (this restricted list is named Lj in the state-chart diagram), and/or by checking the "whisper" box. When it is checked, the previous members who could read the messages of the thread before, and who have been removed of the recipient list, are not any more able to read the new message, which appears in grey in the conversation thread. Or else, if the "whisper" box is not checked, the removed members will still be able to read all the messages of the thread.

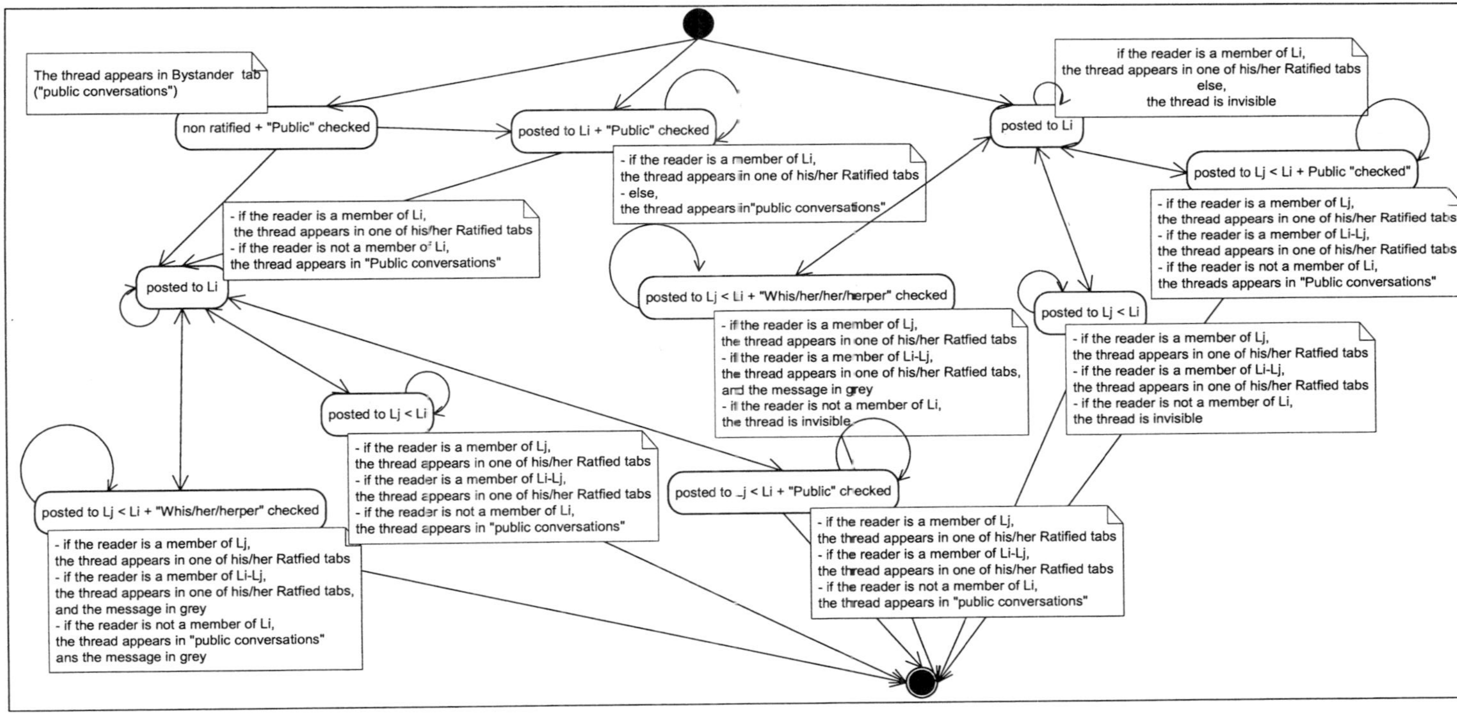

Figure 2. Messages' State-chart diagram and impact on the visualization of the threads in the tabs

To conclude with this presentation of PartRoOM, we could say that our design aim brought us to reconfigure a little bit the participative model, but without distortion. Actually, we can find in PartRoOM the two categories of ratified actors: a member is addressed when he/she is in the "to" field of a message, he/she is unaddressed (in the Goffman sense), or an auditor when he/she is in the "cc" field of a message. We also find two categories of bystanders, but not the same as in the Participative Framework: on one hand, we can not call overhearers the ones which read the messages in the "public conversations" tab, because they do not read them by accident, so we prefer to call them "hearers". And on the other hand, we do not find eavesdroppers in our system –apart from hackers–, because members have to be identified to read messages, but we find another kind of bystanders which we call the "non-hearers", who are the users which see some messages in grey, when they are excluded of a private conversation (the author of the message remove them from the recipient list and checked the "whisper" box).

After having presented the design principles, we are now going to present the use cases of this kind of newsgroup.

3.2. Use cases of a PartRoOM-based newsgroup

As illustrated in the use cases diagram on figure 3, an identified member of a PartRoOM newsgroup is able to:

- Read the existing threads classified in the four different tabs according to his/her participative role in the conversation: (1) a tab where the reader will see all the threads where he/she is the principal recipient of at least a message, named "TO: username", (2) a tab where the reader will see all the threads where he/she is the secondary recipient of at least a message, named "TO: username", (3) a tab named "public conversations" where the reader will see all the threads where he/she is never addressed, but whom members have decided to let the conversation visible, (4) a "past conversations" tab where the reader will see all the archived conversations.
- Participate to an existing conversation: the member can reply to a message, which is a part of a conversation, in several ways: (1) without modifying the list of recipients (a kind of "reply all" in an e-mail system), (2) by restricting the list of recipients if he/she decides to have a private conversation with some members, (3) by enlarging the list of recipients if he/she decides to open the conversation to other members. The second and third ways have some possible extensions. Firstly, when the member wants to have a private conversation, he/she can on the one hand let it visible to the excluded members (as in a meeting, when one is speaking to someone in particular, but the others can here what he/she says), or the second hand, he/she can check a "whisper" box to hide the message which will appear in the thread, but in grey for the excluded members. Secondly, the opening of a conversation could be maximum by checking a "public" box, which consequence is that the whole thread will appear in the "public conversation" tab for the members who were never addressed before in this conversation.
- Create a new conversation (or thread): the user proposes a new subject by posting a message, which can be ratified to some members or not, and public or not. This action of "thread launching" allows him/her firstly to see another tab named "management of my threads", corresponding to the subjects of all the threads which he/she has launched; and secondly to make use of management functions of his/her threads in this tab: closing, and then archiving or deleting them.

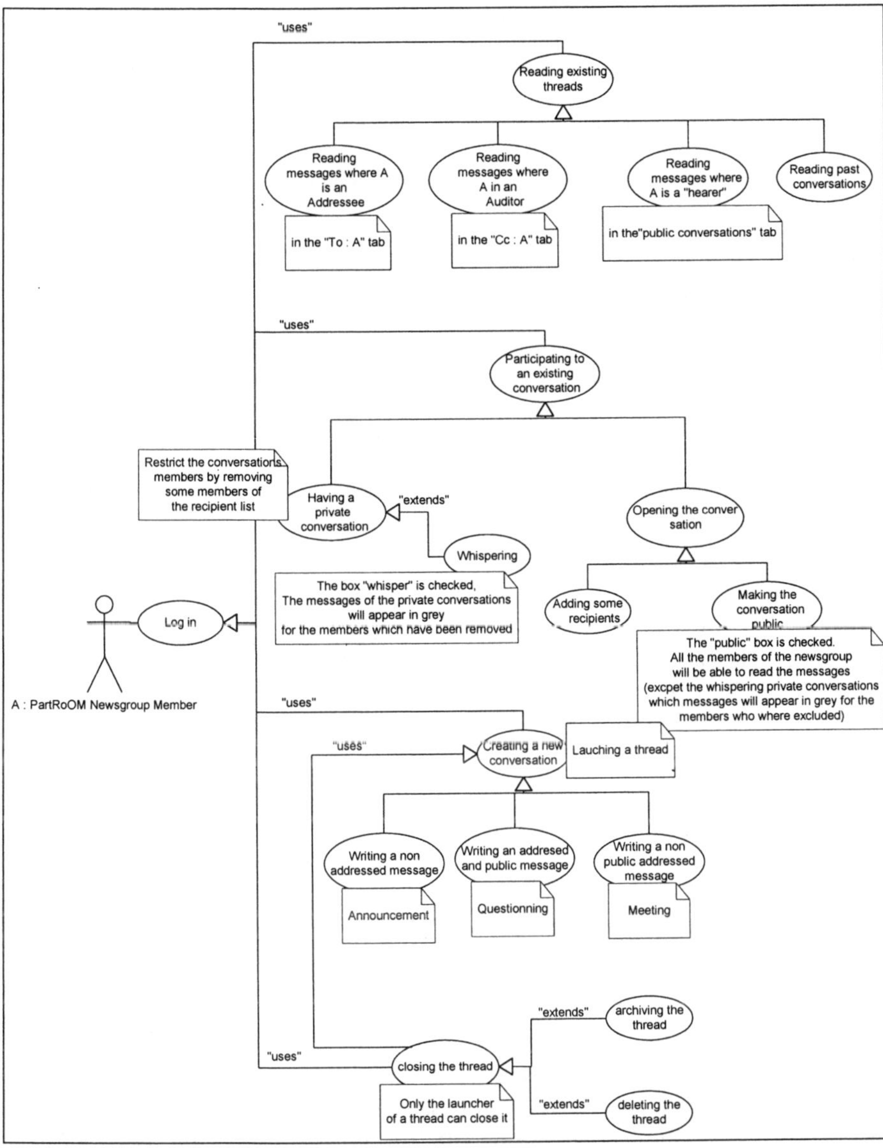

Figure 3. Use Case Diagram of a PartRoOM based newsgroup

After this presentation of PartRoOM and the potential use cases of a newsgroup based on this model, we are now going to propose how, to a certain extent, this kind of newsgroup could fulfil the actual limits of newsgroups.

4. How the use of a PartRoOM-based newsgroup could solve problems with existing newsgroups

4.1. Benefits for structuring and management of discussion

In our hypothesis, a newsgroup which makes explicit the Participative Framework can be resolve or limit the problems described in section 2.

4.1.1. The Participative Framework

The position and the role of each message in the discussion dynamics are defined by its reception format. Within this system, sending a message implies a choice among several audience roles: major recipient, secondary recipient, or bystander. It allows the senders to define the reception format of their messages in a precise and flexible way. The advantage is even more obvious for the recipient: he knows clearly the role allocated to him by the message he reads. Thus, the way the discussion is structured is specific for each participant.

4.1.2. Topical coherence

Making explicit the reception format allows managing fragmentation and emergence of subgroups in an easier way. In fact, the discussion subgroups are perceptible only by the participants to theses groups. Thus, fragmentation becomes a type of discussion management which cannot cause interference on the global discussion.

4.1.3. Readibility of the sequential structure

The problems of "misplacements" of messages in the sequential structure do not sill exist because the structuring based on thematic and chronological sequential becomes secondary in comparison with the structuring based on the Participative Framework, which is different for each participant, according to his/her participative role.

4.1.4. Exchanges length

PartRoOM is supposed to favour collective and cooperative management of the discussion. In relation to this goal, PartRoOM entrusts the participants with the task of managing the discussion sequence they decide to open: sustaining the discussion, formulating summaries of the sequence, closing, deleting or archiving the sequence. This individual management of sequences is supposed to limit the problems of truncated exchanges or "moribund" discussions.

4.1.5. Conversational history

Finally, we will try to develop a specific functionality of PartRoOM, which will allow identifying the participants who share the same knowledge of discussion.

4.2. Benefits for organizational dynamics

A PartRoOM based newsgroup could also improve organizational dynamics. Actually, when an actor can see at first glance the messages where he/she is a principal recipient, it allows him/her to define some priorities in the messages that he has to deal with. The system permits also to reinforce trust, by avoiding eavesdroppers in conversations. It can also be seen in term of decision aid, because private conversations permit users to build coalitions, which is a crucial function in decision making. Finally, this system provides information on actors' importance in the group dynamics, because their role in the exchanges (excluded, included, leader ...) becomes explicit and easily visible.

5. Discussion and further work

This research is based on an application of the Participative Framework model, coming from the multi-party discussion theories, in order to design tools for computer-mediated group discussion. We have presented here an exploratory work, and this paper introduces a diagnosis of communicational problems observed in usual newsgroups, the PartRoOM Model, and our assumption that a tool based on PartRoOM could solve these problems. This work has of course to be completed with an evaluation, as soon as the development of the PartRoOM-based newsgroup will be achieved. This experimentation will allow us to test our hypothesis of better communication with a tool implementing the Participative Framework Model. Besides, it will permit us to precise some potential limits; for example, the role of this tool in relation to other communication devices. More precisely, how could the user choose between posting an addressed message to a unique recipient in our tool or sending an e-mail ? In the same way, what will be the role of our tool in relation to groupware ? We suppose that the elaboration and the practice of use rules would bypass this problem, for instance, the rule of selecting a unique tool for managing the whole communication events in a work group.

Furthermore, we continue our work on PartRoOM in order to implement other features of the Participative Framework Model. For example, PartRoOM could be completed to take into account the recipient's point of view about his/her participative role (in PartRoOM's present version, the participative role of a recipient is defined by the sender of the message). Another interesting function could be the refinement of the choice of recipients: now, PartRoOM allows users to select recipients in a list, and we think about adding the opportunity of a "negative selection" (a kind of "everybody except X").

6. References

[1] Bell, A. (1984). Language style as audience design. *Language in Society* 13: 145–204.

[2] Booch, G., Rumbaugh, J., Jacobson, I. (1998). *The Unified Modelling Language User Guide*. Reading, Mas., Addison-Wesley.

[3] Cabasino, F. (Ed.) (1998). *Du dialogue au polylogue : approches linguistiques, socio-pragmatiques, littéraires. Actes du 3e colloque international Do.Ri.F.-Università*. Rome, CISU.

[4] Clark, H.H., Carlson, T.B. (1992). Hearers and speech acts. In Clark (Ed.), *Arenas of Language Use*. Chicago, University of Chicago Press / CSLI.

[5] Clark, H.H., Schaefer, E.F. (1992). Dealing with overhearers. In Clark (ed.), *Arenas of Language Use*. Chicago, University of Chicago Press / CSLI.

[6] Donath, J. Karahalios, K. Viegas, F. (1999). Visualizing Conversations, In *Thirty-Second Annual Hawaii International Conference on System Sciences*-Volume 2, January 05-08, 1999, Maui, Hawaii: 2023–2034.

[7] Erickson, T., Kellogg, W.A. (2000). Social Translucence: An Approach to Designing Systems that Support Social Processes, *ACM Transactions on Computer-Human Interaction*, Vol. 7, No. 1, March 2000: 59–83.

[8] Fiore, A.T., Tiernan, S.L., Smith, M.A. (2002). Observed Behavior and Perceived Value of Authors in Usenet Newsgroups: Bridging the Gap, In Proceedings of CHI 2002, April 20-25, 2002, Minneapolis, Minnesota, USA, *CHI letters* Vol. 4, Issue 1: 323–330.

[9] Garau, M., Slater, M., Vinayagamoorthy, V., Brogni, A., Steed, A., Sasse, M.A. (2003). The impact of avatar realism and eye gaze control on perceived quality of communication in a shared immersive virtual environment, in *Proceedings of the conference on Human factors in computing systems*, 2003 , Ft. Lauderdale, Florida, USA: 529–536.

[10] Goffman, E. (1981). *Forms of talk.* Oxford, Basil Blackwell.

[11] Golopentja, S. (1988). Interaction et histoire conversationnelle. In Cosnier, Gelas & Kerbrat-Orecchioni (Eds). *Echanges sur la conversation.* Paris, Ed. du CNRS: 69–81.

[12] Grosjean, M., Traverso, V. (1998). Les cadres participatifs dans les polylogues : problèmes méthodologiques. In Cabasino (Ed.). *Du dialogue au polylogue : approches linguistiques, socio-pragmatiques, littéraires. Actes du 3e colloque international Do.Ri.F.-Università.* Rome, CISU: 51–66.

[13] Herring, S.C. (1999). Interactional Coherence in CMC. *Journal of Computer-Mediated Communication* 4(4). www.ascusc.org/jcmc/vol4/issue4/

[14] Kear, K. (2001). Following the thread in computer conferences. *Computers & Education*, 37: 81–99.

[15] Kerbrat-Orecchioni (1990). *Les interactions verbales*, Tome 1, Armand Colin, Paris.

[16] Kerbrat-Orecchioni, C. (Ed.) (2004). *Journal of Pragmatics* – Special issue on Polylogues, N°36 (1).

[17] Kerbrat-Orecchioni, C., Plantin, C. (Eds.) (1995). *Le trilogue.* Lyon, Presses Universitaires de Lyon.

[18] Kreutel, J. , Matheson, C. (2002). From Dialogue Acts to Dialogue Act Offers: Building Discourse Structure as an Argumentative Process. In Bos, Foster & Matheson (Eds). *Proceedings of the sixth workshop on the semantics and pragmatics of dialogue (EDILOG 2002)*, 4-6 September 2002, Edinburgh, UK: 85–93.

[19] Levinson, S. C. (1988). Putting Linguistics on a Proper Footing: Explorations in Goffman's Concepts of Participation. In Drew & Wootton (Eds). *Erving Goffman: Exploring the Interaction Order.* Cambridge, Polity Press: 161–227.

[20] Lewkowicz, M., Zacklad, M., (2000). A guide through the construction of a groupware for efficient knowledge management. In Dieng, Giboin, Karsenty & De Michelis (Eds). *Designing Cooperative Systems The Use of Theories and Models Proceediengs of the 5th Int. Conference on the Design of Cooperative Systems* COOP'2000, Sophia-Antipolis, France, May 23-26, 2000, IOS Press Volume 58.

[21] Malone., T.W., Grant, K.R., Lai, K.-Y., Rao, R. Rosenblitt, D. (1987). Semi Structured Messages are Surprisingly Useful for Computer-Supported Coordination, *ACM Transactions on Office Information Systems* Vol. 5, No. 2: 115–131.

[22] Marcoccia, M. (2001). L'animation d'un espace numérique de discussion : l'exemple des forums usenet. *Document Numérique* 5 (3-4): 11–26.

[23] Marcoccia, M. (2004). Conversation structure and participation framework in internet newsgroups. *Journal of Pragmatics* 36 (1) : 115-145.

[24] Monk, A. F. (1999). Participatory status in electronically mediated collaborative work. In *Proceedings of the American Association for Artificial Intelligence Fall Symposium "Psychological models of communication in collaborative systems".* North Falmouth, MA. Menlo Park, CA, AAAI Press: 73–80.

[25] Monk, A. F., Watts, L. A. (2000). Peripheral participation in video-mediated communication. *International Journal of Human-computer Studies* 52: 775–960.

[26] Padilha, E., Carletta, J. C. (2002). A Simulation of Small Group Discussion. In Bos, Foster & Matheson (Eds). *Proceedings of the sixth workshop on the semantics and pragmatics of dialogue (EDILOG 2002)*, 4-6 September 2002, Edinburgh, UK: 117–124.

[27] Pemberton, L. (1996). Telltales and Overhearers : Participant Roles in Electronic Mail Communication. In Connoly & Pemberton (Eds). *Linguistic Concepts and Methods in CSCW.* London, Springer: 145–161.

[28] Poesio, M., Traum, D. (1997). Conversational actions and discourse situations, *Computational Intelligence Journal* Vol. 13, N° 3 : 309–347.

[29] Reeves, A. J., Healey, P. G. T. (2003). Participation in Community Systems: Indications for Design. 'Digital Cities 3' panel paper for Workshop : local information and communication infrastructures: experiences and challenges. In Huysman, M. Wenger, E. Wulf, V., *Communities and Technologies, Proceedings of the First International Conference on Communities and Technologies; C&T 2003.* Dordrecht, Kluwer Academic Publishers.

[30] Schegloff, E. (1995). Parties and talking Together, Two ways in which numbers are significant for talk-in-interaction. In Have & Psathas (Eds). *Situated Order*. Washington D.C., International Institute for Ethnomethodology and Conversation Analysis / University Press of America: 31–42.

Author Index